Marriage Practices
in Lowland South America

Marriage Practices
in
Lowland South America

Edited by

KENNETH M. KENSINGER

Illinois Studies in Anthropology
No. 14

UNIVERSITY OF ILLINOIS PRESS

Urbana and Chicago

Library of Congress Cataloging in Publication Data

Main entry under title:

Marriage practices in lowland South America.

   (Illinois studies in anthropology; no. 14)
   Bibliography: p.
   Includes index.
   1. Indians of South America—Marriage customs and
rites—Addresses, essays, lectures. 2. Indians of
South America—Amazon River Valley—Marriage customs and
rites—Addresses, essays, lectures. I. Kensinger,
Kenneth M. II. Series.
F2230.1.M28M37   1984   306.8'089980811   83-4924
ISBN 0-252-01014-0

To Robert F. Murphy

"Marriage is a truly peculiar institution. Although it is widely regarded as a natural state, or at least one ordained by deity, it is actually one of the more ingenious traps set for us by society. Consider its dubious benefits. A woman (or women in plural unions) agrees to place herself in lifelong thralldom to a man (or men) for whom she will cook and clean, giving herself sexually to him on demand, and bearing and raising his children. His side of the bargain requires that he restrict his sex urges to his wife (or wives), or at least keep his liaisons secret from her, live with her, and support her children under compulsion of custom or law. Both sides experience a drastic reduction in independence and autonomy and both have had a lien placed against their labors. When children arrive, the burdens on each are multiplied, for they have surely given a hostage to fortune. There is nothing natural about any of this, and the entire business defies common sense. For all mankind, however, marriage has been so much a part of life, so routinized, that people rarely thought to question the institution, and it is a sign of an age of doubt that we are doing so now."

Robert F. Murphy (1979:56)

Preface

This volume had its genesis on a subzero February night in Vermont, when thoughts of warmer climes, seafood in New Orleans, and the forthcoming deadline for submitting an abstract to the American Anthropological Association's December 1973 meetings culminated in a decision to organize a symposium on marriage practices in lowland South America. After drawing up a list of six names, I called Trudie Dole and Pat Lyon, who added to my list more than 20 names of people who "just had to be included in such a program"—they also agreed to participate. During the following 48 hours 22 people agreed to read papers, chair the sessions, or serve as discussants.

The volume consists of most of the papers read during the two sessions, masterfully chaired by Terrance S. Turner and Jean Carter Lave. Professors David Maybury-Lewis, Robert F. Murphy, and Judith Shapiro served as discussants. Shapiro has written the introductory essay, which greatly expands on her comments given at the time of the symposium. Included in this volume, but not presented in New Orleans, are papers by the Whittens and Kracke.

That these essays represent a diversity of approaches and theoretical orientations is no accident. In selecting the participants for the symposium, I consciously attempted to secure representatives from a multiplicity of both graduate schools and eras of graduate training. My goal was to bring together persons with a broad range of perspectives who had worked with tribal societies throughout lowland South America and to focus our attention on a topic defined narrowly enough to perhaps allow us to reach some conclusions that would or could serve as the basis of further research.

Based on my experience while working on my own Cashinahua data, on conversations with others who had done fieldwork in the Amazon basin, and on my reading of the ethnographic literature, I had concluded that the models developed for dealing with societies in Africa, Australia, New Guinea, Oceania, and Asia just did not work well in the South

American context. I hoped that the symposium would document this inadequacy in the available models, and perhaps take several steps toward solving the problem.

In editing the volume, I have not attempted to minimize the differences or to highlight the similarities. The papers are organized by geographic area on the assumption that societies from the same general region are more apt to be similar than those separated by the length of the Amazon river.

In any project of this size, many people become involved and many debts are incurred, far too many to acknowledge individually. To the participants in the symposium and particularly to the authors, I want to express my thanks for their patience and helpfulness. Laura Nowak, Eleanor Moore, Virginia Sandy, Wendy Guerra, Lucille Crane, and Ron Dabney, who typed various versions of sections of the manuscript, edited, checked bibliography, etc., earned more than the few paltry dollars they were paid; they earned my gratitude.

Finally, all of us owe a huge debt to those who taught us, who tolerated our eccentricities, the disruptions we brought to their lives, and our endless flow of questions, who fed us and allowed us to become part of their world for a brief while. Perhaps we amused them and gave them a new topic for discussion; occasionally we may have been able to contribute something to their well-being. To them, our informants, their families and kinsmen, any expression of our appreciation can be a token only.

K. K.

Contents

PART I

INTRODUCTION

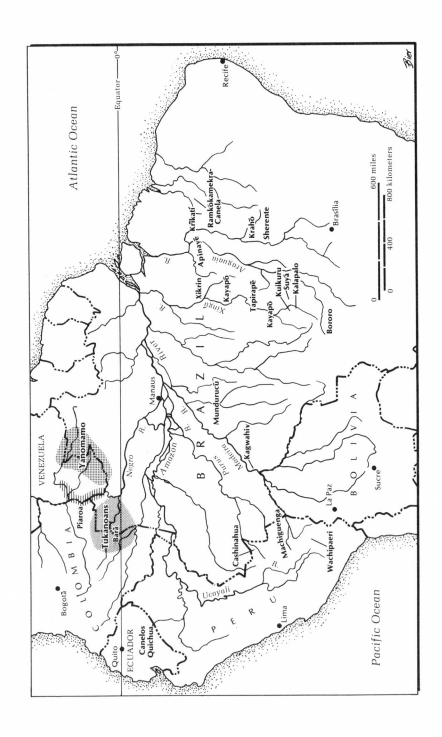

1

Marriage Rules, Marriage Exchange, and the Definition of Marriage in Lowland South American Societies

JUDITH R. SHAPIRO

The major anthropological contributions to the study of marriage over the past three decades have been made by scholars working within the framework established by Claude Lévi-Strauss in his 1949 treatise on kinship and marriage. Lévi-Strauss and his followers, who developed the body of literature that has come to be known as "alliance theory,"[1] concentrated on topics that have traditionally been central to anthropological inquiries into marriage: the rules governing choice of spouse and the relationship between such rules and systems of kinship terminology. They focused on certain basic and recurrent marriage rules, which were analyzed as types of exchange, and interpreted kin classifications as expressions of these marriage rules.

The essays in this volume provide a rich body of data on marriage rules and marriage exchange in lowland South American Indian societies. The ethnographic material presented here and the theoretical orientations underlying the analyses have important implications for alliance theory, and for the more general question of how systems of kin classification are to be interpreted. I will outline some of these implications in the discussion that follows.

I will also be devoting attention to the use of "marriage" as a comparative concept. Though the definition of marriage is not a focus in these essays, it has not been totally ignored either. Two contributors, Kensinger and Dole, have felt it appropriate to consider the general issue of how marriage can be defined cross-culturally. Because their views raise interesting and important points, and because the question of how marriage is defined—both generally and in lowland South American societies—might reasonably arise in the minds of those reading a col-

1

lection of essays on the subject of marriage, I would like to take up the matter here. There will, moreover, be certain points of convergence between my discussion of alliance theory and my discussion of marriage as a comparative concept, since anthropologists working in the Lévi-Straussian structuralist tradition have figured prominently in debate over the definition of marriage (Leach 1951; Needham 1971b, 1975; Rivière 1971).

Marriage Rules and the Classification of Kin

Most of the societies described in this volume are characterized by the kind of kin classificatory system commonly referred to as "Dravidian": the universe of kinsmen is bifurcated along the lines of a cross/parallel distinction and terms for cross relatives are the same as terms for affines. Such a system of classification accords with what some call cross-cousin marriage and others prefer to think of as prescriptive alliance or direct exchange.[2] It has been suggested by one ethnographer of South America (Rivière 1973) that Dravidian systems are a particularly significant diagnostic feature of South American tropical forest societies.[3]

There has been considerable debate among anthropologists about Dravidian systems (see Buchler and Selby 1968:135-48). The term came into the literature through the work of Louis Dumont, who emphasized that certain of the terminologies which in the past might have been labeled "bifurcate-merging" or "Iroquois" could only be properly understood if one recognized the essentially affinal meaning of terms for cross relatives (Dumont 1953a). The distinction between Dravidian and Iroquois terminologies has come to be understood as a matter of the contrast between bifurcate-merging terminologies that reflect a positive marriage rule (through the equation of cross kin with affines and a mode of extending kin terms in accordance with inherited relations of affinity) and those that do not.

This understanding of Dravidian systems of kin classification has been challenged by Scheffler (1971). Scheffler sees the main distinction between Dravidian- and Iroquois-type systems to lie in how they respectively extend terms to more distant relatives. In Dravidian-type terminologies the cross/parallel distinction is applied consistently throughout the system; thus, for example, the children of a man one's mother calls by a sibling term are classified differently from children of a man one's mother calls by a cross-cousin term. In Iroquois-type systems, on the other hand, cousin reckoning depends only on the relative sex of the linking relatives in the first ascending generation; thus, for example, children of male relatives on the mother's side, be they related to the mother as parallel or cross relatives, are classified in the same manner.

It would appear that the pattern of genealogical extensions in Dravidian systems accords with the perpetuation of affinal relations across
the generations, whereas the Iroquois pattern does not. Scheffler, however, is at pains to dissociate Dravidian kin terminology from affinity,
and notes that Dravidian-type genealogical extensions are not always
found in association with the kinds of affinal equations (e.g., MB = WF)
that are usually assumed to characterize this system of kin classification.
He does not present any statistical data on patterns of association among
the various features that alliance-minded anthropologists have considered to be a part of Dravidian systems, and one suspects that the
situation may be less random than Scheffler would have us believe. In
any event, Scheffler's assertion that patterns of genealogical extension
should take priority over the presence or absence of affinal equations,
which Scheffler sees as secondary or epiphenomenal, cannot be justified
on general theoretical grounds but, rather, follows from Scheffler's own
analytic concerns. It is just as easy, perhaps even easier, to argue for
the comparative interest of typologizing terminologies according to
whether or not they have implications for marriage. A particularly good
case for what is to be gained, ethnographically and analytically, from
focusing on the relationship between kin classification and marriage is
made by the essays published here.

It should also be pointed out that the approach taken by Scheffler
involves a relative lack of concern with how people actually reckon kin
ties, as opposed to how they might conceivably be reckoning them. For
example, Scheffler phrases the difference between genealogical extensions in Dravidian and Iroquois systems in terms of how many generations back one goes in distinguishing between same-sex and cross-sex
sibling links. In the foregoing discussion I have rephrased the distinction
in terms of how ego's first ascending generation relatives classify one
another. This seems more appropriate for societies like those of lowland
South America, where genealogical reckoning is generally quite shallow,
and also leaves open the question of whether the ties are being reckoned
consanguineally or affinally. This latter question (should terms in a
Dravidian system be translated as "mother's brother," "mother's brother's
son," etc. or rather as "spouse's father," "classificatory husband/brother-
in-law," etc.) has occasioned a certain amount of abstract theoretical
debate in the anthropological literature, but is more appropriately viewed
as an ethnographic matter. Several of the essays in this volume present
information on how relationships are actually calculated in the societies
under discussion and thus provide information relevant to questions such
as these.[4]

While anthropologists with a genealogical orientation, like Scheffler,
have taken issue with alliance theorists over the affinal significance of

Dravidian terminologies, it is also important to note that their respective approaches are in some ways not as dissimilar as they might appear. Alliance theorists commonly claim that the true referents of kin terms are social categories rather than genealogically defined kinsmen or kin types. Their own approach, however, is equally dependent on genealogical modes of analysis.[5] This dependence may remain covert but often takes the form of lists of genealogical equations. Alliance theorists sometimes apologize for their use of genealogical notation, claiming that it is merely a matter of convenience (Needham 1971b, Rivière 1973), but these disclaimers are unconvincing. What alliance theorists share with avowed genealogists is a relatively narrow focus on the referential properties of kin terms.

This can be seen if we consider the meaning of "prescription" as this concept is used in the literature on marriage rules, where it commonly appears in opposition to the notion of marriage "preferences."[6] This opposition, which in some writings has been associated with the strength of a marriage rule as measured by the proportion of actual marriages that adhere to it, is now most commonly used to draw a contrast between the positive marriage rule encoded in the kin classificatory system itself, which is labeled the "prescription," and any other norms governing choice of spouse, which tend to fall into a residual category, or at least to receive considerably less attention. Divorced both from actual marriage patterns and from the body of lore that exists within a society regarding desirable and undesirable forms of marriage, the notion of a prescriptive marriage rule comes down to a commentary on certain referential properties of the kin terminological system. Such interpretation of a kin terminology is by no means without interest, but it involves a strict limitation on the kinds of ethnographic data that go into the analysis and are rendered more intelligible thereby.

Just as it is impossible to decide from a Dravidian kin terminological system *per se* whether terms for cross kin are best translated in consanguineal or affinal terms,[7] so, more generally, is it impossible to achieve an ethnographically adequate account of the meaning of kin classifications and marriage rules by sorting consanguineally and affinally defined denotata and drawing up genealogical equations. We must instead turn to studies like the ones presented in this collection, which explore the varied meanings of both kin terms and marriage rules, and take into account the wider context of cultural beliefs that give them their significance.[8] These essays show us that what we gloss as "cross kin" may be viewed as either strangers or friends (or both); they analyze how marriage preferences reflect cosmological principles and how marriage strategies are attempts to achieve culturally defined goals that are at once political and spiritual. They enable us to understand how a similar Dravidian classificatory structure operates in conjunction with such differing social organizational arrangements as cognatic kindreds, patrilineal descent groups, and moieties, at the same time presenting us with information on variation within these categories.

To take some examples, both Basso and Kaplan describe the meaning of marriage practices in societies in which cognatic kinship combines with a Dravidian bifurcation of the kin universe. In her analysis of the Kalapalo, Basso devotes particular attention to concepts of relationship and affinity. She analyzes the polysemous nature of the Kalapalo term translatable as "relative," a matter that she has also discussed at length in previous publications (Basso 1970, 1973). The class of relatives may cover the entire range of cognatic kinsmen, classificatory consanguines as well as affines, or it may be construed more narrowly so as to distinguish non-marriageable classificatory consanguines from potential marriage partners. These usages vary with social context, depending on what kind of relationship is being emphasized. When a general principle of kin solidarity is being invoked, the term "relative" will be used in its wider sense; when the particular question of marriage is at issue, potential affines will be excluded from the category of "relative." Basso's discussion of the concept of *ifutisu,* or "respect," as the moral quality characteristic of kin relationships throws interpretive light on this pattern of use. Degree of *ifutisu,* which varies with closeness of relationship (defined not in directly genealogical terms but with respect to household, factional, and village affiliation), differentiates relations of classificatory consanguinity from those of potential affinity. The people one may marry are people with whom one feels socially more distant. As Basso puts it, "Kalapalo marriage is . . . an alliance between sibling sets (*ifisúandaw*) who are considered suitable spouse exchangers because of their social distance, not because of some a priori exchange relationship" (p. 37). Elsewhere Basso has stated that, for the Kalapalo, "affinal categories can be thought of as 'neutral' with respect to kinship as a cultural category." That is, those one may marry either fall into the category of relatives or they do not, a distinction that is not of importance to the Kalapalo; thus, according to Basso, it would be an error to analyze affinity as a subcategory of kinship (Basso 1975:214).

Turning to the Piaroa, we find, in contrast to the Kalapalo, a definite positive value placed on "marrying close." According to Kaplan, this is understood in three different ways. One is in terms of multiple exchange, that is, replicating the marriage of a close kinsman in order to tighten the affinal links between family units. An example is marriage with a brother's wife's sister. This principle does not itself concern genealogical relationship between marriage partners.[9] Genealogical closeness does, however, figure in another definition of marrying close, which is marrying a first-degree cross cousin, either matrilateral or patrilateral. Here one marries within one's close kindred and also replicates an affinal link established in the previous generation. Kaplan sees this rule as part of a conceptual model of the cognatic kindred as a bounded group with continuity over time (see also J. Kaplan 1973). The third definition of marrying close is marrying within the house, a residential expression of the rule of cognatic kindred integrity. Where, for demographic or political reasons, Piaroa marriages do not conform to the ideal of "marrying close," they are ideologically assimilated to the category of marriages between close kinsmen, with the help of such devices as the use of teknonyms between affines (J. Kaplan 1972). Kaplan also discusses a dynamic process affecting the relationship categories of consanguine and affine such that relatively distant consanguines are reclassified as affines and thereafter reabsorbed into the closed cognatic sphere through marriage.

Looking at these two cases comparatively, it seems that the Kalapalo see marriage as creating, but not presupposing, a close relationship: a close tie results from marriage rather than serving as a precondition for it.[10] The fact that the relationship, once set up, entails such rights as further marriage within the same generational level (what has been referred to above as "multiple exchange"), as well as the perpetuation of the marital exchange in the succeeding generation, might seem to pose a contradiction. The solution is apparently that the Kalapalo themselves look at the exchange relationship between sibling sets as a whole, involving two generations.[11]

The Piaroa, on the other hand, view marriage as both presupposing and creating close kin ties. Close marriages confirm the ideal model of society as composed of endogamous bounded kindreds; more distant marriages define new kindred boundaries. Perhaps we may say that, while the Kalapalo think in terms of groups of people *between whom* affinal relations are established, the Piaroa think more in terms of the unit *within which* marital relationships take on their significance. The Piaroa thus deal with marriages that create, rather than presuppose, close kindred ties by seeking to obliterate the distinction between close natal kinsmen and new kinsmen.

A number of other essays in this collection address the meaning of cousin terms and marriage rules with respect to norms for marrying close or marrying at a distance. Kensinger analyzes what marrying close means to the Cashinahua, for whom it is a matter both of village, or more particularly, faction endogamy, and of the special value placed on marriage between first-degree double cross cousins. The privileged nature of the double cross-cousin union, which replicates a sister exchange in the previous generation, is reflected in the Cashinahua classification of marriage types, analyzed in detail by Kensinger, and in the terms used for this particular marriage partner, which combine the terms for "husband" or "wife" with the term *kuin,* meaning "true" or "real." In fact, the Cashinahua distinguish both between marriage with a double as opposed to a single first-degree cross cousin, and between marriage with either type of cross cousin and with a member of the wider class of marriageables defined by the moiety and section system.[12]

On the other side, both Kracke in his study of the Kagwahiv (p. 101) and Dole in her study of the Kuikuru (pp. 55-56) have discussed connections between terms for "cross cousin" and terms for "stranger" or "nonrelative." Dole places the issue in historical perspective, pointing to apparent cognates between cross-cousin terms in other Carib languages and the term used to indicate a lack of relationship among the Kuikuru, who, like the Kalapalo, are a Carib-speaking group of the Upper Xingú region.[13] Excellent descriptions of the meaning of cousin terms and marriage preferences among groups in the Northwest Amazon have been published by Jackson (1977) and C. Hugh-Jones (1979). These studies analyze the range in cousin categories and concomitantly in types of marriage, from an ongoing alliance with a closely related group to the establishment of new marital ties with relative strangers.

These data have implications for the way in which the term "prescription," as used by alliance theorists, can be applied to the lowland South American region. Lévi-Strauss originally developed the notion of prescription in the context of an opposition between "elementary structures of kinship," in which marriage was regulated by a positive kin-based rule, and "complex structures," in which the kinship system operated only negatively with respect to marriage, leaving spouse selection to other mechanisms.[14] It is worth examining more closely what the concept of a positive marriage rule might mean, so that we can better judge the appropriateness of using the term "prescription" for the marriage systems of the different societies we have been discussing.

A kin classificatory system involving a bifurcation of the domain of kinsmen into consanguines and affines may operate in either of the following ways: (1) The universe of relatives, including both consanguines and affines, is part of a larger universe of social relations in which relatives are contrasted with nonrelatives. Here the positive marriage rule, as defined in the kinship system, serves to delimit a set of marriageables in opposition not only to consanguineal relatives but to nonrelatives as well. (2) The relationship terminology constitutes an all-embracing social classification that extends to cover the entire field of social relations. In this case kin terms have a stronger "creative" function (see note 10), that is, they play a greater role in actually bringing into existence the relationships that they designate. Systems of this sort may vary in terms of whether consanguinity or affinity serves as the major idiom for extending the range of kin. Extension in an affinal mode, which is more common in lowland South American societies, poses the problem of just what we mean when we speak of a positive marriage rule.

In 1943 Lévi-Strauss drew attention to the way in which the Nambikwara used affinal terms—in particular, the classificatory "brother-in-law" term—to establish relationships between members of two groups entering into contact with one another. This practice has since been described for other groups, for example, the Yanomama (Shapiro 1972:84-89; 1974). A related pattern is one we might call consanguineal fade-out, in which all but close consanguines can be redefined as marriageable, particularly if relationships can be traced to them in more than one way, as is commonly the case in small-scale societies like those of lowland South America. Where the kinship system has a patrilateral emphasis, as among the Yanomama, the fade-out from consanguinity to potential affinity is more rapid on the mother's side (Chagnon 1968:64, Shapiro 1972:73-77).

In cases like this it is necessary to call attention to a basic asymmetry in the contrastive categories of "consanguineals," or nonmarriageables, and "affines," or marriageables. The first is a relatively fixed and limited set, characterized by a previous history of social relations, while the latter is an inherently expandable one. If we wish in such cases to speak of a positive marriage rule applying to the affinal category as a whole, we can say that marriages are contracted only with people who are placed in a moral and social universe defined by the relationship terminology. This way of putting things has more to do with the culture, or ideology, of social relations than with the amalgam of social organizational and abstract structural considerations that lay behind the original concept of "elementary structures."

Turning back to the various ethnographic cases mentioned thus far, it can be seen that the concept of a positive marriage rule is differentially applicable and has varied meanings. In some cases we may well speak of a value being placed on marriage within a defined category of kin. In others the category of marriageables may essentially be seen as a category of relative strangers; cross relatives may be lumped with nonrelatives. In some societies the kin classification expands to encompass the entire sphere of those with whom one sustains social contact; in others this is less so. In the Northwest Amazon region a closed model of the social order, in which all local groups are viewed as being in some kind of kin relation to one another, seems to coexist with an open model, in which groups to whom one is related are contrasted with groups who are viewed as unknown and unrelated (Jackson 1977:87, C. Hugh-Jones 1979:92-93). In this area one finds positive preferences for marriage with particular close relatives, notably with the father's sister's daughter; the major norm regulating marriage, however, is the negative rule of descent group exogamy.

A historical perspective on marriage in lowland South America suggests cases in which positive rules have given way to kinship systems that regulate marriage through prohibition only. Perhaps one can see a predisposition toward change of this sort in an inherent priority of negative rules. Kensinger's account of the many principles governing Cashinahua marriage, for example, indicates that the most fundamental and only truly inviolable rule is the prohibition of marriage among "real" (*kuin*) kinsmen.[15] The shift from positive rule to negative rule seems to have taken place in the marriage system of the Kuikuru, along with a related change toward the more exclusive use of generational terminology among same-generation kinsmen. To be sure, it is difficult to determine the degree to which apparent differences between the Kuikuru and Kalapalo are to be attributed to the differing analytic orientations of the anthropologists who have studied them. Dole's explanation of the Kuikuru case, moreover, is problematic in that it posits a necessary connection between local group exogamy, the maintenance of a bifurcate-merging kin classification, and a positive marriage rule (Dole 1969). Her argument seems to rest on the idea that kinsmen cannot be distinguished from one another for purposes of marriage if they are living in the same place, a line of reasoning that is questionable on both logical and ethnographic grounds.

While some of the particular explanations that have been proposed for changes in marriage patterns may be overly simple and monistic,[16] the dislocations and severe depopulation brought about by colonialist penetration into the tropical forest area is certainly crucial in cases about which we have information. One such case is the Tapirapé of central Brazil, who have been the subject of ethnographic research for five decades. The Tapirapé prohibit marriage between close kinsmen and have no particular positive marriage rule; their system of kin classification distinguishes same-generation relatives by sex and age only. Comparison with the kin classifications of linguistically related groups provides persuasive evidence for the former existence of a bifurcate-merging, and hence probably Dravidian, relationship system (MacDonald 1965, Shapiro 1968). Factors to be considered in the Tapirapé case include the influence of their Gê-speaking neighbors, who do not share the general patterns of marriage and kin classification we have been discussing here, but also the sudden reduction of Tapirapé population during the first half of the twentieth century and the resulting dislocation with respect to kinship and village organization.

The effects of social change on lowland South American marriage systems, a very important topic that cannot be given the attention it deserves here, is mentioned in several of the articles in this volume. Kracke considers how a historical event like the absorption of a foreign group might have initiated a transformation in the Kagwahiv marriage system; he also inquires into the possibility that the Kagwahiv have acquired their moiety system relatively recently. Changes brought about by the colonial situation are a central concern in the papers by Crocker and Lyon. The particular question of how missionaries have impinged on indigenous marriage practices is treated by Jackson, Sorensen, and Lyon. In the Vaupés, changes in local group composition resulting from the creation of Catholic mission villages have disrupted traditional patterns of residential exogamy. Catholic missionaries in this region have actively sought to do away with sister exchange, an ideal type of marriage as far as the Indians are concerned, since the missionaries consider it a form of selling women (Jackson, pp. 162, 173). Sorensen (p. 189) mentions that missionaries have encouraged the abandonment of language group exogamy, a cardinal principle regulating marriage in the Northwest Amazon area, but indicates that they have made little headway thus far.

Alliance and Exchange

The "classic" model of alliance theory, as it developed in complementary opposition to descent theory, was based on the role of marriage in articulating and maintaining relationships between corporate kin groups through ties of affinity transmitted from one generation to the next. This model is problematic in the lowland South American context, particularly given the general absence of the kinds of corporate groups that figure as units of exchange in descriptions of alliance systems in other parts of the world.[17] Rivière (1973) has suggested that we avoid the term "alliance" altogether in speaking of marriage patterns among South American tropical forest peoples, and that we take care to distinguish terminological "lines" from descent constructs.

In his description of the Kagwahiv, Kracke speaks of alliances between "lines" of patrilineally related kinsmen. He notes, however, that these genealogically defined patrilines are the analyst's construct; they are neither corporate groups nor culturally recognized units. (pp. 108, 118). Jackson considers alliance to be one of the principles governing Vaupés marriage patterns, meaning by this the perpetuation of an exchange relationship between local descent groups (pp. 162-63). Sorensen (p. 192) notes a preference for matrilateral marriage (which exists alongside one for double cross-cousin marriage), but deals with this in reference to individual males in search of wives rather than in terms of relationships between groups. The unilateral preference that is more generally reported for the Northwest Amazon is for father's sister's daughter marriage (Jackson 1977 and this volume, C. Hugh-Jones 1979). Since societies in the Northwest Amazon present more of the familiar features of descent systems, including segmentary organization, than do other societies in lowland South America, one would expect that the concept of alliance would be more appropriate as well. C. Hugh-Jones (1979: 84-100) has discussed the particular value the Pirá-paraná Indians place on a continuing marital alliance associated with father's sister's daughter marriage; such an alliance, however, is one of several types of marriage in a system that is primarily oriented around the principle of exogamy.

Where affinal exchange cannot be seen as a continuing relationship between corporate kin groups, what are the parties involved? And what relationship is being perpetuated?

In studies of lowland South American societies, including the ones in this volume, the parties in a marital exchange are often identified as sibling sets or families. Local group membership commonly affects the norms of exchange between families. These points are well illustrated in Price's (1977) discussion of marital exchange among the Nambikwara of central Brazil. The Nambikwara consider marriage an exchange between two families, ideally taking the form of direct sibling exchange (sister exchange from a man's point of view and brother exchange from a woman's). The social importance of the village is revealed in the different treatment of marriages within and outside the community. When a marriage takes place between members of the same village, there is no insistence on immediate reciprocity. However, when marriage outside the village poses the threat of a loss to the community, direct compensation is sought (Price 1977, personal communication).[18] These data call to mind Maurice Bloch's (1973) discussion of "the long term and the short," in which the moral quality of a reciprocity that is eventual and not too closely calculated is contrasted with exchange relationships in which immediate return is expected or demanded.

If families or sibling sets are commonly the units involved in relationships of marital exchange, the time depth with which such exchange relationships are conceptualized seems to be a span of two generations. This is implied in Basso's discussion of *itsahene* (brother-sister exchange) marriages (p. 37) and is made explicit by Kracke in his analysis of patrilateral cross-cousin marriage, sister's daughter marriage, and the ritual expression of the marriage cycle among the Kagwahiv. Jackson's Bará informants express their preference for father's sister's daughter marriage over mother's brother's daughter marriage in terms of their concern for completing an exchange in the next generation rather than maintaining an outstanding debt (p. 168)—another example of the tendency toward direct and short-term exchange. A two-generational exchange relationship structured around patrilateral cross-cousin marriage has been desecribed for the Matsiguenga, who combine this practice with a preference for dispersing rather than repeating marital exchanges at a single genealogical level (Casevitz 1972, cited in Dreyfus 1977:382). The difference between these marriage practices and the kind of continuing exchange relations with which classical alliance theory is concerned may be likened to the distinction social anthropologists draw between cumulative filiation and descent.

A case of marriage preferences formulated in terms of a greater time depth is presented in the Whittens' account of the Canelos Quichua, who are explicitly concerned with affinal relationships in the grandparental generation. These relationships are in turn referred to a more remote ancestral period, since they are believed to replicate patterns dating from the "Time of the Grandparents," which can be understood in both mythic and historical terms (see, for example, Whitten 1976a:214). The Whittens' focus on the cultural meaning of Canelos marriage preferences leads, however, in a direction quite different from the concerns of alliance theory. Their account, like Kaplan's analysis of the Piaroa, provides an excellent case for studying the dynamic interplay of affinal and consanguineal kin categories in the context of cognatic descent and kindred organization. Both studies show the indissoluble connection between politico-religious leadership patterns and the kinship system, exploring the native concepts that order and link these domains.

In their report of how genealogical considerations enter into the Canelos reckoning of marriage preferences, the Whittens take account of both male and female perspectives. Their paper constitutes an important contribution to the study of parallel transmission, a matter that receives considerable attention in Crocker's essay as well.[19] The data on women's marital strategies are particularly welcome, since studies of marriage patterns, like studies of social organization more generally, have tended to be skewed toward the male perspective.[20] It is to be hoped that students of marriage in lowland South America, and elsewhere as well, will engage in more explicit comparison between the views of male and female informants, since these may differ in interesting ways. In the case of the Canelos, for example, if I understand the Whittens' data correctly, men and women seem to be somewhat at cross-purposes in what each would consider the ideal marriage (pp. 196-97).

The male focus that has generally characterized studies of kinship and marriage takes the specific form in alliance theory of viewing marriage systems as exchanges of women carried out by groups of men. As we have seen in the Nambikwara case above, however, what looks to male informants like an exchange of women may be viewed by female informants as an exchange of men. Crocker discusses why the concept of "exchange" as alliance theorists understand it is inappropriate in the Canela case; according to Crocker, the Canela see their own marriage system not in terms of women being "exchanged" but in terms of men being "moved" (notes 14, 15).

The essays in this collection offer rich cultural analyses of marriage practices in lowland South American societies. Studies like those of Kaplan and the Whittens show how an understanding of cosmological beliefs enables us better to interpret marriage rules and preferences. The Whittens outline the connection between the Canelos' marriage preferences and their beliefs about the transmission of soul substances from one generation to the next, which is partly a matter of inheritance and partly the result of achievement. For Canelos men, the world of kinship and marriage merges with shamanistic aspirations; for women, kin and affinal ties are linked with the passing on of pottery traditions. Kaplan's analysis of Piaroa marriage becomes part of an inquiry into the cosmological significance of dualism in the Piaroa world view. Her essay may be compared with Crocker's analysis of different types of dual opposition in Canela thought, which moves us beyond the concept of binary opposition as it is generally presented in the work of structuralists.

These studies come at a time when the anthropological investigation of social organization has been moving beyond its traditional boundaries to include the kind of material that was often, in standard monographs, treated under such separate rubrics as "religion," "ideology," or "world view." Studies like Christine Hugh-Jones's recent monograph on the Pirá-paraná Indians of the Northwest Amazon (1979) mark what is coming to be a particularly productive period in South American ethnography. What remains to be seen more clearly is how analyses like these can figure in comparative investigation. Structuralists, in general, see comparison to be possible only in terms of fairly abstract notions of formal relations. "Culturological" or "symbolic" approaches tend to entail interpretive schemata that are intended as specific to one society. Insights gained from these kinds of studies must now be formulated in terms appropriate to focused and specific comparative research.

In this volume, investigations of how marriage practices are reflected linguistically in kin terminological systems are supplemented with fuller consideration of how marriage is talked about. Kensinger's paper, for example, provides data on the different ways in which the Cashinahua formulate marriage preferences and evaluate the social and moral desirability of different types of union. He tells us about both the ideals they share and the terms in which they express their disagreements. Sorensen's essay on the process of finding a wife in the Northwest Amazon takes into account the fact that marriage has also to do with love, which is a rather refreshing reminder.

The material presented in these essays is particularly relevant to a topic of perennial interest and debate in anthropological writings on kinship and marriage: the relationship of genealogy to social classification. The so-called genealogical method is something that many anthropologists have come to look upon as at once a methodological convenience (or even necessity) and a theoretical embarrassment. Others have reacted to the limits it has placed on social anthropological inquiry by rejecting the notion of genealogy altogether, on apparently a prioristic grounds. This is an issue that must, however, be formulated as an ethnographic problem. The question of whether a marriage rule should be understood with reference to genealogically specified kinsmen or more general terminologically defined classes, for example, to which much theoretical debate has been devoted, is one that can be answered through close attention to how people talk about marriage.

If genealogical concepts serve as a necessary but not sufficient bridge to an understanding of what are now being called "relationship terminologies" (in an attempt to avoid the taboo term "kinship"), we have to come to terms with why this is so. We must also have more truly "ethnogenealogical" studies of the sort presented here by the Whittens, which show us the meanings attributed to genealogical relationships in particular cultures.

The Definition of Marriage

The question of how marriage is itself defined,[21] which has occasioned a certain amount of reflection and debate among anthropologists, has, for the most part, not been raised in the studies presented in this volume. One reason for this is that the relationships we label "marriage" in lowland South American societies do not present the kinds of features that anthropologists have found particularly problematic—for example, marital unions between members of the same sex or an unusually attenuated relationship between spouses. Marriage, as we encounter it in this region, generally comprises the familiar features of sexual rights and activity, co-responsibility in reproduction, economic cooperation, and co-residence. In a case where those we term "spouses" do not reside or take meals together, as among the Mundurucú (Murphy and Murphy 1974, Murphy 1959), the combination of sexual-reproductive rights and economic interdependence that characterizes the relationship allows it to fall easily within our analytic category of "marriage."

Two contributors to this collection, Kensinger and Dole, do deal with the definition of marriage. Their respective approaches provide a good point of entry into the wider body of anthropological literature dealing with this question. Kensinger is concerned with developing an ethnographically adequate definition of marriage in Cashinahua society and a formulation that is appropriate for cross-cultural purposes. He sees the two tasks as complementary and relates them to one another in terms of the "emic"/"etic" framework, as developed by Goodenough and set out most clearly in Goodenough's general discussion of description and comparison (Goodenough 1970). However, unlike Goodenough, who suggests a single definition of marriage that will cover all ethnographic cases (1970:12-13), Kensinger suggests instead a repertoire of possible features that will be represented differentially in different cases, with perhaps no single feature being found in all (p. 245). Using Goodenough's own analogy, but one that Goodenough did not himself apply to the definition of marriage, Kensinger suggests that we should think of a cross-cultural approach to the definition of marriage as similar to having a phonetic alphabet that corresponds to the sound patterns of no particular language, but provides the basis for comparing them in terms of a range of possibilities.

Dole, on the other hand, feels that some universal, cross-culturally applicable definition of marriage is a prerequisite for cultural anthropological research. The definition she proposes, and that she has herself used for the Kuikuru, is "the socially sanctioned kinship union of two or more persons for the purpose of legitimizing their sexual relations or offspring. Any such union necessarily establishes jural affinal relations and is publicly recognized . . . " (p. 60).[22] In Dole's view, defining marriage in a particular society seems to be a matter of applying some descriptively adequate general definition.

These approaches can be referred to two general positions found in anthropological writings on the definition of marriage. One is represented by those anthropologists who maintain that any search for a single definition of marriage is misguided, since the institutions we have called by that term vary from one society to the next; this view is represented by Leach (1961), Needham (1971b, 1975), and Rivière (1971). Other anthropologists, feeling that the role relationships we term "marriage" in our descriptions of other societies have something in common, have sought to provide a definition that will establish what these common features are.

In order to evaluate what has been written from each of these perspectives, and to bring greater clarity to anthropological discussions of the cross-cultural definition of marriage, it is important to distinguish among the following different questions and to address each separately:

1. Given the fact that we, as anthropologists, require some analytic language with which to describe and also to compare particular societies, can we make a principled choice about which set of culturally patterned relationships in a society's repertoire we will refer to, for comparative purposes, by the term "marriage"?

2. What is the relationship between a comparative definition of marriage that allows for such translation and an ethnographically adequate account of what constitutes "marriage" in a particular society?

3. Does the identification of certain general attributes of marriage necessarily imply an emphasis in comparative work on what all cases have in common? If not, how can we go about doing interesting and valuable work on the cross-culturally variable aspects of marriage?

The first question can and must be answered in the affirmative: we must be able to specify, with respect to comparative considerations, why we choose the label "marriage" for one kind of culturally patterned relationship and not for another. We cannot accept Rivière's position that marriage can only be defined as "one of the forms of relationship between the sexes," and that the question of "which of the forms of relationship between the sexes is, in any given society, to be regarded as the marital one . . . cannot be decided in advance" (Rivière 1971:65). Rivière claims that his approach is less problematic than it seems and that it works quite well in actual practice, since "it seems likely that anyone in any society will be able to tell the inquirer whether or not they are married (*assuming that the linguistic and terminological difficulty can be overcome*)" (1971:65; italics added). Clearly the clause in parentheses expresses the crux rather than the resolution of the problem. As Gough (1959:71) has pointed out, "unless we approach these [different kinds of relationships between men and women] with some guiding concepts of our own, we cannot decide which of them to translate as 'marriage.' " Rivière's own use of the term "marriage" in his monograph on the Trio (1969), his choice of which cross-sex bond to so label, depended not on features peculiar to this group of South American Indians but, rather, on comparative considerations he brought to his analysis.

Turning to the second question, on what basis can we use the comparative, analytic term "marriage" for the differing, culturally defined institutions of different societies? How can we formulate the relationship between the comparative definition and an ethnographically adequate definition of what constitutes "marriage" in a particular society? I maintain that our ability to apply the term "marriage" to a culturally defined class of relationships in a particular society rests on our being able to specify that that class *includes* relationships of a type that can be defined cross-culturally, given that it may include other types of relationship as well; that the relationships in the class *include* features outlined in the general, comparative definition, given that they may include other features as well. I will explain more fully what I mean by this further on in my discussion. For now, let me just point out that when we approach the role relationships that form a category in a particular society, the category presents characteristics that are familiar to us from our cross-cultural experience. That is what enables us to make contact with the category and to make a principled choice of the analytic term by which we designate it. We will, however, need to invoke other considerations in order to come to terms with the category as it is formed in that society. What I am saying may seem self-evident; yet the fact is that anthropological debate on the definition of marriage has generally failed to maintain the necessary distinction between cross-cultural definitions and culture-specific categories, and to suggest a clear way of viewing the relationship between them.

As for the third question, the identification of cross-culturally recurrent features in the institutions we call "marriage" in no way implies that comparative research is a matter of finding lowest common denominators. Indeed, establishing universals or general recurrences is only a part of a larger enterprise that also involves addressing the patterning of cross-cultural variation.

Let us now consider some of the general definitions of marriage that have appeared in the anthropological literature. The most familiar and often-cited of these are the definition proposed by Murdock in *Social Structure* (1949) and the one found in *Notes and Queries in Anthropology* (sixth edition, 1951). According to Murdock, " . . . marriage exists only when the economic and sexual are united into one relationship, and this combination occurs only in marriage. Marriage, thus defined, is found in every known human society. In all of them, moreover, it involves residential cohabitation, and in all of them it forms the basis of the nuclear family" (1949:8). The 1951 edition of *Notes and Queries in Anthropology* defined marriage as "a union between a man and woman such that children born to the woman are recognized legitimate offspring of both parents."

Both of these definitions came under attack by anthropologists who maintained that they failed to cover particular cases, for example, the marriage patterns of the South Indian Nayar, where husband-wife and father-child ties are minimal, or the institution of woman-woman marriage found in a large number of African societies. If we look at lowland South America, we see that the Mundurucú, mentioned above, do not meet all of the criteria proposed in Murdock's definition.

In subsequent attempts at defining marriage, anthropologists sought to avoid these shortcomings and to arrive at formulations that would cover even the most problematic ethnographic cases. Thus Gough (1959: 32) defined marriage as "a relationship established between a woman and one or more other persons, which provides that a child born to the woman under circumstances not prohibited by the rules of the relationship, is accorded full birth-status rights common to normal members of his society or social stratum." Goodenough, seeking to improve on Gough's definition, which focused on legitimacy, proposed one that focused instead on sexual access, which Goodenough deemed more fundamental to the definition of marriage. According to Goodenough, marriage is "a transaction and resulting contract in which a person (male or female, corporate or individual, in person or by proxy) establishes a continuing claim to the right of sexual access to a woman—this right having priority over rights of sexual access others currently have or may subsequently acquire in relation to her (except in a similar transaction) until the contract resulting from the transaction is terminated—and in which the woman involved is eligible to bear children" (1970:12-13). The general orientation revealed in Goodenough's definition, as in many others, can be characterized as "bio-jural"; that is, a highly legalistic view of the conjugal bond is combined with a tendency to derive marriage directly from the "natural" facts of sex and reproduction. One point that should emerge from the following discussion is that such a formulation is more a reflection of how marriage is viewed in our own society than it is a satisfactory cross-cultural characterization of the marital relationship.

Both Gough and Goodenough were attempting to provide a general definition of marriage that could cover all cases, including those that appeared to constitute exceptions to earlier definitions. It seems, however, that that goal of covering all cases has been conceived in a less than satisfactory manner. What we want is a set of concepts that will allow us to establish comparative contact with all the societies we study; this does not mean that our concepts have to address the full range of practices found in each of these societies. As I shall show, our ability to identify the unions between women found in various African societies as "marriages" does not depend upon our having a cross-cultural definition of marriage that is itself broad enough to cover this ethnographic possibility; the existence of such unions does not necessitate a general revision of the definition of marriage along the lines envisaged by Gough and Goodenough. Goodenough's definition is, in any event, inappropriate to the forms of woman-woman marriage found in Africa, since these unions are hardly best understood in terms of "sexual access"; issues like rights in children and/or access to labor seem more to the point (see, for example, Gough 1971 and Krige 1974). In more general terms, one might well ask why a comparative, cross-cultural definition should have to account for practices that are found in some societies and not in others.

Anthropological debate on the definition of marriage has been plagued by recurrent attempts to have general definitions account for phenomena that are best understood in culture-specific terms. To continue with the example of woman-woman marriage, since it is an interesting one and has received a considerable amount of attention in the literature, we might first note that this type of conjugal union is essentially limited in its occurrence to Africa, where it is quite common. This should lead us to inquire into what there is about kinship, marriage, and other areas of social life in those African societies in which woman-woman marriage is found that makes this institution both possible and meaningful. We might begin by noting the importance of exchanges of wealth, as opposed to sexual activity, in defining marital unions and legitimating rights in off-spring. A cultural separation between biological and social paternity is a basic element in the kinship systems of societies in this region, and clearly a contributing factor to the possibility of woman-woman marriage and female fatherhood. Another major consideration is the salience of descent as a principle of social identity: a woman's status as member of a descent group may override her gender in determining the position she occupies. Finally, the very centrality of kinship to the role systems of African societies, combined with the other features just outlined, means that kinship can serve to express the social promotion of women to statuses normally occupied by men.[23]

The need for a culture-specific approach to patterns like woman-woman marriage can be seen even more clearly if we compare the African cases we have been considering to the question of homosexual marriage in our own society. While such unions are not currently recognized by law, many feel that they should be. If same-sex unions make sense to a certain segment of American society, it is certainly not for any of the same reasons that woman-woman marriage makes sense to the Nuer, Lovedu, Nandi, or Yoruba. In order to understand current arguments in favor of homosexual marriage, we must be aware of how the marital bond is viewed culturally, the kind of companionship it is felt to entail, and the role of sexual love in the union. We must also see how the question can be construed as a civil rights issue. Similarly, opposition to homosexual marriage from other segments of society must be analyzed with reference to cultural beliefs that heterosexuality and heterosexual marriage are rooted in nature or in divine will.[24]

Let me at this point suggest a basis for the cross-cultural identification of "marriage" relationships and discuss how my own approach compares with the others I have been considering, including those presented in in this volume.

I propose that we may appropriately label "marriage" that class of relationships, defined as a category in a given society, that includes within it relationships having the following characteristics: that the partners be a man and a woman; that sexual activity be a defining feature of the relationship; that socially significant bonds be established between the partners and any offspring they may have (what anthropologists understand by "filiation"); that the union involve wider social ties between persons related to the respective partners (what anthropologists understand by "affinity"); and that the relationship be a part of the society's system of relations of production.

The component parts of this definition—a cross-sex bond, sexual activity, filiative bonds, affinal relationships, ties to the economic system—are themselves familiar from many other definitions, including the one presented in Dole's paper. I would, however, like to call attention to some points concerning the concepts of filiation and affinity, and to the nature of the relationship I am establishing between marriage and economic systems.

The concept of filiation, as I use it here, contains no assumptions about cultural theories of conception, an issue that is commonly raised in discussions of filiation and descent; it does not rest on beliefs about the physical transmission of substance from parent to child. Nor does the filiative tie between a man and his children necessarily involve a man's having some significant set of rights over or obligations to his children, a matter to which Goodenough has devoted attention (1970:27ff.). What is at issue is that the social identities of both partners in a sexual relationship are relevant to the social placement of children that are believed to be the outcome of such a relationship. As for relations of affinity, these need not be established as a result of the marriage; they may precede the marriage, as in the case of certain "alliance" systems described for Southeast Asia and elsewhere, or in the case of those lowland South American societies described in this volume whose systems of kin classification can appropriately be characterized as incorporating a positive marriage rule. The point is that whether affinal relationships are *presupposed* when a marriage takes place or whether they are *created* by that marriage (see note 10 below), the concept of affinity clearly depends upon the concept of marriage.[25]

The idea that marriage should be viewed from an economic perspective harks back to Murdock's definition. Murdock saw the economic dimension of marriage as a matter of the division of labor between the sexes in the context of the conjugal family. I prefer to see it in terms of a link between sexual and reproductive relations and the wider socio-economic structures of a society. A system of economic relations involves the mobilization and channeling of sexual energies; the replication of roles within that system is tied to reproductive arrangements. The husband-wife pair need not themselves constitute a significant unit of production and consumption, though commonly they do. Their union will, however, express those social categories central to the society's system of relations of production, be they categories of rank, class, caste, lineage, or sex itself.

The definition of marriage I am presenting here differs from others less in its content than in how its range of application is formulated. In order for the term to apply, it is not necessary that all "marriages" in a particular society meet the criteria outlined above, only that the culturally defined class of relationships we, as anthropologists, translate by the comparative term "marriage" include relationships that do meet these criteria. We thus establish our point of comparative contact with the society we are studying by our ability to specify at least a subclass of relationships that fall within a cultural category we choose to label "marriage"; at the same time, we allow for the fact that other types of relationships may be part of that category as well. It is important to keep in mind that our ability to identify these other types of relationships as "marriage" itself depends on their membership in a wider class that we have been able to define with reference to the general definition.

The approach I am taking here posits *implicational* relationships between different forms of marital union: that is, the existence of certain types of marriage, or the identification of certain unions as "marriages," implies the prior existence, or prior identification, of other types of union. Inquiries into implicational relations, or implicational hierarchies, has been basic to typological comparative work in linguistics (Jakobson 1941, Greenberg 1966) and might profitably be considered by social anthropologists. In the study of marriage such an approach would help us to distinguish between universal and variable features, and might also bring more order into the study of those features that vary.

It is of interest to compare the concept of implicational relations with the respective approaches to the definition of marriage taken by Needham and Kensinger. Needham has claimed that the term "marriage" has been used to designate institutions that have no single feature in common. According to Needham, terms like "marriage" are what Wittgenstein called "odd-job" words: they do not designate a class constituted by some universally shared feature or features but are instead based on an overlapping of features, a set of serial resemblances—what Wittgenstein termed "family likenesses" (Needham 1971b:5, 29-30). Needham goes on to argue that this notion of "family likenesses" corresponds to what a natural scientist calls a "polythetic," as opposed to "monothetic," class (1975).

Kensinger acknowledges that some features may prove to be common to all marriage systems, but plays down the significance of this possibility for a comparative approach, which he feels should address itself essentially to the complexity and variation among forms of marriage. He proposes an analogy with the International Phonetic Alphabet: a comparative, or "etic," approach to marriage should consist of developing "a matrix chart wherein various constellations of features can be identified" (p. 245). Kensinger's model has certain structural properties not found in Needham's, though these are not worked out in explicit detail by Kensinger here.

Comparing these two perspectives to the one I have adopted, I suggest that an approach that rests on implicational relations better accounts for how anthropologists are, in fact, proceeding when they do comparative research. I would go further and suggest that this may be the only way they can proceed. In any event, the discussion I have presented above would seem to show that Needham is incorrect when he asserts that the institutions we have labeled "marriage" have no single feature or features in common. The implicational relations model, moreover, has considerable potential as an ordering device in cross-cultural study. The emics/etics model used by Kensinger, while providing a basically sound general analogy for the process of comparative inquiry, also involves certain problems—a subject to which I shall return in a moment.

Both Kensinger's and Needham's discussions are productive insofar as they direct attention to comparison based not just on identity but on variation. It is interesting to note that Needham never followed up on this line of inquiry. The same observation can be made of Leach's (1951) earlier discussion of the definition of marriage; Leach presented a list of the different kinds of rights that marriage could serve to establish in different societies, but failed to pursue further any comparative investigation that might have been suggested by his own consideration of such varying features. Both Leach and Needham instead used variation as a point of departure for arguing the uselessness of all general definitions of marriage. The main reason for this is that both were concerned with dissociating themselves from traditional functionalist approaches in social anthropology in favor of structural analysis in the mode of Lévi-Strauss. What this amounted to was a search for relations of a highly abstract sort, that take the form of a "mathematical pattern" (Leach 1961:2), and that express the "logical and psychic facilities which are elementary resources available to all mankind in the ordering of experience" (Needham 1971b:32). Unfortunately, such an approach, whatever its merits, had problematic implications for comparative research that were not unlike those of the functionalism it criticized: no matter where one went, one was essentially looking for the same thing.

One of the major problems with functionalist approaches was the uneasy and unclear relationship between natives' explanations of their own behavior and the analyst's interpretation of the social order. In Radcliffe-Brown's positivist view, society, or social structure, was a "concrete reality" that could be studied by "direct observation" ([1940] 1952: 190). The essential conflict between this objectivist perspective and the clearly normative approach that Radcliffe-Brown took to the study of social institutions went unrecognized and unresolved in his own work, as it did in that of his predecessor and major source of theoretical inspiration, Emile Durkheim.

In structuralist writings we find an equally disturbing disjunction between the "surface" phenomena recorded by the ethnographer and the "deep" structures that are said to constitute a society's most significant ordering principles. The result can be, once again, an obscure relationship between informants' understandings and the anthropologist's analysis. Rivière's discussion of the definition of marriage is a case in point. In the course of his exposition he criticizes an account by Christopher Crocker of two kinds of sexual union among the Bororo. Crocker had labeled one kind of union "marriage" and the other a "sexual liaison"; Rivière takes him to task for "simply expressing in Leach's terms the criteria which the Bororo themselves appear to employ in making [such] a distinction" (Rivière 1971:58). But is it not the very purpose of analytic distinctions to adequately account for the distinctions made by the people we study? This does not mean that anthropologists confine themselves to native theories of the social system, though such theories do constitute important social scientific data. It is rather the task of the anthropologist to penetrate beneath this more conscious, or ideological, level to get at the tacit and covert conventions that make action meaningful and interpretable.

Kensinger sees the ethnographer's task in essentially these terms. The ethnoscientific tradition within which he is working, however, presents some of the same difficulties as the approaches I have just been considering. If we look at Goodenough's work, for example, we can see an amalgam of a kind of functionalism similar to Malinowski's (or Murdock's) and a structural linguistic approach derived from phonemics, the same ultimate source of many Lévi-Straussian structuralist notions. Goodenough's functionalist orientation leads him to base his general definitions of institutions like marriage in "universal functions" that are defined with reference to biological needs and other "extra-cultural conditions" (1970: 122). His work is also characterized by a dualism that is reminiscent of the unresolved contradiction in Radcliffe-Brown's work, noted above. In Goodenough's case what we have is an opposition between "culture" and "society," in which culture is viewed as a set of shared ideas that can be studied out of the context of social action, while society is, to use Goodenough's terms, "a material-behavioral system of interacting people and things" (1970:103) that is presumably amenable to "objective" study. In other words, we seem to be faced with a gulf between culture as an activity of the mind and society as mindless activity.

This same dualism is behind the emic/etic model of comparative research, as elaborated by Goodenough (1970) and adopted here by Kensinger. The "etic grids" used in comparison are based on an analogy with a phonetics defined in objective, physicalist terms. Paradoxically, this model, besides involving a problematic view of phonology (see Jakobson and Halle 1956), seeks to develop a "cultural semantics" by drawing on just that level of linguistic analysis that does not itself deal with meaning—an observation that is also relevant to the structuralist enterprise.[26] These assumptions may not all be a part of Kensinger's own use of the emics/etics model. Nonetheless, having defined his goal in terms of providing an "emic" analysis of Cashinahua marriage, Kensinger has difficulty relating the rich material on how Cashinahua talk about marriage, which takes up the major part of his paper, to the conclusions about underlying rules that inform Cashinahua behavior.[27] The emics/ etics analogy also fails to provide guidance on how the legal and moral dimensions of marriage in particular societies are connected to a cross-cultural definition of the marital relationship (p. 245).

Another aspect of Kensinger's approach to marriage that grows out of his ethnoscientific orientation is his concern with discriminating between optional and obligatory features of marriage, and with arriving at a definition that will clearly distinguish between marriage and other kinds of relationships. The distinction between definitional and nondefinitional dimensions of marriage is indeed an important one. The question must, however, be approached in a dynamic and subtle manner. We want to consider the possibility that disagreements may exist within a society about what are, or should be, the defining attributes of the marital relationship.[28] Changes that occur over time in the social definition of marriage may be a matter of shifts between the obligatoriness and optionality of various of the relationship's attributes. In general, anthropologists interested in the cross-cultural study of marriage can benefit from the experience of linguists who have found that studying a pattern that is overt, formal, and obligatory in one grammatical system enables them to understand the operation of a similar pattern in another language in which it is relatively covert and less formalized. Finally, too rigid a distinction between definitional and nondefinitional aspects of marriage would leave us unable to address the networks of meaning that give the marital relationship its distinctive cultural significance in any particular society.

The goal of defining marriage in a clear and unambiguous manner must be formulated more precisely and viewed in ethnographic perspective. Not all societies are themselves concerned with unambiguous distinctions between marriage and other forms of sexual union. On the contrary, ambiguity may play a central role in a marriage system (see, for example, Comaroff 1980). It may also be appropriate in some cases to speak of marriage as a matter of degree, as Murray (1976) points out in his description of marriage among the Basotho. One might, in fact, look at Cashinahua marriage in this light, based on the data provided by Kensinger. While Kensinger states that the Cashinahua make a clear distinction between marriages and affairs (pp. 243-44 and note 6), he also provides a tripartite classification of marriages in which one type ("Illegitimate-improper") so totally violates Cashinahua marriage rules that it would not be allowed to persist and another type ("Legitimate-improper") can perhaps be seen as somewhat less of a marriage than the remaining type ("Legitimate-proper") (pp. 240-42). The marriage Kensinger calls "Legitimate-improper" is a socially recognized albeit not approved union between a man and a woman that can form the core of a nuclear or polygynous family and may attach itself to other social units in the village. It may not, however, form the nucleus of what Kensinger calls an "atom of social organization," that is, a nexus of relationships that typifies the ordering principles of Cashinahua society. These marriages thus do not figure in the processes of social reproduction in the same way as "Legitimate-proper" marriages do, a distinction that refers us back to the general definition of marriage outlined above.

In the light of these considerations, it is possible to formulate in more precise terms what we should expect of a cross-cultural definition of marriage with respect to distinguishing between different types of union. The cross-cultural definition should enable us to make an analytically principled choice about which of the unions distinguished by the cultural system in question (insofar as such distinctions are in fact made) we will label "marriage." The choice will be guided by the features of the cross-cultural definition: the term "marriage" will be used for the type or types of sexual relationship most concerned with filiation, affinity, and economic ties (that is, with the process of reproducing the social and economic system). As Kensinger puts it at one point in his discussion, our definition should "allow us to discuss marriage in any society with as little ambiguity as possible, while conveying whatever ambiguity exists in the system itself" (p. 245).

The reason that anthropologists have tended to view the discrimination between marriage and other sexual relationships as a relatively straight-forward matter is that they themselves, for the most part, come from societies in which marriages are brought into being by a particular act or ceremony, be it civil or religious. The phrase "I now pronounce you man and wife," uttered in the course of a marriage ceremony (that is, by an authorized person, in an appropriate setting, when certain conditions have been met), constitutes what philosophers of language call a "performative," since it serves to bring into being a particular state of affairs, in this case a marriage. Marriages in lowland South American societies, on the other hand, are brought about in a different manner. Kensinger makes the very important point that marriage in Cashinahua society must be looked on as a process (pp. 222, 224, 244), a conclusion that emerges from a number of other articles in this collection, including those by Jackson, Sorensen, the Whittens, Kracke, and Crocker.[29] The exchanges associated with a marriage unfold over time, and the conjugal bond is established as couples sustain a particular kind of relationship with one another. Kracke (pp. 112-14) speaks of a simple wedding ceremony among the Kagwahiv, but it is clear that this ritual is not what brings the marriage into being. The Whittens (p. 210) note that the concept of cementing the affinal bond with a single ritual is foreign to Canelos Quichua culture. The group marriage ceremony described by Crocker for the Canela serves primarily to reinforce marriages that already exist (p. 70), and may be seen as having primarily to do with the age grading system that plays such a central role in the social organization of Gê peoples.[30]

With the perspectives provided by these ethnographic cases, we must re-examine Dole's general definition of marriage, which includes the proviso that there be some kind of "marriage act" (see note 22). According to Dole, the marital union must be "publicly recognized, if not acclaimed, by a customary act, even if that act is no more than moving one's ham-mock" (pp. 60-61). The essential point here is to be careful about the meaning of such acts. They may serve to indicate, or announce, that a marriage has taken place; they may provide the idiom in which members of the society commonly speak of a marital union having been established. This does not mean, however, that the social acts themselves bring the marital union into being, as a civil or religious ceremony does in our own society. In other words, the more general category of acts that bear some symbolic relationship to marriage must be distinguished from the narrower category of those that serve as performatives. Kensinger does well to note (p. 244) that a general definition of marriage should contain no assumption that marriage is necessarily an act, a covert assumption we might tend to make because of both our social norms and the properties of our language.

The marriage process in lowland South American societies does not generally involve special rituals or elaborate ceremonies. Given the kinds of socioeconomic systems involved and the lack of significant corporate group organization below the level of the community, marriage does not involve important and formalized transfers of rights over resources, property, and persons. Bride service, rather than bride wealth, is the general practice in the region, which accords with the processual nature of marriage. While relations of affinity are accompanied by relations of exchange, it is not generally exchange that serves to legitimate the marriage. The issue of legitimacy, particularly with respect to the legitimation of offspring, is itself not a central preoccupation. It is interesting to note that the concept of legitimacy figures in Kensinger's discussion of Cashinahua marriage not in connection with the status of offspring but in connection with how well a union adheres to the rules for the proper choice of spouse.

As noted above, the relationships that have been labeled "marriage" in the societies of lowland South America have seemed familiar enough not to have occasioned any problems in the application of the term. The definition of Cashinahua marriage proposed by Kensinger (p. 240)—involving cohabitation, a sexual relationship, and economic cooperation—closely parallels Murdock's (1949:8) definition of marriage quoted earlier. This definition seems a reasonable point of departure for characterizing marriage in lowland South American societies more generally. What we may now proceed to do is augment this definition through the kind of rich ethnography that has come increasingly to characterize South American studies in recent years, so that we may achieve a fuller understanding of the many meanings of marriage for societies in this part of the world.

NOTES

1. In addition to Lévi-Strauss's own writings, other relatively early key contributions to this body of literature include Leach (1951), Dumont (1953a, 1957), and Needham (1958).

2. In descriptions of these systems the term "kin" is used in two different ways: in its more general sense, it covers all classes that form part of the terminological system; when used more specifically, it refers to nonmarriageables only. Since I will want to consider the significance of this polysemous pattern as it figures in a native system of social classification (for example, that of the Kalapalo), I have thought it best to refrain from ambiguous usage in my own comparative discussion. I will therefore use the term "kin" in its broader sense and use the term "consanguine" for the more restricted category of non-affinal kin. I do not thereby imply any ideology of relationship based on shared blood or other physical substance.

3. Several of the groups represented in this collection fall outside the culture areal rubric adopted by Rivière and have different systems of classification; these groups include the Canela, Bororo, and Canelos Quichua. For a general discussion of Dravidian systems among Carib-speaking tropical forest societies, see Rivière (1977).

4. Kaplan's article in particular includes a discussion of affinal as opposed to consanguineal interpretations of Dravidian kin terms, and also contains critical comments on Scheffler's approach.

5. Scheffler himself has made this point repeatedly in his various writings (see, for example, 1977:873).

6. I do not wish to become involved here in the lengthy debate among alliance theorists concerning the terms "prescription" and "preference," but will confine myself to a couple of brief observations. A critical discussion of the prescription/preference debate can be found in Schneider (1965b), which covers the literature up to that point. See also Lévi-Strauss (1967:xvii-xxiii), Needham (1971a:lix-lxxxi; 1973), and Maybury-Lewis (1965). The distinction between "prescription" and "preference" is sometimes, but not always, seen as congruent to Lévi-Strauss's opposition between "mechanical" and "statistical" models (1953).

7. Buchler and Selby (1968:137-88) make this point in their discussion of the controversy over Dravidian terminologies.

8. That the structural analysis of kinship and marriage, as developed by Lévi-Strauss, deals only tangentially with the meaningful systems commonly understood by the anthropological concept of "culture" has been pointed out by Schneider and Boon (1974:802).

9. This concept of multiple exchange is an appropriate characterization of marriage systems in which a prohibition on marriage between relatives is combined with a set of preferences including sibling exchange, sibling polygamy, sororate, and levirate. Such a system is found throughout most of the North American Great Basin, for example (Shapiro, in press).

10. My use of the concepts of presupposition and creativity follows Silverstein's analysis of rules of language use (1976:33-35). The opposition can be applied to the analysis of kin terms: one can speak of a kin term as "presupposing" insofar as its use can be accounted for in terms of separate, preexisting criteria such as genealogical linkage or common membership in a social group; "creative" use of a kin term, on the other hand, itself serves to bring a particular relationship into being.

11. I will return to this point in greater detail below, when I take up the issue of how exchange and alliance can be understood in the societies described in this volume.

12. The Cashinahua have until recently been the only case of a Karieratype section system reported for South America. Another case, however, has been described in Melatti's (1977) preliminary ethnographic study of the Marubo, who live near the Brazil-Peru border at the headwaters of the Itui and Curaça rivers. In this system an individual belongs to the same named section as his or her maternal grandmother.

13. According to Dole, the current pattern of cousin terminology among the Kuikuru is purely generational. I will return to this point in a moment when I take up the question of historical change.

14. He later claimed that he had no particular interest in most of the issues raised in the debate over the meaning of "prescription" (Lévi-Strauss 1967: xvii-xxiii; see note 6 above). Both Leach (1970:105) and Needham (1971a: xcii) have noted problems in how we are to understand Lévi-Strauss's distinction between elementary and complex structures.

15. Dole's (p. 54) observations about the narrow effective scope of the cross versus parallel distinction in Kuikuru terminology may also mean that the pattern of extensions shows Iroquois rather than Dravidian features, which would accord with the absence of a positive marriage rule.

16. This problem is discussed by Needham (1974), who presents and reanalyzes Suárez's account of historical changes in the marriage system and kin classification of the Warao of Venezuela (Suárez 1971, 1972).

17. Problems in applying alliance models in lowland South America involve the question of how descent can be understood in this part of the world—a topic that is beyond the scope of this essay. The examination of descent constructs in lowland South America was the subject of a symposium at the 74th annual meetings of the American Anthropological Association (Descent in Lowland South America 1975, Shapiro and Hunderfund n.d.). The papers given by Murphy and Shapiro in that symposium raise some general comparative considerations. For discussion and debate concerning the role of patrilineal descent in one South American Indian society, the Yanomama, see Shapiro (1972:72-74, 95-102, 197; 1974), Ramos (1972), Taylor and Ramos (1975), Ramos and Albert (1977), and Lizot (1977).

18. A similar point has been made by Townsend and Adams (1973) in their discussion of marriage exchange among the Culina of eastern Peru: strict accounts are kept with regard to exchange outside the village, while within the community there is not the same concern for achieving precisely balanced exchanges.

19. Also relevant to this issue is Kensinger's observation (p. 231) that Cashinahua women reckon their moiety affiliation not through their fathers directly but through relationship to a genealogically more distant female relative.

20. See Shapiro (1981) for a discussion of this issue and references to some of the literature on male bias in anthropology.

21. The argument I am presenting here is developed at greater length and in more detail in an essay entitled "Marriage as a Comparative Concept." Copies of this manuscript, which has been submitted for publication, can be obtained from the author.

22. The passage continues with "if not acclaimed, by a customary act, even if that act is no more than moving one's hammock." The question of what Dole, here following Ackerman, refers to as the "marriage act" will be taken up below.

23. For ethnographic data and analytic perspectives on these points, see

Gough (1971), Krige (1974), O'Brien (1977), Oboler (1980), and Shapiro (1979:283-84).

24. For an analysis of American concepts of kinship that are relevant to this issue, see Schneider (1968). Rosenthal (1979) provides a legal perspective on homosexual marriage that is also culturally revealing.

25. The attempt on the part of alliance theorists to shift emphasis from the conjugal pair to wider marital exchange relations has led to occasional analytic confusion on this issue (see, for example, Leach 1955).

26. I am indebted to Michael Silverstein for my understanding of these points and also for introducing me to the concept of implicational hierarchies. Silverstein's analyses of the ethnoscientific literature have so far been presented primarily in unpublished lectures, but some of the general points are treated in Silverstein (1976).

27. Part of the problem is a covert shift in focus from the classification of marriages to the discrimination between unions that are considered true marriages and those that are not. (I shall be taking up this latter question below.) In more general terms, the ethnoscientific tradition within which Kensinger is operating, based as it is on equating meaning with reference and cultural knowledge with a classification of objects according to their properties, limits Kensinger's ability to appreciate the data he has himself collected on the "pragmatics" of classifying marriage—that is, how classification may depend on features of the social situation in which classification is taking place rather than on features of the marriages being classified. For a general discussion of these issues, see Silverstein (1976). Ethnographic analyses that shed particular light on the limitations of the ethnoscientific method include Schneider (1965a) and Moerman (1971).

28. Rivière seems to find the existence of such differing views about marriage troublesome (1971:59); on the contrary, inquiries into intracultural variation should be central to the ethnographic enterprise and are an intrinsic part of the study of social change, something that functionalist approaches, as Rivière himself points out (1971:59), have never been able to address.

29. Carter's (1977) discussion of Andean marriage is also relevant here; according to Carter, the use of the term "trial marriage" by ethnographers reflects an inability to appreciate the processual nature of marriage in this region. The importance of viewing marriage in certain societies as a process has been emphasized by a number of Africanist ethnographers (see, for example, Roberts 1977, Comaroff and Roberts 1977, Comaroff 1980).

30. The Canela ceremony may be compared with the group marriage ceremony described by Maybury-Lewis for the Akwẽ-Shavante, in which an entire age set is married at once to girls some of whom are still toddlers (1967:79-80). These marriages may or may not endure; the ceremony itself follows an initiation and marks the passage of the age set into a new grade.

PART II

BRAZIL

2

A Husband for His Daughter, a Wife for Her Son: Strategies for Selecting a Set of In-laws among the Kalapalo

ELLEN B. BASSO

The culture of the Kalapalo Indians includes a set of kinship terms which may be ordered along two dimensions of contrast, that of "kinship" and that of "affinability" (see Figure 1). Reference to "kinship" allows a member of the society to classify kin so that only generational distinctions are made. These generational divisions refer not to the relative age of kin but to successive ascendancy and descendancy of sibling sets (*ifisúandaw*) who are linked to each other by ties of matrifiliation and/or patrifiliation. By referring to "affinability," a speaker distinguishes among kinsmen within these generational sets so as to yield categories defined as "spouse exchangers." Depending upon the situation, a Kalapalo may designate the same individual as a "kinsman" or as a "spouse exchanger," or (s)he may classify differently two persons who occupy the same genealogical kin-type position.

With reference to this system of alternate classification, the only statement Kalapalo make about marriage is that persons who are classed as *ifándaw* ("spouse exchangers at ego's generation") are the only kinds of kinsmen who can legitimately become spouses (*iŋiso*) and lovers (*ajo*). These relationships should not occur between other kinds of kinsmen.[1]

However, the Kalapalo cannot clearly state why *ifándaw* are appropriate spouses and lovers, and are unable to explain why they identify certain kin as potential affines and designate others as unaffinable. Yet it is clear that all Kalapalo make decisions about affinability in choosing spouses for their offspring and lovers for themselves. They must decide who among their kin are affinable and then select among several possible

33

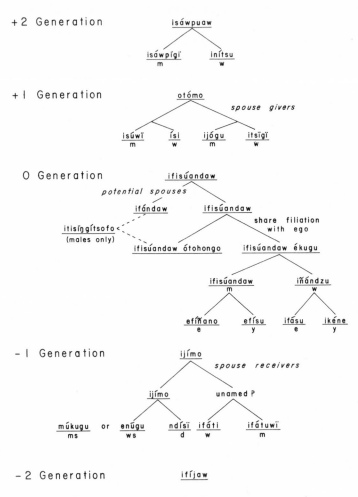

FIGURE 1. KALAPALO KINSHIP CATEGORIES.

affines (including those who are nonrelatives). What, then, are the criteria upon which these decisions are made? Are there benefits that accrue to spouse exchangers possessing certain qualities that mark them as "affinable"? If so, what are the strategies for gaining the maximum possible benefits from a marriage alliance?

It is clear from the way Kalapalo use kinship terms that these are intimately linked with ideas about relationships between people, especially norms (rules for behavior) and moral meanings that indicate the appropriateness or inappropriateness of certain kinds of behavior. Norms and morals are inseparable from the definitions of Kalapalo kinship categories, as they are inseparable from the general Kalapalo notion of "kinship." Thus ideas about relationships and behavior are critical for understanding how kinship terms are used to classify individuals. To understand more precisely the meaning of affinability, we must examine Kalapalo ideas about proper kinship behavior in general, and indicate how these norms are applied in different situations.

The Kalapalo understand all kin to be involved in a continual reciprocal relationship of *ifutisu,* that is, supportive behavior including sharing food and possessions, assisting in communal projects, and verbally defending relatives who have been accused of serious crimes, especially witchcraft. Enactment of these norms indicates that kin have "respect" for one another. Yet despite this ideal code, some persons clearly show more intense *ifutisu* for their kin than do others. Similarly, *ifutisu* relationships are often skewed so that a person receives more deference than (s)he displays. Precisely who among the members of an individual's kindred are involved in relationships of greater *ifutisu* than they receive varies considerably, according to several specific factors.

To begin with, certain kinds of kinship and affinal relationships are defined in terms of normative conduct that requires deference on the part of one member of the dyad. For example, children are expected to defer to the opinions and decisions of their parents, and younger siblings to their elders. Similarly, among affines, a newly married son- or daughter-in-law must defer to the parents-in-law. As a result of these inegalitarian normative obligations, individuals tend to receive greater *ifutisu* from certain kin than they show those persons. In addition, a few Kalapalo receive more respect from a wider set of kin than do the majority. Most Kalapalo have only a few kin who display greater deference than they receive, the majority of a person's relatives being on a relatively "equal" *ifutisu* relationship with him. In any case, the number of a person's subservient relatives is to a great extent the consequences of genealogical fortuities, such as the number of living siblings an individual happens to have, how many children (s)he has, and, of these, how many are male, how many female. However, Kalapalo men who have relatively large numbers of deferential relatives (both kin and affines) tend to be faction leaders because they can command the support of a sizable group of people during disputes over village representation, witchcraft accusations, and decisions about the movement of the community. Therefore, the ideal *ifutisu* relationship, expressed as equal and reciprocal, is modified by the complexity of actual ties between individual kin, with consequences for political organization.

Political relations are not, however, the only determinant of the degree of *ifutisu* one relative actually shows toward another. Persons who are socially distant from one another have ties of relatively less *ifutisu* than do those who are socially proximate. Social distance is a consequence of four hierarchically related principles that form a graded series of decreasing importance. These are residence, factional support, village affiliation, and language group affiliation.

First, regardless of how they are related to one another, relatives who live in the same household must continually share food and material possessions. Also, they tend to present a "common front" against other households, particularly with respect to the jealous guarding of possessions, food, and spouses. Thus members of the same household most closely adhere to the ideal *ifutisu* relationship by continually enacting the norms of kinship behavior on a daily basis.

Second, relatives who support the same faction leader, though they may live in different households, tend to participate more often in communal work groups organized by their leader, and therefore have more interests in common, than do kinsmen who belong to different factions. For example, members of the same faction often work together for substantial periods of time on some subsistence project (such as a major fishing expedition) the products of which will be distributed equitably among them. In these situations men and women work together for their common good. Similarly, because factions are the vehicle for witchcraft accusations, such persons tend to agree with one another about who is a witch, and thus support each other during periods of intense anxiety brought about by sudden illness or a suspicious death.

Third, relatives who live in the same settlement, though they may be members of different factions and household groups, have more frequent contacts than do those who live in different settlements, simply because of physical proximity and the common participation in settlement-wide activity. Yet persons who belong to the same settlement, but to different factions and households, are socially distant in that they are not obligated to one another in the same way that common faction or household members are. In other words, Kalapalo feel allegiance primarily to persons in their own households or factions, and only secondarily to kin in different groups.

Finally, relatives who live in different places but speak the same language are socially closer (simply because they can communicate verbally) than are relatives who belong to settlements speaking different languages. The latter might be described as the most socially distant of all a person's relatives.

It is clear that the simple fact of kinship relatedness does not imply solidarity or obligation, despite the ideal norms of *ifutisu*. As a consequence, it is possible to rank any person's kin in terms of their proximity.

Kin who live together in the same household, and who therefore belong
to the same faction, the same settlement, and who speak the same language, are at one end of the continuum, that of the most intense *ifutisu*
relationship. Individuals who fall within the socially proximate ranges
of this continuum are invariably classed as non-affinable kin. Therefore,
we can say that one important meaning of affinability in Kalapalo terms
is the relative lack of *ifutisu* ties between persons who are supposed to
enact the norms of kinship behavior. Similarly, persons who are not
affinable are those kin who are relatively strong *ifutisu* relationships that
are a consequence of social proximity.[2]

Given this basic meaning of affinability, why does a person's social distance make him or her an acceptable affine? What is the advantage to a
Kalapalo of selecting socially distant kin as spouse exchangers? The answer to this problem lies, I believe, in Kalapalo marriage norms themselves.

Kalapalo marriage is, in the first place, an alliance between sibling
sets (*ifisúandaw*) who are considered suitable spouse exchangers because of their social distance, not because of some *a priori* exchange
relationship. These sibling sets are those of the parents of the individuals
who marry, as well as those of the spouses themselves. Reciprocity between these sets is precisely defined. Rights transferred include (1) the
reciprocal exchange of spouses among persons in a particular generation
(which includes the original or initiating marriage and further levirate,
sororate, and brother-sister exchange [*itsahene*] marriages), and among
persons in succeeding generations (in conformance to an ideal rule of
brother-in-law/sister-in-law marriage, or *itsahene* marriage), and (2) the
continual exchange of material wealth and assistance between sibling
sets of the two generations involved. We can properly view the latter
obligation, in particular, as an especially stringent set of *ifutisu* norms;
indeed, the Kalapalo refer to the relationship between affines as *ifutisu
ekugu*, "great" or "strong," *ifutisu*.

Kalapalo marriage must also be seen as a contractual alliance between
two individuals who are classed as "spouses." Here, reciprocal sexual and
economic obligations define their relationship as distinctive and unique
among persons of the opposite sex. Sexual obligations are necessary because of the demands of one's kinsmen for spouses, faction members,
assistants for communal labor, and contributors of wealth. Since children
are, in the Kalapalo view, directly a consequence of repeated sexual
activity, the latter activity is a responsibility of persons who are married.
Similarly, reciprocal economic duties not only encompass the individual
marriage partner but incorporate obligations to the kin of one's spouse as
well. If marriage is a social contract, then it is clear that obligations

incurred by spouses are very similar to those incurred by persons who are socially proximate. The latter are in fact bonded by the social contract resulting from common residence and factional affiliation.

If Kalapalo marriage is accepted as a contractual alliance between social units and between individuals, it is possible to understand the advantage of designating socially distant persons rather than those who are close and in strong *ifutisu* relationships. The advantage lies in reinforcing *ifutisu* ties, which are diffuse in the case of socially distant kin. Such reinforcement means the establishment of a marked sense of obligation and reciprocity that is demanded by the norms of affinal relationships. In other words, persons who are socially distant become especially close, even (in terms of the duties imposed upon them) closer than the hithertofore closest members of an individual's kindred. A Kalapalo marriage has the effect of bringing together persons who were previously distant and without *ifutisu* bonds, marking the new relationship as close in a special way, different from, but stronger than, the intense *ifutisu* relationship between socially proximate kin.

The specific advantages in selecting socially distant individuals as spouse exchangers can be seen clearly in two cases of Kalapalo seeking appropriate spouses for their children. In each case the parent was fortunate in having more than one option; several trial selections and false starts were made before a "final" decision (if such ever occurred) was arrived at.

The first case involves the search for a husband for W., a young woman whose parents were affiliated with the Kuikuru village (see Figure 2). In the fall of 1966 the Kalapalo learned that W. had been promised to K., the only son of A., leader (*anetu*) of Aifa. A year before, K.'s first wife had left him and their only child, a boy of seven, to return to the Kuikuru household of her eldest brother and her mother. After failing to convince

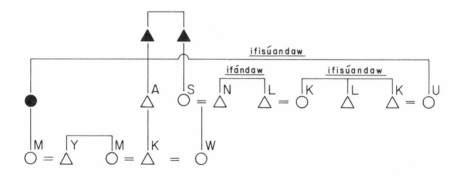

FIGURE 2. SIMPLIFIED GENEALOGICAL RELATIONS IN W.'s CASE.

her to return, K. and his father began to look around for another wife. The arranged marriage between K. and W. was not unusual, because the girl's mother was *ifisuagï* to A., and of sufficient social distance to be an appropriate affine. Thus K. and W. had always been considered "potential spouses" (*ifándaw*). Although K. had two other female *ifándaw* who were as yet unmarried, only one was unengaged. She, however, was a member of the Tupi-speaking Kamaiura. Furthermore, her father was a senior factional leader who would have demanded that K. move to his own settlement. Because A. was also in this political role, K.'s position was one of an "up-and-coming" young man among the Kalapalo group. Thus it would have been difficult for him to move permanently away from his own faction. W. therefore seemed to be the only choice from both K. and A.'s point of view.

The fact that W. had not been committed to a man until her last year of puberty seclusion was quite unusual, however, since most girls are engaged several years before they begin to menstruate. Furthermore, her unengaged status could not have been for lack of suitors, since at the time there were few girls of her age set but many older men who were as yet unmarried. In fact, her father had rejected all the proposals of his fellow villagers, including that of one individual whose relationship to W. was that of "potential spouse." Instead N. chose as a son-in-law a young man who lived in another village, and a person whose own father had been declared a witch. Because of the intense acrimony the new engagement caused in his own settlement, N. found himself in a highly ambiguous position. N. was one of those individuals so common in the Upper Xingú, who find themselves belonging, by reason of birthright or sentiment, to none of the settlements in the area. Allied by kinship to only one man, whose household he shared, he was accused of witchcraft by many of the Kuikuru. This in itself would not have been a problem, since most adult men are accused of this crime by at least some persons, but the fact that N. did not have the support of a large number of relatives, who would block his assassination in the event of a crisis, made him highly vulnerable in case of a sudden death.

On the other hand, N.'s wife S. had several distant kinsmen in Aifa, members of A.'s powerful faction. Thus it was highly advantageous to the parents to arrange a marriage for their daughter with the son of a man who was the leader of this faction. Although this would mean that W. and her parents would have to leave their own settlement permanently to live in Aifa, they would have the advantage of asylum from their Kuikuru antagonists among their Kalapalo affines, leaving behind the single supporting kinsman among the Kuikuru. For S., the move would have the additional advantage of allowing her to live close to her only living kinsmen, especially a "sister" with whom she had close emotional ties.

Finally, the couple would be able to live in the same village as their daughter, thus permitting them to make demands from K., a new son-in-law. In any case, N.'s insistence upon living in Aifa, in the very house of his son-in-law, was inconsistent with his own social position. Behaving as if he was a man of great influence and prestige, he disrupted the household of a man who was actually more powerful than he, and demanded continual obedience from his son-in-law even though his daughter was still in seclusion. Such behavior was only acceptable for a man whose son-in-law had moved in with *him,* not vice versa.

After living in the Kalapalo settlement about two months, it was evident that W. was receiving a number of men in her seclusion chamber at night. Her parents, sleeping on the other side of the seclusion wall, were apparently unconcerned about this, but one night her betrothed heard someone scrambling over the wall. This led to K. chasing and briefly scuffling with the man, something highly uncharacteristic of Kalapalo men (who tend to vent their jealousy on their wives). The young man who was caught was a kinsman of K., the son of S.'s "sister." Because the fight took place outside the house of this man's own future parents-in-law, the incident greatly embarrassed many people.

The next day the Kalalapo left for the Kuikuru village, where they were to participate in a long-planned trading ceremony. N. and his son joined the general party of travelers, leaving S. and W. behind in Aifa. N. was said to be very upset that his daughter was publicly known to have lovers. However, one reason for his going to the Kuikuru village was to bring back to Aifa the large quantity of manioc flour he had left behind. The fact that all the Kalapalo men would help him carry the flour to Aifa would publicly and formally indicate his decision to change his village affiliation.

In the Kuikuru settlement was K.'s first wife, who now seemed anxious to return to Aifa. That night she went to sleep with K. in the house where the visitors had slung their hammocks. One of the Kuikuru who had been angered by the engagement of K. to W. informed N. of this. He (perhaps sensing that this would be an appropriate excuse for breaking off the relationship) surprised the pair with a flashlight and, enraged, declared that the engagement was broken. His excuse was that he did not want his son-in-law to have two wives. If this were so, it would mean that K. would be allied once again to his first wife's brother (and his household), who were living with the Kuikuru. This would, in fact, establish K with a very strong factional group, making him unequivocally a powerful person in the Kalapalo village, and his father-in-law (N.) somewhat subservient. At any rate, the broken engagement satisfied K. completely, since he was not happy with N. as a father-in-law. As the ceremony had ended that same day, next morning the Kalapalo (together with N.) left.

A few days later K. again went to the Kuikuru, returning to Aifa with his wife. As soon as the couple arrived at Aifa, N. and S., together with their children, left unceremoniously for the Kuikuru, thus ending the relationship they had initiated.

At another ceremony held in the Mehinaku settlement the next rainy season, W. left seclusion, her hair being cut by the Mehinaku leader (this ritual is usually performed by a woman's husband, who thus releases her from puberty seclusion at the same time that they become formally married). She was still unmarried, as N. could not decide on another son-in-law. Many individuals, most unrelated to either N. or S., had proposed an engagement, but they had all been refused. Indeed, several of these men had offered to pay bride price for W., though the Kalapalo say a father should not expect this after his daughter has left puberty seclusion.

Finally, in the fall of 1967, a second Kalapalo man successfully asked to marry W. L. was a young man whose sister was married to N.'s single supporting kinsman among the Kuikuru. Another sister of L. was married to the son of S.'s "sister" in Aifa. Furthermore, L.'s elder brother was married to that same sister. L. thus had several types of affinal links to N. and S. L.'s strategy was to visit his sister in the Kuikuru settlement and live with his brother-in-law and N.'s family in order to convince the latter to give W. to him. For several months L. stayed with this household, helping the two senior men during the piqui harvest. He was apparently successful, for he returned with W. to Aifa in November, remaining in the same household as his older brother and brothers-in-law. This time N. and S. remained behind with the Kuikuru. Having publicly insulted K. and his father at the ceremony during which their daughter had been released from seclusion, they could hardly re-establish friendly ties among the Kalapalo.

All seemed to go well with L. and W. and, as an added benefit, with W. and the senior woman of her new household, who was, after all, her mother's "sister." W.'s relationships with the women of this household were thus relaxed and comfortable, even though she was a newly married, in-marrying bride. Therefore, it was a shock to this group when N. returned to Aifa after only a month to take W. back to the Kuikuru. His excuse was that these very women were mistreating his daughter. Highly indignant, they denied this and sought to find who had spread the story. The source was a man from Mïgiyapey whose Kuikuru *ifisuagï* had been a claimant before W. had even entered puberty seclusion. The Mïgiyapey man had acted on his brother's behalf, hoping that a divorce would result in the latter finally being able to marry W.

N. apparently was still adamant about not allowing his daughter to marry a Kuikuru, however. L. insisted on traveling once more to his former father-in-law, against the advice of his many relatives who by this time were beginning to speak very strongly against N. Once again L. was successful in bringing W. back to Aifa, but only after he had paid N. with shell ornaments. Yet in the end N. was not satisfied, and W. had to return to the Kuikuru. Thus the situation remained when I left the Upper Xingú in 1968. When I returned in 1979, they were married and living with N. and S. in the Kuikuru settlement.

Despite the special appropriateness of marriage between L. and W., owing to the complex affinal relationships between his sibling set and those of both S. and N., the latter were unable to accept this union because it conflicted with their own personal interest in remaining free of both witchcraft accusations and witchcraft performed against them. Threatened with the harm that would come to his daughter if she were permanently married to a man who incurred the jealousy of too many Kuikuru contenders, and fearing for his own life because of the poverty of his relationships with Kuikuru factional alliances, N. could not at the time permit his daughter to marry someone who belonged to a faction that claimed his undivided loyalty. Thus, two years after exiting puberty seclusion, W. was still an unmarried woman.

The second case consists of the marital and engagement history of a young Kalapalo man whose mother was one of A.'s sisters (see Figure 3). His case is interesting because it illustrates the succession of wives and fiancees which a man sometimes goes through until he is able to successfully settle down with one woman. The succession results not from marital instability alone but from the vagaries of epidemics and personal incompatibility between potential spouses. Yet, like the preceding example, the selection of spouses for E. conformed to the strategy

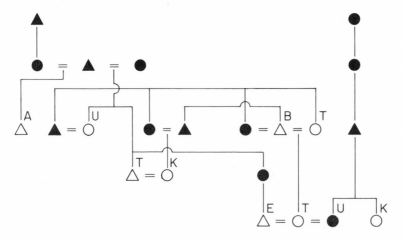

FIGURE 3. SIMPLIFIED GENEALOGICAL RELATIONS IN E.'S CASE.

of maximizing one's relationships with distant kin for the purpose of political alliance and refuge from witchcraft accusations.

The first wife selected for E. was a girl in puberty seclusion, whose father was an *ifisuagï* of A. and E.'s mother. Unfortunately, before they had been married long, this woman died suddenly, allegedly the victim of witchcraft. Therefore, her younger sister, also in puberty seclusion, was selected as E.'s second wife. This woman had refused E.'s seductive advances, however, and so he refused to marry her. On the day of their wedding, when she came to his house to remove his hammock and carry it back to her father's household, he fled out the back door, leaving her crying in the doorway. His mother's *ifisúandaw* had made arrangements for the marriage despite his request to end the alliance. Such a marriage was not only an appropriate *ifándaw* marriage but conformed to the sororate rule. A third engagement was attempted by another *ifisuagï* of E.'s mother who lived with the Yawalipiti. Although it was highly inappropriate to do so, this man suggested directly to E. that he marry a daughter who had been divorced several times by Kuikuru men who accused her of having too many lovers (in fact, E. was one of these). E. rejected this proposal indirectly by suggesting to the older man that the proper person to speak with about it would be his mother. Yet he never told the older woman since he did not like the girl because of her promiscuity, and did not want to live with the Yawalipiti, whose language he did not speak. E.'s mother and her *ifisúandaw* were annoyed that he did not tell them of the request of his *ifau*'s father.

Eventually, the older sibling set engaged E. to the eight-year-old daughter of B., a strong factional leader and Kalapalu *anetu*. Here, again, a complex network of relationships between B. and his wife T., on the one hand, and E.'s mother's *ifisúandaw* on the other justified several times over the exchange of spouses between them. Furthermore, after making the alliance known to E., he would stand in between the rival factions of A. and B., allied to each but able to provide a bridge between them.

In both examples Kalapalo parents' initial selection of spouses for their children followed the rule of "affinability," which defines persons labeled *ifándaw* as potential spouses. In each case the decision was made to choose a distant *ifisuagï*'s child as a spouse for the unmarried person. Thus the initial strategy was to conform to the most explicit norm of mate selection, that referring to the concept of social distance, which defines certain categories of kin as affinable.

However, a more subtle strategy, one which perhaps overrides the original one, also figured in each case. This was a scheme by means of which an alliance for political purposes, motivated by witchcraft accusations, became more critical than the consideration of kinship ties. The need for security against potential public indignation forced the accused witch (however secure at a particular moment) to seek what can only be described as asylum among a set of powerful affines who might have prevented his execution by outraged members of his own community. In N.'s case a change of residence was made to avoid an immediate threat against him, but more usually, as in E.'s case, a more far-sighted strategy is used to reinforce existing ties that are becoming diffuse through the creation of new factions that draw away support from earlier alliances. Clearly, then, Kalapalo arranged marriages do not only affect the establishment of ties of reciprocity between people who may or may not happen to be related by kinship. They also maintain the delicate balance of power between factional groups that are opposed by the rivalry of their leaders for political power, but that use witchcraft accusations and consensus about who is a witch as an idiom of this opposition. Hence it is important to reinforce ties between socially distant kin and between persons who are non-kin in order to expand one's domain of refuge should one someday need to flee. The most judicious means of reinforcing these ties is through the establishment of affinal alliances.

NOTES

1. This does not mean that the Kalapalo have a positive rule of *ifándaw* marriage, however, since nonrelatives may equally legitimately be married or become lovers.

2. Earlier I indicated that the Kalapalo are unable to explain why some people are affinable and others not. Similarly, when asked to whom they owe "great" *ifutisu,* Kalapalo informants simply list every relative they have, stating that they have "great *ifutisu*" for everyone. To admit that one does not conform to the ideal kinship relationship (*ifutisu*) is to admit that one is not a proper kinsman, and is therefore somewhat less than a model member of one's society. It also suggests that one does not wish to accept one's kinsmen as such. To deny a kinship relationship (or to hedge on it by saying that one's feelings of *ifutisu* are not strong in a particular case) is so serious a breach of the *ifutisu* norm itself as to result in witchcraft accusations against the speaker in question. Such a person is considered motivated by unknown and inexplicable antisocial feelings. It is no wonder that Kalapalo refuse to rank individuals in terms of their *ifutisu* toward one another.

3

The Structure
of Kuikuru Marriage

GERTRUDE E. DOLE

Introduction

For over a hundred years anthropologists have recognized the importance of marriage ties in forming and maintaining social, economic, and
political alliances among kin groups, but only in the past few decades
has a structural theory of alliance been developed. As a consequence of
this development it has recently become fashionable to consider the data
of all marriage and kinship structure in primitive societies in the light
of alliance theory.

Certainly maintaining family or kin group alliances through marriage
is an ideal objective among many preindustrial peoples. However, some
societies do not achieve that objective or make a concerted effort to do so.
The Kuikuru of the Upper Xingú region in central Brazil are one such
society. In the 1950s Kuikuru society appeared to be in flux as a result
of demographic changes, and its structure seemed to lack regularity in
both rules and practices (see Dole 1966, 1969). As a noted writer once
put it with reference to another society, "There is just enough social
organization to keep order in the tribe and no more" (Niles 1931:ix).
This interpretation has been questioned, however, and an attempt has
been made to represent Kuikuru kinship as an internally consistent system of alliances (Basso 1970).

In this paper I will outline briefly the aspects of Kuikuru organization
that bear on the structure of marriage, describe Kuikuru marriage practices, and finally discuss the extent to which marriage[1] in that society does
or does not conform to alliance structure.

Kuikuru Organization

In 1954,[2] before being moved and relocated in the Upper Xingú Parque Indígena, the 145 Kuikuru lived in a single tribal village. A total of 34 nuclear families were unevenly distributed among nine multifamily houses averaging about four families per house. By "nuclear family" I refer to the minimal kinship group comprising one or more dyads of primary relatives and including at least one adult. The dyads of primary relatives are husband-wife, parent-child, and siblings. Among the Kuikuru the nuclear family is the basic economic and residence unit.

The norm for this basic unit is to settle in the natal community of the husband, patrivincial residence in Carrasco's terms (1963:133). Similarly with respect to the multifamily dwellings the norm is to reside patrivirilocally, that is, with the husband's father (see Wedgwood 1952: 456) in patridomestic units (Carrasco 1963:133). However, in reality the place of residence does not follow any rule consistently; residence arrangements are irregular and unstable with respect to both house and tribal settlement, as well as with respect to the type of focal relatives (see Bohannan 1957). This is because observance of the norm is often inhibited by a number of factors, and the ideal arrangements are interrupted by frequent changes made in response to various contingencies.

One important factor is a strong norm of initial uxorilocal residence that sometimes amounts to a period of trial marriage during which the husband hangs his hammock above his new wife's in her own home, which is also usually that of her parents. This initial period of uxorilocal residence is variable, lasting from a few days to many years. The length of time depends on compatibility, family structure, the economic status of the groom, and the marital history of the partners. If the bride accepts the man as her husband, they may remain with her parents for a few months or until the birth of their first child, sometimes even longer until the young man has paid off with bride service the debt incurred by taking a wife. It is said that formerly young men lived for a longer period with the wife's family and did more for them; today the custom is considerably relaxed.

If, however, the bride has no strong male relatives in the household and especially if it is not a first marriage for either partner, the initial period spent with the woman's family may be very brief, after which the couple moves to the community and house previously occupied by the groom, normally that of his parents.

Other factors that produce mobility include internal tensions. Rather than risk confrontations or loss of face, disgruntled Kuikuru often move to another house or to a different village, where they take up residence with the family of a friendly relative. This is a common occurrence when couples are divorced. Other factors that may precipitate such moves are the imminent birth of a child and the accidental destruction of a house by fire or wind storm. One instance of natolocal residence (see Barnes 1960:853) resulted when a jealous wife in a polygynous family drove her younger co-wife from their house, after which the latter woman went back to live in her father's house with her infant, even though her marriage remained intact.

To sum up, a considerable amount of variation can be seen in the residence patterns exemplified by the nuclear families at any one time. Nevertheless, *if it is understood that a wide circle of patrikin are included as foci* in the "patrilocal zone" (see Kopytoff 1977; cf. Heinen 1972), the number of families that may be interpreted as following the norm of uxoripatrilocal residence is greater than the unadjusted statistics suggest.

There is a long-standing and still current argument in anthropological literature about the relation of residence practices to other aspects of kinship structure. On the one hand, Murdock (1949:183, 202) and Goodenough (1956), following Lowie (1927:62) and Kroeber (1938: 307), conclude that the association of people resulting from residence arrangements determines other kinship relations to a large extent. In opposition to these findings, Fortes (1953:36) and Kopytoff (1977: 556) theorize that local ties do not form bonds of kinship, descent, marriage, or "citizenship," but that residence patterns themselves are determined by political, economic, and ritual interests or relations, which in turn are shaped by the kinship structure.

This is a complicated and, it seems to me, confused argument. It is commonly accepted that property and political ties are important factors in determining residence patterns. However, this does not negate the common findings that the choice of residence is an important factor in shaping the form of kin groups and kin relations. Because of their mobility the Kuikuru illustrate how these two aspects of social structure are related. As we shall see, the Kuikuru data on residence and marriage suggest that a *norm* of regular uxoripatrilocal residence is associated with a common pattern of marriage and family household unit. On the other hand, because it often happens that the ideal residence pattern cannot be realized, variation in this aspect of structure brings the immediate consequence of variation in the forms of family household units.

With the exception of one fraternal group, extended family residence groups in 1954 were bilateral or composite,[3] rather than either simply patrilocal or uxorilocal units. Analysis shows that the presence of married sisters in some otherwise patrilocal groups cannot be accounted for on the basis of initial postmarital or postpartum uxorilocality. Conversely, nuclear families of own brothers and first male parallel cousins are sometimes dispersed among separate houses and even in more than one tribal settlement. This is not to say that adult brothers do not cooperate in subsistence activities somewhat more intensely than do sets of nonrelatives, but it does emphasize the variety of family residence groups and the degree to which they fail to conform to the stated norm.

The Kuikuru lack any form of unilineal kin groups. Kinship is reckoned bilaterally, and all individuals assume some degree of genealogical relation to most other members of the community, even though genealogical ties frequently cannot be traced. In addition, terms of kinship are generally extended to all members of the local group whether or not actual consanguinity is acknowledged, much as among the Nhadju Dayaks, for example, where "an individual refers to all his fellow villagers as cognates, even if there is no evidence of a genealogical tie. Frequently, the fictitious relationship is assumed to be a real one. . . . For instance a person refers to most of his affines . . . as cognates" (Miles 1970:304). Hence the entire community may be regarded as a cognatic kin group. It is a *local kin group,* not merely a local group (see Dole 1969:111, 113), in which for any ego people may be conceived of as being arranged in concentric circles of kinship, demonstrable kin being at the social center, with stipulated (assumed) genealogical relatives around them, and on the periphery those individuals with whom ego does not claim a genealogical tie but for whom he or she nevertheless uses an appropriate kin term.[4] In general, kin terms are polysemic, the same terms being used for persons in all three of these categories with varying degrees of specificity.

Variation in residence patterns and forms of extended families is matched by a corresponding irregularity in the norms and practices of marriage. It is not much exaggeration to say that there is general disagreement among the Kuikuru about rules of marriage. Because of in-law avoidance and other interpersonal tensions and because some Kuikuru, who speak a Carib language, have spouses who speak only an Arawakan or a Tupian language, there is a remarkable lack of communication among families; each family, it seems, develops its own tradition of what practices are necessary and proper.

No prescription exists with respect to local exogamy. One may take a spouse from within the community, even from one's own household. Some men expressed a preference for wives from other tribal groups (local *and* kin group exogamy), but others asserted that it was best for Kuikuru women to marry within the community (local and kin group endogamy). The discrepancy in these expressed norms may be related to a temporarily acute shortage of nubile women. Informants may have been thinking in terms of both an ideal marriage pattern of group exogamy and the actual scarcity of eligible women. At any rate, about 75 percent of the marriages I have analyzed were endogamous with respect to the *kin community*.

It is understood that upon marriage a man will have sexual access to his bride's unmarried sisters as well as the woman he formally marries, and that his brother may also have access to his wife (anticipatory sororate and levirate). However, the Kuikuru do not recognize any category of persons one must marry. Some informants expressed a preference for a particular matrilateral cross cousin as a mate for their offspring, others a preference for a patrilateral cross cousin. Others felt it was preferable to marry more distant relatives, and still others preferred as mates persons whom they regarded as not related. Thus among the Kuikuru there is no prescriptive marriage pattern; there are only preferences that vary from family to family, and probably also according to contingent circumstances. Parenthetically, the preference of some for cross-cousin marriage is based on the very widespread tendency for parents to try to provide suitable spouses for their offspring by negotiating with their own close relatives, as will be explained.

The only rule with respect to Kuikuru marriage structure is a proscriptive one, namely that persons may not marry within the nuclear family or with first parallel cousins, parents' own siblings, own siblings' children, grandparents, or grandchildren, which is merely a statement of minimal incest prohibitions. This is not a prescriptive rule, since there is no category marked by a distinctive term from which mates must be chosen. By including other persons than the preferred categories, such as "nonrelatives" and even foreigners, as potential mates, the circle of eligible mates is widened and becomes infinite except for close consanguines. As Löffler and Baer point out, opening the marriage system to include people who are not affines obscures the distinction between kin and affine. A system "can in actual fact only remain free from contradiction as long as the affinals for the affinals are neither marriageable nor permitted to marry each other, i.e. as long as they behave like siblings. . . . This can no longer be controlled when the endogamy limitations cease to exist . . . " (1974:278, 279).

It is a tautology to label prescriptive a marriage system in which all persons are defined as affinable except close consanguineal kin. The circularity of such reasoning has been expressed by Schneider: "A prescriptive system is one in which ego has no choice but must marry a 'marriageable woman'. A 'marriageable woman' is a woman from a wife-giving unit. If this is a prescriptive system, what then is the opposite type?" (1965b:66). Moreover, if marriage patterns are not obligatory, "alliance" loses much of its meaning when applied to marriage structure. To represent such a system as alliance would indeed be simplistic.

Returning to a description of marriage practices among the Kuikuru, when girls reach the age of puberty they are secluded for from two months to two years; boys are normally secluded for two years or more. Although prepubertal intercourse is generally frowned upon, both males and females may freely engage in sex after they have been secluded. Men like to marry women immediately after the latter leave seclusion. Because men are somewhat older when they enter seclusion and usually remain in seclusion for a longer period, a woman is ideally three or more years younger than her husband. In actuality, however, because of a continuing shortage of eligible mates, marriages, especially secondary ones, unite persons who differ in age considerably more; that is, women may marry men who are either considerably older or considerably younger than they are.

If a young woman is engaged at the time of her seclusion or if her father approves of her suitor as her future husband, he may permit the young man to visit her privately behind the seclusion screen. However, if a young woman should bear a child before her marriage, the infant would probably not be allowed to live.

Infant betrothal is not uncommon, and girls are usually promised before they are ten years old. However, informants made it explicit that these arrangements are not binding but are subject to the wishes of the young people when they reach sexual maturity and are ready to marry.

If all parties agree, the marriage takes place, but if a woman's fiancé is not her own choice and she does not like him as a partner, she "sends him away," and he does not press his suit; the match may also be broken up by their respective lovers. Moreover, if the parents think the young man is lazy, they may prevent the marriage by stalling and other indirect devices.

Divorces occur because of barrenness, ill humor, adultery, spending too much time away from home in one's natal settlement, and probably laziness, although this last was not made explicit with respect to early marriages. Both men and women have extramarital sex partners, whose identity is usually well known to other members of the society in spite of the principals' attempts to hide it. In the absence of stable residence kin groups there is very little control over private interpersonal relations outside the nuclear family.

Polygyny occurs, but few men are able to attract and keep more than one wife. The Kuikuru say that formerly only the headman or a champion wrestler had plural wives. Some informants now consider polygyny to be bad because co-wives fight with each other. As a matter of fact, most polygynous unions are unstable, whether sororal or not.

Ideally a man and his sister try to arrange for the marriage of their children. Thus these two go-betweens (*kitofo,* "speakers") are father's sister (*etsi*)[5] and mother's brother (*auaju,* or *jogu*) to the prospective mates.

As most Kuikuru perceive it, it is a young man's father who takes the initiative in making arrangements for his first marriage. Even though a youth has made his own choice of a mate, it is his father who undertakes negotiations. "When a man finds a girl he wants to marry, he asks his father to talk to the girl's parents about it. If the girl's parents are willing and the girl has been secluded, they can marry immediately," after her father's brother or mother's brother cuts her bangs, which have been allowed to grow and cover her eyes during seclusion. From the point of view of the girl also, it is sometimes her father who negotiates for her marriage by speaking to her prospective husband's parents. "A man speaks to his daughter first and asks if she wants to marry his sister's son. Then he talks with his sister about it." If a young man has no father, his widowed mother asks her brother to promise his daughter as a future wife for her son, even if the daughter is still an infant.

Among the Kuikuru the role of cross aunts and uncles as helpers in *arranging* marriage appears to predominate over the concept of wife giver and wife receiver. This interpretation is supported by the fact that one's mother also sometimes is referred to as *isogu* (third person possessive form of *jogu*), and by the fact that the terms *etsi* and *auaju,* or *jogu,* are spoken with obvious fondness and respect (*ifisu,* which the Kuikuru translate into Portuguese as *vergonha,* "shyness, shame"; compare the Kalapalo *ifutisu,* "good kinship behavior," in Basso 1970, 1973, 1975). Even before marriage the intended mates show great respect for prospective parents-in-law (*ifisofo*) by avoiding contact through touching, looking at, or speaking to them or speaking their names.

Although brother and sister often cooperate in arranging matches between their adolescent offspring, it sometimes happens that own allo-gender (opposite sex; see Dole 1957:144-45) siblings do not live to negotiate marriages for their offspring. In such instances avuncular relatives, own or classificatory, serve as surrogate parents, thus widening the circle of preferred mates to include second cousins by negotiating marriages with their own offspring.

It appears therefore that first and second cross cousins are frequently promised to each other, and in some instances they honor the promise. However, even when the arrangement does result in marriage, many of these first, arranged marriages are brittle and of short duration. An individual may have several other mates consecutively before a compatible match is made. It is felt that marrying lovers (*ajo itsómitï*) is good and that such marriages last longer.

What amounts to a formal announcement of an engagement occurs when a man deposits outside his future mother-in-law's door a load of prized hard firewood that he has split and brought from his garden. She gives some of the logs to her sisters and special women friends (*ato*), who also thereby assume the status of the man's mothers-in-law.

On the occasion of a woman's first marriage the groom gives to his parents-in-law several items that require considerable time or expense to provide. Although a woman's brothers may also use the affinal relationship as an excuse to exact favors and gifts from her husband, his gifts to these brothers-in-law are less costly. Nevertheless, brothers-in-law are socially very close. They ask freely from each other, even taking from each other without permission or repayment. But they also help each other in times of need, as when a man cannot cultivate his own garden because of illness.

The Structure of Marriage

As I have already noted, about one-fourth of the marriages unite Kuikuru with mates from other communities. However, there are reasons to believe that this figure is abnormally low. In a community of as few as 145 people it is often necessary to find spouses outside the local group. In 1954, for instance, several unmarried men were looking for wives at a time when there were no Kuikuru girls in seclusion being prepared for marriage, whereas in the neighboring and closely related Kalapalo community three girls were in seclusion.

From genealogical data covering five generations of Kuikuru, local exogamy appears to have decreased since 1905. This change has occurred in part through *locally* endogamous marriages that have united Kuikuru with members of former tribes who had already moved to the Kuikuru village. Reduced by disease and the resulting hostilities, those tribes had ceased to exist as separate local groups, and some members of remnant families had sought refuge among the Kuikuru. It should be noted that, although locally endogamous, the first of these marriages were tribally exogamous and are so regarded by the Kuikuru (see Dole 1969:110).

Even if there were enough eligible mates within the community, it would be important to create and perpetuate ties outside the community, as well as outside the immediate family and household. In addition to special friends (*ato*) that a man has in each of the tribal settlements and whom he visits to trade, it is also important to have kinship ties to provide for hospitality during intertribal ceremonies and refuge from interpersonal tensions or accusations of witchcraft, as well as to prevent intertribal conflict. The Kuikuru have in fact established kin ties with all the other Upper Xingú tribes.

Given both the negative consideration of scarcity of eligible mates within the community and the positive advantages of having relatives in other settlements, it is understandable that parents should try to arrange "cousin" marriages between their children and the children of relatives in other settlements, thus perpetuating intertribal ties through kinship. If repeated over several generations, the marriage of either first or more distant cross cousins, together with exchange marriage, sororal polygyny, levirate, and sororate, would result in alliance structure. Let us see to what extent Kuikuru marriages conform to this pattern.

It has been possible to trace genealogical relations between the partners in a significant number of current betrothals and marriages. In many instances the partners are related in two or more ways, and in the following discussion I have used the closest relation in each case.

Only five contemporary marriages united first cross cousins. One of these couples separated without offspring soon after marriage. Another was separated by death within a year of marriage. In my sample four men were married, and another was engaged, to second cross cousins. Again, one of these unions lasted only a few days.

With respect to exchange marriages, it is rare that siblings obtain spouses from the same nuclear family among the Kuikuru, or from families that are closely related to each other. In one instance brothers married women who were parallel cousins to each other, and in another sisters married parallel cousins. I have not found evidence that when this type of exchange occurred in the past, the alliance was maintained in subsequent generations. In the single instance of current sibling exchange, the marriage of two brothers to two sisters, one of the couples separated after a few days, reportedly without consummating the marriage with sexual relations.

Although not mandatory, and subject to the same individual preferences as primary marriages, levirate and sororate unions are common, but these secondary marriages necessarily produce fewer offspring to maintain the alliances than do primary ones.

It is clear from these data that marital alliances among closely related *families* seldom last over more than two generations among the Kuikuru. Nevertheless an alliance structure could be established if members of two *categories* were regularly united by marriage. As we have seen, however, no such intermarrying categories occur among the Kuikuru.

A significant finding in this respect is that Kuikuru marry parallel as well as cross relatives. For example, men were married to first and second parallel cousins (M 1/2 SiD, MFSiSoD, MMSiDD, and MF 1/2 SiSoD). In a system of alliance each of these marriages would necessarily have united people who were in the same marriage category. The same is true of some marriages that link persons whose ancestors were found to have married each other, as for example the marriage of men with their FMBWDD and BWBDD. All of these marriages would tend to remove a distinction between "wife-giving" and "wife-receiving" categories. Such unions are not regarded as abnormal by the Kuikuru, suggesting that beyond first cousins they make little distinction between cross and parallel relatives with respect to marriageability. By contrast, it is reported that the Kalapalo prohibit marriage with any relative other than cross cousins (*ifándaw;* Basso 1970:410-11).

Among the Kuikuru, on the other hand, marriages to cross cousins are fewer than marriages to other types of relatives, including numerous cross-generation marriages. In many instances, however, it is not possible to determine whether the partners would be "affinable" in a two-section alliance system because informants often do not distinguish lineal from collateral relatives in reckoning their genealogies.[6] A brief digression is necessary here to clarify the relation of consanguinity to affinity among the Kuikuru.

People usually reckon their relation to others by referring to their relation to an intermediate relative, often a member of parents' generation, or by the kin term used by the referent. The following examples illustrate these principles:

X is my classificatory sibling (*ufisï/ufisuïŋgï*) [because]

1. he/she is my *auaju indisïpe* ("MBD")
2. he/she is my *auaju mu(ku)gu* ("MBSo")
3. his/her F is *auaju* ("MB")
4. Y [who is X's F] is *ujogu* ("MB")
5. *eu primo, veu?* ("I am his cousin, see?").

X is my affine, *apaju ifitsï* (FW).

X is my son; he calls me *ama* (M); or *isʉuï ugé* ("I am his father").

X is my daughter [because] *meu primo papa* ("my cousin [is her] father").

X is my nephew [because] Y [X's F] is my *ufisï* (B).

X is my grandchild [because] Y [X's M/F] says *"ama,"* or *"etsï"* (FSI), [to me]; or he/she says *"kokojó"* (GM).

In each instance the connecting relative is classificatory. It is interesting to note that some informants rely on what kin term the referent uses rather than on demonstrated genealogical ties, thereby accepting a stipulated relationship.

Now brother and sister terms are used regularly to refer to both parallel and cross cousins of any degree (the Generation pattern). In spite of the fact that Bifurcate Merging terms are used in $+1$ and -1 generations, since one's parents refer to all their kin in their own generation as brothers and sisters, ego learns to know them all, both cross and parallel, as MSi/B and FSi/B, instead of distinguishing them as "kin" and "affines." This means that sets of siblings who are in fact a parent's cousins are telescoped into "parent's siblings." In this way, not only are near and distant relatives merged, but also the distinction between cross and parallel, or kin and affinable, is lost to subsequent generations. Thus designating *etsí* and *auaju* as a category of spouse givers would imply an affinal opposition that does not fit either the Kuikuru marriage practices or kinship terminology.

Everyone of course knows his or her own or supposed biological parents, and probably grandparents as well. However, people remember with less precision the names of collaterals and more distant ascendants. In genealogies distinctions between matri- and patrilateral relatives, between cross and parallel relatives, and between siblings and cousins are often blurred. An example of the pervasive confusion of sibling sets appears in Basso's account of a Kalapalo-Kuikuru genealogy in which two Kuikuru men, "Nahu" and "Luis," are represented as own brothers (1975:223). According to genealogies obtained from these men in 1954, they were actually related as second cross cousins (FFBDSo). In another instance a woman chose to overlook the affinability of her FSiSo and referred to his wife as sister-in-law, an affine, thus bringing her own male cross cousin into a "brother" relationship.

Clearly if the Kuikuru think in terms of "sibling" sets, those sets include both cross and parallel cousins. An individual is acknowledged as both kin and affinable in different contexts, and different kin terms are used for the same relative depending on whether a supposed consanguineal or affinal link is alluded to. In informant responses there is a good deal of indecision and vacillating between these alternate terms. Thus attempts to maintain marital alliances among the Kuikuru are continually frustrated by the terminological confusion of cross and parallel relatives.

As noted earlier, some informants explicitly preferred as mates persons who not only were not first cross cousins but who were regarded as unrelated. The Kuikuru express unrelatedness by the word *telo,* which contrasts with *telófiŋï* (not unrelated) and *iɟisuïŋgï(pe)* (relatives). Terms that are cognate with *telo* are used among the Galibí and Caribs of the Maroni River in the Guiana region. In those societies *tewô* and *ti:wo* respectively refer to a man's first cross cousin (Arnaud and Alves 1975).

Used in general contexts, *telo* has the meanings of "other" and "different." In the context of kinship and marriage it was defined or explained by the term *ñailï* (nothing, no relation). The use of *telo* differs from one informant to another. Under identical conditions, for example, being asked to indicate one's relation to other Kuikuru as presented to the informants in alphabetical order, some informants gave a kin term for every other Kuikuru whereas one informant of apparently pure Kuikuru ancestry used *telo* for a considerable number of Kuikuru. Others admitted to being uncertain about their relation to a few people. It is used variably in other situations to mean "distantly related," "related but in an unknown way," "affinable by reason of being unrelated," and "foreign" (that is, a member of a different tribe, for example, Kalapalo). A sample of the persons who were referred to as *telo* were found to be related to the speakers as follows:

1. Cousins: first cross cousin, first cross cousin once removed, first parallel cousin once removed, first cousin twice removed, second cross cousin, second parallel cousin, second cousin once removed (one of whom was also a step-father to the speaker), step-mother's sister's daughter.

2. Affines: step-daughter's husband, half-sister's husband.

3. Niece: daughter of a half-sister who had married into another group.

4. Mother's affine: mother's half-brother's wife.

Some of these are clearly cross relationships and would conform to alliance structure, but others are parallel relationships. Still others are not clear, since the method of reckoning the relationships is not made explicit and they would be cross or parallel depending on whether ego reckoned descent through males alone, which is generally not true for the Kuikuru, or through females, for which there is even less evidence.

From the above example, together with statements from informants, it is apparent that *telo* is frequently used to indicate persons with whom ego claims no demonstrated or stipulated relationship or to whom he does not know that his parents claimed a relationship. By using this term also for parallel and distant cross relatives along with persons in other tribal communities, ego changes their status from consanguine kin to potential affines.

In the context of marriage, use of this term supports informants' statements that they felt they should marry someone who was unrelated. But relatedness itself is conceived of as being quantifiable. In one instance when the offspring of a brother and sister were discussed as potential mates, they were classed as *telo* instead of the usual *ifisuïŋgï* (relatives), increasing the social distance between them. One informant said it was not good to marry a first cross cousin and specifically rejected the idea of his daughter marrying his own sister's son, preferring that she marry a young man who was *telo*. When it was pointed out that the informant had been referring to that young man's mother as "sister," he said, combining Kuikuru and Portuguese, that her son was *telo poquinho* (a little bit unrelated). Another informant described a woman as being *telo* to her lover. But when her relation to him (second parallel cousin) was pointed out, the informant added that they were *ifisuïŋgï kotsifïŋï* (not close relatives).

These examples illustrate the importance of fictively increasing genealogical distance in the context of both extramarital sex and marriage. It appears that by labeling as *telo* genealogical relatives who are regarded as potential marriage partners, some Kuikuru purposely remove them from the category of consanguines in order to justify their marriage plans.

In analyzing data on Kuikuru marriage I found a seldom-used term for cross cousins, *ufaï*, that appeared to be a clue to former marriage structure. On the basis of the manner in which this term was used by the Kuikuru, together with comparative data on the kinship nomenclature of 15 other Carib-speaking societies and research on the process of change in kinship nomenclature, I interpreted *ufaï* as a term that had once been commonly used to designate a category of affines, namely male cross cousins and brothers-in-law (Dole 1957:294ff.; 1969).

Subsequently Basso studied the use of a corresponding Kalapalo term, *ifaú* (third person possessive of *ufaú*). Approaching her data from a structuralist orientation, she took exception to the necessity of adducing factors of change and explained the term as "an integral, viable part of the system by which kin and affines are classified" (1970:42ff.). Further, on the basis of an unspecified amount of time spent with the Kuikuru (remembered by them as three days) at their new settlement Afanítafagï, called Lafatuá by the Kalapalo, as well as with the Carib-speaking Matipú ("Wagifitï") and remnants of the Nafuquá ("Jagamï") at Magiapé, Basso generalized about kinship and marriage among all "Xingú Caribs,"[7] implying homogeneity of marriage norms and practices as well as kinship nomenclature among all those groups (1970:403-4).

This is not the place to describe all the differences in terms and usage between the Kuikuru and Kalapalo. However, a discussion of the use of the term *ufaï* is important to an understanding of Kuikuru marriage structure.

ufaï

It is true that among the Kuikuru as among the Kalapalo *ufaï* is "rarely heard in speech and even more rarely used by young people" (Basso 1970: 411). Beyond this, however, Kuikuru usage differs considerably from that of the Kalapalo, where Basso speaks of a prohibition on the use of affinal relationship terminology within the hearing of affines, and states that "a term marking a specific affinal category is never uttered within the hearing of such an affine of the speaker. The terms seem to be confined to contexts where the need arises to specify an affinal relationship to an ignorant listener" (1970:412).

Among the Kuikuru, although affinal terms are not used to address parents-in-law or allogender siblings-in-law, other specific affinal terms are used freely within hearing of the affines. Spouses often address their mates as *uño* (husband) or *ufitsï* (wife), and men especially use the term *ufametigï* in its specific sense both in addressing and referring to brothers-in-law. A man may openly and purposefully address a prospective or actual brother-in-law as *ufametigï* with the intent of thereby imposing on the latter the affinal obligations of freely giving goods and services.

Nor is the less common term *ufa̧ï* restricted among the Kuikuru to contexts of myths or explaining affinal status as among the Kalapalo (see Basso 1970:412). In fact it was not used by Kuikuru either in the context of eliciting genealogies (*ifïsuïŋgï afefïjï,* "writing relatives") or in response to questions about actual or potential marriage. It was heard most frequently in response to alphabetically arranged lists of names presented to informants for the purpose of eliciting relationship terms. In other contexts informants stated that it was "a good word" and could be used in address as well as reference with no embarrassment (*ifïsu*). It is used by both males and females to designate any cross cousin (*"auaju mu(ku)gu,"* MBCh, or *"etsí mu(ku)gu,"* FSiCh). Although informants made the relationship explicit in these ways, in fact the cousin ties referred to are distant; I have not been able to trace precise genealogical links between persons designated as *ifa̧ï* (third-person form of *ufa̧ï*).

With the definition of *ufa̧ï* as cross cousin in mind and the frequency of marriage to persons other than cross cousins, it becomes significant that although some informants felt that marriage with *ufa̧ï* was good, others merely said it was permissible. One man explained that a person could have sex relations with *ifa̧ï* (*"ufai kupitsï ake"*) and added in Portuguese that they could legitimately either marry or be lovers (*"casar ou namorar"*). *"Quando etsí tem filha, eu pode trabalhar a ella"* (when father's sister has a daughter I can have sex with her). A man's father's sister "can give" her daughter to her brother's son, reminding one of Yalman's explanation of the relationship between cross cousins among the Sinhalese: "It is said that they have blood claims . . . upon each other. They already belong to each other from their birth since they find themselves in categories of kinship established by the kinship position of their parents" (1962:565).

While it is clear that *ifa̧ï* are considered to be among one's cross relatives, some informants felt that the relationship was too close for marraige. One man who raised his *ifa̧ï*, a small orphan girl, in his own home seemed to regard her as a close relative and would not have intercourse with her. As explained above, some preferred marrying more distant relatives or persons not known to be related and referred to first cross cousins as *telo* in order to imply affinability by reason of distance if they were attracted to a specific first cousin.

In my earlier paper I proposed the hypothesis that abandonment of special terms for cross cousins is in general associated with a breakdown of exogamous kin groups and an increase in marriage within a kin group

(1969:119). Actually there is evidence for a recent change away from cross-cousin marriage among the Kuikuru. An informant stated that formerly *ifą̈* married each other *"bem direito"* (very strictly), but that the Kuikuru were abandoning that practice. He noted that a man can now marry *ufati* (SiD) if they are *"poco longe"* (a little distant) and that one man had married his "mother's sister" and one woman her "mother's brother." Many cross-generation unions between both parallel and cross relatives do in fact occur in the Kuikuru genealogies. The same informant commented that such marriages *"atropalha muito"* (mix things up a lot).

Before leaving the discussion of *ufą̈*, it should be noted that an alternate term, *pamï*, was borrowed from the Carib-speaking Bakairí formerly in the Upper Xingú region. It is clearly cognate with *ufą̈* and with the form *ibamuy* used by the Island Carib in 1665 (see Dole 1969: 112). This borrowed form is used by Kuikuru in exactly the same sense as is *ufą̈*, and not exclusively for an *ifą̈* who is also a special friend (*ato*), as reported by Basso for "Xingu Carib" (1970:412). It is interesting in this connection also that the conservative forms *pa:mï* among the Moroni River Caribs and *paman* among the Galibí are used along with *ti:wo* and *tewô* (cf. Kuikuru *telo*) for FSiSo and MBSo (Arnaud and Alves 1975).

Conclusion

Among the Kuikuru marriage structure is not clearly an alliance system. There are few recognizable exchanges of spouses, either direct or delayed. Siblings usually marry members of different sibling sets, different house "factions," and different sets of cousins. Moreover, the not infrequent marriage of parallel relatives counteracts any tendency to establish categories of affinables as opposed to consanguine kin. Instead of a neat system of alliance, Kuikuru norms provide a wide range of variation of appropriate marriage patterns and support them with appropriate rationales. In practice, marriage exhibits an even wider variety. In this respect Kuikuru structure resembles that of the Tsimihety, of whom Southall says, "Nowhere is there any suggestion of a marriage alliance pattern between groups. All kin groups (with the exception of a few important royal ones) are genealogically shallow . . . " (1971:154).

By contrast among the Kalapalo—who speak a similar Carib dialect, have a generally very similar culture, and intermarry with the Kuikuru to some extent—marriage structure is described as "an alliance between two sets of siblings . . . who are considered suitable spouse exchangers . . . " (Basso 1975:212), with "the majority of marriages conform[ing] to the same general formal pattern of 'affinal repetition' within a single generation . . . " (Becker 1969:85). If the Kalapalo do in fact marry cross relatives regularly, they may indeed maintain an alliance structure more strictly than the Kuikuru. However, in seeming contradiction to her generalization about alliance marriage among the Kalapalo, Basso indicates that she found "no examples of such exchanges occurring over more than two generations" and adds that "the present system does not contain elements of permanency. . . . The kinship-based [intermarrying] groups have no definite existence beyond a single generation" (Becker 1969:85). My observation of Kuikuru marriage agrees with these findings.

I also agree that the use of *ifaï* for a category of affinable cross relatives is explainable in terms of marriage alliance structure. This point is not at issue. What is at issue is whether structural theory can explain the fact that the term is not used regularly among the Kuikuru. Its relatively infrequent use among the Kuikuru is not explained by its structural meaning.

The current regular, public term for cross cousins is the same as the one that is used for siblings and parallel cousins (*ufisï, ufisuïŋgï*). Unless one is convinced that terms similar to *ifaï* that were used regularly for cross cousins or affines among 16 other Carib-speaking groups, dating from as early as the seventeenth century, are independent of the Kuikuru tradition, the conclusions are unavoidable that this term was once used more generally among the ancestors of the Kuikuru to designate cross cousins or affines or both; that a sibling term has been extended to cousins in regular usage; and that the infrequency of the current use of the Carib cross-cousin term among the Kuikuru requires explanation in terms of culture change.

A structural approach neither conflicts with nor replaces the study of culture change; the one complements the other. A structural analysis describes the system in its ideal form; the developmental (in this instance "devolutionary" rather than "evolutionary") approach may explain the lack of functional correlation between the ideal pattern and actual practice.

NOTES

1. Despite Leach's view (1961) that any attempt at a universal definition of marriage would be vain, I believe it is absolutely necessary to make such an attempt in order to communicate on the subject and to make possible comparative studies of marriage. I therefore suggest a definition with cross-cultural application in mind.

In this paper I use "marriage" to mean the socially sanctioned kinship union of two or more persons for the purpose of legitimizing their sexual relations or offspring. Any such union necessarily establishes jural affinal relations and is publicly recognized, if not acclaimed, by a customary act, even if that act is no more than moving one's hammock (cf. Dillingham and Isaac 1975:60-61). To distinguish the act of becoming married from the structure of marriage, the former has been aptly referred to as a marriage act (Ackerman 1964).

The above definition is compatible with those found in Webster's Seventh New Collegiate Dictionary (1965): "marry: to join as husband and wife according to law or custom . . . ; to take as a spouse . . . ; to enter into a close or intimate union," and "marriage: the state of being married; the mutual relation of husband and wife; the institution whereby men and women are joined in a special kind of social and legal dependence for the purpose of founding and maintaining a family. . . . "

Such a definition of marriage in terms of practices or customs allows one to describe, discuss, and compare marriage as a culture trait, whereas definitions such as "a set of native concepts . . . which serves to justify requests for spouses" (Basso 1970:402)refer only to the ideas about and rules for the conduct of marriage practices. Requesting a spouse is an integral part of marriage as a culture complex, and therefore it cannot logically be justified by the thing of which it is a part, namely marriage as concepts. Rather, marriage is *based on* a set of concepts, including "native beliefs," and it *exemplifies* those concepts and beliefs to varying degrees. In addition, marriage involves a customary social agreement between human partners and an association of those partners in a special kinship unit. In order to be able to study marriage practices themselves, it is essential to keep in mind these aspects of marriage as well as the concepts, beliefs, and rules for behavior.

2. Data in this paper were collected in 1953 and 1954 in the Kuikuru settlement of Lafatuá, also called Lamakuka, which was located near Lake Lamakuka a few miles west of the middle Kuluene River in the Upper Xingú basin of Mato Grosso. I am indebted to Robert Carneiro for additional data collected by him in 1975 at the settlement of Afaŋítafagï, one of the two current villages on the Tuatuarí (or Tïfatïfagí) affluent of the lower Kiliseu.

3. Composite extended families are organized on the basis of two principles, in this instance lineality and bilaterality, resulting in groups that include the nuclear families of parents and of both male and female offspring.

4. Although the Kuikuru do not claim actual genealogical ties with many members of other groups than their own, they extend kin terms to the latter, and it seems likely that as of 1954 members of all the Upper Xingú tribal groups were interrelated, even though the relationships may not be remembered.

In the present discussion only kin terms of reference are considered, although most of the same terms may be used in address as well.

5. Unlike Kalapalo, Kuikuru words are regularly accented on the penult. Accents are indicated here only when the pronunciation differs from the regular pattern.

6. Another difficulty in tracing genealogical relations, and therefore marriage ties, is the use of four or more different names during one's lifetime: two baby nicknames, one given by each side of the family; adult names also

given from each side of the family ancestry; and finally at least one other
name taken from an ancestor if a person lives long enough to give his or
her own name to a grandchild. In talking about kinship relations,, individuals
speak the names that have been given by their own progenitors and not those
given by affines. Hence different people use different names for the same
person. In addition, various people pronounce names differently, sometimes
using shortened forms and different dialect renditions.

7. The Kuikuru, Kalapalo, and Matipú live not on the Xingú but in an
area drained by five rivers that meet to form the Xingú. The area drained by
those tributary rivers is properly referred to as the Upper Xingú basin.

4

Canela Marriage: Factors in Change

WILLIAM H. CROCKER

Ethnologists have not usually utilized diachronic materials in resolving synchronic problems, or even for adding the perspective of time
to their ethnologies, either because they lacked earlier pertinent studies
of sufficient substance or because they simply have not tried to reconstruct the past, believing such attempts to be unreliable. For this study
focused on the institution of marriage, however, an earlier monograph of
sufficient significance has been available, and the researcher has specialized
in developing techniques for reconstructing certain aspects of tribal life
reaching back as far as 1900 for some trends, and earlier for others.
Many of these changes, though included as relevant to the institution
of marriage, are also pertinent to other institutions both in the two tribal
societies analyzed herein as well as in closely related tribes being re-
searched by other ethnologists. This paper should serve to clarify certain
trends and changes in these other culturally related societies, or at least to
offer alternative materials for debate.

The Gê-speaking Ramkókamekra- and Apanyekra-Canela live in Brazilian savanna country (*cerrados*) some 100 miles from real *hiléia* tropical rain forests (W. Crocker 1972a:225-28) and about 400 miles southeast of the city of Belem at the mouth of the Amazon. They were "pacified"
in the last century (Nimuendajú 1946:28-35),[1] are now in close contact
with local farmers and ranchers, and have been cared for by the national
government Indian services since the 1930s. Although they have adopted
most of the technology and agricultural practices (slash-and-burn) of
their Brazilian backwoods neighbors, and lost some of their old socio-
cultural patterns, they nevertheless still carry out most of their traditional
customs. The greatest changes have come from a "loosening" of the

63

authority structure. As a result, the older generations have lost considerable control over the younger people (W. Crocker 1961:82-84).

Both populations are growing; the Ramkókamekra now number somewhat over 700 and the Apanyekra around 300 (just over 400 and around 225 in 1970) and occupy circular villages about 30 miles apart. Both are characterized by uxorilocal residence, matrilateral extended families, and bilateral personal kindreds, but no corporate, full-time descent groups (W. Crocker 1979:237-40). The two Canela tribes differ from the other Timbira tribes (Krahó, Krĩkatí, Pukóbye, Gavião, and Apinayé)[2] mostly in their village size (important), more complete maintenance of their age class systems, the greater extension of the R-Canela Crow-like characteristics, and the relative permanence of their marriages when there is a child to cement the union.

The Canela marry persons they consider to be "nonrelated" (ca'krit), where the genealogical relationship has been "lost," forgotten, or become very attenuated by social or spatial distance. All members of ego's kindred (R-C: mehũũkyê; A-C: me'kwë)[3] even out to third and fourth collaterals, and further if parallel cousins, may at least in theory be considered "blood relatives" (mei-caprôô-kwë, my blood group). When these are of the opposite sex, they are unavailable for marriage or sexual purposes, at least in theory—their theory. They also sometimes "commit incest" (to ayprë) with relatives as close as third or second cross cousins.[4] First cross-cousin sexual relationships and marriages, which occur very rarely, are held to be shameless and life-shortening. Uterine sibling sexual contacts are thought to cause madness or death.

Quite clearly, there are no prescriptive or preferential marriage rules, nor do formal or statistically related alliances exist. The sororate (cf. Nimuendajú 1946:124) is practiced only occasionally but nevertheless is theoretically favored,[5] whereas the levirate is not. Brothers do not marry into the same uxorilocal family.

Sexual relations begin for girls between the ages of 10 and 13, and for boys between 12 and 15, that is, usually as young as possible. A lad is initiated into sexual relations by an experienced woman in her late teens; formerly, he was then ordered by his "grandfathers" to have sex only with older women in their forties and fifties for several years. When a young male takes a girl's virginity (córmã 'cuuni, "she is still whole"), he has the choice of staying "married" to her (mehikwa, "they lie down") or of withdrawing from the relationship, after which his kin must pay a significant fine (cute-cukën ya'pan-tsä-'nã, "his-having-broken-in payment"). Every effort is made (largely exhortation by his kindred and the elders) to keep a couple together,[6] and the girl's family "buys" the young husband (meiwawë 'nã hämyõr, "our-son-in-law for paid") by means of a large meat pie ceremonially delivered to his family house late in the afternoon. (Meat pies increasingly today are exchanged between both families.) The meat pie purchase of the son-in-law usually used to occur before sexual relations began, but now this rite almost always takes place afterward. This is an individual matter and apparently these alternatives existed at the turn of the century as well as now, but there has been a quantitative shift. Engagements between children often were arranged by their families—an old and current practice (*cute meaypēn tê,* "they for-each-other restricted"), but individual preferences prevail later. Just prior to and after puberty these engagements could be broken if the boy's kin made a small payment for his release.[7]

Until the birth of a child, young couples did not live in the same house. Although they were "married," young people were supposed to have sexual relations only very infrequently with persons of their own generation (including their spouses), so a young man would only occasionally cohabit with his wife, and then usually just at night, on a platform bed in her house raised high under the rafters for this purpose (cf. Nimuendajú 1946:118), returning to the plaza before the early morning dance. Nevertheless, the Canela do call these liaisons "marriages." During this early childless stage, before the girl has delivered a whole deer to her mother-in-law and had her ceremonial belt and body painted red (*urucu: Bixa orellana*) in return, the publicness of her extramarital activities is restricted (W. Crocker 1964a:28 and 1974:187). After the belt-painting ceremony, however, which amounts to a more complete acceptance of her by her husband's family, she is expected to go openly, assigned as a girl associate (*cuytswë*), to accompany male groups for purposes of group sex. Her husband must not be jealous, though he increasingly objects these days, and maybe always did so even in aboriginal times.[8] Between her loss of virginity and childbirth, she is classed as a *men-crecrer-re* (slippery, free) person and must please most men with her sexual favors (W. Crocker 1962:115), especially after the painting of her belt (formerly mostly only after the termination of her postpuberty restrictions). If she does not, a group of men will waylay her to teach her to be generous. The group sex practices and the waylaying still occur among the Ramkókamekra but were abandoned long ago by the Apanyekra, an interesting and very important acculturative difference.

In these two periods—i.e. between virginity loss and belt painting, and from the belt ceremony to conception—a girl often used to be "married" several times. In the 1970 marriage case history study, however, the Ramkókamekra average for these periods was 1.5 marriages, while it was 1.8 marriages for the entire life cycle. With conception and the survival of a child, moreover, divorce is (and was, they say), almost impossible (seven cases in 96 marriages);[9] there are numerous separations, however, some lasting as long as a year. In contrast, divorce regardless of children is rampant among the Krĩkatí (Lave 1967:249) and easier among the Apanyekra than the Ramkókamekra. This Canela difference is remarkable, since uxorilocal tribes are noted for their relatively high frequency of divorce.[10]

The main point of friction in the Canela sociocultural system *is* nevertheless between husband and wife. Tribal schisms, difficult to bring about, do occur, and political rivalries between age class leaders exist but are relatively mild and suppressed owing to the high cohesiveness of the social structure and the great emphasis on generosity of spirit. Noncompetitiveness and overt cooperation rather than a show of hostility are traits that are seen as being manly. "Women, animals and *cupẽ* (local Brazilians) fight," the Canela say, "but Canela *men* bear up (*awcanã: aguënta*) under problems and adversity." I estimate that at least 80 percent of the cases coming before the tribal council involve marital disputes.[11]

Nimuendajú claims (1946:129) that adultery *was* grounds for divorce. A trend may be developing in this direction but was certainly not the case in Nimuendajú's time for couples with children, that is, for most of the adult population, though childless couples sometimes parted for this reason. A Ramkókamekra might come upon a man having relations with his wife on their platform bed, but even such a disrespectful act (especially on the part of his wife) is said not to be grounds for fighting, let alone divorce; it would, nevertheless, be sufficient reason for a payment to be made between the two extended families to alleviate the husband's shame.

Canelas can divorce and remarry if they are not raising children born to them. This happened in 1973 to a Ramkókamekra couple in their early forties, Tsêp-kä and Pre-'capaa. There are numerous other childless couples, however, who remain married for a lifetime. (I counted 14 in the village of Ponto in August, 1960.) The oldest Ramkókamekra, Pï'tô, about 81 in 1970, died in May, 1973, ending a lifetime, childless marriage. His widow, Kïy, was in her late seventies. In the 1970 R-Canela marriage case histories, however, three young men left their wives, set free by their children's death, and just two older men left their wives precisely because they could not bear children.

Great love, attachment, and personal care can be seen between many Ramkókamekra couples. When I asked if a spouse was considered a "blood relative" or not, there was some question in the informants' minds because after years of sexual intercourse it is believed that a couple's blood has become interchanged. It was agreed that this mingling was enough to require the illness taboos to be maintained between the couple, as among uterine siblings, but that spouses were nevertheless *not* considered *me-caprôô kwë* (persons'-blood group).

When a Canela husband is traveling "in the world" (i.e., in Brasília, Recife, Salvador, Rio, etc.), as they often do for several months, a young wife without children lives in "mourning" conditions (no sex, singing, dancing, or body painting, and her hair growing long) with her mother-in-law's family (cf. Nimuendajú 1946:126-27). Oldtimers say the change in this practice (the internment used to be in the wife's mother's house) is due to fear of her husband's now unsuppressed jealousy (*incrïc-tsii*), of therefore losing him, or of having to make big payments in his family's favor to "erase the shame from his face" that accrues especially in modern times. A wife's husband's family would surely confine her with greater care than her own mother's family.

When a wife dies, particularly if she leaves children, her family tries to persuade the widower to marry again into their family for the sake of the children, and because they do not want to lose an economic asset, if he is a reasonably good one. The widower, nevertheless, usually leaves after several weeks of mourning if he has paid the grave diggers himself, or he is allowed to depart in three to six months if the deceased wife's family has paid the grave diggers. Quite similarly, after her husband's death, a widow is carefully watched by her deceased husband's family to see that she keeps her mourning restrictions for about six months; whoever breaks her sex restrictions has to pay a fine to her family if he does not stay with her, i.e. marry her.[12]

It is interesting that only a man's departures are restrained by fines. (These constitute "reverse exchanges," in goods rather than people. See da Matta 1979:120.) If a woman absolutely does not want a man, and even if they have been married for some time and she has had children by him, he must leave and neither of the parties' kin pays a fine, but this rarely occurs.[13] Thus, although a husband can be coerced by pressure from his bilateral kindred and the council of elders, this formal lecturing being reinforced by fines, once a wife has taken a determined stand, no one expects influences of this sort to change her mind.

Husbands are economic assets that can be bought, controlled, used, reasoned with, and restrained. Wives, however, are "seen" as the immovable solid blocks of society. (For female immutability, see da Matta 1979:123 and Vidal 1977:116.)[14] They may have great sexual flings between the belt-painting ceremony and the birth of their first child, but later become embedded in the female matrix of domestic life, held strongly in place through uxorilocal residence and dominated by the great matrilateral extension of their kin ties. Moreover, there used to be occasional pressure visits from special patrilateral counselors. Women are restrained, in the most ultimate situations, by the fear of vicious female gossip and the danger of illness and death through witchcraft if they are not reasonably cooperative and generous. Thus in contrast, whereas it is their security in the permanence and continuity of generation after generation of strong social position backed by kin and supportive traditions that limits adult female behavior, it is pressures from his kindred, the council of elders, and the fear of fines that influence an adult man's comings and goings with respect to females. Consequently, women are so secure on the personal level that they can afford to be irritable, changeable, and demanding while their husbands must put up with such abuses.[15]

In the marital balance, the women are seen as suffering more: ripped in losing virginity and in childbirth, perspiring when carrying wood and hauling water, and held stationary by raising children and maintaining a household for their husbands. Consequently, the husband is continually rebalancing the marital "scales" by working hard and making small payments to his wife's family.

In modern times, however, the balance is changing because the husband, as a son-in-law, is becoming freed from the ancient social pressures (kindred and elders) that forced him to stay with his wife's family for the sake of the children. He is now becoming a great asset because of his ability to contribute economically (sometimes even reading and obtaining odd jobs) to the increasingly important family group, which is oriented around his father-in-law rather than around his wife's MBs and "GPs."

Nimuendajú reported that in earlier times a majority of Ramkókamekra youths were married in a collective wedding just after they had completed their age class initiation cycle (1946:122). After the termination of the final Pepyê initiation ceremony (their "graduation" into being an adult age class), each youth was taken to his bride. It has fortunately been possible to verify in detail the former existence of this ritual. As Nimuendajú wrote, this ceremony *was* last held around 1913 and was *not* carried out in 1923 after the end of that ten-year initiation cycle. Considering the loss of this obviously significant ceremony, at least two important questions must be answered: (1) how did age class sanctions affect marriages, and (2) what changes have been brought about by the loss of this obviously important institution?

Reconstructing distant past events from just the memories of any people, whether tribal or urban, is a notoriously difficult and not always reliable undertaking. Fortunately, however, I had the help in 1959 and 1960 of old Kä'po, who was about 34 in 1913. Mïïkrô, the Canela-recognized tribal "culture historian," whose class did go through the 1913 ceremony, also helped extensively. So did Rop-kä, the very class leader himself, whose wife's pregnancy just after the 1923 initiation festival made it unpropitious to carry out the ensuing "marriage" rite that year at all; thus it was abandoned. Moreover, the lucid memories of certain old women like Pyê-'kär, maybe 70 in 1964, and the female leader, Ter-kwëy, have served to round out the picture.

Each age class "graduate," whose woman was not already pregnant, was led in turn from the plaza by a councilor (*pro-kãm*), usually some "grandfather," to the house of his present or future parents-in-law where he was placed to lie, limbs intertwined, with his fiancee or "wife" while they were both admonished to care well for each other. The councilor then received a meat pie from the bride's relatives and took it back to the plaza as a gift to the councilors. The procession was repeated for each youth, with the councilors marching in file. A ceremonial individual followed separately, considerably behind, singing a traditional chant that was special for the rite.

The class leader, as on other occasions, was the first to undertake his class's activities. But when his wife had become pregnant before the rite was to be performed, the councilors must have believed it would not be propitious to carry out the ceremony for *any* members of the age class. Class leaders are *hämren,* that is, high in ceremonial status and strong in magical powers and prognostic sensitivity (see W. Crocker 1978:17), unlike the class commandant and class deputy commandant (Nimuendajú 1946:193), who are purely political figures. Therefore, it is easy to understand that when an age class's "seer," with group-protective and danger-sensing abilities, cannot be the first participant in the ceremony to test its propitiousness, it might well be safer and wiser not to carry out the rite at all. Moreover, until after the young men had been brought to their spouses' houses in this manner, they were not supposed to visit these structures in the daytime, but when most of the young husbands and even the class leader himself were seen to be ignoring this rule, there was little reason for the councilors to carry out an act one of the purposes of which was to enable the youths to do what they were already doing.

The ceremony described above certainly was a marriage rite, but it should be realized that almost all of the youths being led to their brides in this manner were already "married" to these girls in the sense that Canela use both the Portuguese expression *casado* and their own *mehikwa.* A man (the "social" husband and maybe the genitor) with his own "biological" children[16] and their mother (the genitrix) are totally married and he cannot become detached and married to anyone else by an act of sexual intercourse. If his wife's children are not seen as his "biological" children, however, and he has made an unattached woman pregnant, he would have to leave his wife and her children to marry the single girl with his "biological" child. Consequently, the rites of "contracting" marriage (*meto aypẽn tê*) before sexual intercourse has taken place, "adjusting" it afterward (*me aypẽn pa,* "they to-each-other listen"), and even the group ceremony conducted by the councilors, do not constitute the crucial

act in becoming married: it is the performance of private sexual intercourse itself in connection with the woman's open demand and the man's
public admission, when neither the man nor the woman is tied to another
person of the opposite sex by a "biological" child, that constitutes the principal elements in having become "married."[17]

Understood in this way, it is certain that most of the youths who were
taken to their "brides" during the traditional age class wedding were
already "married" to them; the ceremony served principally to reinforce
and establish the permanence of the marriage. In the eyes of the councilors and most of the tribe, a youth was placed in a symbolic marital
position with his fiancee or "wife" so that all these people could bear
witness to the fact of their union. Thus, through the collective wedding,
most people in the tribe were placed in such a position that they would
necessarily become somewhat embarrassed if they should ever allow the
marriage to dissolve.

This is a characteristic Canela behavioral pattern. A self-respecting
Canela will not give orders or instructions, or witness acts, unless he
expects the recipients to obey and comply; otherwise, he experiences great
shame. Thus a principal purpose of the collective age class wedding was
to bring virtually all the men in the tribe into a position of being obligated to enforce the various marriages. This may account to some extent
for the relatively low Ramkókamekra divorce rate in spite of uxorilocality
and the matrilineal-like characteristics.

These collective weddings ideally took place at a relatively late point
on the progressing-into-total-marriage continuum for most of the young
brides and bridegrooms.[18] My old informants of both sexes believed that
most of the girls taking part in these weddings were considerably older
than present brides and fully grown and well formed, and that the young
men graduated as an age class considerably older than they do these days,
perhaps between the ages of 16 and 25, or even 20 and 29. (I have been
able to verify Nimuendajú's claim that a new Ramkókamekra age class
is formed about every ten years.) Considering the extramarital possibilities, it is hard to believe that the novices would not somehow have been
trapped into "fatherhood" by the time they were 18, and certainly by 22,
but some arrangements were built into the system that would have helped
some of them avoid it until they were much older. Their postpuberty
restrictions required not only very little sex for several years (maybe two
or three) but also almost no sex with young girls, including their wives,
because such contacts would weaken them. On the other hand, the alternative and recommended sexual outlet—the experienced women in their
late forties and fifties—were believed to magically impart strength and
courage to them. Besides, with postmenopausal women, they would not

run the slightest risk of contact with the very contaminating effect of mere traces of menstrual blood.

By the time a youth was 16 to 18, having become a clear-seeing hunter (*me-nto-capôc*) and a midday-sun endurance runner through the maintenance of these restrictions, he might have begun relaxing these postpuberty taboos. Nevertheless, the very available married women, with or without children, were not entrapping because although seminal contributions were believed to help create a baby, such accretions still would not have made *him* the responsible "social husband," i.e. a principal father (pater), even if she publicly claimed him as a "contributing father."[19]

A young man was caught into entering the first stage of "matrimony" only (1) if he had taken a virginity, (2) if an unattached nonvirgin (with or without children) had proved too alluring, or (3) if he had broken a widow's mourning restrictions. In all three of these cases he easily could have avoided solidification of the marriage, however, (1) if he had bought his release, (2) if some other man had later won over his "wife," or (3) if she had sent him away in dislike, any one of these events occurring before she had become obviously pregnant *while* he was her recognized "social husband." Thus it seems quite possible that a young man might be "married" several times without becoming caught as the principal father and therefore in an "enduring" marriage, until he was 25 or 29, or even later. His personal tactics and the advice of the significant counselors among his kindred surely depended on his position in his age class, namely, whether he were older or younger. Social and family pressures on the young man were certainly very strong and effective in those days.

A girl was caught in an "enduring" marriage only with the man who happened to be her social husband at the time she became pregnant, and even then, if she lost the fetus or the baby in childhood, he might leave or she might send him away.[20]

Some of the brides were virgins at 10 to 13 and had been engaged, that is, contracted in childhood marriages with the older men in the age class. It is clear that an age class collective wedding to a virgin was so binding (see Nimuendajú 1946:119) that the councilors could take a chance on the marriage solidifying during the three to five years until likely pregnancy.

Other arrangements tended to delay the arrival at an enduring marriage for women. A girl maintained postpubertal restrictions for perhaps one year, when she was supposed to have sex rarely and then only with men in their later forties and fifties. Moreover, until she had won her ceremonial belt as a girl associate of a men's society and had had it painted by her mother-in-law, both her husband and other men tended, relatively speaking,[21] to let her alone sexually, especially if she were of high ceremonial status. These practices helped to reduce the chances of conception. However, after the painting of her belt, she became fair game for all nonrelated men, privately and in the group arrangements, a fact that would certainly have tended to bring on a pregnancy more quickly than if she were just left to her husband, a clandestine lover, or an occasional old man.

The old informants were very clear about the point that girls received their belts at an older age in earlier times. Husbands and youths were supposed to respect a girl who had not yet won her belt, having sex with her only rarely. The high-status girl associates (Pepcahäc, Kêêtúwayê, Pepyê, and Wë'të) and the younger of the middle-status girl associates (Häc, Cukrïtre-'ho, Rop, and certain plaza group girls) had to be taken into these men's societies as virgins and parents tried to keep them as such so that they could be chosen to fill such positions. In contrast, the older middle-status and the definitely low-status girl associates (Côcayu, Cukên, Me'kên, and certain plaza moiety girls) were brought into the men's societies as nonvirgins precisely for sexual purposes to be used by the whole troop (see Nimuendajú 1946:228), but only at prescribed times. Thus it should be clear that service in men's societies and having to wait for the belt to be painted did tend to delay pregnancy.

The earlier Ramkókamekra collective wedding, as I reconstruct it, is characterized by (1) the exclusion of a certain number of the older novices and their wives because they had become fathers and mothers and were therefore no longer model individuals with respect to the ideal traditional marital process; (2) an average age of participating men of around 24, with a range of ages between 20 and 29; (3) the presence of either 10- to 13-year-old virginal fiancees, who would lose their virginity almost immediately, or 14- to 20 (or higher)-year-old nonvirgins. Fathers, obviously pregnant women, and mothers are similarly excluded from many other festival roles.

In the late 1950s, when the old Ramkókamekra spoke about the times of their ancestors, which really amounted to what their parents and grandparents had told them about life during the middle of the last century, they always emphasized the fierceness and strength of the political chiefs, the councilors, and the GFs (including MBs and "MBs") in their dealings with their GCs. They told of a long free period in the lives of young men and a shorter one for girls when they were quite unattached and had great sexual freedom and fun. Younger men (the internees or novices, the youngest graduated age class, and, for a few years, the next highest age class) lived as much or more for their age class activities as for their responsibilities to consanguines or affines, and roamed the countryside under the direction of their commandant and/or deputy commandant (not their class leaders). At night they danced, sang, and slept in the plaza with the childless women, younger than about 30 (and sometimes more aged), whether older and barren or young and between their belt-painting rites and childbirth. The ungraduated novices and the pre-belt-painted girls were kept away from these fun-generating activities by the generalized force of the older generation, exerted through the individual's kindred, by his or her name giver, by chiefs in the course of public lectures, and through the direct orders of class commandants and/or class deputies (for boys). Ramkókamekra novices were publicly shamed and hazed for violations by their GF category counselors before a line of dancing women and the tribe assembled in the plaza. In 1958 and 1975 the Apanyekra held a public shaming ceremony in the plaza for couples who had had sexual relations in spite of the Pepyê festival internment restrictions of the young men.[22]

Freedom ended for the girls with childbirth and the need to take proper care of their children. For men, freedom continued in the form of their age class activities even after they became fathers. Their consanguines and affines did make certain demands on them, but they still spent a lot of time with their age classes until they were much older, some informants insisted. Their estimations of age were expressed in terms of the four active age classes. The first graduated age class, the one just above the novices (average age over the ten-year period, about 30), was said to have been relatively free of consanguineal and affinal duties and to have marched everywhere together, whereas the second age class (average 40), being of the same moiety as the novices, was reported to have been very active in singing, dancing, and other pursuits, but nevertheless was gradually settling down to consanguineal and affinal responsibilities. By the time a man had reached the age of the third age class above the novices, his group seldom assembled except for formal situations. By this period he would be in his middle forties and early fifties and would have children and maybe even grandchildren.

The oldtimers pointed out that the ancestors were fierce (*valente; hääprär*) (see W. Crocker 1978:17-18). It was not that the men fought each other all the time but rather that they recognized a "pecking order" based on a combination of real tribal authoritative power and real fighting ability. There were continual showdowns between men but only rarely open hositilities, because internal harmony was most highly prized. The old woman Pyê-'kär said it must have been miserable to have become recognized as a soft man in those days (the last century) because there were stories of fierce men pulling weaker ones away from women in the very act of sexual intercourse and simply taking over. Any ensuing hostilities would then be frustrated by almost any other nearby men, and continuing hatreds, pouting, and revenge were very much counseled against and lost in the all-consuming activities of age class life.

A man had very little influence in his marital home and in the disciplining of his children. His wife's actual and classificatory brothers and mothers' brothers were responsible for counseling and ceremonial purposes and took a hand in controlling the children; they also provided food by leaving more than a token portion of the game they killed. Thus a man gave a sizable piece of game in his Zs' and M's house and became seriously involved in their domestic problems as well. Moreover, a young man usually saved some of his game for his WMB. The surprise in these accounts is that old informants attribute significant *economic support* as well as ceremonial and juridical roles to male matrilateral relatives. Therefore, if we look back far enough into their history, the neat division between the F's and the MB's roles—i.e. nurture versus ceremonialism—may not be as clear cut for the Ramkókamekra as some Timbira specialists would like to have us think.

Quite obviously, the memories of the oldtimers about their ancestral life are idealized and exaggerated but, if evaluated carefully, do present clues about the past.

Returning to the question of what changes have been brought about by the loss of the age class collective wedding ceremony as a significant Ramkókamekra institution, I think it is preferable to see this loss as just one of the many changes that have occurred because of the "loosening" of the authoritative relationship between the Ramkókamekra generations. The question, therefore, cannot be fully handled here. Let a few of the contributing factors, and lines of thought, suffice.

With the loss of warfare as a partial way of life, the fierceness described above, which was decried by some local Brazilians as being "savage," ceased to have a raison d'être. By the beginning of the twentieth century, however, the Ramkókamekra image of themselves had evolved to the point where they did not see themselves as savages—like their ancestors, eating rotten wood and raw meat and killing people. Nevertheless, certain vestigial remains of this fierceness could be expressed during occasional rituals, such as the hazing of youths for their infractions of the puberty restrictions directly before a line of women. With the arrival of the federal Indian service personnel in 1938, however, even this form of discipline had to be discontinued for fear of embarrassment, and with it went the last real shaming, and therefore effective, traditional sort of control that the older men could bring to bear upon the younger ones.

The above description is a gross simplification of what actually has been going on between the Ramkókamekra generations for over a hundred years, but it serves to make the point that the aboriginal control of the old over the young was partly derived from a kind of personality expression through which the youths were terrorized into considerable submission. When we realize that the elders, in the roles of the GF and the MB, largely prevented their GCs and ZCs from having sexual relations with members of their own age group and allowed sex only with older men and women, we can well imagine how quickly this custom would be dropped once the elders had lost their power, and this is exactly what happened.

The old Rop-kä, whose age class was interned roughly between 1913 and 1923, said in August, 1960, that he and his age class mates still had sexual relations mainly with older women and seldom with girls their own age during their two to three postpuberty years, and that sex with young girls had to be largely hidden from their "GFs" (including "MBs")[23] for fear of drastic hazing and shaming in the plaza. For Caapêr-tïc, the deputy commandant of the age class being formed between 1923 and 1933 (Nimuendajú 1946:182), sex with the older women was still the practice but relations with young girls were easier because the "GFs" caused less trouble. In contrast, the age class of Caarä-'kre, 1934 to 1940, only occasionally had sexual relations with the older women, and the age class of the younger Caapêr-tïc, 1941 to 1951, *never* had sex with older women. He said it just was not done anymore out of respect for their age.

Another contributing factor in the breakdown of authority is the loss of tribal self-sufficiency. It is not possible to know exactly when the two Canela tribes first became deficient in supporting themselves. Old Brazilians of the region assure me that the Ramkókamekra were agriculturally self-sufficient and even affluent in a village site (A'krä-'kä-'tëy) they occupied between the middle 1890s and about 1904. Nimuendajú also gives this impression for his period (1929-36). Apparently, however, between about 1905 and 1917, when they were living away from the Santo Estêvão stream, and again between 1936 and 1940, they suffered serious agricultural deficiencies. The arrival of Indian service post personnel after 1938 (principally Sr. Olímpio Martins Cruz) reversed this process temporarily, but ever since 1947 the Ramkókamekra have not raised sufficient staples in their farm plots to prevent endemic semimalnutrition, and the Apanyekra have had a similar record starting somewhat later.

The Canela response to this problem in both tribes has been to abandon their circular villages during the lean part of the year, about September through January, and to spend it fragmented into small groups living beside hinterland farm communities within a 50-mile radius of their home villages, trading their labor and services for food and handouts. During these periods the postpubescent youths and girls do not see their

"GP" counselors for long periods at a time; thus they neglect their post-pubertal restrictions and perhaps begin to believe that these taboos are not very important after all. Moreover, the leaders of these groups are necessarily the F, not the MB, who is foraging elsewhere with his W and children. As a result of this change in group composition and leadership, a shift in authority to the F has been taking place. But the F and M had not traditionally dealt closely with the puberty restrictions, sexuality, and extramarital aspects of their adolescent children's lives. Thus these facets of growing up have changed and continue to change quite rapidly.

Most of the trends are in the direction of greater simplicity, ease, and immediate satisfactions for the young people, and also toward local Brazilian practices. These changes can be understood in the perspectives of: (1) the loss of authority of the "GP" counselors, the "MB" and "FZ" name givers, the tribal political chiefs, the council of elders, and the older generations as a whole, and (2) the shift in power from the GP class (including the MB and FZ) to the F and M and then in turn to the M's and her Zs' DHs.

I want to emphasize that not all of the factors contributing to these changes have been mentioned, let alone described and related diachronically to the consequent trends and changes. Such a treatment of material would have required a volume in itself. Some of the other factors, however, are: (1) impoverishment of existing gallery forest soils; (2) limitation of especially the Apanyekra to a small geographical area (rectified recently); (3) reduction in aboriginal abundance of game; (4) the turning away for prestige reasons from excellent aboriginal crops (peanuts, sweet potatoes, yams, corn, etc.) to less nourishing local Brazilian bitter manioc as the principal staple (dry rice cultivation is not sufficiently abundant); (5) elementary schooling by the federal Indian service post personnel since 1944, which at first was so effective that six youths learned to read and write to some extent; (6) continual exchanges with local farmers and ranchers arriving in the Canela villages almost daily to sell and trade food and goods; (7) disillusionment with the Indian Protection Service when they terminated their paternalistic policies around 1958; (8) the effects of both Nimuendajú and Crocker living in their midst (largely the Ramkókamekra) as cultural acceptables; (9) the effect of several Indian Protection Service agents and National Indian Foundation personnel in setting the example that some non-Canelas were "good people," leading to a breakdown in the strong Canela conviction that only their traditional way of life was decent, worthwhile, and satisfying; (10) a messianic movement (Ramkókamekra) oriented toward the Brazilian way of doing things and this cult's demise, and the effect of these occurrences on their faith in their aboriginal way of life; (11) effects of a Summer Institute of Linguistics missionary and his family living in their (Ramkókamekra) village circle since 1968 (but prohibited since 1978); (12) conspicuously more effective medical treatment in the 1970s and early 1980s, by the National Indian Foundation, legal acquisition of Canela lands by the foundation, and an obvious increase in the foundation's interest in their support and protection;[24] and surely many other acculturative factors of almost equal importance.

Although Nimuendajú has left us with several sizable problems that have to be handled in any paper on Canela marriage, I have chosen to deal indirectly (or in footnotes) so far with most of our points of divergence (adultery, high platform bed "bundling," what constitutes marriage, the sororate, etc.). However, I must deal more directly with his statement that the Ramkókamekra had matrilineal exogamous moieties (1946:79).

I agree with Lave (1967:110; 1971:341-43) that Nimuendajú erroneously saw matriliny in the all-pervasive uxorilocality and matrilaterality (including matrilines of up to four generations) of Canela society. In those days the concept was not always clearly defined and professionals did talk loosely about a society being "matrilineal" even if there were no clearly defined, daily operating, unilineal descent groups (W. Crocker 1977:269-70; 1979:239-40). Nimuendajú did not identify any groups of this nature in a definitive manner, though there actually were several *occasionally* operating, *ceremonial* matrilineal descent groups. It is these festival groups, which could be found in only about a quarter of the extended families and were not characteristic of all families, that must have enabled Nimuendajú to label the Canela as being "matrilineal." Thus, if the Canela were not unilineal, they quite clearly could not have had "matrilineal exogamous moieties," at least not in postcontact times.

A fascinating demographic point is that old informants claim Ramkókamekra men married much younger women—about ten years younger— but what should the expression "married" significantly mean in this context? As explained earlier, conception cements the relationship between a woman and the man who happens to be her social husband. Hence I am taking the average spouse age difference of first conception-cemented marriages as being the principal measure of ideal marriage age separation between couples.

Reliable data for husband-wife age differences in "early" (no previous marriages) first conception-cemented unions and "early"-formed but nevertheless long enduring childless marriages were rare for husbands over 50 in 1970 because of remarriages owing to the deaths of spouses, but in four cases the average age of marital separation was 6.5 years.[25] For the five marriages of this sort with husbands in their forties, the average age of separation was 10.0 years, while for the men in their thirties the difference was 4.3 years in 20 cases.[26] This same figure for 12 husbands in their twenties was approximately 5.1 years. Including "delayed" (husbands and/or wives previously married) first conception marriages, however, the figures for the same four categories in descending order are 7.3 (8 cases), 9.1 (16), 4.8 (27), and 5.4 (13); if marriages of *any* sort are examined, the four categories become 9.4 (10 cases), 9.2 (20), 5.3 (31), and 5.4 (13).[27]

Considering these data, it is indeed quite likely that, formerly, men in "early" and "delayed" first conception-cemented marriages (ranging between 5 to 15 years in spouse age separation), or in marriage taken as a whole (ranging from zero to over 20 years in spouse age differences), were married to women about ten years their junior.

The substantial marital debtor-creditor cycle described by Melatti (1970:168; 1979:69-70) and by Carneiro da Cunha (1978:42) for a man in relation to his affines among the Krahó exists for the Ramkókamekra only to a considerably lesser extent. (Stronger aspects of this affinal relationship can be found among the Apanyekra). This may be because the status of the Ramkókamekra son-in-law is rising in significance, so he is not in the weak position of owing his affines considerable amounts of material goods, though he certainly is obligated to pay them respect and services. I have seen fathers-in-law give new shotguns to their sons-in-law to keep them happy and working. Men, however, are always providing small gifts and doing nice things for their wives' relatives, in order, they say, to retain these persons' good will and assistance in keeping their wives interested in them rather than because of a strong debtor-creditor relationship. They also say they want these affines to counsel their wives favorably.

I would guess that this Ramkókamekra-Krahó contrast might be due to current acculturative differences. It seems that the Krahó are more economically and agriculturally self-sufficient than the Canela, a contrast that gives a Krahó son-in-law less economic status than his Canela counterpart, whose labor is desperately needed. Apparently some Krahó even own cattle, which was almost impossible among the Canela (calves were eaten in hunger), though there are a few Ramkókamekra modern exceptions. Another reason for the difference might be the Ramkókamekra son-in-law's ability to blackmail his in-laws if he discovered his wife to have been unfaithful even during festival situations. Both the Apanyekra and the Krahó may have become acculturated beyond this problem, their wives relatively speaking having far fewer chances at extramarital relations. Consequently the sons-in-law have less leverage with which to cause trouble for their parents-in-law, and therefore are in a weaker position.

Moreover, individualization may have evolved more extensively among the Krahó so that a young husband does not want to live under a standing debt[28] to his in-laws, and therefore pays it off early to be free to leave his wife when he may need to apply such leverage against her family.

It seems, from studying the comparative literature on the Timbira, that the Canela are the least acculturated and best preserved tribes (the Apanyekra less so than the Ramkókamekra, because of their fewer numbers and the severer encroachments on their lands during the last century). Both tribes, however, were fortunate to have been living near the headwaters of streams and therefore out of the way of national river-borne commerce (and currently from highways), and the Ramkókamekra were especially lucky to have maintained a higher living-group population than any other Timbira tribe.[29] Moreover, there happens to be less rainfall in the Canela area (about 40 inches per annum) than in the areas farther west (near 60 inches). Thus the Canela savannahs may have been less advantageous to cattle ranchers and the gallery forests less interesting to local farmers than around the Krahó. Both tribes, whether or not these factors account for their better state of preservation, represent models of the past that Timbira specialists must consider in their studies of the other Timbira and Northern Gê tribes. The Ramkókamekra cannot be simply subsumed under the category "Eastern Timbira" as largely identical to the Krahó and Krīkatí (cf. Maybury-Lewis 1967:301-9).

Whether because of their state of better preservation or because of pre-pacification differences, or both, the Ramkókamekra appear to be the most nearly matrilineal of the Timbira tribes; this is reflected in their more extensive Crow-like characteristics, such as certain families' ceremonial-only, corporate descent groups or lineages. Marriage ties were very weak until the first child was born. These loose affinal connections were then compensated for by extrafamilial institutions in the form of the age classes and the council of elders, and in a sense by the bilateral personal kindreds ("grandparents"), so that the opposite effect was achieved, resulting in almost unbreakable marriages even though the husbands were still very much involved in the activities of their mothers and sisters and their age classes. The dramatic changes in the aboriginal consanguineal-affinal balance were largely brought about by the loss of authority of the GP class of individuals (MBs and FZs included), so that persons who are first-linked to female ego (or merged as such: F, M, Z, B, H, MZ, MZD, etc.) have assumed the principal responsibilities in the power vacuum. My suggestion is that a number of Krahó, Krīkatí, and Apinayé acculturative characteristics may be viewed and accounted for by the utilization of similar longitudinal perspectives.

On a still broader scene, Scheffler and Lounsbury (1971:179) have compared the Ramkókamekra-Canela with the Apinayé, Kayapó, Nambikwara, Sirionó, Inca, and other societies, in the claim that certain " . . . basic structural principles are fairly apparent . . . " in the kinship systems of all these peoples. One of these distinctive principles they call "parallel-transmission," whereby in formal analysis " . . . there is a pronounced tendency for cross-collateral kintypes to take the terminological statuses of their parents of the same sex" (1971:179). I find from field data that their parallel-transmission rule (1971:110) does resolve the Canela consanguineal *and* affinal relationship systems in a more satisfactory manner than if a fortuitous mixture of Crow and Omaha Type-III reduction equations (Lounsbury 1964) is used (Lave 1977:323).[30] Moreover, from other published data (da Matta 1976:177-81, Bamberger 1979: 136, Vidal 1977:52-53, and Turner 1966), I agree with Scheffler and Lounsbury that these rules can also be applied advantageously to the Apinayé and Kayapó relationship systems. This greater suitability will eventually be demonstrated in a monograph that is already in preparation.[31] Briefly contrasting these three tribes, however: the Canela stress uterine line succession bringing out Crow-like features, the Kayapó a kind of substitutive agnatic line transmission manifesting Omaha aspects, and the Apinayé both alternatives. There are still, nevertheless, the matters of cognitive validity and the identification of related social structural correlates, both of which must be satisfactorily handled in order to establish the "parallel-transmission" rules as being an accurate representation of *an* underlying cognitive reality of these relationship systems.[32]

If one talks to Canela informants about descent, systematic succession, or the replacement of one relative or affine by another, one soon finds they use the expression *hatsä yaahêr-tsä kãm* ("his/her-place fill-er in": the person who fills in his or her place). Thus it is clear that they do think in terms of physical substitution of one person by another. By far their strongest association and most likely volunteered response in this context is that a woman will "fill in" her mother's place, and there is an extensive ideology for explaining this.[33] After discussing same-sex sibling substitution, they will soon come around to pointing out that a man does fill in his mother's brother's place (his *quêt*), but he does this, really, because he is very closely related to and responsible for his uterine sister. They are of the same "blood" (*caprôô*) or "substance" (see da Matta 1973:281). In fact, he takes his mother's brother's place most effectively when she takes her mother's place. It is also clear, secondarily, that a man can take the place of *any* other relative in his *quêt* kin category, especially the position of his "naming uncle,"[34] but this creates a rather diffuse situation with respect to male replacement or succession to terminological kin status.

Informants do not volunteer that a man "fills in" the place of his father, but when it is pointed out to them that he does do this just in three different situations, they recognize this process as "replacement," using the same expression *hatsä yaahêr-tsä kãm,* for male intertribal (Timbira) membership, for "exchange peace chief" (*täm-häc*) succession (Crocker 1978:16-17), and for the man who becomes the next "ceremonial chief of the whole tribe" (*krĩ cuuniá mehõõpa'hi*).[35] The point is that while they feel strongly about D/M equivalence and explain this to be the case through the expression *me-ipipẽn* ("they the-same") and consequently also recognize the associated ♂ / ♂ MB (or more properly ♂ / ♂ ZMB) replacement, they, in contrast, see other "ZS"-"MB" relationships as being considerably less important. The S/F succession is scarcely even thought about but is nevertheless recognized as very real ceremonially; it is also real to the considerable extent that ceremonial status performance does carry over into daily life role behavior.

Turning again to the Kayapó, instead of the D/M substitution line being strongly emphasized, it is the relationship of a man to his "adoptive" father that is held to be significant ceremonially and politically, giving the kinship system its Omaha-like terminological appearance. Similarly, a man's much greater importance and integration into his affinal rather than his consanguineal home stresses the H = W tie over the B-Z relationship, again reinforcing Omaha-like cross-cousin terminological results (da Matta 1976:191; Turner 1966:447; 1979:183).[36] The Apinayé situation is intermediate, reflecting both terminological resolutions (da Matta 1976:193). Thus, among other factors, it is the *relative marital balance*—the importance to a man of his family of orientation (Eastern Timbira) versus his family of procreation (Kayapó)—which is closely related to the appearance of Crow-like or Omaha-like cross-cousin terminology. Whereas a Canela gradually moves from—or partly still remains in—his house of orientation after marriage (Nimuendajú 1946:126), the Kayapó breaks this relationship more completely and soon forms strong bonds in his family of procreation (Vidal 1977:141).

The Sirionó, also characterized by parallel-transmission according to Scheffler and Lounsbury (1971), differ from the Canela-Apinayé-Kayapó (the Northern Gê) principally in that they have a MBD-FZS "Spouse Equation Rule" so that marriage takes place between matrilateral cross cousins instead of with "nonrelatives" (*me-ca'krit*) as it is for the Northern Gê groups (unless certain communities have grown too small). This does seem more appropriate to forest-dwelling, small-band endogamy, so one is tempted to see a proto-Canela form in the Sirionó: that is, if early Sirionó-like bands were to have expanded to become 500, 1,000, or more in population, they would quite reasonably have lost their matrilateral cross-cousin marriage practice and married "further out," manifesting their more Crow- or more Omaha-like alternative characteristics depending on the ecology, culture contact situations, and other factors. Weakly supporting this hypothesis for the Canela—that they emerged from an "elementary" system similar to the one of the Sirionó—is the interesting "coincidence," perhaps a cultural vestige found in current Canela terminology, that *atoctïyti* (your GM) or *atoctïyyê* (your HZ) (both female-to-female usage) could be the same person (♀ FZD or ♀ HZ) in a matrilateral cross-cousin marriage system. Similarly, in reference to a male speaker, *aquêtti* (your MB) and *apreequêt* (your WF) could be the same person (see W. Crocker 1977:268).

While the Gê specialists generally see Crow or Omaha cross-generational terminology as being related to the basic dualism and fundamental compartmentalization among these societies—public/private, forum/household, social persona/physical substance (Maybury-Lewis 1979: 305); one generation/another generation, male/female (da Matta 1979: 123)—I have come to appreciate an alternative but not very different associated structure. Namely, parallel-transmission cognitive patterns rather than Crow-Omaha principles characterize the relationship systems, the political and social structure, the marital balances and consequent family role responsibilities, as well as this basic dualism and fundamental compartmentalization. This appreciation has been derived from a detailed and intensive field study (1978-79) of related Ramkókamekra *ideology* in the areas of marriage and family role relationships.

The Ramkókamekra speak of life as a constant movement outward in every direction (especially to the west), horizontally, of "a descendant" (*tämtswë*) from his ancestors (*quêt/tïy*); and that any marriage (or even an affair) transforms this flow (*quêt/tïy* to *tämtswë*)[37] so that an identical blood (*caprôô* or "substance") group is formed between all persons who have become "first-linked" through continual sexual intercourse and its products: H = W, M = D, F = S, M = S, F = D, B = Z, Z = Z, B = B.[38] Beyond this range, second- and further-linked people (a grandkin supercategory) are essentially the same (*quêt, tïy* or *tämtswë*)—the mainstream of the "spreading" flow of humanity—though classificatory first-linked relatives do form an intermediate category for certain replacement purposes. With each genealogical link further away, nevertheless, the substance held in common between ego and alter becomes reduced, diluted by the "contributions" in marriage from another line of descendants. Thus it is really through *marriage* that both the consanguineal *and* affinal relationship systems are generated (and both are extensive),[39] because before a marriage—in their thinking—there was simply an ancestor-to-descendant "spreading out," with marriage making its continuation possible but altering *just* the first-link (and classificatory first-link) terminology. In the Ramkókamekra case, because of matrilocality, this model amounts to matrilines spreading outward from a center with a brother attached to each woman at each generation— matrifiliation. Thus a MB and a MF (or, similarly, a FZ and a FM)[40] are terminologically the same *because* they are second-linked (which amounts terminologically, also, to being further-linked) with respect to ego and also because they are not reducible to first-link foci (the common blood group) through same-sex-sibling, half-sibling, step-kin, or Crow-Omaha III rules—or, more suitably, I believe, through parallel-transmission rules. Again, it must be pointed out for emphasis that the cross-generation terminological characteristics can be largely accounted for in this manner—in the basic first-/further-link terminological and ideological distinction (compare da Matta 1976:188 and 1979:106).

The above reporting applies to the family of orientation, but the extended family of procreation (or the extended affinal system) can be treated similarly. The result is that there is conspicuously more than just " . . . a pronounced tendency for . . . [across-marital-bond] . . . kin-types to take the terminological status of their parents of the same sex," which amounts to applying the parallel-transmission pattern to the affinal domain (Scheffler and Lounsbury 1971:181). It happens to be the case that the agnatic lines can be "seen" more distinctly in the extended affinal relationship system.[41]

Whether Crow- or Omaha-like cross-cousin terms appear as parallel-transmission alternatives depends on the kind of marriage that dominates from tribe to tribe, as has been pointed out before. Even the ideology with respect to what goes into forming a baby changes with this shift of emphasis from the uterine line to the agnatic line, for while the Eastern Timbira believe that both father and mother contribute equally to forming the substance of the fetus, the Kayapó stress the father's role (Vidal 1977:89), as do the Suyá (Seeger 1974:140 and 1981:123) and the Sherente/Chavante (Maybury-Lewis 1967:63).

It has become very apparent to me that the parallel-transmission rules must represent a very deep Northern Gê (and perhaps a central Brazilian) cognitive pattern, partly because these rules resolve the Canela consanguineal and affinal terminologies so very well (both the ideal models and their legitimate ideological variations) but also because they fit a general cognitive pattern I have derived in other ways. Ramkókamekra dualism is characterized by both positive and negative "pairing" (*aypen catê,* "in-relation-to-each-other a-pair"), and this pattern of culturally perceived similarities, including even some crucial opposite characteristics, can be found in the domains of the festivals, relationship systems, colors, shapes of three-dimensional objects, village plan and activities, religious syncretism, and many other domains.

Some pairs are necessarily "oppositional" (*aypēn cunáá-mã*, "related opposite-each-other"),[42] such as "good" versus "bad" and one age class moiety against the other one. There are, however, ways for transforming certain oppositional pairs into complementary pairs (*ipipror*, "two only," in parallel) or even into sets of overlapping complementary pairs (*hapää*). Probably the best example of such transformations is that men and women, in general, are seen to be a pair (*aypēn catê*, "related a-pair," oppositional or complementary), the two categorical members of which are in an *oppositional* relationship with each other, whereas when they marry, they are described as being in a *complementary* one.[43]

Similarly, a uterine sister and brother are "in parallel" (by blood "equality"), as are distant cousin cross-sex "siblings" after they agree to put their names on a same-sex child of such an opposite-sex sibling (*amyi-pitär*, "for-self take-over") to convert their oppositional relationship into a complementary one. Turning to a more complicated transformation, one pair of siblings and another pair of siblings, each pair with one sibling in common, form a *me-hapää*[44] of three "equivalent" persons. Three festival societies may be paired in this overlapping manner to form a *me-hapää* in opposition to the one festival society across the plaza.

The pertinence of the parallel-transmission rules is that they transform oppositional human structures into complementary relationships—the great Ramkókamekra "genius." Moreover, they "fit" the across-the-plaza village integration design, i.e., the web of patrilateral extensions of the generally matrilateral extended families, one of the principal tribal integrative networks. These across-the-plaza bonds begin their existence with a young man crossing to the other side of the village to marry a nonrelated girl, so that "opposing" families are neutralized by having a pair "in parallel." Once the marriage is secured by a child and some time has passed, the connection "out" along the generational lines between this man's family of orientation and his family of procreation lies in the relationship of this man with his sister (and her descendants on one side of the plaza) and with his daughter (and her descendants on the other side of the plaza). This relationship between the two extending matrilines may continue long after the death of the original man who crossed over the plaza in order to marry, consequently making a *me-hapää* by being paired in a complementary manner first with his sister and then with his wife, and eventually with his daughter who is "the same" as her mother. In this context a woman's MMMBDDD would be her third cousin, and though they would still have some attenuated "blood" in common, and males and females at this genealogical distance still should not marry each other for this reason (though today they occasionally do), nevertheless the parallel-transmission rules can "formally reduce" this somewhat distant quasi-oppositional kin relationship "into" its equivalent, the

♀ BD kin type ("GD"), reconstructing a formal *me-hapää*. Thus a woman and her MMMBDDD, while still not "in parallel" or "identical," are nevertheless very close (*aypẽn catsúwa*, "relation-to-each-other toward") since they are formally in the same *me-hapää* or "bridge." In this way, certain distantly linked relatives become "equivalent" in the formal sense to second-link relatives, and whenever they want to utilize this actual terminological equivalence, they can behave in a manner very similar to a second-link relative.[45]

In summary, following the lead of Scheffler and Lounsbury (1971), it does *appear* that the parallel-transmission rules fit the Canela-Apinayé-Kayapó relationship systems (W. Crocker 1977), and that there are numerous social structural correlates and cognitive congruencies to support this representation for the Ramkókamekra-Canela. Field research must still be carried out (or provided in published literature) in order to cull additional Kayapó and Suyá details in support of this approach for representing an underlying cognitive pattern for the Northern Gê, or perhaps even for central Brazil and parts of Bolivia. With the MBD-FZS matrilateral cross-cousin marriage understood as a special feature of the Sirionó (and of the Suyá), however, it becomes easier to perceive a Sirionó-Canela basic resemblance, both characterized by *a* parallel-transmission-like *cognitive* pattern reflected in the relationship systems.

Finally, it is important for our understanding of the above materials to recognize: (1) that the Ramkókamekra see marriage as initiating the first-/further-link dichotomy in kin terminology and that such compartmentalization is manifested in a similar manner in several other domains;[46] (2) that ideologically they emphasize uterine line "position filling in" rather than the nevertheless coordinated ZS-MB replacement, but yet agree to three distinct examples of S/F succession; (3) that ideologically *both* parents contribute to forming the fetus for the Eastern Timbira tribes, while just the father contributes for the Kayapó and Suyá, and that this change in ideology corresponds with the shift in emphasis from the matriline to the patriline expressions of the parallel-transmission alternatives; (4) that the cross-collateral form of the parallel-transmission rule "fits" the patrilateral across-the-plaza network of integration of the Canela village plan, and the tribal structure, in its marriage-initiated cross-sibling "bridge" (*me-hapää*); (5) that this cross-collateral form of the parallel-transmission rule may even explain for the Kayapó why the brother-sister bond is weakened while the marital tie is strengthened (no genealogical *me-hapää*) when the agnatic line of reduction equivalence is given priority (i.e. patriline emphasis); (6) that eventually such comparisons may be extended to include parallel-transmission-related variations found among the Suyá, Sherente/Chavante, Bororo, Nambikwara, Sirionó, and other tribes; and (7) that the parallel-transmission pattern is congruent with the great Canela "genius" for transforming opposing paired elements into complementary ones. In contrast, with the B-Z bond disregarded or broken for the more agnatic-line-oriented societies that still are nevertheless all uxorilocal, the analyst would expect the agnatic line expression of *a* parallel-transmission-like *cognitive* pattern to increasingly assume either ceremonial and political forms rather than genealogical ones, such as the F to S inheritance of the political chieftainship among the Xikrin-Kayapó (Vidal 1977:150), or to increasingly manifest agnatic line characteristics such as a group of full brothers marrying a group of full sisters, as among the Suyá, or patrilineality itself, though shallow, as among the Shavante.

In final summary, an ethnography of *marriage* and *separation* was first presented, and close attention was paid not only to the *balance between the sexes* but also to how this intersex relationship and the institution of marriage have been *changing* over the years. Some special questions—such as the *differences with Nimuendajú,* the poorly understood institution of *age class marriage,* and the nonexistence of *matriliny* and *exogamous moieties*—were largely resolved, at least for postcontact times. Then the focus was shifted to the relative position of the Canela on the Northern Gê and central Brazilian scenes, at least hypothetically, and the possibility of the existence of a basic cognitive pattern ("psychological reality") represented in the relationship systems in terms of formal *parallel-transmission* rules (Scheffler and Lounsbury 1971) was examined. Through this inspection, the nature of Canela *dualism* was seen as being closely related to these parallel-transmission patterns, and the nature of marriage and marital roles was shown to vary depending on which aspect of the rules (Crow-like or Omaha-like, or uterine line or agnatic line) was given more emphasis in each particular society. Whereas marriage played a significant societally integrative role among the *genealogically* oriented, uterine-line-emphasizing Canela, it seemed to be less important as a societally integrating factor among the less genealogically oriented, more agnatic-line-stressing Kayapó, where *political* factors seemed to predominate.

NOTES

1. Much of the material for this paper can be found in Nimuendajú (1946) but has also been collected independently by myself. Rather than referring to that great Brazilian ethnologist's volume in every paragraph, I wish to acknowledge an overall personal and professional indebtedness of very sizable proportions. Beyond these expressions of general recognition, I

will cite his important works only to support or to differ with the most critical points.

Most of this research has been carried out with the support of the Smithsonian Institution and, in Brazil, under the auspices of the Museu Paraense "Emílio Geoldi."

2. Krahó: Melatti (1970); Krĩkatí: Lave (1967); Pukóbye: Newton (1971); Gavião: Laráia and da Matta (1967), Arnaud (1975), and Arnaud *et al.* (1977); Apinayé: da Matta (1971, 1976, 1979).

3. The orthography utilized herein is largely based on a phonemic analysis by Jack and Jo Popjes (SIL workers) (1982). The Portuguese vowel system is utilized, with the tilde indicating nasalized phonemes. The values of the non-Portuguese phonemes /ï/ and /ë/ are written according to Pike (1947:5), /ä/ and /ã/ are middle, open, back, unrounded vowels. The phoneme /h/ is split into its allophones [h,?], with the apostrophe " ' " representing the glottal stop. The distinction between /k/ and /kʰ/ is expressed as "c" ("qu" before "e's" and "i's") in contrast to "k." The alveolar or alveopalatal, voiceless affricated consonant phoneme is written "ts." Phonemic vowel length is expressed by double vowels, and /w/ and /y/, when syllable final, are "glides."

4. Sixty-nine R-Canela couples in 1970 believed themselves to have been consanguineally "nonrelated" before marriage, whereas 30 considered themselves to have been related. I found one couple to be related as first cousins; two as first cousins once removed; two, second cousins; five, second cousins or further (because of their genealogical uncertainty); one, third cousins; six, third cousins or further; two, fourth cousins or further; four, knew they had been related before marriage but could not figure out how; and one couple were GC of *amyi-pïtär* "siblings" (i.e., distant cross-sex siblingship strengthened by the naming of one of each other's same-sex child). Four couples had married each other as siblings through "contributing father" relationships, one pair were step-relatives, and another were S and GD of siblings by adoption. These latter six cases are most likely all nonrelatives consanguineally, though they do reckon themselves as kin, so there were, in 1970, *at least* 24 consanguineal marriages genealogically (one-quarter). From a little different point of view, namely, what the couples believed they had called each other before marriage (two had forgotten) rather than what I could discover their genealogical relationships to be: thirteen had addressed each other as "B" and "Z"; nine as "GF" and "GD" (includes MB and [m.s.] ZD); two as "GM" and "GS" (includes FZ and [w.s.] BS); two as "F" and "D"; and two as "M" and "S."

5. Six examples of the sororate were found through analyzing 204 individual R-Canela marriage life histories in 1970. The deceased W's Ps like to retain their DH for the raising of her children by providing the widower with the deceased W's Z, "Z," or some other woman who can be easily brought to live in the same household. In contrast, only two examples of the levirate were found.

6. Of the 96 marriages included in the 1970 R-Canela marriage life history study, 40 (41.7 percent) were first marriages for both H and W. There were also 40 other people who had been married only once, making 120 (58.8 percent) out of a total of 204 alive-married and alive-formerly-married persons in the study who had been married only once.

7. The distinction must be made between "contracting" marriage (*meto aypẽn tê*, "they for-each-other restricted") and "adjusting" the marriage (*me aypẽn pa*, "they assemble to-hear"—hold council). The former arrangement, though not commenced by any rite, constitutes an enduring relationship between the two families, including a casual and continuing exchange of services, whereas the latter situation amounts to some members of the two families holding an informal meeting and consenting to the marriage as well as counseling the couple either just before or soon after the taking of virginity. If there was no "adjusting" before virginity loss, the girl is said to have been "stolen (*hä'kĩya*) or that they came together because of "liking each other" (*me aypẽn kĩn*). If she then failed to obtain the seducer's admission or prove her case in identifying him, she would be said to have "lost her money" (*i'pore pictor*). The acculturative trend is moving from "contracting" through "adjusting" first to "stealing" and "liking each other" and "adjusting" afterward, but not toward the virgin "losing her money."

8. Lyon questions whether aboriginal sexual jealousy is a human universal (1974:183). Old Canelas in the late 1950s insisted, however, that sexual jealousy was traditional rather than learned from local Brazilians. Ramkókamekra males only create a fuss when confronted by talk or evidence of "infidelity." It is a question of loss of face, the anger depending on who took the advantage, a friend or competitor. As a form of one-up-manship, an anxious husband will usually try to "catch" the competitor's wife in return. I suspect the old Canela informants were right and that a wife's infidelity with a culturally unauthorized person amounted to an invasion of her husband's sphere of limited but recognized control. What he did not know would not hurt him, but when others knew he knew, he had to act. Thus, if such jealousy is a near human universal, the suggestion here is that such "possessiveness" would have a high sociopolitical component.

9. A decidedly "crazy" (very emotionally disturbed) father left his wife and then later a second one, both mothers of a child of his; another father of a child was sent away by its mother (his wife) as a half-wit; one woman was abandoned by an Apanyekra returning to his tribe; another mother was left twice, and one of these two ex-husbands was later interned in the Indian Foundation national correction center in Minas Gerais for other antisocial reasons; and one father who was sent away in 1970 returned in 1971. Viewed from 1970, however, this amounts to seven father-child separations.

10. Some reasons for Ramkókamekra marriage stability are: (1) very extensive extramarital sex practices (W. Crocker 1974); (2) extreme focus on the welfare of children (pre- and postpartum taboos, teknonymy, principal ceremonial roles, etc. [W. Crocker 1971:326]), including that ego's family of orientation exists primarily for the raising of ego; (3) social

sanctions applied by ego's "GPs," the tribal council, and chiefs of the tribe, which cause a man to return to his wife (W. Crocker 1964b:344); (4) the many sources of satisfactions in Canela life other than the marital link (group singing and dancing, hunting, racing and sports, festivals, joking relationships, extended family and council meeting verbal outlets and recognition of personal problems, etc.) (W. Crocker 1962:120); and (5) factors such as age class ridicule and coercion.

11. Other cases coming before the tribal council involve theft, damage to crops, nonconformity with certain attitudes, and, formerly, accusations of witchcraft.

12. For a man, deserting a widow after her first intercourse is like leaving a virgin after hers; i.e., a similar payment must be made in either case.

13. There were only two examples in the 204 life history cases of women requiring their social husband, the pater, and a believed-to-be genitor of their children, to leave the marriage entirely.

14. Since there is no direct or indirect formal exchange of spouses between marriage groups among the Canela, and for that matter since there are *not even any marriage groups,* there can be no question at all about whether it is wives *or* husbands who are "exchanged" in the classical sense. Quite clearly a son-in-law, and his services to her family, are exchanged on several different occasions for ceremonial foods and his wife's services to him. Although the exchanges are seen as being between the extended families of the spouses, this interfamilial bond is not strengthened generation after generation into a traditional alliance pattern because brothers and their sons do not marry into the same families. They say that even full brothers may marry into the same household—there is no law against it—but actually they do not do this, and informants offer no taboos or reasons why full brothers and classificatory brothers avoid marrying into the same household and generally even into the same extended families. I suggest that brothers are not welcomed into the same matrilateral family group because the first-married wife's kin want to be able to control the later marrying-in sons-in-law, who if they were brothers or "brothers," might offer too much collective resistance to their traditional role of initial subjugation.

15. In Canela thinking, it is sons-in-law who "move" rather than wives who are being "exchanged," as in classical theory. A husband is portrayed as crossing the plaza diagonally, like a shooting star, to stay at the house of his wife on the village circle for one generation, thus enabling their sons to cross over diagonally to *different* houses, generation after generation—specifically not returning to the same houses because incest is at least theoretically reckoned to the second and third cross-cousin range, and further between parallel cousins. In addition, matrilines are "seen" as potatoes along a vine (a succession of daughters) to which men cross over from other vines to make possible the formation of a new daughter potato growing further down the vine. Moreover, we must think of the Canela women's daily dance line that is fixed in space in the plaza while the men move before and around it. Also, in their imagery—including their complementary dualism, on which more later—

women are portrayed as being passive, generative, and sustaining while men are mobile, activating, and impermanent. Nevertheless, it was the women who used to take the initiative in setting up the traditional engagements between pre-nubile couples, and who still play the more active roles in seeking out effective sons-in-law—when the young people leave it to them. A girl's mother approached a prospective son-in-law's mother, and if agreement was reached, they would then turn to their respective male kin for support. It is *clearly* sons-in-law who are exchanged for ceremonial food (meat pies, deer, etc.) in several rites, each step binding the young man more tightly to his wife's family. Whereas the ultimate control and command may have been theoretically held by the mother-in-law's male kin, it was certainly, then and now, the women who were and are more actively engaged in attracting and securing the young, married-in, work-force males of the matrilaterally extended family. These days, however, it is most likely the girl herself who chooses her mate by presenting her mother and their male relatives with a fait-accompli situation through her loss of virginity and his admission as the taker.

16. It does not matter whether or not ego's MH is actually his/her genitor because it is believed that any man who has had sexual intercourse with a woman after her pregnancy has become evident is a "contributing father" in the sense that his semen has helped to form the fetus. Each contributor is later named by the mother as a "biological" father, but the "social" husband (pater) nevertheless is held as the principal father even though conceivably, in modern scientific terms, he may or may not be the actual biological father.

17. Other elements in having become married, especially with nonvirgins, are: (1) a man moving into a woman's house and supporting her; (2) what persons making love say to each other and their relatives about their intentions, i.e. whether marriage is eventually expected or not; (3) whether a man might be engaged and waiting for his fiancee to grow up or not; and (4) the relative political power of the parents and relatives of either party brought to bear upon the interpretation of all other marital approximation factors.

18. There are eight acts in the solidification of a marriage, and the age class rite was a ninth event which might have occurred at different stages of the continuum for different individuals. The first four steps are contracting, intercourse, and adjusting the marriage, followed often by a meat pie payment or, increasingly today, an exchange of meat pies. The next step follows when the girl wins her ceremonial belt and her mother-in-law paints it red. Later there is evident pregnancy, childbirth, and the rite ending postpartum restrictions. Ideally, the age class marriage rite would have occurred between belt painting and pregnancy.

19. At childbirth, the mother names the principal men with whom she has been having relations during her pregnancy; a messenger then goes around the village circle to publicly indicate the "contributing fathers" so they can immediately commence a kind of couvade.

20. According to my Ramkókamekra demographic data submitted for the Sept. 1, 1970, Brazilian national census, in 38 cases with materials sufficiently

reliable and pertinent to the study, the mother-firstborn age difference average (where no miscarriages had preceded) was about 16.5, making the conception age average about 15.75 years. Old informants reveled in their memories of the extensiveness of the fun and extramarital activities that used to occur between the belt-painting ceremony and childbirth. Married and unmarried childless girls and women used to sleep in the plaza (too visible to be done today) on the opposite side from their husbands, animating their companions until they became pregnant. Many shifts in spouse alignments consequently used to occur (unlike today), with men winning over wives of other men or leaving their wives because of jealousy, until a couple was caught, in a procedure not unlike "musical chairs," by her pregnancy and obliged to stay together for as long as they were raising their children.

21. As soon as she had lost her virginity, usually to her "husband," other men occasionally tried "catching" her for private sexual relations, but she was not indicated by the chief in a morning council meeting as one of the girl associates to accompany the men's daily work group or an age class moiety hunting expedition until after her belt had been painted, nor was she expected to join the festival extramarital sex occasions.

22. A Ramkókamekra hazing rite has been fully described elsewhere (W. Crocker 1961:78-79), but an Apanyekra one was as follows. Pepyê novices were made to kneel sitting on their heels in the plaza in a row facing their similarly "sitting" sexual partners, whether wives or otherwise. Chiefs and elders then proceeded to give them blistering lectures for their infractions, the severity of which I have never experienced among the Ramkókamekra.

23. The institution of the platform bed high under the rafters furnished to the young H and his W in the house of her kin, is inconsistent with the general rule of no sexual intercourse being formally allowed young people by their GF category relatives. Only the WMF, among all her GF kin and none of her H's GF kin, however, witnessed the young H's occasional, quiet nocturnal visits to his W's platform bed, since just he (the WMF) was a resident of the W's kin's house, but he would have said nothing. All informants, however, have been very amused by the idea that youths might have climbed up to a girl's high platform bed without having had sex with her (see Nimuendajú 1946:118). They say this could never have been the case because desire among youths is too overpowering, and that the bed was elevated only after the girl had lost her virginity to her young husband and that he was the only visitor. I witnessed the elevation of my adopted ZD's platform bed just after she had won her belt in 1957 and heard the relevant noises from my adjacent quarters below. In sexual matters the Canela become embarrassed by what is seen, not by what is heard. A nonvirginal, unattached young woman, of course, might have a variety of visitors.

24. The Ramkókamekra lands were legally demarcated, very much to their tribal advantage and against some local rancher opposition, between 1969 and 1971. A jeep or truck road directly from the *município* capital of Barra do Corda to the Ramkókamekra village of Escalvado was completed in 1970, and it was extended to the Apanyekra village of Porquinhos in 1973. In

1970 and 1971 a sizable new post building and a schoolhouse were built in Escalvado as well as a soccer field. These buildings and the village are now lit by lights at night by electricity made by a gasoline generator that also draws water from a deep well and supplies a sending-receiving radio. As a "model post" with several guest rooms and running water, there has been an excellent Indian agent in charge, Sr. Sebastião Ferreira, and also a nurse and a school teacher. A special tuberculosis medical team has identified prospective cases and prescribed medicines for the actual patients, and carried out a relatively successful program by convincing many of the Canela patients and their families of the necessity to submit to medical treatment continuously over a long period of time, with the consequence that by 1979 tuberculosis had all but been eradicated.

25. This figure for men over 50 in 1970 (average age difference between spouses) has most probably been reduced (biased) by the death of the older men in the age classes.

26. The custom of youths sleeping with older women was abandoned between the initiation times of these last two age classes, namely, the group of the principal chief, Caarä-'kre (age 49 in 1970), and the group of the younger Caapêr-tïc (age 38 in 1970).

27. In a number of late remarriages as well as for several obviously incompetent males, spouse age differences of over 20 years can be found.

28. The three ritual payments sometimes made by the wife's relatives to secure her husband (his meat pie "purchase," a deer at the belt-painting ceremony, and further meat pies at the postpartum contributing fathers' rite) are repaid by the husband partly in his daily services rather than by extensive gifts, as described for the Krahó. The rest of the debt remains to be paid in case he should leave his wife. In that case, values that must be paid for are: (1) the wife's loss of virginity, (2) the three ritual payments if they were made, (3) the birth of children, (4) the breaking of a widow's postmortum sex restrictions, (5) sexual relations when a wife was not interested, and (6) any insults or injuries she may have suffered because of her husband and his family. These debts are reduced by: (1) a return meat pie payment from his family to hers, (2) shame the husband may have suffered because of her infidelities before his eyes, (3) her negligence in the performance of domestic duties, and (4) insults and injuries he may have suffered because of his wife or her relatives.

29. Apinayé in 1962 (Lave 1967:20): 150 and 80; Krahó in 1963 (Melatti 1972:4): 169, 49, 109, 50, and 130; Gavião in 1962 (Laráia and da Matta 1967:138): 23 and 17; Krĩkatí and Pukóbye in 1964 (Lave 1967: 19): 152, 58, 90, and 25; Apanyekra in 1959: about 170; Ramkókamekra in 1960 (W. Crocker 1972:240): 269 and 143, but in very close contact and recent (1956) separation. Around 1936 (Nimuendajú 1946:13-36) it appears that the Ramkókamekra were just under 300 and that all other Timbira villages were well under 200.

30. It has to be assumed (lacking space for clarification herein) that the professional reader knows about "formal analysis" of kinship systems through

Lounsbury's approach (1964), namely Crow and Omaha Type-III extension or reduction equations, and through Scheffler and Lounsbury's orientation (1971) emphasizing parallel-transmission rules. (See Nogle 1974:22-26) for a critique including other forms of semantic analysis.) Crow-Omaha principles, where most pertinent to the Canela, stress the MB/ZS terminological equivalences (through linking relatives), while the parallel-transmission rules emphasize uterine and agnatic line extensions or reductions (through linking relatives). Among the Ramkókamekra, however, the kinship ideology is more emphatic in its relationship to matrifiliation than to avuncular replacement, so the parallel-transmission rules seem very much more pertinent. Moreover, a technical advantage of the parallel-transmission rules lies in their closer "fit" to the empirical data. For instance, a person's spouse's cross sibling's spouse is a spouse ($WBW = W$, $HZH = H$), just as a parent's cross sibling's spouse is a spouse (or an affine, if ego and alter are of the same sex; $\delta MBW = W$, $\female FZH = H$; $\female MBW = \female BW$, $\delta FZH = \delta ZH$). These kin types are never addressed as consanguineal relatives, as they are in Crow and Omaha Type-III on one side of the paradigm, unless they actually are such "blood" relatives by birth, which does occur quite frequently. (Obviously, the reciprocals of these affinal kin types follow the same form.) The really greater advantage of parallel-transmission's better "fit" is found in the reduction of the very long affinal kin types crossing one or even three marriage bonds. Uterine and agnatic line terminological equivalences, through linking relatives, do exist, depending on certain known priorities, *wherever* ego and alter are further-linked (two links away or more), *and* involve cross collaterals or include a marital bond, provided that certain subcategory terms can be recognized correctly as being part of their principal category, semantically.

31. The field data were collected in 1966, 1969, 1970, and 1971 and reconfirmed in 1975. The possibility that these data may support parallel-transmission rules among the Ramkókamekra was presented in a paper to the American Anthropological Association in 1976 (W. Crocker 1976), with copies distributed.

32. Conceivably the parallel-transmission rules, together with several other more basic rules (Scheffler and Lounsbury 1971:127), might resolve the terminological systems, i.e. reduce all kintypes to their categorical foci in a satisfactory manner—or extend all kin categories out to their various kin types—without reflecting or being congruent with native thought or their social institutions. Thus it is necessary to demonstrate a relatedness between the rules (etic) and the structure of the data from the field (possibly emic). Surely there are several culturally significant cognitive patterns in any society; surely representations of the same pattern differ from one level of psychological reality to another. Thus the question of congruence herein is at least difficult and may be even spurious, but I believe nevertheless it should be pursued.

33. One belief is that a woman, her daughter, her granddaughter, etc. all come off the same umbilicus and so are "the same," at least as paired. (A

woman is not, however, quite "the same" in "blood" composition as her granddaughter.) Another belief is that women are like squash or melons on a vine, growing on and on from mother to daughter to granddaughter, etc.—the same "blood." Still another belief is that the afterbirth materials are buried in a corner of the mother's birth enclosure room, that her daughter's similar materials will be added there, and that her granddaughter's will be interred there too, etc., always in the same *position* on the village circle (villages move), *forever,* or until the line dies out for lack of daughters. The "permanence" of a female line at one point on the village circle, "forever" as they say, is very powerful symbolically.

34. Name transmission is stressed among the deculturated Krĩkatí as forming the principal social and ceremonial structures (probably because they have lost most other integrative networks), but among the Ramkókamekra this "MB" to "ZS" name giving is only important ceremonially. It is the actual mother's brother (*quêt*), however, or some other *quêt* kin category counselor, who is usually far more important in the socialization of his sister's son than that boy's naming uncle. "Brothers" and "sisters" (i.e. cousins of varying degrees) preferably transmit names to one same-sex child of such a cross-sex sibling in order to create a closer relationship between each other in a large society, so why should they exchange names with a uterine sibling who is already close?

35. Among both Ramkókamekra- and Apanyekra-Canela, Eastern Timbira tribal membership is by sex filiation—a woman belongs to the tribe of her mother and a man to that of his father "out" along the line "forever," they say. Similarly, a peace exchange ceremonial chief (a *tämhäc*) took the place of his father, or his father's brother, or his father's father (contrast Nimuendajú 1946:99). The institution of the ceremonial chiefs of the whole tribe began around 1908 in order to unite the Ramkókamekra, who were split into two villages, each under a different political chief, both very hostile to each other. Such a ceremonial "peace chief" was chosen in each village by the other village; he was the "honorary chief" in the other village whom they could visit and who would protect them. The villages did in fact join in 1912, and these two "honorary" patrilines still exist today and are enshrined very prestigiously in an intergroup peace-keeping dramatization in the Pepcahäc festival—the most highly honored *api-craw-craw-re* rite. It is conspicuous that where there are no institutions like uxorilocality to prevent the "expression" of agnatic lines "spreading" (*me-ipicrän*) "in parallel" (*me-ipipror*) with uterine lines, this psychological "parallel" reality does seem to manifest itself. Curiously they do say that these two intertribal descent lines are "in parallel" with each other, which seems inconsistent with the more characteristic male-female opposition, but items that are "in parallel" can be seen as such from different points of view—in this case, diachronically, where oppositions are nonexistent, instead of synchronically.

36. It may be pertinent that when the Canela refer to their ancestors, they use the expression *me-nquêtyê* (the mothers' brothers or the parents' fathers),

but the Kayapó talk of their "fathers" (*djun-iyê*) (see Turner 1966:Ap. 1, xxvii).

37. In this case they really utilize the plural form of *tïy* (FZ, FM, MM), namely *me-mpuptswëyyê*, which I have not included here in order to avoid confusion. They also draw a line of "descendants," as if *quêt, tïy,* and *tämtswë* were all of the same supercategory, distinguished only by the "arriving" *tämtswë* (either sex) and the "departing" old *quêt* (male) or *tïy* (female). But when a man from one file of "descendants" crosses to marry a woman in another file of "descendants," then all the other terminological categories are created, largely because of (1) shame surrounding the ongoing sex acts that one-link consanguines of the spouses must not think about, (2) the obvious conflicts of interest between affinals, (3) the need for consanguines to protect each other's rights, and (4) the necessity to keep the sons-in-law working and in their places.

38. The mingling of male and female fluids, perspiration, and body odors in sexual intercourse soon make a husband and wife of the same "blood," as are their children with each other and with their parents. As a result of sharing almost "identical" blood, these persons have to maintain strict food and sex restrictions for each other when any one of these first-linked persons (*not* classificatory first-linked relatives) is ill or in a weakened condition. Linguistically there is a distinction between those one-link relatives "who carry out restrictions for me" (*mei-ipiyakri-catêyê*) and all other relatives who share more attenuated, less similar blood (*mei-yũũkyê* or *mei-kwë*). This semantically discrete and nonoverlapping distinction exists at some levels of Ramkókamekra thought and not at other levels (see W. Crocker 1977:272), but nevertheless it most certainly results in an attitudinal and behavioral dichotomy.

39. Gê specialists who do not know the Ramkókamekra-Canela believe that all the Northern Gê did not extend their consanguineal and affinal kinship systems very far. From empirical data, I know of fifth cousins (parallel, and connected through all female links [♂ MMMMMZDDDDD]) who still consider each other to be "brother" and "sister," and third cross cousins (through all female links except one [♂ MMMBDDD]) who call each other "uncle" and "niece." Quite obviously the spouse of such a "brother" may treat his "sister" as an affine (♀ BZ), and the spouse of the "uncle" would most likely address his "niece" in the same way (♀ BZ). Moreover, the across-the-plaza affinal terminological structure can sometimes cross two or three marriage bonds (♀ HMBSW = ♀ BW or D; ♀ HMMBDSW = ♀ BW only).

40. Consequently, it must be clear that the recpirocals, a ♂ ZC and a ♂ DC or a ♀ BC and a ♀ SC, are terminologically the same, as are all GCs regardless of sex (*tämtswë*).

41. Examples of "across-marital-bond" further-link uterine and agnatic lines are the following: HMM = HM = HZ = HD = HDD . . . ; WFF = WF = WB = WBS; WMBW = WMBD = WMBDD . . . = W; HFZ = HFZD = HFZDD . . . = HZ; WMF = WMB = WMBS = WB.

42. This expression *aypēn cunāā-mā* is just one of a number of ways of expressing an oppositional but yet paired relationship, *aypēn cuurê-tswën* (relationship inimical) possibly being the most hostile one; in contrast, *aypēn kay-nā* means "they are *off* with respect to each other" with no question of their being paired in any way. Not every relationship can be expressed in dualistic terms; in fact, most items are not paired at all.

43. Gê specialists have generally been aware of only one kind of dualism in these tribes (unlike Maybury-Lewis 1979:312), but the Ramkókamekra do pair certain entities positively (+ or //) and others negatively (− or X). For instance, while the village (*krī*) and the untouched forest (*a'cuuni*) are *oppositionally* paired (−), the plaza (*cää*) and the houses (*ikre*) on the village circle are perceived to be in a *complementary* paired (+) relationship. But a garden (*pur*) is in a thicket (*a'kêt*), the burning of which helps it grow (+); a thicket is part of (+) the forest and the garden helps the village survive (+). Thus by overlapping complementary pairings the Ramkóka-mekra have created an all-complementary *hapää* (village//garden//thicket//forest) between two distinctly oppositional entities (village X forest). (Contrast Melatti 1979:79.)

44. The morpheme *"me"* (really *"mẽ"*) indicates the plural and also that Indians are involved, but that these persons must understand each others' languages. Thus *"me,"* besides indicating the plural, also means "Timbira" for the Canela, a distinction that excludes the Kayapó, whom the Ramkókamekra scarcely comprehend, and the Shavante, who are completely unintelligible. (Presumably the Apinayé and Krahó would have a different perspective, being nearer to the Timbira boundaries.) It is interesting that while *pī-yapää* ("poles three-or-more-in-parallel") means "bridge," usually across a stream, *me-hapää* implies that there are two or more pairs of Timbira persons (or groups) "overlappingly" in parallel, and *hapää* suggests that there are two or more pairs of "items" (animals, *civilizados*, non-Timbira-speaking Indians, and things) with one item always in common to each pair. (I have usually found the overlapping feature to be necessary, but sometimes informants will align rows of positive and negative objects opposite each other without pairing them.)

45. Just how congruent to social structures and native thought does an etic "formal" principle have to be in order to be accepted as "representing" an emic pattern? As an example, let us take the nature X culture opposition, which is best represented in the Canela-Indian X game-animal relationship (*me-hīī* X *prïi-re*). A young hunter purifies his "body" by undergoing very thorough food and sex restrictions, which themselves are "in parallel" with this same youth in training (*me-hīī//ipiyacri-tsä*), so that the game animal grows to like him and even tries to approach him when the hunter (*me-into-capôc*) goes hunting (*me-into-capôc//prïi-re*). Thus an *hapää* exists (*me-hīī//ipiyacri-tsä//me-into-capôc//prïi-re*) and the poor beast is thereby easily shot dead. Other "bridging" examples are the following: Timbira X ghosts, but Timbira // shaman and shaman // ghosts; thus Timbira//sha-

man//ghosts, or *me-hũ*//*cay*//*me-carõõ*. That is, ordinary Canela cannot deal with the supernatural, but a shaman can do this for them.

46. Quite obviously, this paper throws some light on the Central Brazilian dialectical organization so extensively discussed and portrayed by the researchers of the Harvard Central Brazil Project (Maybury-Lewis 1979). I have been aware of the nature of the material presented in Professor Maybury-Lewis's introduction (1979:12-13) for some time, and therefore was very pleased to find some of his "oppositions" and "harmonious syntheses" expressed in certain Ramkókamekra linguistic terms. It might interest the reader to know what a careful study of the semantic fields of such terms has revealed. Taking such expressions from Maybury-Lewis (1979:311), "nature" and "culture" have been handled already in the "forest" X "village" and "game animal" X "Timbira Indian" oppositions. Another example is "raw meat" (*hũ-täm*) X "cooked meat" (*hũ-tsär*), which becomes complementary as "raw meat" // "fire" (*cuhü*) // "wood" (*pĩ*) // "cooked meat." "Individual" and "society" can be expressed *amiyá-'kôt* X *harkwa-kôt* ("one's-own-initiative following" X "orders following"), a very important Ramkókamekra opposition. "Male" and "female" have been dealt with already, and "ceremonial" and "instrumental" can be portrayed in *me amyi-'kĩn catêyê* ("Timbira festival people") // *me to-ipïyapar catêyê* ("Timbira something-raising/cultivating people"), but note that these elements are positively rather than negatively paired.

"Public" and "private" was not a contrast that I could identify in Ramkó-kamekra terms, unless it is the same as "society" and "individual"; almost every situation seemed to be "public," even household rites for individuals. From Maybury-Lewis (1979:305) "forum" (*cää*) and "household" (*ikre*) are paired in a complementary manner, as are "social persona" (*me-haprë*, Timbira names) and "physical persona" (*me-caprôô*, Timbira "blood" or physical substance), but the social persona comes just as much or more from a principal counselor (*to hapac-kre catê*) as from a name giver (*haprë yõr catê*), though both are traditionally of the *quêt* kin category. Professor Roberto da Matta stresses male-female differences (already discussed) and generational contrasts (1979:123), but it is interesting that Ramkókamekra informants will not allow either complementary or oppositional pairing to exist between parents and their children: there are no diachronic oppositions, only synchronic ones. Children are seen as the products of "cultivation" by the parents, as are crops. Adjacent Ramkókamekra generations *are* generally in opposition, however, but this "gap" is bridged for parents and their children by the blood identity of genealogically first-linked people.

In summary, it seems that while some of the components of dualism are in opposition, other components are paired in a complementary manner, and that some pairs are "in opposition" under some circumstances and "in parallel" (complementary) in other situations. Most of the paired contrasts presented in Professor Maybury-Lewis's volume could be adequately expressed by Ramkókamekra paired linguistic terms, but the public-private contrast could not be found (maybe a tribal difference), the social persona was seen as including another important element, and generational differences (Professor da Matta), where important to the kinship system, were interpreted as neither oppositional nor complementary but rather as diachronic products. The suggestion is that Central Brazilian Gê dualism is quite varied, but the paired components are of several kinds, and that further study in the various tribes is needed.

5

Kagwahiv Moieties:
Form without Function?

WAUD H. KRACKE

The Kagwahiv Indians, who inhabit the east bank of the Madeira River
in Brazilian Amazonia, claim to regulate their marriage through patrilineal, exogamous moieties.[1] In this the Madeira Kagwahiv—often de-
noted "Parintintin," a term that may be derived from the language of
their long-time enemies the Mundurucú (Nimuendajú 1924:201)—are
unique among tribes that speak Tupi languages in the narrow sense of
the Tupi-Guarani family.[2] They differ even from the closely related
"Tupi-Cawahib," encountered by Rondôn and later Lévi-Strauss on the
Machado, who possessed numerous patrilineal clans, and from other
remnants of the old "Cawahiwa" tribe that scattered westward from the
Tapajos in the nineteenth century.

At first consideration, the system of moiety exogamy appears simple,
harmonious, and unitary, firmly established as the regulatory principle
of Kagwahiv marriage. As one examines their system more closely, however, the apparent neatness and uniformity of the system prove illusory.
One encounters not simply individual exceptions to the rule of moiety
exogamy but a whole category of Kagwahiv who occupy an ambiguous
position, marrying indifferently with members of one moiety or the
other. Further investigation reveals other principles at work in marriage
determination, principles that perpetuate patterns of marital choice
which are, from the point of view of moiety exogamy, indiscreet.

A thorough account of the Kagwahiv system of marriage choice reveals three separate systems, operating at different levels: a dual organization of exogamous moieties that remains exacting at the ideological
level; a covert triadic system of exogamous clans, partially coterminous
with the formal moieties, that is discovered in the actual marriage practices and is grudgingly acknowledged by perceptive informants who

strain to reconcile it with the dual ideology; and a system of alliances between discrete "lines" embodied in the practices by which marriage choices are, or should be, actually determined, embodying a complex set of rules that tends to preserve the discrepancy between the first two systems. Neither the first nor the second system is irrelevant for the selection of a marital partner, but the third is the most immediate set of considerations in the choice of the first spouse, and tends to carry the most weight.

The discrepancies between these three systems offer the individual Kagwahiv considerable latitude for weighing his own personal considerations in marriage choice, considerations political, practical, or of the heart, introducing an element of flexibility into what might abstractly seem a rigorously restrictive system of determination of marriage choice.

Such coexistence of dyadic and triadic systems, or the discovery of triadic systems in apparently dyadic social organizations, has been observed in other South American lowland societies, understood in quite different ways by Lévi-Strauss (1956, 1963a) and Maybury-Lewis (1967). I do not here propose any further discussion of the essence of dual organization, nor the intrinsic relationship between dyadic and triadic systems as such. These questions have been quite thoroughly discussed (Maybury-Lewis 1961; Lévi-Strauss 1960; Ortiz 1969:5-8, 136-37; Kensinger n.d.), and I have no new geometric or other perspectives to add to them. What I will discuss here is the persisting coexistence of such divergent and apparently incompatible models for choice of marriage partner within a single society, the mechanisms that make such continuing coexistence possible, and the ways in which Kagwahiv try to reconcile the resulting incongruities.

The very existence of such intracultural heterogeneity, of conflicting prescriptive models within a single domain of a social order, is itself a phenomenon of considerable interest. Such variation within a society has become increasingly a focus of theoretical interest in anthropology, as admirably formulated by Robert Murphy (1972). One intention of this paper is to explore the consequences and implications of such diversity of conceptual models within a culture.

The Theory of Moiety Exogamy

The Madeira Kagwahiv society is divided into two theoretically exogamous moieties, each named after a bird—*Mytum* (Portuguese *mutum*, "curassow") and *Kwandu* (*gavião real*, "harpie eagle"). So basic are these moieties to social definition of the person that a Kagwahiv identifies himself by his moiety affiliation before his personal name. Nimuendajú reports that when he first contacted them he was intensively quizzed about *his* moiety affiliation, his inquisitors being incredulous that he did not belong to either. The automatic answer to the question "What kind of person is he?" is always to give the moiety affiliation of the individual in question.

Kagwahiv terminology of kinship and affinity is in perfect accord with a system of exogamous moieties. It is two-line in nature: the terms for father's brother and mother's sister, *ruvy* and *hy'y*, are derived from those for father and mother (*ruv* and *hy*)[3] and are extended, respectively, to all older men of the parental generation (G + 1) in one's own moiety, and to G + 1 women in the opposite moiety. The reciprocal for all these is *ra'yr*, "child." *Tuty* refers to father-in-law and all G + 1 men of the opposite moiety, including MB; *jaji* similarly refers to mother-in-law, and to G + 1 women of one's own moiety, including FZ. The reciprocals for both these terms include *ti'i*, a man's son-in-law or his sister's son, and *'ai*, a woman's daughter-in-law or her brother's child. In one's own generation members of one's own moiety are called by sibling terms: *kuvy* for a woman's brother, *rendy* for a man's "sister," *irũ* for a "sibling" of the same sex (see Figure 1). For same-generation members of the opposite moiety there are descriptive terms such as *nhanhimemby*, "child of my *jaji*," but the most common term is *amotehe*, undoubtedly related to Surui *amutehéa*, which Laráia (1963) glosses as "lover." In Kagwahiv this term has been so fully absorbed into the moiety system that it has been extended to mean not only any cross cousin (of either sex) but even any member of the opposite moiety—or any person considered "unrelated." Other Indian tribes are referred to as *kagwahiv amotehe*.

The birds after which the two moieties are named can be readily placed in conceptual opposition to one another: the harpie eagle (*kwandu*) is the largest of the South American hawks, fierce, carnivorous, high-flying, nesting high in treetops or crags, and considered inedible as are other predators. The curassow (*mytum*) is a large, gallinaceous, turkey-like terrestrial bird, all black except for its bright red comb, and highly prized for eating. Feathers of both are used in headdresses and for fletching arrows, and harpie eagles used to be kept in large cages as "pets" for their feathers.

In addition to its eponymous bird, each moiety is associated with other birds, by whose names they are sometimes called, which carry through and underline this opposition. The birds associated with the Mytum moiety are mostly other kinds of curassow, the *gwyra'yreru* (flute bird, Portuguese *urumutum*, "nocturnal curassow"), a kind of *mytum;* the *jakupem* (superciliated guan), another dark-colored relative of the curassow; and the *inamuhũ*, a dark brownish-colored tinamou, very similar in appearance and habits to the *mytum* (Santos 1952:24, 127, 133). These are all dull or dark-colored terrestrial birds that are delectably edible and rather gentle. The two alternative birds representing the Kwandu moiety

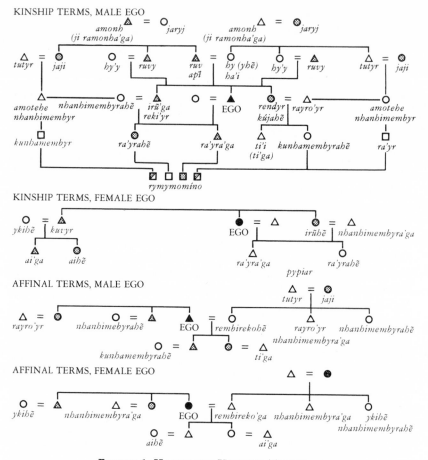

FIGURE 1. KAGWAHIV KINSHIP TERMINOLOGY.

Division into "kinship terms" and "affinal terms" is for expository convenience; in general, there is not a sharp distinction in Kagwahiv, so that for the most part terms for siblings-in-law are practically interchangeable with those for cross-cousin, etc.

Notes: suffixes "-'ga" and "-hē" are (human) masculine and feminine gender markers, respectively.

membyr, which in other Tupi languages means "own child, woman speaking," has dropped out of Kagwahiv except in the compounds nhanhimembyr (jaji + membyr, "cross cousin, child of my jaji") and kunhamembyr (kuja + membyr "sister's child"). It has been functionally replaced by the less frequently used pypiar, "woman's child." Ra'yr, which in other Tupi dialects often refers to a man's child only, in Kagwahiv does duty for anyone's child.

△ = male
O = female
□ = both
▲ ● = EGO
▨ ▲ ⊘ = of ego's moiety

I have omitted a number of frequently used sibling terms used by elder siblings to younger and vice versa, or to refer to one's next younger sibling.

are somewhat more diverse than the Mytum alternates, but follow the characterization of high-flying, high-nesting, big-beaked, inedible birds. Unlike the harpie eagle itself, they are both bright-colored; what they share with the harpie eagle is being prized for their feathers. The principal alternate bird names used for the Kwandu are *apyawytang* (or *ararovy*) and *tarave* (or *maracanã*), both members of the macaw family—brightly colored, very high-flying birds, with large, hooked, parrot-like beaks and long, brilliant tails. Macaws nest deep in the jungle, flying out at great heights to the river early in the morning to feed and flying back late at night. The macaws are relatively large, but the maracanã are by no means the largest of the family. Like the harpie eagle, though, they are considered inedible, and are prized rather for their feathers.

Another bird sometimes associated with the Kwandu moiety is the *japu* (oropendola), a relatively large, long-tailed oriole with a thick beak and bright yellow feathers among its black ones, with pendulous nests hanging in groups high in the trees. The *japu* is reputed to be voraciously omnivorous, eating anything at hand, including other birds' eggs (Santos 1960:213-16). Not being so high-flying a bird, nor so high-nesting, it seems less similar to the harpie eagle in these respects than is the macaw. Its meat, though not prized, is sometimes eaten. On the other hand, it would appear to possess the aggressiveness that characterizes the harpie.

There seems, then, to be some asymmetry in the relationships among the various birds representing each moiety. The birds referring to the Kwandu moiety seem much more divergent from one another than those representing the Mytum. They are all dramatic and prized for their feathers, but the *tarave* and *japu* are much smaller than the *kwandu,* and in fact smaller than many of the birds associated with the Mytum moiety. And, as I have noted, the *japu* lacks many of the characteristics shared by the *tarave* and the *kwandu.* Even its aggressiveness is somewhat more covert than that of the *kwandu.* Nunes Pereira, a widely traveled naturalist who has visited the Kagwahiv and published some of their myths (1967, pt. IV), suggested (personal communication) that the *japu* might represent a third clan.

Moiety exogamy is enforced by very strict sanctions: the result of violating it is automatic supernatural retribution, causing the death of a parent or child of the culprit. Even Brazilians are believed to suffer from such sanctions, for a Brazilian's loss of his father and children was blamed on his parallel cousin marriage. One middle-aged man felt considerable guilt over an adolescent liaison with a classificatory sister (FFBSD), fearing that it might be responsible for his aged father's current illness— 15 or 20 years subsequent to the liaison. (Less consciously, he feared it might have caused the death of his own child as well.)

Yet certain incongruities are striking. Despite the centrality of the moiety division to the Kagwahiv concept of man, and the strength of the norm of moiety exogamy, I could find no myth of origin for the moieties. In fact, in all of the mythology I and others have collected (Nunes Pereira 1967, Betts and Pease 1966), there is no reference to the moieties at all, with one possible exception: in a story involving a dance of birds, my (Kwandu) informant identified some species as belonging to the Kwandu moiety. Furthermore, despite repeated probing, I could not find any role the moieties played as such in any of the ceremonies (no longer performed) my informants described. The only other function these psychologically important moieties seem to have is in the assignment of personal names. Each moiety is said to have a fund of names for each stage of the life cycle. But even this is rather loose in practice, since some names are held by individuals from both moieties, and there are inconsistencies in the lists of names assigned to one moiety or the other. The lack of integration with other aspects of Kagwahiv life and culture leads one to wonder whether the moieties, for all their psychological importance in individual identity, might not nonetheless be a somewhat recent acquisition of the Parintintin, grafted superficially onto their institutions.

Gwyrai'gwara: The Clandestine Clan

Further research led to the discovery of some more fundamental incongruities. Genealogies, which a few informants could give me back three or four generations, turned up a rather large number of incestuous marriages between members of the same moiety, both in past times and among presently living individuals—including the son-in-law of the old chief Homero, who was my best genealogical informant. Virtually all of these incestuous marriages, furthermore, were between members of the Kwandu moiety, none between Mytum. In addition, it seemed to run in families: many of these Kwandu individuals who married other Kwandu had siblings or fathers or grandfathers who had made similar incestuous marriages. When I pressed my informant on this fact in one instance, he conceded that there are two kinds of Kwandu—Kwandu proper and Kwandu-Gwyrai'gwara.

The Gwyrai'gwara, Homero asserted, are a shameless, incest-prone group of Kwandu who will marry indiscriminately Mytum or other Kwandu.[4] He claimed that they were completely promiscuous in their choice of marital partners: they would even marry among themselves. But my genealogical data suggest a different hypothesis: they do not seem to marry each other, only Mytum or Kwandu proper (i.e. non-Gwyrai'gwara Kwandu). In other words, they form, in effect, a third exogamous clan, Gwyrai'gwara, who marry into the other two clans, Mytum and Kwandu.

Yet, except for this scandalous peculiarity of their marriage patterns, and the name denominating them, the Gwyrai'gwara are assimilated into the Kwandu moiety. The alternative names most used to refer to members of the Kwandu moiety—Tarave and Apyawytang—definitely include the Gwyrai'gwara; there seems to be no denomination referring to members of the Kwandu moiety excluding Gwyrai'gwara. (Though for convenience with my principal informants I used the term "Kwandu-hete," "real Kwandu," to distinguish non-Gwyrai'gwara in my genealogies, even this term in common parlance can include the Gwyrai'gwara.) Thus, while the Gwyrai'gwara in effect comprise a third exogamous clan, conceptually—for the sake, perhaps, of preserving the moiety ideology—they are completely merged with the other members of the Kwandu moiety.

One other name, however, does seem to be used by some informants more or less exclusively for them. Although I was at first given *japu* as a bird associated with the Kwandu moiety generally, I have not heard non-Gwyrai'gwara Kwandu spontaneously referred to as Japu. Homero refused to limit the term to Gwyrai'gwara, but other, younger informants used the term to specify that a certain individual was a member of this "nonconformist Kwandu" group. LaVera Betts (personal communication) reported that on the death of one Carlo Paquiri, a Gwyrai'gwara, one of the Kagwahiv pointed to a passing *japu* bird and said, "There goes Carlo's soul." The *japu* bird, then—the one that lacks some of the characteristics shared by the harpie eagle and the maracanã—seems to have specific associations (at least for some informants) with the Gwyrai'gwara, thus giving weight to Nunes Pereira's hunch that the Japu might be a kind of third clan.

Homero, the informant who first conceded the existence of this anomalous clan, was also able to present me with a history of its development—or, at any rate, with his theory of its origin. The ancestors of the present Gwyrai'gwara, he said, were enemies of the Kagwahiv who were assimilated into Kagwahiv society after their defeat two or three generations before pacification by Homero's Kwandu grandfather, Uparahu, who then promulgated an edict that no Kwandu should marry one. When a Gwyrai'gwara named Hajikwari wished to marry one of Uparahu's daughters, Uparahu refused to accept bride service or bride payment from him. The daughter nonetheless eloped, but Hajikwari's later attempt at reconciliation by bringing Uparahu a tapir was again spurned. Uparahu's children, however, seemed to have no such objections to *their* children marrying Gwyrai'gwara: Hajikwari's brother Pireró married a daughter of Uparahu's son Tukáia (a half-sister of Homero's), and cross-cousin marriages in the succeeding generations led to a welter of intermarriages between this branch of the Gwyrai'gwara and Uparahu's descendants. At the same time, Hajikwari's sister made a "proper" marriage to a Mytum, and many of her Mytum offspring made cross-cousin marriages to her brothers' Gwyrai'gwara children. In other words, these Gwyrai'gwara— and other branches that intermarried with descendants of Uparahu and other Kwandu, as well as with varied Mytum—came to marry like a third clan, although in name and concept they maintained their affiliation with the Kwandu moiety.

The Gwyrai'gwara are evidently in a very ambiguous social position. Their existence is not readily acknowledged: it was only when I ferreted out the inconsistencies in the genealogies that informants admitted their existence; the Summer Institute linguists who had been studying Kagwahiv for several years and were well versed in Kagwahiv culture had not heard the name. Indeed, of the several anthropologists who had visited them over the years since pacification, only Nunes Pereira suspected their existence.

Not only scholars but some Kagwahiv themselves—informants who have no close kin married to Gwyrai'gwara—seemed genuinely vague about the status of Gwyrai'gwara in the society. One old Mytum man I knew well concluded that since the Gwyrai'gwara he was acquainted with were married to Kwandu, the Gwyrai'gwara must be a branch of the Mytum moiety![5] Such misconceptions, if at all widespread, could have led to considerable confusion about what marriages would be legitimate with a Gwyrai'gwara—though my Mytum informant may well have been simply evading the topic.

The anomaly of the Gwyrai'gwara within the Kagwahiv social system has radical implications for the moiety system itself. It means that the moieties no longer serve the principal function for which they are alleged to exist. The regulation of marriage has for several generations been carried out not by the moieties but by a system of three exogamous patrilineal clans.

The apparent ease with which the Gwyrai'gwara were (in practice, as opposed to ideology) integrated into the system as a third *de facto* clan, and the fact that the system continues to function without in the least disturbing the ideology of moiety exogamy, raises further questions about the nature and function of Kagwahiv moieties. If their principal function were, as ideology maintains, the regulation of marriage, one might expect the change in the actual system of marriages to lead, over three or four generations, to a gradual erosion or modification of the moiety ideology. It might be modified, for example, into a three-clan system on the model of the Eastern Shavante (Maybury-Lewis 1967:75). Yet the moieties seem as strong today as when Nimuendajú contacted the Kagwahiv 50 years ago. It is as if the addition of a third clan in the marriage system is almost irrelevant to the dualistic ideology of moieties. Granted, the third clan has been kept highly clandestine, but the three clans continue to be the real units that regulate marriage.

The persistence of this situation, in which the ideal rules governing marriage contradict the patterns followed in practice, is made possible by the existence in Kagwahiv society of a third alternative conceptualization of the determinants of marriage choice. Although this conceptualization is strictly embodied in only one category of Kagwahiv marriages— the normative arranged first marriage—and is not nearly as saliently emphasized by informants as the moiety system, it may well be as fundamental to the Kagwahiv conception of marriage choice as are exogamous moieties. This third conception can be reconciled either with moiety exogamy or with a system of three exogamous clans, and even makes it possible to account for the clandestine persistence of a triadic system in the face of the continued dyadic ideology.

Infant Betrothal and the Cycle of Marriage Contracts

Ideally, the initial marriage of a Kagwahiv is arranged by his or her parents while he or she is still an infant. Although this infant betrothal is not loudly proclaimed by Kagwahiv to outsiders, it is part of a complex system of marriage choice that is basic to the Kagwahiv conceptualization of marriage. Until recently, betrothal in infancy seems to have been the rule for Kagwahiv. Yet Curt Nimuendajú (1924:225-26), the first anthropologist to visit the Kagwahiv, was unaware of it. José Garcia de Freitas, who accompanied Nimuendajú and was long-time *encarregado* of the SPI post, noted that "parents determine their daughters' marriages" (1926:68) but was unable to say at what age or how marriage partners were chosen. Joaquim Gondim, an early visitor, remarked on the existence of infant betrothal (1938:31) but failed to appreciate the extent of its practice or the complex sequence of commitments of which infant betrothal is a part.

The betrothal takes place on the occasion of the child's being given its first name. This "play name" (*mbotagwahav*) is bestowed upon the infant by one of his mother's brothers, who thus places his claim on the infant as a spouse for his own recently born child when they should reach maturity. He thus "betrothes" (*opojiká*) his own child to that of his sister.

Such betrothals are part of a larger cycle. The brother who thus puts his claim on his sister's child is not randomly chosen but is one to whom the sister (or her husband) already has an obligation, dating from her own marriage. When a woman is married, two of her brothers (real or close classificatory) are chosen to give her away (*gwerová*) in marriage to her husband. In receiving his wife from her two brothers, the new husband incurs an obligation to reciprocate by giving one of his own children (sex not specified) to each of these two brothers of his wife, to marry a child of his. When a child is born to the new bride, if it is opposite in sex to a child recently born to one of the brothers who gave her away, that brother lays a claim to the child for betrothal to his own by naming his sister's child. When these two children grow to maturity, they marry; two brothers are chosen to give the girl to her husband, and the cycle continues.

An example: Gabriela was given to Homero by her favorite brother Pope'i, her father's brother's son Tauat, and one other classificatory brother, Py'róva. Tauat had a boy, Sergio; shortly afterward, Gabriela had a girl, Emilia. Tauat came joyfully to Gabriela and gave her daughter her play-name, thus claiming her to be betrothed to his infant son.

When Sergio and Emilia grew to maturity and married, Emilia was given to Sergio by two of her classificatory brothers, one of them Jovenil, thus establishing obligations to give each of them a child to marry one of their children. The contract with Jovenil might not, under current social conditions, be fulfilled—although one of Jovenil's four unmarried sons might marry one of Sergio's daughters. One of the sons, in fact, was working for Sergio a few years ago, but vehemently denied that it had anything to do with a possible forthcoming marriage.

Ideally, the brother chosen to give the woman away is a real brother. If none is available, as close an agnatic parallel cousin as possible is chosen. A man who gives his real sister to another man thus establishes an especially close bond with his brother-in-law. Once Sergio, trying (while inebriated) to ingratiate himself (and coax some alcohol from my medicine kit) by offering me a wife, said—somewhat apologetically— "I don't have an unmarried sister, but I have a cousin," and proposed to ask his cousin's father to give her to me in marriage. Quite frequently— especially to judge from the frequency of first cross-cousin marriages in the genealogies—it *is* a woman's real brother who gives her away and gets her child betrothed to his. In such instances, carried out generation after generation, the net effect is an exchange of women between the patrilineal descendants of the two men involved in the first transaction. The overall effect is, at it were, an exchange between two (genealogically defined) "patrilines," though they are neither conceived as such by the Kagwahiv nor named, and certainly do not form corporate groups. From the observer's point of view, therefore, one may view this cycle of marital exchanges as (ideally) implicitly approximating a pattern of exchanges between genealogically defined but not natively recognized "patrilines."

The existence of this third mode of determining marriage choice may throw some light on the absence of concern about the contradiction between the ideal system of moiety exogamy and the actual three-clan system, and the fact that some Kagwahiv seem hardly aware of it, having only the fuzziest notion of how the third clan fits into the "moiety" system. One would think that such vague notions might lead to some considerable confusion about who is an acceptable marriage partner. The problems of this situation are much alleviated, however, if marriage choice is thought of as primarily determined neither by moiety exogamy nor by exogamy of clan but by a system that assigns a marriage partner in a manner which could be consistent with either moiety or clan exogamy. If one chooses a marriage partner in a way that replicates the marriage of one's parents, by marrying the offspring of one's mother's brother, then whatever particular kind of exogamy the parental marriage may have represented will *automatically* be guaranteed by the marriage of their offspring. By such a system of marriage determination, the exogamic relationships of the major units of the society—be they moieties or clans—will be preserved and continued, without the individuals choosing marriage partners necessarily being aware that they are preserving such relationships.

Indeed, with this system of determining marriage choice one can see how even a single intramoiety marriage, as long as it is properly carried out, would almost automatically snowball into a *de facto* segmentation of a moiety along "lineage" lines. If a couple both of Kwandu affiliation marry, then they are obliged to give one or more of their children to marry children of the wife's brothers who gave her away, resulting in a permanent alliance of marital exchanges between the wife's brother's "line" and the husband's. With the continuation over successive generations of the sequence of cross-cousin betrothal and marriage, this would soon lead to a segmentation of the moiety into two intermarrying "clans."

Although the data are not available so far back on who gave whom away in marriage, the genealogical data on the intermarriages between the Gwyrai'gwara crypto-clan and other Kwandu support this account of its development. As the accompanying charts show, a number of the marriages between Gwyrai'gwara and other Kwandu—and, for that matter, between Gwyrai'gwara and Mytum—are the result of cross-cousin marriages of the offspring of four or five such marriages in the generation of Homero's father, around the turn of the century, as already

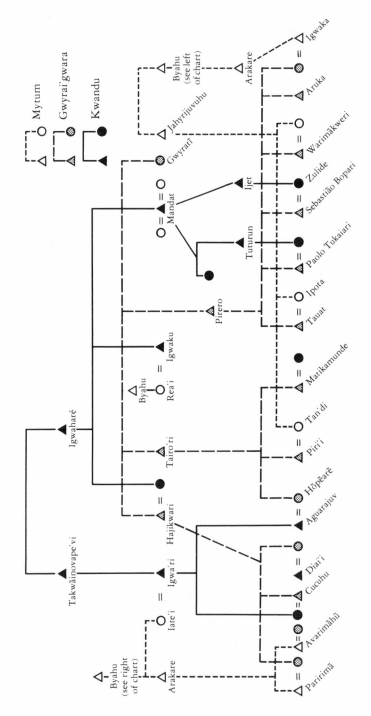

FIGURE 2. GWYRAI'GWARA I: HAJIKWARI AND HIS SIBLINGS AND THEIR DESCENDANTS.

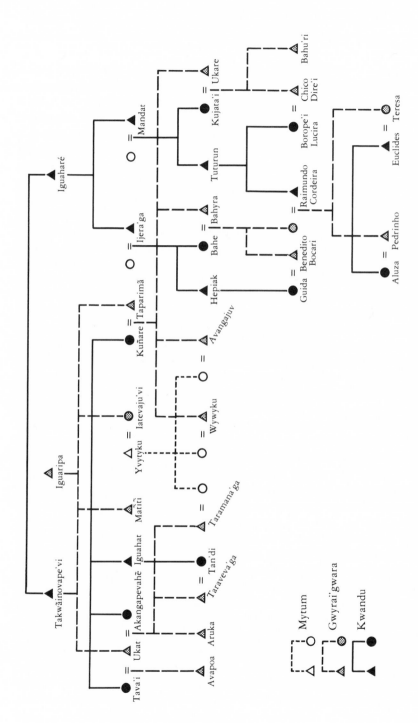

FIGURE 3. GWYRAI'GWARA II: IGUARIPA AND HIS DESCENDANTS.

described in the middle of the preceding section. Another line of Gwyrai'gwara also intermarried primarily with the lines of Homero's father and of Igwari (see Figures 2 and 3).

The Marriage Cycle:
Its Articulation with Ritual

In contrast to the moieties, which play no part in ceremonies, infantile betrothal and the other events of the marital exchange cycle are integrally woven into the sequence of ceremonies demarcating the Kagwahiv life cycle, an index of how deeply this cycle of marital exchange commitments is embedded in Kagwahiv social structure. The "giving away" of a woman by her brother, the act that initiates the cycle, is a central part of the symbolism of the simple wedding ceremony. Subsequent stages of the cycle—the infantile betrothal that turns the general obligation into a concrete contract, and the event of the "first marriage" that fulfills that contract—are parts of two major (now defunct) life-cycle rituals, the infant's naming ceremony and the girl's puberty rite.

A wedding was initiated either by the bride's father or, almost as frequently, by a real or classificatory brother, who would ask the father to give his daughter to so-and-so in marriage. Whoever initiated the proceedings, the girl's father took the formal initiative, either approaching the prospective son-in-law himself or, more properly, asking one of his own brothers to act as an intermediary. This paternal uncle of the girl would speak to her and to the prospective groom, persuading both to marry. The reluctance with which both bride and groom responded to these overtures, so regular and stereotyped as to appear traditional, seems yet to have been quite real. The girl was often quite young, since girls were married as soon as possible after puberty (avowedly to avert illegitimate pregnancies), while a boy resented giving up his freedom for bride service. The brothers giving the girl away might join her father's brother in persuading and pressuring both their sister and the potential groom. Gabriela recalls being beaten by her brother Pope'i into submitting to marriage with Homero.

When the couple is persuaded, the relatively simple wedding ceremony is carried out. The groom is seated on a hammock, the bride's appointed brothers carry her to him and place her next to him in the hammock. Thereupon bride and groom embrace and are lectured in their conjugal duties by the presiding bride's uncle—and/or, some informants assert, by the headman of the group. The wedding is then festively celebrated by singing, playing of *jiru'a* and *yreru* flutes, and dancing.

The next stage of the cycle is likely to follow shortly, when the newly wed couple have their first child. If one of the wife-giving brothers of the mother has recently had a child of the opposite sex, or has one shortly thereafter, he proposes to perform the naming ceremony for her child. If she accepts, he comes after singing all night to her hammock, where she is sitting with the baby on her arm, and in a brief and simple ceremony bestows on the child a play name (*mbotagwahav,* often a descriptive name referring to a characteristic of the child) and in return asks that the child be given, later on, in marriage to his child.

No special form of relationship seems to obtain between the two betrothed children during the early years of their lives. Children appear to be free to indulge in sex play indiscriminately with children of the opposite sex, as long as they are also of the opposite moiety. But in late latency or early adolescence the boy of the pair may be adopted by his future father-in-law, moving in with him and working along with him, to learn the duties of a son-in-law. For a while the relationship is simply an educational one, but as the betrotheds approach puberty, the man approaches his young helper—or, more properly, asks one of his sons or brother's sons to approach him—and makes the proposal of marriage.

Once the two partners are reconciled, the wedding traditionally takes place following the ceremony that ends the girl's seclusion at first menstruation. The girl, who has been sitting in her hammock for approximately ten days immobile and observing rigorous food taboos, is carried down to the river where a ritual bath formally terminates her seclusion. She is then taken by her father's brother and by her own appointed brothers and placed beside her groom in his hammock. In this act they establish a new contract whereby the groom is obligated to give each of them a child of his.

The marriage is only fully completed, however, on fulfillment of bride service, which (for a first marriage) seems to have averaged about five years. During this time the couple remain part of the bride's father's family, slinging their hammocks in the same corner of the *ongá* (longhouse) and using the same cooking fire. The groom works for his bride's father (or, if he is deceased, for one of her brothers) in his fields, fishing and hunting for him, etc. Only at the end of this period may the couple leave the bride's natal household, to establish—if they stay in her settlement—a separate cooking fire and a separate spot in the *ongá* to hang their hammocks. (Nowadays, couples build their own Brazilian-style one-room family houses.)

The traditional cycle of marriage determination, then, is articulated with many of the main Kagwahiv life-cycle rituals. This contrasts with the slight role of the moieties in Kagwahiv ceremonial life, giving further evidence that this cycle is at least as basic to the Kagwahiv conceptualization of their system of marriage choice as is the moiety system.

Parameters for Flexibility

The marriage cycle I have just described provides a basic model for the Kagwahiv conceptualization of marriage contracts, at least for the first marriage. If all first marriages were arranged exactly along the lines of this traditional pattern, it would seem to create a rather inflexible system, leaving little choice to the partners themselves.

In practice, however, while many marriages are carried out in consonance with the cycle of infantile betrothal, not all—not even all first marriages—conform neatly to this traditional model. Indeed, given both the mortality rate and the degree of mobility in a warlike tropical forest society like the Kagwahiv, it would be impossible for a system that designates one's marriage partner so specifically from birth to function with full accuracy. The likelihood is considerable that a person's betrothed will have died or moved to a distant area before the marriage can be carried out. Thus the very rigidity with which the system determines a person's first marriage partner, under Kagwahiv demographic conditions, requires a degree of flexibility in the execution, and parameters are introduced that pragmatic Kagwahiv can exploit for the expression of personal preferences:

Homero gave Lucira in marriage to Mohã'gi, at the request of Lucira's father Igwa, who had adopted Homero as a child and brought him up. In return, Mohã'gi's and Lucira's deeply loved only daughter Aluza was betrothed to Claudio, Homero's oldest son by Gabriela. But Claudio, in resentment for his parents' refusal to permit his union with a neighboring Brazilian girl, left the area to work for Brazilians. While he was away, Mohã'gi married Aluza to Jovenil, since those two had been fond of each other for many years. It is not clear whether Claudio's prolonged absence was the reason for this marriage or the excuse for it; the latter seems more probable, since Aluza and Jovenil claim to have been engaged for several years before their marriage. Gabriela has still not forgiven Mohã'gi for this.

The practice of having two or more brothers give away their sister in marriage to some degree reduces the demographic vagaries of the system, making it more likely that at least one of them will have a child of appropriate age and sex to betroth to one of her first children. If not, her husband himself may have given one or more of his sisters away to other men, establishing new bonds to choose from. All of these alternatives reduce the likelihood that there will be no partner available for any given child, but they also create numerous conflicting obligations, not all of which can always be met. These conflicting obligations in themselves provide an additional element of flexibility and choice.

Gabriela, as described above, was given to Homero by her favorite brother Pope'i, her first parallel cousin Tauat, and his brother Py'róva, thus establishing potential bonds with all three.

As we have just seen, Gabriela's first child with Homero, Claudio, was betrothed in fulfillment of obligations established by Homero's giving his sister Emilia to Mohã'gi. This left her second child, who was named and claimed by Tauat for his son Sergio, whom she eventually married.

Now Gabriela also had a step-daughter, Camelia—the issue of Homero's earlier marriage with Gabriela's deceased older sister—about whose naming Gabriela gave conflicting reports. At one point she said Tauat named her also, but later she said Camelia was named by Pope'i, who thus claimed her for his son Janoari. She also asserted that when Camelia took herself another husband, Emilia fell to Janoari as *his* betrothed. (I am not sure what became of Janoari; he has disappeared from the scene—fortunately so, if Gabriela's statement can be credited, thus avoiding a conflict with Sergio's claims on Emilia).

Py'róva, the third "giver" of Gabriela to Homero, seems to have dropped out of the picture—perhaps because his son, Samuel Piroba, was betrothed to the daughter of Ukarepuku, who had given his own sister to Py'róva.

As important a consideration in making a match as the mutual attraction of the partners is the ability of the bride's father to get along with her husband, who must not only do several years' bride service but is also a candidate to stay on and become one of the core of his father-in-law's following. I know of at least one potential marriage that was not carried through because of antipathy between the man and his potential father-in-law. In Sergio's case, on the other hand, a factor in his acceptance of his contract-fulfilling marriage was his admiration for Emilia's father, Homero. Even more frequently a man's desire for a promising son-in-law may influence his decision—even, in one case, to breaking the betrothal of his daughter to another man.

The renowned leader Tupaiaku gave three of his daughters in succession to Homero in marriage, although no prior bond had been established by infant betrothal nor (as far as I know) by Homero's father giving a sister to Tupaiaku. The third daughter Tupaiaku gave to Homero was Gabriela, who was betrothed to another young man. Against her will and that of her betrothed, it is rumored, Tupaiaku married her to Homero— a fact deplored by Homero's current detractors, and thrown up to him by Gabriela when she is angry at him. Homero, in turn, very definitely regards these marriages to Tupaiaku's three daughters as an expression of confidence on the part of Tupaiaku, and of Tupaiaku's personal desire to maintain a close relationship with Homero.

Even if the arranged marriage is carried through, various mechanisms allow the couple considerable freedom for further choice. Institutional polygyny permits a man to have a wife of his choice in addition to his betrothed, if he wishes. This, however, was not frequent. Nimuendajú (1924:225) believed the Kagwahiv to be strictly monogamous, and Garcia de Freitas (1926:72) knew of only three cases of polygyny (although I can document a number of instances of at least temporary polygyny from the early days of pacification). Informants are rather amused at Aguarajuv's five wives (at least three of which were simultaneous), considering it rather unwise of him. Polyandry, while occasionally practiced, did not afford women an equally attractive, socially sanctioned alternative, since the few cases I know of were provisional affairs of the nature of Surui "polyandrous arrangements" (Laráia 1963). But for the woman who is discontented with her husband's choice of a second wife, or who is unwilling to share him—or simply looking for an excuse to leave him—it is considered quite acceptable for her to refuse to accept a co-wife and leave. In some cases this may prevent the second marriage, but in others it provides an occasion for the nullification of an arranged marriage that was not to the mutual satisfaction of the couple.

Ukarepuku carried through a traditionally arranged marriage with Teresa, the daughter of his mother's real brother Paririmã. Teresa, quite young, was far from ready for the responsibilities of marriage. Somewhat later Ukarepuku took steps toward marriage with a second woman he was attracted to. Teresa's objection did not stop him, and she took the occasion to walk out on him. Ukarepuku's second wife bore a good many children for him, and they remained together to her death. On her death Ukarepuku persuaded Teresa—since remarried and widowed—to return to him, and spent his last few years with her.

Another instance did not turn out so satisfactorily: Homero's second wife tried to leave him when he married a third, her younger sister, after the decease of his first. Homero, however—a fierce warrior—retrieved her and beat her brutally, for which public opinion roundly condemned him.

The husband's taking a second wife was not the only occasion for the dissolution of marriage. Separation is rather easy in Kagwahiv society; many individuals, both men and women, have had two or three spouses, and not a few have gone through many unions. The submission to authority implicit in bride service, and in the frequent uxorilocal residence (since it is often difficult for a husband to persuade his wife to leave her father's settlement), puts additional strain on the marriage bond. Even a loyal follower and (more or less) devoted husband like Sergio feels the restrictions that marriage and service to his father-in-law place on his freedom.

Yet many marriages are quite stable, and not a few couples have close, enduring marriages that last a lifetime. There does not, interestingly, seem to be much difference in this respect between arranged marriages and those in which the partners chose one another. Two of the strongest marriages I know are Mohã'gi's arranged marriage with Lucira and Jovenil's voluntary one with Aluza.

Thus the occasions and rationalizations for terminating a contract are numerous at any point in the contractual cycle. Similarly, new contractual cycles may be initiated at virtually any point, without the prior contractual bonds necessarily having been formed.

Some marriages later in life will pick up on earlier commitments of the marriage cycle that were not carried through originally. José Bahut's marriage to Camelia after the death of his first wife might be regarded as a fulfillment of the contract between his father, Bahut, and Camelia's father Homero. Bahut was one of those who gave Homero's first wife to him, but was not repaid by the betrothal of any of his children to one of Homero's. It is not clear whether José's marriage to Camelia could be regarded as a belated fulfillment of this contract, since Camelia is a child of Homero's second marriage, not of the first wife given him by Bahut, and Homero has not mentioned this marriage as the fulfillment of a contract. But this may have been a factor in his acceptance of José Bahut as a rather troublesome son-in-law.

If the contractual exchange model of marriage determination were strictly adhered to, it would be highly restrictive in determining marriage choices, at least for initial marriage. But sufficient parameters are built into the system to allow much greater flexibility than the outward form of the system would seem to permit; the very specificity with which the system determines marriage partner in itself becomes a source of flexibility through the frequent unavailability of the specified partner.

Yet all this does not mean that the marriage exchange and childhood betrothal cycle is unworkable, or that it does not play an important part in shaping the pattern of Kagwahiv marriages. While the system is sufficiently flexible to allow for alternatives when the assigned partner is unavailable, or when the partners to a marriage (bride, groom, or father-in-law) have strong preferences for a different arrangement, many marriages on which I have full data have followed this traditional form; sequences of cross-cousin marriages in earlier genealogies, for which informants cannot recall the actual wife givers and infantile betrothals, suggest that many of these early marriages may well have followed the same form as well. The parameters I have described simply provide an escape hatch for strong-willed individuals whose preferences run counter to what their parents have chosen for them, or for those whose situation makes it impossible to fulfill past commitments.

Summary and Conclusions

I have presented three models of marriage determination, all consciously held in Kagwahiv society: a moiety system that seems deeply ingrained but does not correspond to the actual arrangement of marriages; a triadic clan system that is highly dissembled and even incompletely understood by Kagwahiv, but that is closer to the empirical distribution of marriages; and a complex system of progressively more specific contractual arrangements that amounts to alliances between patrilineal "lines" (not conceptualized as such).[6] All of these models are relevant to Kagwahiv marriage choice, but no one of them corresponds completely to the actual patterns of marriage determination—least of all the most official model, that of moiety exogamy.

The coexistence of the ideology of moiety exogamy with the *de facto* three-clan system invites comparison with the Eastern and Western Shavante moiety system described by David Maybury-Lewis (1967). At an approximation, the Kagwahiv system seems to be similar to that of the Eastern Shavante, whose three intermarrying clans are grouped into two moieties. Yet a subtle but important difference must be noted. While the Shavante triadic system is officially acknowledged and merged with the diadic one in a more complex ideology, the Kagwahiv triadic system is covert and denied, marriages between the two clans of the Kwandu moiety still regarded as dimly tinged with incest. The contrast becomes even more striking when the comparison is made with the Western Shavante, whose situation is a precise inversion of that of the Kagwahiv: the Western Shavante present a *formal* system like that of the Eastern Shavante, with a triad of clans grouped into moieties, but *in fact* the moieties are exogamous, so that the division of one into two clans is superfluous from the point of view of exogamic relationships. Where the Kagwahiv, then, have a dualistic ideology covering a triadic system of exogamous clans, the Western Shavante have a triadic ideology covering a real system of exogamous moieties.

It seems surprising that the ideology of moiety exogamy can persist so strongly, not only as an ideal but as the Kagwahiv description of their own marriage system, in the face of its blatant incongruity with the actual marriage patterns. True, many Kagwahiv—perhaps the majority—can ignore the existence of Gwyrai'gwara (or at least maintain only a dim awareness of the category), as they are not directly involved in affinal links with Gwyrai'gwara, nor are their close agnatic kin; they can, without any serious confusion arising in their own kin relationships and terminology, go on thinking of the marriage system in terms of moieties. Yet one would think, if marriage was primarily determined in fact by the system of three exogamous clans, it would require consciousness of that system on the part of all Kagwahiv to maintain the exogamic boundaries properly. Such conscious awareness of the triadic clan system would, one might think, conflict with the maintenance of the theory of moiety exogamy.

The third model, I have shown, can explain how either the moiety or triadic system could persist even without full understanding on the part of the participants. To the extent that marriage contracts are carried through, the continuity of exchanges between different "lines" is maintained, perpetuating existing affinal relationships between particular groups of agnatically related individuals within each clan, thus indirectly preserving the distinctness of the clans themselves.

Speculating further, one may show how this model of marriage determination could lead to the establishment of the Gwyrai'gwara as a third *de facto* clan, even in the face of the theory of moieties. If moiety exogamy had been the overriding concern in choice of a marriage partner in Kagwahiv society, one would expect that, even if the first generation of Kwandu-Gwyrai'gwara persisted in their incestuous marriages with brother Kwandu, later generations of Gwyrai'gwara, having learned proper Kagwahiv behavior and become more "acculturated," might make more proper choices and limit their marriages to Mytum. Instead, they persisted in the error of their parents' ways and, far from being more discreet in their affections, perpetuated their parents' anomalous marriages. The mechanism by which the first-generation incestuous marriages were perpetuated in their children's was the bilateral cross-cousin marriage promoted by the third model, the contract cycle. Almost all of the current Gwyrai'gwara marriages to other Kwandu are thus derived from one of the few original such marriages a few generations back. A few intramoiety marriages in the first generation might, through the process of betrothing a child of the wife to a child of her brother who gave her away, lead directly to the founding of a third clan.

Various indications suggest that the third model, of contractual marital exchange through infantile betrothal, may be at least as fundamental to Kagwahiv thinking about marriages as the official model of moiety exogamy. For one thing, in contrast to the moieties, which are virtually absent from Kagwahiv mythology and ceremony, the process of contractual exchange is woven deeply into the sequence of life-cycle rituals.

The very perpetuation, through contractual exchanges, of marriages that were anomalous with respect to moiety exogamy confirms the importance of this model.

Additional confirmation of the fundamentality of the cycle of infantile betrothal as a Kagwahiv concept of marriage choice comes from comparative evidence from other Tupi-Guarani tribes. Although no other Tupi-Guarani tribe, as far as I know, has an identical system for determining marriage choice, variants of it occur in some, and some of its elements are quite widespread in these cultures. As Baldus documents (1970:293-94), childhood and infantile betrothal is widely practiced among other Tupi-Guarani and can be traced back to the early Tupinambá. Patrilateral cross-cousin marriage—which embodies the principle underlying the Kagwahiv marriage cycle, of a child being given in return for a wife[7]—is favored by the Akuawa-Asurini (Laráia and da Matta 1967:39-41); sister's daughter marriage, in which the exchange of a sister for a wife is even more direct, is a common Tupi-Guarani practice.

By contrast, the concept of moiety exogamy is unique to the Kagwahiv among Tupi-Guarani. The Mundurucú, who have exogamous moieties, are probably of a more distantly related branch of Tupi stock (Rodrigues 1965). Mundurucú moieties, moreover, are of a completely different nature from Kagwahiv moieties, consisting of two rather loose amalgams of phratries rather than the (theoretically) unsubdivided halves into which Kagwahiv society is split (Murphy 1960).

Exogamous clans, on the other hand, do occur with greater frequency. The closest known relatives of the Kagwahiv (other than the recently contacted Juma), the "Tupi-Cawahib" first visited by Rondôn, though lacking moiety divisions, have numerous named bands that Lévi-Strauss calls "clans" (1961:328) or "sibs" (1948:303), with the reservation that they only tend toward exogamy. His genealogies (1958) suggest that these group names are also those of patrilineal clans, but the 20 clan names he lists (1958:332-33) are names of trees, plants, and geographical formations, not bird species. The Surui, however—more distantly related Tupi speakers living in the Xingú—are divided into five exogamous patrilineal clans (Laráia, in Laráia and da Matta 1967:43), and the name of one is translated *gaviaõ*. The moieties could be the Kagwahiv variant of the patriclans that appear in other Tupi-Guarani-speaking tribes, including other branches of the old "Cawahib."

These three models of marriage choice all have their own validity. Each in a different way is deeply embedded in Kagwahiv social structure. But they are applicable in quite different (though often overlapping) contexts. The diversity of models available even in a society as small and technologically simple as the Kagwahiv facilitates individual adaptation to a variety of special social circumstances within the society, as well as permitting the expression of differing individual proclivities. Parameters accepted in the society for adapting models to one another, or to circumstances, create sufficient flexibility in Kagwahiv marital norms to allow considerable exercise of individual choice, whether on the basis of politics or of personal preference.

This analysis may be compared with Lévi-Strauss's discussion of the Bororo in his article on "Social Structures of Central and Eastern Brazil" (in 1963b). A system that is at first glance formulated in exogamous terms is seen on closer inspection to contain a set of alliances that create groups of an implicitly endogamous cast—although in the Kagwahiv case the linked "patrilines" do not have any hint of the hierarchical ordering that Lévi-Strauss rather tenuously attributes to the endogamous groupings he ascribes to the Bororo. But my argument goes a step beyond his: even these ostensibly endogamous units apparently formed by exchanging pairs of "patrilines" are themselves only a formal property of the ideal system; in practice, the system is so unworkably complex as to allow considerable individual choice in marriage partners, with a resultant virtual overruling of the system of exchanging lines that appears so neat on paper. In the end, both normative systems of marriage choice—the descent-based moieties and the structure of alliances—are equally fictitious.

Recent theoretical writing, in redress of functionalist excesses of balanced integration, has stressed the contrast between norms and behavior, in dialectical opposition to one another. Robert Murphy (1972) contends that a certain degree of ambiguity in a social system is essential for its continued existence and operation, consistent with Lévi-Strauss's view (1963b) that a people's cultural formulation of their own ideal system is of necessity a deceptive disguise for reality, permitting flexibility and choice for the practitioners of the system. A new task for anthropology, undertaken in this paper (and in others in this collection), is to examine the ways that social systems provide (or that people devise) for manipulating the norms, or " 'playing' with the systems" (Murphy 1972:158).

The three different types of "real-unreal" opposition that Kensinger (this volume) describes in Cashinahua thought—real versus unreal on an ideal, absolute level, real or unreal in the real situation limited by the available possibilities, and real or unreal in the judgment of the speaker—might well be useful analytic categories for social anthropology, providing for greater precision than our simple dichotomy of "normative" and "deviant" behavior. Certainly, they are useful for understanding the considerations that go into a Kagwahiv's decision on marriage.

The different models of Kagwahiv marriage choice presented in this article—in particular, the two models of exogamy—exemplify a second phenomenon, related to the flexibility just discussed, that is receiving increased recognition of late: the existence of considerable change within traditional societies such as those of the Amazon—change that takes place even without, or apart from, contact with Western "civilization." The addition of the third Gwyrai'gwara clan to the previously existing moiety system constituted a radical restructuring of the Kagwahiv social order. Informants' histories of the development of the Gwyrai'gwara "clan" trace it to the influence of a foreign group of conquered people incorporated into the Kagwahiv tribe. In this paper I have suggested at least a possible mechanism by which a few incestuous marriages by these foreigners, who were initially assimilated into the Kwandu moiety, led progressively to the development of what is effectively a third clan (though still not described as such).

This change came about—at least so it appears—in the last few generations before permanent contact with Brazilian society. While warfare with Brazilian society may have had some indirect effect in stimulating the population movements that brought the Gwyrai'gwara tribe in contact with the Kagwahiv, this change in Kagwahiv society cannot be directly attributed to contact with Brazilians in any way. In the more distant past the adoption of the moiety system itself may well have occurred in the process of the disintegration of the nineteenth-century upper Tapajós "Cabahiba" (Nimuendajú 1924) and the westerly wanderings of the Kagwahiv. At least the absence of moieties in any other known "Cawahib" group seems to suggest that moieties must have been a Kagwahiv innovation at some point, although there is no hint as to what internal process or external contact may have brought this about.

These instances of social change through mutual contact among lowland South American tribes are not isolated. Nimuendajú (1942:19-20) reconstructs that the Sherente clan system was altered in a somewhat similar way by the incorporation of alien Gê groups, and Arthur Sorensen (1967) has shown that in the Northwest Amazon such intersocietal contacts, and resulting intrasocietal changes, are commonplace. The relatively static and unitary models of society that have served anthropology in the past do not comfortably fit the realities of native lowland South American social systems.

Our image of "primitive" societies as uniform, simple, and static is yielding to a more dynamic and complex view of their social order. The situations we encounter in societies like the Kagwahiv invite greater attention to contradictions within a society—contrasts between ideology and practice, the coexistence of inconsistent models of (and for) social praxis, and the diversity of ways in which norms can be manipulated for individual purposes. These contradictions themselves are dynamisms that energize thought and the innovation of cultural forms (one of the lessons Lévi-Strauss took from South American societies). Attending to these inconsistencies, rather than trying to deny them by deciding which is the "correct" representation of the social form or by fitting them all into a higher-level static model, may lead us to further understanding of change in social systems and of the creative contributions of individuals in their attempts to adapt their needs to their social order.

NOTES

1. The research on which this paper is based consists of nine months of contact time in 1967-68, supported by NIMH fellowship 5-F01-MH-29, 905-03 and NSF grant FA-1402; an additional two months of contact in 1973, supported by a grant from the Research Board of the University of Illinois at Chicago Circle; and several months of library research at the Museu Nacional in Rio de Janeiro, who kindly opened their facilities to my use in 1966-68. I am also most grateful to Peter Rivière, Joanna Kaplan, and Kenneth Kensinger for their valuable comments and suggestions on this paper.

2. The Tapirapé, neighbors of several Gê groups, have adopted *agamous* moieties but no exogamous ones, while the Mundurucú, who do have exogamous moieties, speak a language of a different branch of the broader Tupian stock, not strictly of the Tupi-Guarani family (cf. Murphy 1960:7; Rodrigues 1965 and personal communication).

3. Terms of address: *apĩ* and *ha'í,* and *hu'gwý* for *ruvý.* In transcriptions of Kagwahiv terms and names in this paper, *y* represents a high, back, unrounded vowel, like Russian yerih; *v* a bilabial fricative; and *ñ* a palatalized *n* as in Spanish. Other sounds are as in Spanish or Portuguese. Nasalization is indicated by a tilde except in certain common words in which nasalization is indicated by a final *m* or *n* as in Portuguese, a usage the Kagwahiv themselves follow when writing. In all Kagwahiv words and names stress is on the final syllable unless otherwise indicated, although Portuguese names are stressed (and pronounced) as in Portuguese. The transcription generally follows that of Helen Pease and LaVera Betts, with a few modifications generally in the direction of more phonetic transcription where theirs is more strictly phonemic.

4. Gwyrai'gwara means literally "eater of small birds," and was identified by one informant as a smaller *gavião* (hawk), the *gavião-tesouro,* "swallow-tailed kite." Note that the word for "to commit incest" is *oji'u,* literally "to eat oneself."

5. A Kwandu informant (brother-in-law of the one just mentioned) identified Carlo Paquiri, who I later learned was Gwyrai'gwara, as a Mytum.

6. In some ways this situation is an inversion of that observed by Nimuendajú among the Tukuna, whose complex system of alliances among individual clans worked out to a *de facto* moiety system without the individuals in the system being aware of the fact—or, at least, without acknowledging it (Nimuendajú 1952). Roberto Cardoso de Oliveira (1959, 1961) has suggested an analysis of the particular exchanges between "demonstrable unilinear descent groups" in Tukuna society that in some ways parallels the argument of this paper.

7. It is perhaps of theoretical interest to note that the Kagwahiv marital exchange cycle, while taking the *form* of bilateral cross-cousin marriage, is nonetheless conceptualized by its practitioners in terms of "short-term cycle" exchange like that characterizing patrilateral cross-cousin marriage (Lévi-Strauss 1969). The difference, of course, is that while Lévi-Strauss considers the items exchanged to be women, the Kagwahiv consider infants of either sex to be suitable "items of exchange" to pay back the receipt of a woman.

Tupi societies are those *par excellence* in which avuncular marriage is practiced. As Lévi-Strauss notes, this extreme of short-cycle exchange coexists in such societies with long-cycle bilateral cross-cousin marriage. But the short-cycle avuncular marriage is congruent with the Kagwahiv *conceptualization* of cross-cousin marriages as if they were short cycle.

PART III

WESTERN AMAZONIA
(Colombia, Ecuador, Peru, and Venezuela)

6

Dualisms as an Expression of Difference and Danger: Marriage Exchange and Reciprocity among the Piaroa of Venezuela

JOANNA OVERING KAPLAN

In lowland South American thought we find a recurrent appeal to pairs of opposites of various sorts, in cosmological doctrines, in accounts of natural phenomena, and in the understanding of proper social ordering. In the complicated dual organizations of the Gê and Bororo societies of central Brazil such dichotomous classifications of reality are exhibited in their ceremonial life, and each village itself is bisected by a moiety system, or series of moiety systems, opposed by dyadic classification and between which relations of logical complementarity are ritually played out, made formal through ceremony in elaborate ways (see Lave 1977, 1979; da Matta 1979; Melatti 1979; J. Crocker 1979; Maybury-Lewis 1979). When compared with the highly ritualized social organization of these central Brazilian societies, the endogamous cognatic kinship groups of Guianese Amerindians appear fluid and amorphous in shape. While in Gê and Bororo societies, the Amerindian understanding of society as a process within a specific cosmological scheme of things is laid out spatially before our eyes—through ritual and in their circular or semicircular village layout—in the Guianas there exists no complex spatial configuration reflecting the order of social life: there are no naming groups, no moieties in ritual exchange with one another acting out ceremonially a particular vision of cosmological ordering, or expressing an eternal ordering of "another world" from the mythic past. In short, there exists no ritual to declare the elaborate interlocking of the units of which society is comprised.

127

A prescriptive marriage rule associated with variations on a Dravidian type of relationship terminology[1] is, to the best extent of our knowledge, universal to Guianese Amerindian groups (see, for example, Rivière on Carib organization, 1974; J. Kaplan on the Piaroa, 1973, 1975; Lizot on the Yanomam, 1971). Throughout the Guianas the privileged union, in Lévi-Strauss's sense of the term (1969:120), is within one's own local group, itself identified as a unit of close kinsmen (see Rivière 1969; Henley 1979; Albert on the Yanomam, in Ramos and Albert 1977; J. Kaplan 1975). The traditional local group usually dwells together within a large communal house as an endogamous cognatic kinship group; membership in the house is based upon a principle of affinity, for an adult should be married into the house, have affines within it, to join it. Its structure is one that I have previously classified as an "alliance-based kinship group" (1973, 1975), one which maintains itself as a unit of cognates by ideally restricting exchange to within itself, its unity as such a group being associated with the number of marital exchanges among men within the local group itself. It is ironic that in the very societies where the prescriptive marriage rule is of such overwhelming importance to the organization of local groups within them, there is no evidence of a dual organization through which ritual or, indeed, social life should be played out,[2] while in the organization of moiety relationships within Gê and Bororo societies, the exchange of women between moieties plays a relatively minor part in the Amerindian understanding of moiety interaction (Lave 1979, da Matta 1979, Melatti 1979, J. Crocker 1979, Maybury-Lewis 1979). Thus in lowland South America dual organization is often not associated with a prescriptive marriage rule; conversely, the presence of a prescriptive marriage rule by no means implies the presence of one. This is a topic to which I shall return below.

Despite the contrast between the organization of the central Brazilian societies noted above and those of the Guianas, underlying their very dissimilar social structures is a similar philosophy of society, one that is probably common to many Amerindians of tropical South America. As the Guianese example in this discussion, I shall focus on the Piaroa Indians of Venezuela,[3] for within Piaroa mythology and related cosmology we find expressed a very clear statement about the nature of society, the nature of social relationships within it, their proper and improper enactment, their dangers. On this level, the cosmological, we can more easily see a strong similarity between the organization of the Guianese society and the dual organizations of central Brazil, a similarity more difficult to grasp when the focus is upon social structure alone. Maybury-Lewis, in his introduction to the edited volume of articles on the Gê and the Bororo, states (1979:13) that these essays "show how each society strives to create a harmonious synthesis out of the antithetical ideas, categories, and institutions that constitute its way of life . . . to create balance and harmony by opposing institutions"—hence the title of the collection, *Dialectical Societies*. For the Piaroa, as for the Gê and the Bororo, the universe exists, life exists, society exists only insofar as there is contact and proper mixing among things that are different from one another (see J. Kaplan on lowland South American social organization, 1977a). The Piaroa, and the Guianese Amerindians in general, do their best in local group organization to suppress such differences, while the Gê and the Bororo stress them. The recognition of such variation among Amerindians in their overt emphasis upon social differentiation—or its suppression—takes one a long way in understanding variation in the social structures of the Amerindian groups of lowland South America.

Below I shall discuss the relation between Piaroa social organization and cosmology. It is my stance that Piaroa social structure is not so much "reflected" or "replicated" in the cosmology: rather, the cosmology—and the philosophy of social life contained within it—informs with meaning social relationships which, although acted out in the idiom of kinship and affinity, are also metaphysically loaded relationships and, as such, entail far more than kinship obligation. In Piaroa mythic times the world began as an undifferentiated whole, where all of its differences were contained within one being, Ofo Da'ae, the supreme deity. The history of mythical beings tells of their separation, being made different, then being brought together again in interaction with one another. To a certain extent the Piaroa moiety system replicates this structure; the clans, each comprised of beings of one category distinct from all others, are spatially separate from one another both in pre-society time and in the afterworld. In contrast, society exists only through the interaction of the members of different clans. The interaction in mythic time of cultural heroes and in social time of members of different clans is consistently expressed not only as relationships of affinity but also as ones that entail danger. In general, one way the Piaroa do look at the relationship among things of different kind is in terms of affinality, and the danger forthcoming from such interaction is viewed as the result of unfulfilled reciprocity (J. Kaplan 1981).

After making a few remarks on Piaroa territorial organization, I shall begin the discussion with a description of the Piaroa moiety system, for in its structure we are given direct evidence of the Piaroa view of society as of necessity being comprised of beings within categories different in kind.

The Piaroa dwell along the relatively turbulent tributaries of the Middle Orinoco that flow from the Guiana Highlands. The characteristic residential unit of the Piaroa is the multiple-family and semiendogamous kinship group (the *itso'de*), which normally is comprised of 14 to 60 members. Piaroa land itself was traditionally divided into 13 to 14 autonomous political territories, an organization that is now breaking down with the recent and continuous migrations of Piaroa to the lower reaches of their rivers.[4] Each territory was comprised of six to seven *itso'de* (houses), which were separated from one another within the territory by approximately a half-day's journey along a river or jungle path. The political organization of the territory is still based upon the loose and competitive ordering, hierarchical in nature, of *ruwatu* (religio-political leaders) within the territory (J. Kaplan 1973, 1975, n.d.). There is no kinship principle placing order on territorial organization; rather, political alliances among men within the territory give the territory its identity (J. Kaplan 1975, n.d.). The communal house, on the other hand, is a local residential unit that is kinship structured (J. Kaplan 1975).

The Piaroa Moiety System

In Piaroa cosmogony their social life had its beginnings in the intermarriages enacted between the members of the first Piaroa clans, in themselves infertile since comprised of brother and sister pairs. The classification of cosmic habitats that distinguishes the *iyaénawátu* (clans) of the Piaroa moiety system is one that opposes "those of the sky" (of *mariwéka*) and, not surprisingly, "those of the earth" (of *hu'tó'hu*). Within these moieties the different clans are named by the conjunction of *hakwáwa* ("within"), *yo'u* ("the lake of"), and the name of the physical or organic object to which the lake belongs. For the moiety of *mariwéka* the latter are land animals, inanimate objects, and insects; for *hu'tó'hu*, birds, the stars, and fruit that grows high on trees. For example, there are *hakwáwa ofóyo'u* ("within the lake of the tapir"), *hakwáwa ináekwayo'u* ("within the lake of the stone"), *yawíyo'u* ("the lake of the jaguar"), *chiríkoyo'u* ("the lake of the star"), and so on.

The names recount the places of creation for the Piaroa: the Piaroa's creations are unique from one another and recorded as such by the names of the different *iyáenawátu* (clans), which also specify the different localities of origin; in one of several versions of the myth of origin, Wahari, the culture hero, creates the first pairs of Piaroa men and women in separate acts of creation at each of the sacred lakes of *mariwéka* and *hu'tó'hu*. One's "place of creation" and the afterworld are conjoined in Piaroa thought: the human soul (*aweta*) returns to its "place of creation" after death, and the members of each clan (*iyáenawang*) live together in a settlement spatially separate from all other *iyáenawátu*—separate from affines, and also from animals, from all beings different from self. Just as the human soul returns to its "place of origin" after death, so too, after it is killed, does the soul of the animal. The Piaroa afterworld, where like entities are departmentalized, represents nonsociety and, as we shall see, a state of nonfertility. Society, and thereby fecundity, can exist only by the interaction of entities that are on the contrary kept separate in the after-world (M. Kaplan 1970, J. and M. Kaplan in press).

The *iyáenawang* to which the individual returns after death is also that of his father, in accordance with a principle of patrifiliation. There one passes time in the afterworld in infertile fornication with a sibling, and since both plant and animal kind are separated from self after death, one consumes one's own flesh for food, endocannibalism most literally ob-served. In describing death the Piaroa also describe in rather eloquent fashion their vision of society; in their view existence in the afterworld entails a state of being that is stripped of all that is necessary to social living. In social life beings significantly different from one another must mingle, while in death there is a separation of differences. The social "I" is separated from the social "other," and the eater "I" from the eaten "other": kin dwell in an abode set apart from affines; man has no contact with animal kind. At the same time, in death, there is the dissolution of uniqueness among beings, male and female, leader and follower, who do dwell together: the attributes characteristic of gender are lost, those that distinguish men as fertile beings from women in their fertility; so too are shed the critical powers of the shaman, or the fertility peculiar to his status—his voice, his songs, his *ta'kwa ruwang* (his "master of thoughts")—all traits that distinguish in social life the leader from the follower. For the individual there are no affines after death, no fertility, no animal food, no food from the gardens. In short, there are no dangers (M. Kaplan 1970, J. and M. Kaplan in press). Lévi-Strauss speaks at the conclusion of *The Elementary Structures of Kinship* of the "bliss of the hereafter" where women will no longer be exchanged, i.e. "removing to an equally unattainable past or future the joys, eternally denied to social man, of a world in which one might *keep to oneself*" (1969:497, italics in original). In the Piaroa view it is both past and future, but for man to live there must be entities, those of a different kind from self. Indeed, social life is defined by the Piaroa in terms of the necessary commingling of different entities in society and the immediate consequences thereof.

The spatial distinctions of the *iyáenawátu* afterworld make it in concept somewhat akin to the Bororo "land of *aroe*," where in the topography of the underworld all the dead members of a single clan live together in the geographical wedge allocated to it (J. Crocker 1979); it is also similar to the Northwest Amazonian Pirá-paraná "waking-up houses," the stone houses of the sibs that exist separate from another in the changeless and timeless state of *He,* and from where the souls of the new-born come and to which go the souls of the dead (S. Hugh-Jones 1979, C. Hugh-Jones 1979). It is on the level of social action that the clan system of the Piaroa departs so radically from that of the Bororo and the Amerindians of the Northwest Amazon; in both of these societies the social life of the individual is to a large extent determined by one's membership within one's clan or sib and his interaction with others. In the Northwest Amazon, for instance, the distinction between major cosmic habitats—land, earth, and sky—underlying "Endogamous Groups" identification becomes a root distinction of sameness and difference in social relationships, and as such has a startling degree of classificatory strength in the ordering of Vaupés marriage exchanges (see C. Hugh-Jones 1979).

In contrast, the classification of cosmic habitats that distinguishes the clans of the Piaroa moiety system, one that opposes "those of the sky" and "those of the earth," is not a dualism projected back onto the marriage system: the Piaroa show litttle interest in their moiety system as a language for ordering their marriages, which they easily could do insofar as their marriage system is ostensibly one of "symmetric exchange." Moreover, the spatial distinctions of afterlife and of creation are pointedly not replicated in Piaroa social life, the former two being states quite contrary to earthly and social life where through intermingling the clans completely lose their spatial distinctiveness. Although the Piaroa place great emphasis upon the intermarriages of the first sets of Piaroa, for it is through these intermarriages that all Piaroa are cognates today, the individual's clan membership in no way obligates him in this life. The moiety system refers not to social groupings but to the sacred places of creation and, because after death one returns to his group of creation, to mortuary subgroups.

The Piaroa identify society with both difference and danger and, inversely, nonsociety with identity and safety. They very explicitly state in general the association of difference with danger—the danger of the strong for the weak, animals for humans, affines for oneself. However, it is also their belief that the association of like items (e.g., "kin" with "kin"), although safe, denotes a state of nonsociety: society itself is equated with affinity, the coming together of unlike items (affines). Throughout the remainder of this essay I shall discuss how the Piaroa handle the dilemma with which they are faced, i.e., that society must be comprised of the interaction of unlike entities which, potentially at least, are highly dangerous to one another.[5]

The *Itso'de* and the concept of *Chawáruwang*

The members of an *itso'de* (communal house) form a kinship-structured local group, and, by the Piaroa's view, it is a group of close kinsmen cooperating as such (see J. Kaplan 1973, 1975). *Chawáruwang* ("my kinsman"),[6] a concept that carries with it the notion of consanguinity, is the principal and the most general term through which the Piaroa discuss and explain categories of kinsmen and the obligations associated with these categories of relatives (J. Kaplan 1972, 1975). Highly relevant to the understanding of this concept is the fact that the Piaroa believe an individual to be related equally to his mother and his father. As a physical entity created through sexuality, he partakes of the blood, the flesh, and the bones of both parents.

For any ego the term *chawáruwang* (pl. *chawáruwae*) has multiple references. Although the Piaroa lack interest in genealogies, they nevertheless believe and express the notion that they are all related to one another cognatically through common descent from the first men and women created in the mythic past. Thus all Piaroa are *tawáruwang* to one another. It is important to point out that the first people do not take on the character of focal ancestors: they remain vague in nature and assume no significance as the focus of an ideology of descent. Rather, the Piaroa emphasize the intermarriages of the first sets of Piaroa, and these intermarriages led to the intricate ties of kinship that hold today for their descendants. Here we are clearly introduced to the Piaroa notion that marriage and consanguinity are not to be separated conceptually, that marriage leads to kinship.

Second, the term *chawáruwang* is extended metaphorically to all individuals with whom one engages in peaceful social interaction, whether Piaroa or non-Piaroa. In this context the term takes on the meaning of "friend." Third, a Piaroa uses *chawáruwang* to signify those individuals who comprise a network of kinsmen with whom he interacts on a more or less regular basis: the members of his own territory or individuals in neighboring territories with whom he maintains social, economic, or political ties. Finally, in its most restricted sense *chawáruwang* is used for the members of a person's immediate kindred, *tük'ú chawáruwae* ("my close kinsmen"), as opposed to his *otomínae chawáruwae* ("my distant kinsmen"). Ideally, the members of one's immediate kindred, comprised of all close genealogical kinsmen related to ego through both parents extending to the first cousin level, should live with him and, indeed, comprise in total the population, with himself, of his *itso'de* (house). In short, the two elements of which the category *tük'ú chawáruwae* (close kinsmen) is comprised—close genealogical relatives and the members of one's house—are ideally isomorphic.

It is common usage for a Piaroa to apply the term *chawáruwang* in referring to his own house (*itso'de*) as a discrete grouping of kindred members or "one family,"[7] although some Piaroa tend to use the phrase *tütáe itsótu* ("my own family," "my own kind") to refer to one's own house and its members. Likewise, *chawáruwang* in broader context can refer to the house of others: *chawáruwae ta'hu* signifies "two houses" and the two "families" of which they are comprised. We see, then, that the Piaroa conceive of the house and its inhabitants as a discrete kinship group, one whose membership is based on a principle of consanguinity, or *chawáruwang*ship. The Piaroa also share the common Amerindian belief that domestic intimacy—living, eating, and sleeping together within a confined space—leads to a sharing of physical essence, whether the relationships involved are genealogical ones or not (see for example W. Crocker 1977, Melatti 1979).[8]

The house (*itso'de*) is ideally endogamous: the preferred, or privileged, marriage is with a *tük'ú chawáruwang* of the house. One marries within one's close kindred and lives with its members as well: with one's parents and parents-in-law, with one's sisters and brothers, and their spouses. Thus membership in the *itso'de* implies conjugality as well as kinship, and in this model of close kindred endogamy one's kindred by birth and conjugal kindred should be identical. Here we see that the Piaroa picture of Piaroa land—where all Piaroa are kinsmen of one another through the initial intermarriages of the first people—is in macrocosm identical to the picture they have of their local group, the *itso'de.* Through intermarriages within it the house becomes a unit comprised of close cognates and, as such, reflects the idealized ordering of Piaroa land as a whole. The *itso'de* has a corporate identity that distinguishes it as a group of cognates who live together on a named site, to be contrasted with the membership of other houses, each of which is also located on its own named site.[9] The members of the *itso'de* believe "We are all one, *tük'ú tawáruwang* of one another," that is, a group of consanguineally related and intermarried kinsmen.

For many reasons, both demographic and political, individuals often do not *in fact* marry within their immediate kindred or house (see J. Kaplan 1973, 1975). Nevertheless, the Piaroa always act *as if* their marriages were endogamous to both the house and the close kindred of birth.[10] By marrying either into a house or into a person's personal kindred, one becomes incorporated as a close kinsman of that respective group and into alter's immediate kindred. Often enough, the parents of bride and groom become united in residence through the marriage of their children, and the *itso'de* thereby becomes after the fact an endogamous unit. Those who do not marry endogamously to their kindred of birth are replaced in practice—as far as group membership goes—by those who do marry in. In fact, one tends to slough off close collateral kinsmen with whom either self or spouse has no affinal tie within one's own generation: one can live with an affine, who may be distantly related genealogically, but not with a first cousin who has not married within ego's close conjugal kindred. As mentioned above, the *itso'de* is an affinally structured group, for a principle of affinity is responsible for both group formation and group continuity. The Piaroa perceive the *itso'de* to be a group of cognates, and talk about it as such; yet at the same time it must, in accordance with their own understanding of society, be comprised of beings of categories different from one another, i.e. in-laws. With this understanding we can interpret their use of their relationship terminology as a device for classifying kinsmen both within the *itso'de* and outside it.

The Dravidian Relationship Terminology and the Prescriptive Marriage Rule

As I have argued elsewhere (1972, 1973, 1975; cf. Rivière 1969; Yalman 1967), the most sensible account of the Dravidian relationship terminology insofar as it is *used* by the Piaroa is that of Dumont on South Indian systems (see, for example, 1953a, 1953b, 1957, 1961, 1975; also see Good 1980). It might be noted that the analyses of Scheffler (see, for example, 1971, 1977, 1978; Scheffler and Lounsbury 1971) and his arguments against Dumont (Scheffler 1971, 1977, 1978) are not very persuasive to the South Americanist attempting to understand the Amerindian's classification of his social universe through the use of his relationship terminology as symbolic orientation. Although Scheffler claims that he wishes to show how Dravidian systems "really work" (1971:223), he falls far short of such a goal, for he is not a *social* anthropologist: his aim in formal analysis is to analyze "systems of kin classification rigorously and independently of the social contexts in which they are used" (1978:85). The question is not whether Scheffler is right or wrong in his attempt to uncover cultural universals, but simply that his results as he presents them are uninteresting to the social anthropologist.[11]

The Piaroa relationship nomenclature is a straightforward Dravidian-type terminology, and it is through the categories of the terminology, which differentiate in the three medial generations of ego's kinship universe "kin" and "affine," that marriage is regulated among the Piaroa (see Chart 1). Their prescriptive rule of marriage is that a man must marry a woman who is related to him, according to this relationship terminology, as *chirekwa* (a woman must marry a man who is related to her as *chirekwo*), a category of relationship that includes among others within his own generational level the genealogical specification of MBD or FZD. Chart 1 shows the structure of Piaroa marriage, and Chart 2 provides specifications for the terms (but see below). Since I have elsewhere presented a description of the Piaroa relationship terminology and the prescriptive marriage rule associated with it (Kaplan 1972, 1973,

Gen.	(kin)	(affines)
+2	(GF, GM) *chiminya (bu)*	(M-in-law, F-in-law)
+1	(F, M) *chad'o (bu)* (MB, FZ) *chad'o (a)*	
0	ego *chu'buo* (eB) — eB *chibawa* (yB) — yB eZ *(a)*, yZ *(bu)* *chad'o (bu)*	(MBS, FZS) *chisapo* (B-in-law) (MBD, FZD) *chirekwa* (spouse)
−1	(S) *chitti*, (D) *(bu)* (BCh) (ZCh) (S-in-law, D-in-law)	(MBSCh, FZSCh) (S-in-law, D-in-law) *chuböri (bu)* (S, D) (MBDCh, FZDCh) *chitti (bu)*
−2	(GS, GD) *chu'do (a)*	

CHART 1A: MALE AND FEMALE TERMS (Male Ego) AND FILIATION. (Feminizing suffixes are *a* and *bu*.)

<table>
<tr><td>+2</td><td colspan="4">(kin)
cha'do (a) (GF, FM)</td></tr>
<tr><td>+1</td><td colspan="2">(kin)
(F, M)
cha'o (hu)</td><td colspan="2">(affines)
(MB, FZ) (M-in-law F-in-law)
chiminya (hu)</td></tr>
<tr><td>0</td><td>(kin)
chú'buo (eB)
chihawa (yB)</td><td>(kin)
(eZ) (a)
ego
(yZ) (hu)</td><td>(affines)
(MBS, FZS)
chirekwo
(spouse)</td><td>(affines)
(MBD, FZD)
chóbiya
(Z-in-law)</td></tr>
<tr><td>−1</td><td>(affines)
chuhöri (hu)
(S-in-law, D-in-law,BCh)</td><td colspan="2">(kin)
(S,D) chitti (hu)
(MBSch, FZSCh)
(Zch)</td><td>(affines)
chuhöri (hu)
(S-in-law, D-in-law,
(MBDCh, FZDCh)</td></tr>
<tr><td>−2</td><td colspan="4">(kin)
chu'do (a) (GS,GD)</td></tr>
</table>

CHART 1B: MALE AND FEMALE TERMS (Female Ego) AND FILIATION.
(Feminizing suffixes are *a* and *hu*.)

CHART 2: PIAROA RELATIONSHIP TERMS.

Terms of Reference and Address for Male Ego:

1. *cha'do:* all males of second ascending generational level.
2. *cha'da:* all females of second ascending generational level.
3. *cha'o:* F, FB, MH, MZH, FFBS, MMBS, FMZS, MFZS, etc.
4. *cha'hu:* M, MZ, FW, FBW, FMBD, MFBD, MMZD, FFZD, etc.
5. *chiminya:* MB, WF, FZH, MMZS, MFBS, FMBS, FFZS, etc.
6. *chiminyahu:* FZ, MBW, WM, FFBD, MMBD, FMZD, MFZD, etc.
7. *chú'buo:* eB, FBSe, FFBSSe, MMBSSe, MZSe, all males of third ascending generational level, WZH, etc.
8. *chú'bua:* eZ, FBDe, FFBSDe, MMBSDe, MZDe, all females of third ascending generational level, WBW, ZHW, etc.
9. *chihawa:* yB, FBSy, FFBSSy, FMZSSy, MFZSSy, MZSy, all makes of third descending generational level, WZH, etc.
10. *chihawahu:* yZ, FBDy, FFBSDy, all females of third descending generational level, WBW, ZHW, etc.
11. *chisapo:* FZS, MBS, MMZSS, FMBSS, WB, ZH, DHF, SWF, etc.
12. *chirekwa:* FZD, MBD, MFBSD, FFZSD, W, BW, etc.
13. *chitti:* S, BS, FBSS, MZSS, FZDS, MBDS, WS, etc.
14. *chittihu:* D, BD, FBSD, MZSD, FZDD, WD, etc.
15. *chuhöri:* ZS, FZSS, MBSS, FBDS, MZDS, WBS, ZHS, DH, etc.
16. *chuhörihu:* ZD, FZSD, MBSD, FBDD, MZDD, WBD, ZHD, SW, etc.
17. *chu'do:* all males of second descending generational level.
18. *chu'da:* all females of second descending generational level.

Terms of Reference and Address for Female Ego (where they differ from those used by male ego):

1. *chirekwo:* FZS, MBS, MMZSS, FMBSS, H, ZH, HB, etc.
2. *chóbiya:* FZD, MBD, MFBSD, FFZSD, HZ, BW, etc.
3. *chitti:* S, ZS, FBDS, MZDS, FZSS, MBSS, HS, etc.
4. *chittihu:* D, ZD, FBDD, MZDD, FZSD, HD, etc.
5. *chuhöri:* BS, FBSS, MZSS, HZS, BWS, etc.
6. *chuhörihu:* BD, FBSD, MZSD, HZD, BWD, etc.
7. *chiminya:* Identical to terms used by male ego, except for spouse's parent: HF.
8. *chiminyahu:* Identical to terms used by male ego, except for spouse's parent: HM.
9. *chú'buo, chihawa:* Identical to male ego, except for sibling-in-law's spouse: HZW, BWH.
10. *chú'bua, chihawahu:* Identical to male ego, except for spouse's same-sex sibling's spouse: HBW.

1975), I shall here review only some of the more salient reasons for my insistence that the Piaroa marriage rule enjoins marriage not between cross cousins but between "affines of the same generation" (see, of course, Dumont 1953a, 1953b, 1975).

In reckoning which of his relatives one can marry, ego distinguishes two classes of relatives within each of the three medial generations, the members of which, by Piaroa interpretation, are respectively "affines" to one another. The Piaroa frequently describe the prescribed marriage category (*chirekwa/chirekwo*) by reference to the first ascending generation: they state that one marries the child of a *chiminya* and/or *chiminyahu* ("affines of first generation," a category to which, of course, MB and FZ belong as parents' siblings-in-law) or—and this is more usual—the child of father's "brother-in-law" (father's *isapo*)[12] or mother's "sister-in-law" (her *kóbiya*). MBD is, by the marriage rule, the "child of father's brother-in-law," and the relationship is thereby traced through the father and not the mother. In contrast, FZD, by the marriage rule, is the "child of mother's sister-in-law"; the relationship is traced through the mother and not the father. That this is the case follows not only from the manner in which the Piaroa express the marriage alliance but also from their notions of correct and incorrect marriages. The Piaroa consider a marriage to be fully legitimate only if the father of the bride and the father of the groom classify each other as "brother-in-law" (*chisapo*) and/or the mother of the bride and the mother of the groom classify each other as "sister-in-law" (*chóbiya*) (see J. Kaplan 1975:Table 21, p. 136). A marriage with the child of a person classified as a "parental cross-sex sibling," one whom ego's mother classifies as "brother" or whom ego's father classifies as "sister," is considered slightly incorrect unless the former prerequisite also holds. On the other hand, marriage with one who is classified as "parent's affine's child"—the child of father's *isapo* or mother's *kobiya*—but not also categorized as the child of a parent's "cross sibling" is perfectly legitimate; a man whom ego's father classifies as "brother-in-law" often is not classified as "brother" by ego's mother; a woman whom ego's mother classifies as "sister-in-law" may not be classified as "sister" by ego's father (J. Kaplan 1975:Table 21). The point of this rather tedious digression is that for the Piaroa the fact that one marries into the category to which his "cross cousin" belongs is irrelevant to the prescriptive rule. The expression of marriage in terms of "parental affines," in particular in terms of father's "brother-in-law," coincides with the manner in which the Piaroa contract most marriage exchanges: two "brothers-in-law" arrange a marriage between their children.

All Piaroa informants were emphatic on the point that all marriages must be between the categories *chirekwo/chirekwa*. Clearly, however, in a small in-marrying population like that of the Piaroa, one is usually related to one's spouse in a number of ways. If one is related to a woman as both distant "sister" and as distant "potential spouse," the latter relationship is emphasized and claimed to be "the closest." When previous terms of address are not consistent with the marriage, ego corrects his relationship terms and thereafter addresses his wife and most of her kinsmen by terms appropriate to a marriage of the prescribed category. They likewise correct their terms of address for him and his close relatives. There is one type of "incorrect" marriage that the Piaroa very occasionally allow, that between a *chiminya* ("father-in-law") and his *chuhörihu* ("daughter-in-law"). Such marriages between "affines" of adjoining generations follow a specific pattern. In all three cases in my data of such marriages, they were extremely important politically, two of which drew large *itso'de* together into one house. They were all contracted as second marriages by powerful leaders; in each case not only was the marriage between generations distinguished terminologically, but physiological generations separated husband and wife as well: the husband was at least 20 years older than his bride. It is crucial to point out that such marriages are, as with normal marriages, arranged by two *chisapomu* ("brothers-in-law"), but instead of exchanging children, one man takes as wife the daughter of the other. The Piaroa refer to the marriage as one in which a man "marries his *isapo*'s ('brother-in-law's') daughter." The Piaroa are highly ambivalent about the legitimacy of such marriages, and they rationalize their occurrence at great length. There is ambivalence as well over the degree to which terms of address are to be changed so as to coincide with the marriage: the husband and wife concerned always correct for the marriage, but for the two men involved in the marriage exchange and their close male relatives, both the terms of address used before the marriage and those appropriate to the marriage are considered to be legitimate. A certain degree of terminological confusion results, where choice of terms of address and reference become determined by social and political context.

It is no more appropriate to classify such marriages among the Piaroa as "ZD" marriage than it would be to classify their marriage into the prescriptive category of *chirekwo/chirekwa* as "bilateral cross-cousin marriage." In neither instance is the focus upon a consanguineal link; in both the marriage is reckoned through ties of affinity; in the proper marriage a man marries the child of his father's "brother-in-law" or his mother's "sister-in-law," while in the *chiminya/chuhörihu* marriage he marries the child of his "brother-in-law." It cannot be too greatly stressed that these glosses are in accordance with Piaroa description and, in the case of proper marriage, with jural rule. Moreover, unlike some of their neighbors, as with the Trio (Rivière 1969) and the Pemon (Thomas 1979), the Piaroa have no ideal or preference for marriage with the "ZD," whether she be near or distant in relationship. The Piaroa do not in fact marry into the category to which she belongs (*chuhörihu*), for they correct for proper marriage. Also, unlike marriage with "ZD" among these neighboring Carib peoples where an age difference between spouses is negligible (Rivière 1966b, 1969; Thomas 1979), as similarly is the case among South Indians who are reported to practice elder sister's daughter's marriage (see, for example, Rao 1973, Beck 1972, Good 1980), marriages among the Piaroa that cross terminological generations involve partners who are widely separated in age, unusual for normal marriages with them. A marriage that crosses both terminological and physiological generations, as with the Piaroa *chiminya/chuhörihu* marriage, is a considerably different institution from the Carib and the South Indian cases of "ZD" marriage just noted.

One of the hallmarks of Piaroa marriage is a stress on marriage between age mates, while a hallmark of their social structure is a clear distinction between generations. It is the confusion of generational levels among male affines following in the wake of a *chiminya/chuhörihu* marriage that is bothersome to the Piaroa[13]—the fusion of brother-in-law and father-in-law into one person, and brother-in-law with son-in-law. The status relationships of relative inequality and equality that should hold between different types of affines, between whom a distinction of status is based to a certain extent upon a difference in status of age, have become muddled: the father-in-law and the son-in-law have become age mates, while brothers-in-law, who should be equal, have become separated by a physiological generation.[14] The jural and political focus of a house (*itso'de*) is in theory a set of brothers-in-law,[15] reflecting a notion of proper group ordering in keeping with the horizontal structure of jural relationships that in general holds among lowland tropical forest Amerindians (J. Kaplan 1977b; also see Lizot on the Yanomami concept of *mashi,* 1977; and Kensinger on the Cashinahua, 1977). The reason that such intergenerational marriages *are* allowed among the Piaroa is that they do fulfill, as I shall discuss below, the requirement of reciprocity within the group, an endogamous one where the emphasis is upon multiple ties of affinity among male affines within it. From the viewpoint of two male affines who are engaged in establishing a series of marriage exchanges with one another within a house, the *chiminya/chuhörihu* marriage can be seen as merely one more exchange possibility through which such affinal ties can be reaffirmed and/or initiated. The possibility that the oblique marriage might be disruptive to an ongoing "cycle of exchange" (Lévi-Strauss 1969:448) is irrelevant to the structure of reciprocity within the endogamous group, as too would be a concern for direction of exchange (see concluding section).

So far I have been speaking about the prescriptive marriage rule per se, and not the Piaroa preferred marriage choice. As indicated above, the privileged union among the Piaroa is marriage within the house with as close a kinsman as possible; given the prescriptive marriage rule, this would be the MBCh/FZCh. As I have written elsewhere (1973, 1975), the Piaroa ideal of "marrying close" (marrying *tük'ü*) can be accomplished in a number of ways, by participating in an ongoing marital exchange (e.g. a man marrying the sister of his brother's wife) or by marrying a MBCh/FZCh. The latter union, though rare for demographic reasons, is the ideal marriage among the Piaroa, where ego is able to replicate in the closest manner possible the marriage of his parents (and stay home with them). As I have argued before (1973), we must not confuse the prescriptive marriage rule, which refers to category, with an ideal of marriage with a close kinsmen. While the one is obviously not mutually exclusive to the other, the logical consequences of each for group formation, and certainly for its interpretation, may vary considerably one from the other. By referring to one symbolic system or subsystem of classification at one moment, and to another the next, the Piaroa play with such logical consequences. In accord with such juggling they can stress the affinal nature of group relations—the differences within it—or its character as a group of cognates, as being comprised of beings of one kind with another. Indeed, it is only by understanding the dialectical interplay of the two—the prescriptive rule and the preference—that we can come to a satisfactory understanding of Piaroa social organization.[16]

The Piaroa can use in reference an optional lexical marker that distinguishes actual from distantly related kinsmen; the use of this marker reflects within its structure their preference for marriage with as close a kinsman as possible. The Piaroa do not distinguish between "true" and "false" relatives. Rather, if one wishes to distinguish between one's father and father's brother, the latter and more distantly related members of the category *cha'o* can be referred to as *cha'o paehkwaéwa*, while no lexical marker is used for ego's father; he is merely referred to as *cha'o*. *Paehkwaéwa* means "one over the other," or "next to each other," like leaves on a thatched house or building blocks. The expression *wüü paehkwaéwa* refers to sexual intercourse, literally "sex on top of one another." Thus *paehkwaéwa* is a particularly apt metaphor signifying kinship linkage, and one that is appropriate to a culture whose members talk of such ties not as being based on a concept of common substance but as marriage links. In reckoning close or distant kinship to another, a Piaroa usually discusses not a blood tie the two may share because of descent from a common ancestor but the number of marital links that separate his kinsman from himself. Through the use of the same marker, *paehkwaéwa*, siblings can be distinguished from classificatory siblings, children from classificatory children, and so on. However, no distinction can be made between parents' cross-sex siblings (or their siblings-in-law) and parents-in-law, between a man's male cross cousins and his brothers-in-law, and so forth. None of the following denotata can be used with the lexical marker: MBS, FZS, WB, or ZH; each is always *chisapo* and never *chisapo paehkwaéwa.* The brother of a man's brother-in-law can be referred to as such.

Several comments are in order about the distinctions the Piaroa can make through such lexical markers. It is not clear from their use whether or not the foci of what are affinal categories by prescriptive rule are in this instance consanguines or affines; the meaning of the unmarked term remains ambiguous.[17] MB and FZ are after all respectively father's and mother's sibling-in-law. There is evidence that the Piaroa think of such relatives as both kin and affine, and whether or not the MB is considered as "kin" or "affine" is not really the question here. While the Piaroa do hesitate over classifying an actual cross cousin as a consanguine, they do view MB, FZ, ZCh (m. speaker) and BCh (f. speaker) as close kinsmen, indeed, as closer relatives than grandparents. A young man may well emphasize the kinship aspect of his relationship with his mother's brother; to verbalize his affection for and trust in him as such, he may address the elder relative as *cha'o,* the category to which his father belongs. However, if the young man should marry the daughter of his mother's brother, from that moment on he would address him as *chiminya* ("father-in-law"), the category in which the mother's brother is properly placed. He would be set firmly in mind as "affine," and the political aspect of the relationship—the mother's brother as brother-in-law of his father— which might be ignored and held inert before the marriage, would be activated with it.

There is no reason why the terms of a relationship system cannot at one and the same time be used to refer to biological family relationships and to social categories. Nevertheless, having said this, it makes little sense when discussing the manner in which the Piaroa use their terminology for the classification of all but the most immediate kinsmen to talk of such use as genealogical extensions from "primary" kinsmen. Although a Piaroa can give the "correct" category for any of the denotata comprising the genealogical chains presented in Chart 2, it does not mean that a particular relative so related to ego would be so classified. Alter is related to ego through a multiple of kinship ties, and the Piaroa man, for instance, tends to trace relationships past first cousin range through a number of different relatives, and often as not through marital and in-law links (as with WFBW or W"B"). Through inconsistent reckoning he is able to establish himself as affine—"father-in-law," "brother-in-law," or "son-in-law"—to most men within his territory, and can thereby potentially set into motion marriage negotiations for their children or siblings, both with respect to his own marriage and to the marriages of all other members of his family (J. Kaplan 1975). The precise genealogical tie, to the extent it is even known or remembered, is not only overridden but also often irrelevant to the task of structuring marital and political alliances within the territory.[18]

The obvious point is that relationship terms are polysemic, but not necessarily in the sense Scheffler and Lounsbury see them to be. Each term has multiple referents, and its meaning depends upon which referents are being stressed for symbolic orientation in any given instance. Witherspoon (1977:94) notes that for Navaho terms there exists an exchange of meaning among all referents, and the meaning of any particular term can be viewed as a set of semantic elements analogically linked together.[19] I would argue that the same holds true for Piaroa terms: the significance of their cosmological referents informs the affinal content or biological familial meaning of a term, investing it with political, sacred, and metaphysical significance. The affine relationship as it existed in mythological times entailed unmitigated danger, acted out in power battles over elements of the universe and expressed through pointed nonreciprocity. As such, it is not a model of exchange to be copied in social life, but its content nevertheless provides a language that the Piaroa use for the discussion and understanding of both kin and affine relationships in their social world.

Dualisms in Mythic Time:
Mythic Space and Mythic Affines

The supreme god of the Piaroa, Ofo Da'ae, Tapir/Anaconda—a chimerical being who still today dwells in his home beneath the earth—was genitor to two different sets of beings who are classified respectively with the domains of land and water. These two classes of beings, those of land and those of water, are related once again in mythic time through the affinal relationship of the masters of these domains: Wahari, the Tapir son-in-law, and Kuemoi, the Anaconda father-in-law. Much of mythic time was spent in the playing out of power battles between these two mythic beings for the control of the various domains of the universe and of all the elements of which they are comprised.

Wahari is the master (*ruwang*) of the land, the mountains, the rocks, and the sky. He is also called *Pihae Ruwang,* "Master of the World," for most of the earth's features are his creations. He also was the creator of the Piaroa. To acquire the power and the knowledge for the task, he was taught beneath the earth with the hallucinogens of Ofo Da'ae, his grandfather, Anaconda/Tapir supreme deity. During mythic time Wahari was *Ruwang Itso'de* ("Master of the House") of the jungle animals, and he gave both form and knowledge to them. Although master of land, Wahari was a fisherman: he fished from land, from the rocks of the rapids he had created, and he ate from the domain that was not his, from the aquatic domain.

Kuemoi, Wahari's father-in-law, is fire and was born in water: he is the master of water. His mother is Isisiri, the dangerous "Mistress of the Lake," and his father is Ofo Da'ae, the Tapir/Anaconda (see Figure 1 depicting the kinship relationship between Kuemoi and Wahari). The crocodile, the cayman, and large fish are Kuemoi's family (*awáruwa*), as are the opossum and the vulture, the former an omen of death for, and the latter an eater of, jungle animals. Kuemoi is also grandfather of sleep and the master of darkness: he dwells in a house called "Night" (*Yo'dorei*). It was there that he created all the poisonous snakes of the world and the jaguar.[20] In brief, all dangerous and biting animals and all things poisonous in this world, for beings classified as "jungle animals" (*dea ruwa*, a category to which the Piaroa belong),[21] are his creations and classed together as "Kuemoi's thoughts." He poisoned all large rock formations and the streams; he is grandfather of boils, the father of biting and poisonous fish, and the creator of poisonous toads; the bat is his spirit (*a'kwáruwang*). He himself is anaconda, and he transforms himself at will into jaguar. Kuemoi is *Kwaewae Ruwang*, "Master of all edible fruits and vegetables in the world," their first owner, and father of the garden plants: maize, squash, yuca, and guamo.[22] And, as Wahari is a fisherman, Kuemoi is a hunter: he also eats from the domain that is not his and brings death to its beings.

Both Wahari and Kuemoi are great sorcerers, and as the respective masters of land and water, of day and night, and as the reincarnations of Tapir and Anaconda, they are in their distinctiveness a fractionalization of their primordial genitor,[23] the Tapir/Anaconda (Ofo Da'ae); as such they are earthly embodiments of the two opposing aspects of his nature, the united force of which remains beneath the earth. Wahari takes Kuemoi's daughter, Maize (*Kwaewáenyamu*) as wife, and through the intermarriage of these two aspects (see Figure 1), opposed through their association with distinct domains of the universe—their origin within

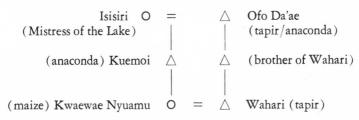

FIGURE 1. KINSHIP RELATIONSHIP BETWEEN KUEMOI AND WAHARI. (See n. 23 for an explanation of why Wahari's genealogical father is also his brother.)

earth[24] and within water—social relations on earth and in mythic times came into existence. But the exchange relationship so established was highly precarious, for it was not reciprocated. Kuemoi, the father-in-law, received nothing, not even a grandchild, in return for the daughter he gave, nor for his gifts to his son-in-law of cooking fire, cultivation, and cultural artifacts. Thus Kuemoi spent most of mythic time trying to eat his son-in-law and other creatures of the jungle (*dea ruwa*) who were of the family of Wahari. In Kuemoi's attempts to turn the flesh of Wahari into meat to be eaten, it was food he saw as due to him on a number of accounts. If Wahari had reciprocated the gifts received from Kuemoi, he could have canceled out his own status as a being totally different from Kuemoi and, as such, his father-in-law's food.

The mythic message is a clear one, and the Piaroa understand it this way: the relationship between wife giver and wife receiver is an inherently dangerous one, since in-laws are strangers who may eat you. The safe exchange relationship is the reciprocated one, and it is only through such reciprocity that the peril intrinsic to the in-law relationship can be averted. In recognizing that society can only exist through the interaction of differences, of beings unlike one another, and in understanding that such mingling is very hazardous, the Piaroa expend a good deal of social structural energy in masking the principle of difference toward the end of achieving safety. But here caution is in order, for this observation by no means holds for all Piaroa behavior: within the communal house (*itso'de*) certain affinal relationships are veiled, while in relationships between houses within a political territory they are stressed.

Politics, Affinity, and Mythic Classification

In keeping with the view that society can come into being only through the coming together of unlike beings, the jural relationship in Piaroa society is with in-laws, and political relationships within the territory are acted out in the idiom of affinity. One competes politically with one in an affine category but never with one classed as a "father," "brother," or "son." In political battles one's opponent—a *chisapo* ("brother-in-law"), *chiminya* ("father-in-law"), or *chuhöri* ("son-in-law")—is given the attributes of Kuemoi: his power is power out of control, he is a user of too powerful hallucinogens, he transforms himself into anaconda, becoming Kuemoi in so doing. He is a sorcerer who sends fatal disease, becoming in this action a cannibal, for disease is always considered by the Piaroa to be a process of being eaten.[25]

We see, then, that the Piaroa use mythic categories—where "I" am Wahari, power in control, and "you" are Kuemoi, power out of control—to structure political battles between houses within a territory. Such use of mythic classification does not imply an ordering that is metaphoric in nature but, rather, speaks of specific metaphysical states: in one's drugged state under the influence of hallucinogens, one sees oneself as the beautiful Wahari and one's opponent as Kuemoi. The use of such categories emphasizing essential differences of being as exist between political competitors structures relationships between those classed as affines of different local groups, and their use relates to the hierarchical ordering of shamans within the political territory. We see that the classification of mythic beings, where distinctions of essential difference are made through distinctions of separate origin, are used for talking about and understanding aspects of social distance, of the distinction between kin and affine. Hence the mythic in-law relationship, where the affine can be both anaconda and cannibal, informs the postmythic in-law relationship, thereby actively structuring experiences in the social world.

Such language, taken from the classification of the elements within the cosmos, must not be used to structure relationships within the house (*itso'de*): one must never stress the essential difference to oneself of affines living with one. If political competition within the house becomes serious, the house immediately fissions. Thus it is the *potential* affine who is Kuemoi the cannibal, that is, one with whom no marriage exchange has been contracted or with whom one's ties of actual affinity are weak. The giver of disease, the cannibal, is one with whom one's relationship is unfulfilled reciprocity or, indeed, negative reciprocity. The relationship between actual affines who live together within the *itso'de* must not be modeled upon the relationship that held in mythic society between the two archetypical affines who were enemies of one another, Kuemoi, the guardian of water, and Wahari, the guardian of land. Safety with the actual affine is partially achieved through proper reciprocity, and it is for this reason that the marriage exchange among the Piaroa is firmly based upon a principle of reciprocity carried out through the serial and multiple repetition of affinal ties.

The Endogamous Marriage and Multiple Affinity

For the Piaroa, society itself comes into being through the dangerous association of dissimilar elements: both mythological history and cosmological ordering give this message. It is this understanding about the nature of things in the social world that the Piaroa do their best to ignore in their relationships within the *itso'de*. If the Piaroa were to use the mythic classification of the domains of land and water as the language for ordering their marriage exchange—as is the case in my earlier example of Northwest Amazon Indians—or, indeed, the distinction of "above" and "below" underlying their own moiety system, they would also be making the overt statement that actual affines are creatures who are essentially different from one another and as such liable to devour each other. Thus, to ignore such divisions is one method of overriding the dangers of difference, of masking the very elements of which society consists, or, if you will, masking any dualism of which it must be comprised. The Piaroa are not willing to accept the implications forthcoming from the assumption of essential difference, and it is through their very strong ideal of endogamous marriage that they manage to understate the necessity of essential difference to social life within the local group. The most obvious device they use in ignoring difference toward the end of safety is marriage with a close or at least well-known relative within the house. This ideal of local group endogamy, so strongly stressed by most Guianese Amerindians, is but the other side of the coin of their equally emphasized fear of the stranger (see, for example, Rivière 1969, Henley 1979).

As noted in the section on *chawáruwang* ("my kinsman") and close *chawáruwang* marriage, close consanguines who do not marry into one's close kindred of birth are replaced by actual affines. It is through the application of a system of teknonymy that affines are transformed into close kinsmen, and all marriages thereby become endogamous ones; the empirical world is transformed to make it agree with the ideal (J. Kaplan 1972, 1975). The teknonym declares the father-in-law a consanguine to his son-in-law through their relationship to one another as traced through the younger man's child: they become respectively in relationship "grandfather of my child" and "father of my grandchild," while a spouse becomes related as "parent of my child."[26] The Piaroa themselves interpret their use of the teknonym system within the house as being a symbolic statement on its unity as a group of consanguines. Through it they are able to legitimize on a kinship basis, so as to make it congruent with their ideal model of endogamous marriage, any group composition founded upon a specific set of marriage exchanges, no matter how fleeting these alliances may be. Thus the larger houses among the Piaroa, within which dwell almost all of each member's conjugal kindred, frequently do at least on an ideological level approximate the ideal. The great fiction is, of course, that society as the isolated endogamous group that replicates itself through time (J. Kaplan 1972, 1973, 1975) becomes comprised of the association of "like" items, consanguines who are safe to one another, and not of dangerous "unlike" affines. Here we have with the Piaroa an interesting dialectic between society as an ideal world of endogamous kindreds and society that includes the wider whole: potential affines and political opponents.

The teknonym system, however, only proclaims kinship among same-sex affines when of different generations; in keeping with the horizontal structuring of jural relationships within the house, a system based upon sets of same-generational affines, it still retains within it the same generational in-law relationship. "Brother-in-law" of male ego and "sister-in-law" of female ego become through the use of teknonyms "fathers-in-law" and "mothers-in-law" of ego's child.[27] The teknonym system thereby retains within it the crucial "marriage alliance" by focusing upon the marriage of ego's children rather than upon ego's own marriage, which was dealt with by the primary relationship terminology.[28] Because it retains within it elements of affinity, the teknonym system alone in its use as a classificatory device is not sufficient to the task of maintaining safety among affines of one's own generation: multiple marriage exchanges among such affines do make their relationship a safe one.

The endogamous marriage not only implies safety both by keeping everyone home with close relatives and by making fuzzy the distinction between "kin" and "affine" but also is the marriage reciprocated, for through it previous affinal ties within the group are reaffirmed. In Piaroa theory the more marriage exchanges enacted between two affines, the safer the relationship and the more unified the group as a unit of cognates. It is a type of marriage exchange found throughout the Guianas (Rivière 1969, Henley 1979, Arvelo-Jimenez 1971), where the viability of the affinal relationship, the political alliance, and the unity of the group are correlated with the number of marital exchanges established among men within the local group. In making such exchanges, all unmarried, dependent relatives of the men involved are fair game. A man may arrange the marriages of younger brothers and sisters, his daughters and sons, and young widowed relatives who dwell with him. In the process kinship ties are often re-reckoned, and as a result the marriages within the house become highly complex.

In theory, the reduplication of any affinal tie within the group—as when a set of brothers marries a set of sisters, a common Guianese practice—is a marriage both replicated and reciprocated, from the point of view of the group as a whole. Within an endogamous group a marriage tie does not need to be directly reciprocated as in brother/sister exchange: any marriage within the group is at least indirectly reciprocated, as in indirect exchange, insofar as every man within the group ideally receives a wife from within it. In one sense, through endogamous marriage, the very notion of marriage exchange, and not only its dangers, has been erased. Ironically, it is through the marriage exchange, especially the one re-enacted time and time again within the house, the gift continually returned, that differences are annulled and safety achieved. If one views reciprocity, as does Lévi-Strauss (1969:84), as the most immediate means of integrating the opposition between the self and others, the Piaroa have through the endogamous marriage, where self and others are not only unified but become of a kind with one another, carried this principle to its logical extreme.

In that society itself for the Piaroa is equated with affinity, the coming together of unlike items (affines), endogamy becomes a philosophy of society for them, a "half-way point" that overcomes to a certain extent the dangers of the social state and the dictum that says that society can only exist by the coming together of different and dangerous elements (J. Kaplan 1981). In short, endogamy as an ideal expresses the Piaroa fear of the social state, thereby becoming a principle underlying a society suspicious of its own social nature.

Conclusion: Elementary Structures of Reciprocity

I think it possible to say in general of tropical forest Amerindians that their notions of proper and improper reciprocity entail a philosophy of the relationship of things that are the same and the relationship of things that are different;[29] from this perspective we can come to a clearer understanding of the proliferation of dualisms within these cultures, no matter what their content or how they are played out. We have among the Piaroa the cosmological expression of the conundrum, which I think very general to lowland South American Indians and of considerable importance to an understanding of certain ambiguities in the ordering of their social universes, that states the necessity of differences to social life in a world where the coming together of differences implies danger, while the conjoining of like elements implies safety and nonsociety, or antilife.

Both the Bororo and the Gê avert the dangers of social differentiation through elaborate ritual transactions between moieties, through which "ritual roads" are established between name sets (see, for example, J. Crocker 1979, da Matta 1979, Lave 1979, Melatti 1979). Through the ritual inversions common to these systems, where "I" becomes "other" and "other" becomes "I"—where the chief of one moiety is chosen from the other or the ritual representation of the totems of one moiety is acted out by the other—identity and difference between social categories become as blurred as through the endogamous marriage of the Guianas. In each of these societies the principles of exchange are to some extent principles of metaphysics, where the emphasis is not so much upon the attainment of a particular type of group formation but upon the achievement of proper relationships among beings of categories that are viewed as significantly different, but necessary to one another for society to exist. Whether these distinctions relate to the classificatory logic of names, to symbolic attributes of male and female, or as in the classic case, to "kin" and "affines" or to the "marriageable" and the "unmarriageable" as implied by a prescriptive marriage rule, in each example such contrasts are employed in the elaboration of exchanges that are clearly "elementary" in form. As J. Crocker comments (1979:296-97) on the elaboration of structures among the Gê and the Bororo, categories founded on other sources of distinctions than those forthcoming from a prescriptive marriage rule "can possess precisely the same inexorable implications for social interaction which must express a logical model as the most rigidly prescriptive 'elementary structure.'" Instead of "elementary systems of kinship and marriage," we can speak more generally of "elementary structures of reciprocity," and thereby treat both Guianese Amerindian societies and those of central Brazil as so many examples of one basic structure.

The implications for Amerindian social life of the elementary structure of reciprocity ordering it is that society itself becomes a logic for maintaining a balance, a proper relationship among items in the universe that allows society to perpetuate itself. Reciprocity itself can thus be equally viewed as a particular mode of self-perpetuation. Finally, it can be added that for the individual the acting out of life as a social person within such a society is acting as well on a philosophical plane. Among Amerindians of lowland South America, society as social rules—or as social structure—cannot be clearly distinguished from cosmological rules and cosmological structure. For them the cosmological and the social form one multidimensional system, and whereas no one ordering can possibly unravel such a system, each aspect of it tends to give meaning to the next.

NOTES

1. See, for example, Dumont (1953a, 1953b). Also see Lounsbury (1968: n. 134) and Scheffler (1971, 1977), but see comments below.

2. Lounsbury (1968:n. 134) remarks that Dravidian-type systems are not generally "founded" on clan or moiety reckoning, and Scheffler (1971:233-34) comments that moieties or sections are not invariant structural features of societies with Dravidian-type kinship terminologies. Although Scheffler is quite correct in his insistence that such terminologies are not dependent upon dual organizations, he is incorrect in assuming that they are inconsistent with one. His reason is that male and female ego classify their joint offspring by the same term, but if a principle of patri- or matrifiliation or unilineality were *superimposed* upon the system, it would work perfectly well within the context of a moiety system; see, for example, below on the Piaroa mortuary clans, where husband and wife are separated after death, and siblings remain together. As Scheffler himself insists, the terminology is a flexible one with respect to jural rule. Needham (1973) makes the same point.

3. My research among the Piaroa throughout 1968 was financed by a grant from NIMH given to my husband, M. R. Kaplan. For six months of fieldwork with the Piaroa in 1977, my research was financed by several sources: SSRC grant HR5028; Central Research Funds of the University of London; London School of Economics Research Funds; Institute of Latin American Studies travel funds. The SSRC has also given me a research grant (HRP 6753) that has allowed me to rewrite and update this article. I warmly thank all of these institutions for their aid.

4. In 1968 the Piaroa political organization was intact; the migrations down to concentrated settlements along the lower reaches of their rivers began, with government encouragement, in the early 1970s.

5. Much of Piaroa ritual and taboo structure can be understood as an integral part of such a view of society. All ritual, such as the chants protecting against the diseases of the animals, eating ritual and food taboos, and hunting magic, is an attempt to maintain such balance through the prevention of the dangers to humans resulting from the interaction of categories—plants and animals, man and animals, kin and affines, humans and gods—that differ "essentially" one from the next.

6. In previous publications I have written *chawáruwang* as *chuwaruwang* (1972, 1973, 1975). After detailed work with dialect differences in 1977, I have decided that *chawáruwang* is preferable. As with most Piaroa nouns, *chawáruwang* is a possessed noun:

tü chawáruwang—my kinsman
uku kwawáruwang—your kinsman
chu awáruwang—his kinsman
yahu kwawáruwang—her kinsman
uhutü tawáruwang—our kinsman
ukutu kwawáruwang—your kinsman
hitu tawáruwang—their kinsman

There are three pronouns signifying "they": *nitu*, signifying men and women; *naetu*, signifying all women; and *unmaetu*, signifying all men. The suffix *ae* pluralizes *chawáruwang: chawáruwae.*

7. See Henley (1979:152-3) on the Panare term *Piyaka* ("another of the same kind"), which is very similar in use to the neighboring Piaroa's term *chawáruwang.* Its meaning is dependent upon context; it can refer to all who live within the same settlement as ego, or to primary kin. It is used in opposition to *tungonan*, "those of a different kind," e.g. those of other settlements or in-laws and potential spouses.

8. W. Crocker (1977) notes that the Eastern Timbira say that, over time and through physical contact, a husband and wife become more closely related in blood composition than either with their respective siblings. Many of the food restrictions and couvade practices of Amerindians, where parents must not eat certain foods for fear of harming the child, are explained by a belief in the physical and not necessarily jural or spiritual unity of those who share a common residence.

9. It should be stressed that in lowland South America corporate group structure is rarely based upon the ownership of scarce resources such as land or domesticated animals: the "corporate group" has no perpetuity over time as a property-holding unit. See J. Kaplan (1977a) and J. Crocker (1977).

10. See J. Kaplan (1972, 1975) on the Piaroa teknonym system, a relationship system that converts all affines, save the sibling-in-law, within the house into "kin."

11. Keesing (1972) also stresses the importance of context to the meaning of relationship terms, and makes the observation, with which I agree, that because formal analysis does not take into account such context, it is not speaking of "emic" meaning.

12. *Isapo* is third-person singular. All kinship terms are possessed nouns; the terms listed in Charts 1 and 2 are for first-person singular. The declension of *cha'o* ("my father") is as follows:

tü cha'o—my father
uku kuwae'o—your father
chu hae'o—his father
yahu kae'o—her father
uhutu tae'o—our father
ukutu kuwae'o—your father
hirü tae'o—their father

13. As various authors have noted (Rao 1973; Rivière 1966a, 1966b, 1969; Good 1980), "ZD" marriage and cross-cousin marriage are often enough associated, and with no terminological confusion; indeed, the former can well be congruent with a "symmetric prescriptive marriage rule."

14. Among the Trio (Rivière 1969) and the Pemon (Thomas 1979), where age difference between spouses is negligible, the "ZD" marriage is viewed with favor; with it, one sheds a "father-in-law" (WF = ZH), or at least the asymmetry of the father-in-law/son-in-law relationship that age difference between affines imply.

15. Such a focus is reflected in the teknonym system. Through its use ego converts affines of first ascending and first descending generations into kin; in contrast, by applying a teknonym to his sibling-in-law, ego stresses the affinal nature of his relationship to him (see J. Kaplan 1972 and the discussion of teknonyms below).

16. It might be added that far too little attention has been paid to the structural consequences of specific preferences associated with particular prescriptive rules (see J. Kaplan 1977a). Scheffler in his discussion of variation in preferences associated with Dravidian-type systems (1971:237) in effect dismisses the problem: having noted such variation, he states that it in itself "suggests that the presence of Dravidian-type systems of kin classification is not in the least dependent on the presence of any sort of marriage rule. . . . " What he is doing is confusing the rule with the preference. Needham (1973) states clearly that we must distinguish among terminological structure, prescriptive rule (jural rule), and behavior. It is equally clear that

we must differentiate between different types of jural rules (prescriptive and preferences), and then understand both the interplay among them and the interplay between jural rules and behavior (also see Keesing 1972).

17. Certainly it is the case that in many kinship systems consanguinity and affinity imply one another (see Dumont 1961:6, where he says for South Indians that kinship equals consanguinity plus affinity); thus one can use as base either to produce the other. See Wordick's reanalysis (1975) of the Siriono kinship terminology. Contrary to Scheffler's insistence that the use of lexical markers as described above for the Piaroa is proof of a structural "primary meaning" (Scheffler 1971:236; 1972:314-15), their use can just as well provide evidence that individuals think both ways; mother's brother is also father's affine. If one wishes to view the classification of distant relatives as "an extension out" from close relatives, the Piaroa "extend out" the terms *chisapo* and *chiminya* because the distant relatives are "affine-like," not because they are MBCh-like or MB-like.

18. As I have already noted, affine links are traced not through cross-sex sibling links but through same-sex affines; the former can just as well be seen, then, as epiphenomenal to the latter.

19. Keesing (1972:18) talks in a similar manner by suggesting that we understand the relations among kinship terms as having a "family resemblance . . . such that the relational pattern among features is preserved through a series of topological transformations."

20. Neither jaguar nor poisonous snakes are classified by the Piaroa as *dea ruwa,* or "jungle animals," the category to which the Piaroa themselves belong and a label of self-denomination used by them.

21. In other words, Kuemoi created all creatures and things dangerous to *dea ruwa,* creatures over whom Wahari is master.

22. It would be interesting to compare the inversions of this system—where Wahari and Kuemoi eat from domains that are not their own—with the inversions so characteristic of Gê and Bororo moiety systems (see especially Lave 1979, J. Crocker 1979).

23. Wahari is both son and grandson to the tapir/anaconda. Wahari's elder brother, Buok'a, was born within the crystal womb box of Ofo Da'ae and later withdrew his younger brother from his right eye with the help of Ofo Da'ae (see Figure 1).

24. Wahari grew up and, as already noted, was given knowledge within the earth in the land of Ofo Da'ae.

25. When a Piaroa is ill, the modern-day, as opposed to the mythic, master of animals is within him eating, as is the grandfather of the disease. Sorcery also is a process of eating: within the quartz stone the sorcerer shoots into the body of an enemy is an animal or an insect that eats the victim.

26. The teknonyms are always used in address for individuals within the house who have children, whether they are actual or classificatory affines.

27. Also in keeping with the emphasis upon the affinal nature of jural relationships of those in the same generation within the house, individuals related to male ego at WZH, who by the relationship terminology should be

within the category of "brother," are consistently addressed, if not an actual brother of ego's, as "brother-in-law." All other relationships are made congruent with the marriage (see J. Kaplan 1975). I wish to thank Jonathan Parry for discussing with me the analysis of the structure of affinity within Piaroa communal houses.

28. See J. Kaplan (1972, 1975).

29. See J. Kaplan (1981) for a similar discussion of "elementary structures of reciprocity."

7

Vaupés Marriage Practices

JEAN E. JACKSON

Introduction

This paper discusses some of the characteristics of the marriage system of the Vaupés, a region in northwestern Amazonia. Data are from informant statements and a sample of 684 marriages. Specifically examined are: (1) direct exchange, (2) kinship between spouses, (3) language group exogamy, and (4) distance between spouses' local descent groups.

The relationship between marriage principles as verbalized by Vaupés natives (here called Tukanoans) and the marriage patterns themselves as revealed by the sample raises an important theoretical question: to what degree are the latter "objective," and what is the significance of the lack of fit between the two kinds of data on Vaupés marriage? Another question concerns the kinds of decision-making criteria used in marriage-related behavior.

Marriage can be seen as purposive behavior which is ultimately comprehensible and predictable to the degree that marriage choices are based on shared cultural (rather than idiosyncratic) criteria, that the circumstances in which individual marriages occur are similar to one another, and that this information is available to the investigator. At present, criteria relating to the participants' goals and their assessment of the particular situations in which individual marriages occur fall into three kinds of areas: (1) environmental constraints, (2) social structural principles, and (3) a set of shared decision-making rules for ordering and choosing among the alternatives presented by (1) and (2) for a particular marriage.

Ethnographic Background

The Vaupés territory in this paper refers to the Colombian sector of the central Northwest Amazon, in particular to the Papurí drainage

and upper Tiquié regions where most of the data were gathered (see
Figure 1).[1] The Vaupés and adjacent Brazilian territory comprise the
central Northwest Amazon, a region characterized by multilingualism,[2]
linguistic exogamy, and the use of Tukano as a lingua franca. The
intermarrying units of the Vaupés, henceforth referred to as language
groups,[3] are patrilineal descent units. Each unit is identified with a distinct
language (its father-language; see Sorensen 1967). At least 16 of these
are found in the central Northwest Amazon, and they are the focal
point for this discussion.

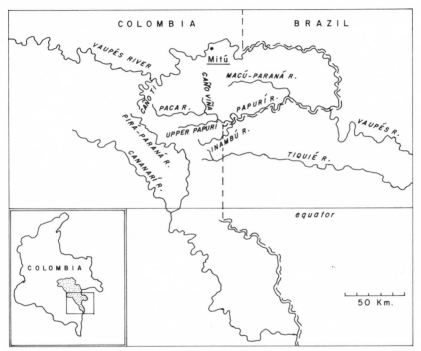

FIGURE 1. THE EASTERN COLOMBIAN VAUPÉS.

Population density has been given for the Comisaría del Vaupés
at roughly .2 inhabitants per square kilometer, including non-Indians
(*Atlas de Colombia* 1969:xiii). Sorensen gives an estimate of about
10,000 inhabitants for the central Northwest Amazon, and compares
its size to that of New England (1967:670).

The Tukanoans considered in this discussion are sedentary swidden
horticulturalists, living near streams and rivers in a lowland tropical
forest environment. The women grow manioc and other crops in fields
cleared by the men, who hunt and fish. Multifamily longhouses are the
traditional settlement type, and are separated from each other by two

to ten hours' canoe travel. Residence is patrilocal, and at present four to eight nuclear families inhabit a longhouse.

Vaupés social structure is segmentary, following the rule of patrilineal descent at all levels. Its units, in ascending order of inclusion, are the local descent group, the sib, the language group, and the (at present poorly understood) phratric unit (see Chart 1).

The language group has usually been referred to as a "tribe" in the literature on the Vaupés. However, no single generally accepted definition of "tribe" exists. Those definitions most frequently offered list such traits as (1) tribal territory; (2) political, ceremonial, or warrior roles as tribesmen; (3) more intratribal as opposed to intertribal interaction; (4) some proportion of marriages occurring within the tribal unit; or (5) a certain number of significant cultural differences separating neighboring tribes. None of the definitions utilizing this list of traits permits calling the language group a "tribe," and it is misleading to continue this usage merely because of the language and various other differences separating one language group from another.

At the present time the language group is psychologically the most important identity group, at least for the inhabitants of the Papurí drainage. The members of a given language group observe a rule of exogamy, terminologically distinguish at this level agnates from other kinsmen (however, agnatic terms are sometimes extended to the more inclusive phratric level), and identify with co-members as "brother-people." Distinguishing features that serve as significant symbols of identity are: (1) the language and name themselves, (2) separate founding ancestors and distinct roles in the basic Tukanoan origin myth cycle, (3) the right to ancestral power through the use of certain ritualistic property such as sacred chants, (4) the right to manufacture and use certain kinds of ritual property, and (5) a traditional association with certain ceremonial or near-ceremonial objects. The difference between points (4) and (5) is that the latter type of object may be manufactured or owned by Tukanoans not of the language group associated with it. Although all these traits symbolize membership in different language groups, at present language is the most important of these (see Jackson 1972, 1974, 1983).

Regardless of the specific language group to which a particular individual belongs, all Tukanoans share a homogeneous culture. Language and the other differences between language groups in themselves do not *ipso facto* indicate that cultural differences separate the language groups. These differences, though highly significant, are perhaps best seen as facilitating interaction within a single social and cultural system, in much the same way that unmistakably different uniforms aid the interaction of a football game.

CHART 1. VAUPÉS SOCIAL STRUCTURE

	1														2		3
I	1														2		3
II	Bará											Tukano	Yurutí	etc.	Tuyuka	etc.	etc.
III	*waí mabá*				waíñakoroa			wamútañara			etc.	(approximately 30 sibs)	etc.				
IV	A (*bará yóara*)	B	C	etc.	M	N	O	X	Y	Z	etc.						

I. Phratry   An unnamed unit composed of various language groups. Members of a phratry do not intermarry and describe co-members as siblings.

II. Language Group   What is commonly referred to as "tribe." Membership is determined by a rule of patrilineal descent, and members share a father-language.

III. Sib   Named groups occupying one or more longhouses along a stretch of river. Sibs are ranked, and membership is determined by patrilineal descent.

IV. Local Descent Group   Co-agnates who are one another's closest agnatic kin who share the same settlement (usually a longhouse). Can be coterminous with the sib.

Explanation of capital letters in Level IV:

     These represent current locations of local descent groups who are known by their settlement name. The sib name is permanent, but the settlement name changes when the local descent group moves its longhouse site. For example, A = *pûmanaka buro* in 1970.

Vaupés language groups do not occupy discrete territories in any exclusive sense (see Figure 2). However, the distribution of local descent groups over the landscape is neither random nor totally integrated with regard to language group affiliation. Specific language groups are clearly represented by local descent groups in some and not other regions of the Vaupés. Nor are language groups corporate groups in any sense. Largely owing to the effects of the rule of language group exogamy, the majority of interaction situations take place between Tukanoans of more than one language group. Membership in these groups is permanent and public; if anything is known about a given Tukanoan, it will most likely be this aspect of his or her social identity.

Vaupés Marriage

A brief introduction to the more important marriage principles operating in the Vaupés will be given here, followed by consideration of a few of the more interesting characteristics of the system. For a more comprehensive discussion, the reader is referred to the previously noted ethnographic material.

All of the following characteristics of the Vaupés marriage system are to some extent observable in behavior related to marriage and, more important, can be verbalized as norms by Tukanoans. In this sense we can call them "principles." Tukanoans have a prescriptive marriage system: the category of marriageable people of any given ego is covered by a single kinship term (see Jackson 1977 for a discussion of Bará terminology as it relates to marriage). The category designating potential spouses includes ego's bilateral cross cousin. The kinship terminologies of several Vaupés languages are Dravidian in structure.

Another principle is that of symmetrical, or direct, exchange. This rule applies to all marriages. In its ideal form a man obtains a wife by exchanging his real sister for another's man's real sister. Although this ideal is seldom completely realized in practice, many marriages are exchange marriages, and any marriage involving only one couple is seen as incomplete, for the wife-giving local descent group considers itself owed a woman until given one in return.

A third principle is a stated preference for marriage with a genealogically close kinsman or kinswoman.[4] Thus marriage is prescriptive in that one must marry a kinsman in one's own generation who is neither a sibling nor a parallel cousin (in Bará, and presumably other Vaupés languages, everyone who is not a Makú or non-Indian is a kinsman). Marriage is preferential in that a Tukanoan ideally marries a close kinsman in this category.

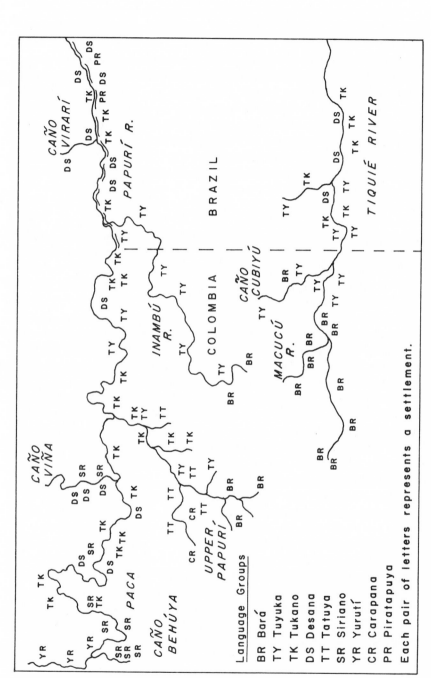

FIGURE 2. LANGUAGE GROUP DISTRIBUTION OF SETTLEMENTS OF A SECTION OF THE VAUPÉS.

Another principle is residential exogamy. The few exceptions to this at present occur in towns founded by Catholic missionaries who brought members of more than one language group to live in the same place, a revolutionary change in Vaupés social and spatial arrangements.

A fifth principle is the previously mentioned one of language group exogamy. This is the one which is the most perplexing to non-Tukanoans—missionaries, local Colombians, and anthropologists alike. Despite the far-sweeping changes brought about by acculturation, linguistic exogamy is still very much the rule (excluding Cubeos), in terms of both marriage patterns (this was the case for over 1,000 marriages recorded in the Papurí-Tiquié region, with one questionable exception) and conclusions drawn from numerous discussions with many informants.

A sixth and final principle is that of alliance. This simply means that two affinally related local descent groups consider it advantageous to continue to exchange women over time and to some extent can be seen to achieve a proportion of marriages that conform to this goal.

It is important to note that "principle" is intentionally a loosely defined word. The degree to which the kind of behavior resulting from a given principle actually occurs is at this stage a goal of investigation rather than a known fact. Although these marriage principles are consciously stated norms agreed upon by almost all Tukanoans, they are not rigidly enforced rules in any way. In the first place, they are not highly predictive of marriage patterns. Nor can we even say that these principles strongly influence all decisions about marriage and are simply less visible in the resulting patterns because of the monkey wrenches thrown into the system by demographic and similar constraints. The degree to which these principles influence decision making about marriage is complicated, variable, and at present quite inconclusive. Nonetheless they are "principles" in that for Tukanoans they represent the culturally approved patterns of marriage. In general (but not necessarily in every case), they represent the ideal type of marriage from the viewpoint of any given Tukanoan.

A final point should be made about the way in which marriage is conceived of in this paper. Marriage is to be viewed not only as a relationship between two people but also as a kind of movement between two local descent groups—of people, goods, and intangible commodities such as prestige. It is an extremely important activity, influencing almost every sphere of life. Tukanoans spend much time and energy either actively engaged in marital arrangements or observing and discussing the activities of others. Furthermore, marriage is to be seen not as only one or several events but as an ongoing process that is initiated long before a woman moves to her husband's settlement and that continues long after the couple is seen as having a stable marriage.[5] To the degree that a marriage establishes or continues an alliance, the movement between local descent groups resulting from an initial marital agreement is a permanent process outliving any of the participants.

We can now consider each principle in greater detail.

Direct Exchange

The idea of "sister exchange" can also be described as "exchanging our daughters for daughters-in-law." As mentioned above, to some degree the undertaking always involves a pair of local descent groups as well as the two pairs of prospective spouses. An exchange of actual sisters is the ideal outcome of several strategies employed while arranging marriages. For example, although an exchange can be completed in the next generation, this means that for a considerable amount of time one local descent group will be indebted to another, which has been deprived of a woman. Also, it is risky to expect people to live up to obligations incurred at a much earlier time. A man has the most influence over his actual sisters. Classificatory sisters are as acceptable for an exchange, but are most influenced by *their* brothers and fathers. A man's real sister will be more likely to consider marrying a particular man if by so doing she can help her brother get a wife, as opposed to a more distantly related co-residential agnate.[6] Furthermore, a man is more likely to be able to persuade his actual sister to return to her natal local descent group should his wife leave him. Thus an exchange of two women is seen as a means of guaranteeing a greater amount of marital stability, and an exchange of actual sisters is seen as the best type of arrangement for accomplishing this.[7]

The Bará terms for marriage describe the exchange itself. The term *hikaníyā* (*hiká,* "one") can be glossed as "one-couple marriage," and *püaníyā* (*püá,* "two") can be glossed as "two-couple marriage." A married woman will be a *hikáyā mahkó* or a *püáyā mahkó,* depending on whether or not she was part of an exchange marriage. While the distinction between one-couple and two-couple marriage is made, the principle of exchange is involved in both cases, as indicated above.

Only women can be exchanged for women. According to alliance theory: ". . . marriage forms . . . may be regarded as partial and incomplete expressions of certain underlying principles of reciprocity" (Buchler and Selby 1968:103). Marriage in the Vaupés is, indeed, part of a larger relationship, between families and between pairs of local descent groups. However, no goods can be given in lieu of a woman, whose loss is compensated for only by another woman given at that time or promised for the future. Goldman speaks of a headman's prestige and "perhaps affluence helping him get a second wife through bride price alone" (1963: 145), but this is not my impression of what actually happens when a man obtains a wife without exchanging a woman for her. If a man, even a headman, receives a woman without giving one, then he and his local descent group are in a position of indebtedness that he cannot completely clear with bride price.

The fact that only a woman given compensates for a woman received is frequently offered by Indians as a reason behind a general disapproval of polygyny. A man with a second wife (usually a headman) is indebted to the local descent group where she was living—even if she was a widow, a divorcée, or without close kinsmen. The unavoidable implications of polygyny, therefore, are that such men have used two of their close female agnates in exchange for their wives, or that one or two are owed to another local descent group. Although a headman's wife works very hard and can be seen as more deserving of the help of a co-wife (although she may not see it this way), his position as a headman does not formally entitle him to contract two marriages. A man is entitled to one wife, for there is a general belief that that is all there are to go around.

In general, bride and groom do not differ markedly in age at marriage (particularly when compared to certain other lowland Amerindian groups), which might permit more polygyny, and it is felt that all men deserve to have a wife rather than just the older ones, the best hunters, or whatever.[8] Thus monogamy is seen as the most equitable arrangement for all concerned. In a sample of 672 marriages, only six were polygynous, and four of these were made by one rather remarkable Tukano, who was persuaded to send three of his wives back to their natal longhouses by the local priest when the situation was discovered.

A marriage made at the Bará longhouse *púmanaka buro* demonstrates the operation of the principle of exchange in the absence of brother-sister pairs. Estribino, the headman Mario's eldest son, took a Tuyuka wife, Isabel; she came from a family of three sisters and no brothers that lived downstream. A week later Isabel's father, Armando, arrived, saying that he wanted Estribino's younger sister, Maximiliana, in exchange for his daughter. This precipitated a huge quarrel, mainly between Armando and Mario, Estribino's father. Armando said that he was owed a woman and that he had a right to a second wife because he had no sons and therefore no daughters-in-law, and who would look after him and his wife when they were old and their daughters had all married? Mario retorted that Armando already had a wife who could still bear children, that he was too old, and finally, that Maximiliana did not want to marry him anyway. Armando took his daughter, Isabel, back home with him, although against her will; he was obviously counting on Estribino to pressure Maximiliana into going with Armando. Armando's plan was not successful, and Isabel was not allowed to return to *púmanaka buro*.

When Armando and Mario had discussed the upcoming marriage, no mention had been made of an exchange of women, since the demographic imbalance and the fact that Armando lived alone with his family (a quarrel had led to his leaving his natal longhouse) meant that the potential bride, Isabel, had no classificatory brothers with a strong claim to her in exchange marriage. Armando waited until Isabel was firmly established at *púmanaka buro* and then came forward with his demands, when his bargaining position was strongest. Using his daughter as leverage in this fashion with this particular family was perhaps the best possible strategy, for it was common knowledge that Estribino had been trying to get married for a number of years (he was at least 26). The pressure on him to marry was particularly strong, since a headman's eldest son should be the first to get married and the first to have a son of the new generation of local descent group males.

It is difficult to speculate about the incidence of *püaníyã* in earlier times, although "one-couple" marriages might be more frequent today because of acculturation, depopulation, and out-migration. However, the principle of sister exchange as a norm is still quite strong, and Tukanoans who are quite aware of the changes in marriage patterns owing to acculturative influences agree that *püaníyã* is still the best arrangement, regardless of the disapproval of the Catholic missionaries who consider it a form of selling women, and who have prevented exchange marriages taking place.

Table 1 gives the incidence of two-couple marriage for a sample of 423 marriages among Tukanoans. The figures in the table represent only those marriages that were specifically described as *püaníyã* marriages. Furthermore, they are all completed exchange marriages, in that both marriages of the exchange are included in the sample (thus the number of exchanges is half the number of exchange marriages). Some of the marriages coded as "missing observations" were in fact described to me as *püaníyã,* so certain were the informants that the other half of the exchange was imminent, but since it hadn't occurred at the time the information was gathered, the preceding marriage was excluded. (For further discussion of the sample, see Jackson 1972).

Kinship Relations between Spouses

When specifically asked, Tukanoans will state a preference for marriage to a genealogically close kinsman within the category of potential spouse.[9] The advantages of marrying a closely related cross cousin are several. Since it is the woman who marries out, it is better from her point of view not to move into a totally strange longhouse group. Usually a longhouse with the closest cross cousins of a particular woman will also be relatively nearby, another consideration both parties take into account. Furthermore, not only is the longhouse where a woman's closest cross cousins are living likely to be familiar territory inhabited by familiar

TABLE 1. EXCHANGE OF WOMEN.

Relationship	Absolute Frequency	Adjusted Frequency	Cumulative Frequency
Both or one of the wives were actual sisters of the husbands	79	18.7%	18.7%
The wives were the husbands' long-house parallel cousins ("sisters")	61	14.4%	33.1%
An exchange was made involving agnates from the same longhouses but of a different generation	102	24.1%	57.2%
The wives were patrilineal parallel cousins, but not from the same longhouse	24	5.7%	62.9%
Known that no exchange was made	157	37.1%	100.0%
Total	423	100.0%	–
Information not available	249		
Not applicable	12		

people, but most of these people are kinsmen of hers through several links in addition to the affinal one being established. Should trouble arise, an in-married woman will be seen in her role not only as daughter-in-law but also as close niece of several of the residents. Living with the real or close classificatory siblings of her parents, whether on her father's, mother's, or both sides, probably helps to resolve marital difficulties more easily. She also speaks the father-language of the longhouse where a real or close classificatory MB is living, and is very likely to speak the long-house language where a real FZ is living. (However, she will be familiar with the father-language of any longhouse belonging to her mother's language group, and only some of them will contain genealogically close kinsmen.)

While a woman remains a member of her local descent group through-out life, her membership in a residential group shifts at marriage from her natal longhouse to her husband's. At times this places the woman in a position of conflicting loyalties. A woman's children are members of the local descent group and residential group of her husband, and her loyalties to them sometimes divide her from her continuing allegiance to her own local descent group when quarrels arise between the two groups. A pair of local descent groups will experience more pressure to resolve disagreements equitably when they have a long-standing exchange relationship involving more than one married couple, even though it is these very affinal relationships that are frequently the root of many of the disagreements that arise. A pair of allied local descent groups has much to gain from continued contact and much to lose from a permanent rupture, since so many individual relationships are involved. Both groups will be more likely to keep their promises, therefore, and work at resolving conflicts when there is more than one in-married woman connecting them.

Not much information is available in the general ethnographic literature dealing with the desirability, from either the native or the structuralist viewpoint, of marrying a genealogically close, as opposed to a more distant, kinsman in a bilateral exchange marriage system. Most of the literature deals with the desirability of marrying a genealogically close MBD[10] over an FZD when the marriage system is already structured that way—when it is an asymmetrical matrilateral prescriptive system.[11]

In the Vaupés not only are both MBD and FZD "potential affines," but a preference is actually stated for a genealogically close spouse. This is particularly interesting in light of some prescriptive marriage systems that prohibit marriage between relatives who are in the category of potential spouse and who are genealogically quite close (usually first or double cousins). Dumont (1957:13) gives examples and states that marriages with a double cross cousin are "condemned and are *kunda-munda cambandam* 'ball-ball marriage' " (see also Maybury-Lewis 1965: 223 and Spencer and Gillen 1962:64).

This is the opposite of the situation in the Vaupés, where actual MBDs and FZDs not only are married but are actually the preferred marriage partners.

Arguments about sentiments and authority (Needham 1962, Lounsbury 1962, Schneider 1965b) might not be applicable to unilateral prescriptive marriage systems or many bilateral prescriptive systems, but the issues these debates focus on are of interest in a situation like the Vaupés if we are careful not to confuse distinct levels of causal explanation. At present, nothing resembling a section or moiety system organizes the Vaupés region, and this fact may be connected to the stated preference for a genealogically close kinsman within the prescribed category of allowed marriage partners. Questions of territorial arrangements may also be pertinent, since in some situations where marriage with a genealogically close relative is prohibited, the rule is sometimes expressed in terms of such marriages being "*too* close." Formal proscriptions on marriage to genealogically close kinsmen (whether of a type derived from other structural principles—as in section and subsection systems—or similar to the situation among the Pramalai Kallar, where a single explicit rule guards against marrying too close) may relate to the disadvantages to the group of forming an exclusive alliance with one other local group. The creation of sanctions that avoid this perhaps arises in part because marriage with very close kinsmen is deemed advantageous by the individual parties involved.[12] Yengoyan's (1968:185) description of section systems as functioning to regulate interaction over a delimited area, thus serving as a means of "ensuring" utilizable resources, is an instance of such reasoning.

Various other factors in the Vaupés system may adequately prevent the formation of too exclusive and intensive an alliance between pairs of local descent groups. This would allow the very real advantages of close kinsmen marriage to the individual spouses to be formalized into a conscious norm as well as implicitly stated in the kinship terminology.

A second issue concerns the advantages of marrying more closely through *one* of the patrilines connecting the spouses as opposed to the other. For example, it might be seen as more advantageous to have a wife related through her mother's line (FZD) than through her father's (MBD). Speaking from a male ego perspective, Bará informants stated a preference for marriage with an FZD rather than an MBD. However, their explanation of this preference relates to structural principles rather than to advantages arising from the relative genealogical distance involved. FZD marriage is preferred to MBD marriage because it is "getting back a woman (FZD) for the one we gave out in the previous generation (FZ)." Marriage with an MBD, on the other hand, makes the debt to the affinal group a double one, since MBD's local descent group has now given both M and MBD. This preference for FZD conflicts with some of the ethnographic reports from other societies with prescriptive bilateral marriage, in which natives sometimes state a preference for MBD as opposed to FZD (Elkin 1953, Radcliffe-Brown 1953).

These two consciously stated preferences concerning genealogical relationship between marriage partners cannot be combined into a single composite preference (e.g. "the ideal marriage is with a true FZD"), since informants argue them from different grounds. However, it should be noted that from a woman's point of view it is preferable to be both an FZD and a genealogically close kinswoman of her husband, for she would then be marrying her MBS and moving into her mother's natal longhouse, with which she would always have warmer ties than would be the case with a longhouse her FZ has moved into, when these are not the same.

It is necessary to emphasize that while Tukanoans may state that marriage to a genealogically close kinsman is preferred, and with an FZD/MBS as compared to an MBD/FZS, what Tukanoans actually *do* when arranging marriages is influenced by many other considerations as well. While neither a Vaupés woman nor a man can be forced into a marriage, it often happens that conflicts of interest arise, and considerations such as the indebtedness of a potential bride's or groom's local descent group will influence an individual's choice of spouse as well as general principles of preference and his or her personal predilections.

Tables 2, 3, and 4 deal with the question of kinship genealogically traced between spouses in the Vaupés. It should be pointed out that Tables 2 and 3 produce an ordinal scale; thus the cumulative percentages are important measures of kinship relationship as well as the percentages for each value. Three marriages included in the "actual FZD" category are in fact between a man and his actual sister's daughter. Informants initially described these as "actual cross-cousin" marriages, claiming ignorance about the wife's mother or giving her a different name. The real nature of the marriages was ascertained by examining genealogical data and having subsequent discussions with informants. Such marriages are considered improper, since they cross generation lines. Table 4 shows that no significantly closer relationship obtains between spouses through either the wife's mother's line or the wife's father's.

TABLE 2. KINSHIP RELATIONS BETWEEN SPOUSES TRACED THROUGH WIFE'S FATHER.

Relationship	Absolute Frequency	Adjusted Frequency	Cumulative Frequency
Wife's father is brother of husband's mother	15	4.2%	4.2%
Wife's father is classificatory brother of husband's mother	21	5.8%	10.8%
Wife's patrilocality is same as husband's mother's	19	5.3%	15.3%
Wife's sib is same as husband's mother's	17	4.7%	20.0%
Wife's language group is same as husband's mother's	75	20.8%	40.8%
Wife's language group is different from husband's mother's	213	59.2%	100.0%
Total	360	100.0%	–
Information not available	311		
Non-Indians involved	13		

TABLE 3. KINSHIP RELATIONS BETWEEN SPOUSES TRACED THROUGH WIFE'S
MOTHER.

Relationship	Absolute Frequency	Adjusted Frequency	Cumulative Frequency
Wife's mother is sister of husband's father	14	5.0%	5.0%
Wife's mother is classificatory sister of husband's father	19	6.8%	11.9%
Wife's mother's patrilocality same as husband's	15	5.4%	17.3%
Wife's mother's sib same as husband's	19	6.8%	24.1%
Wife's mother's language group same as husband's	52	18.7%	42.8%
Wife's mother's language group different from husband's	159	57.2%	100.0%
Total	278	100.0%	–
Information not available	393		
Non-Indians involved	13		

Language Group Exogamy

As has already been indicated, the language group is the clearest exogamous unit in the Vaupés, from the point of view of both the marriage sample and Tukanoan normative statements. Table 5 gives a list of the language group affiliations of the spouses in the sample. With the exception of a two-year union between a Tukano man of the mid-Papurí and a woman of Yavareté, no marriages occurred between members of the same language group. Informants were reluctant to discuss this union, saying at times that it was not really a marriage at all and at other times that the *ahpükeria* (a low-ranking Tukano sib) group to which the woman belonged was actually a different language group, with a language of its own.

Tukanoans see the rule of language group exogamy as extending far beyond the Papurí–Tiquié–Pirá-paraná region. Indians are quite critical of Cubeos intermarrying among themselves. Bará war stories generally finish with the victors going north and killing off all Cubeos except a brother-sister pair, who then *had* to marry each other in order to start the Cubeo people again. This is given by Tukanoans as the reason why Cubeos "marry their sisters" at present.

TABLE 4. CROSSTABULATION OF FZD RELATIONSHIP BY MBD RELATIONSHIP.

Count Total Percent	MBD						
	Wi Fa is Br of Hu Mo	Wi Fa is class. Br of Hu Mo	Wi Patri-locality is same as Hu Mo	Wi Sib is same as Hu Mo	Wi lang. group same as Hu Mo	Wi lang. group different from Hu Mo	Row Total
FZD							
Wi Mo is Si of Hu Fa	1 / 0.6	0 / 0.0	0 / 0.0	0 / 0.0	1 / 0.6	9 / 5.0	11 / 6.1
Wi Mo is class. Si of Hu Fa	0 / 0.0	2 / 1.1	0 / 0.0	1 / 0.6	2 / 1.1	7 / 3.9	12 / 6.7
Wi Mo Patrilocality same as Hu	1 / 0.6	1 / 0.6	1 / 0.6	0 / 0.0	1 / 0.6	5 / 2.8	9 / 5.0
Wi Mo Sib same as Hu Sib	0 / 0.0	1 / 0.6	0 / 0.0	0 / 0.0	4 / 2.2	9 / 5.0	14 / 7.8
Wi Mo lang. group same as Hu	1 / 0.6	1 / 0.6	2 / 1.1	0 / 0.0	9 / 5.0	26 / 14.4	39 / 21.7
Wi Mo lang. group different from Hu	11 / 6.1	9 / 5.0	1 / 0.6	3 / 1.7	20 / 11.1	51 / 28.3	95 / 52.8
Column Total	14 / 7.8	14 / 7.8	4 / 2.2	4 / 2.2	37 / 20.6	107 / 59.4	180 / 100.0

TABLE 5. LANGUAGE GROUP AFFILIATION OF TUKANOANS IN SAMPLE.[1]

Language	Men	Women	Total
Bará	104	86	190
Tuyuka	160	117	277
Tukano	153	162	315
Desana	65	77	142
Carapana	40	20	60
Tatuyo	28	40	68
Siriano	73	50	123
Yurutí	16	25	41
Piratapuyo	8	13	21
Uanano	4	8	12
Cubeo	8	25	33
Barasana	5	25	30
Taiwano	1	6	7
Makuna	3	9	12
Tariano	0	11	11
Curripaco	0	2	2
Carihona	1	1	2
Makú	0	1	1
Wahüná (Pisá-Tapuyo?)	0	2	2
Metuno	2	0	2
Arapaso	2	2	4
Non-Indians	11	2	13
TOTAL	684	684	1,368

[1]This is not representative of relative population sizes, since this sample was mainly gathered in the Papurí drainage region.

How long the rule of language group exogamy has been in effect is open to speculation. Koch-Grünberg reports it (1909-10), but whether it was as strongly enforced as is the case today is not known. Wallace (1889) reports marriage with blood relatives, presumably cross cousins, while Kirchhoff (1931) states that tribal exogamy was practiced by Tukano groups, blood relative marriage being practiced by Arawak groups. Goldman correctly points out that the two statements are not contradictory (1948:780).

According to C. Hugh-Jones (1979) and Arhem (1981), data from the Pirá-paraná region indicate that the language-affiliated unit and the endogamous unit are not always coterminous. However, Tukanoans state that this should not be the case, and that people "shouldn't speak like their cross cousins." They also state that presently intermarrying units that speak the same language spoke different languages in the past.

The strength of the rule of language group exogamy is made more interesting when we consider the degree of acculturation in the Vaupés, particularly in the Papurí drainage region. Change agents, especially Catholic missionaries, have actively discouraged cross-cousin marriage and consider the language group exogamy rule as silly. Despite missionary effects on other areas of Vaupés culture, the marriage system has remained viable. Table 6 shows the language group affiliation of the marriage partners in a sample of 534 marriages involving eight language groups.

Distance between Spouses' Local Descent Groups

The physical distance between a pair of local descent groups is obviously a variable in an analysis of the probability of marital interaction between them. It is evident that settlements in the Vaupés do not marry within a tightly constricted geographical field, yet it is also the case that some marriages are between local descent groups so far away from each other that they are statistically very improbable and are seen as such by Tukanoans because of distance factors alone. Figures 3 and 4 show marriage movement between one local descent group and its affinal settlements during a period of three generations. The figures show that mar-

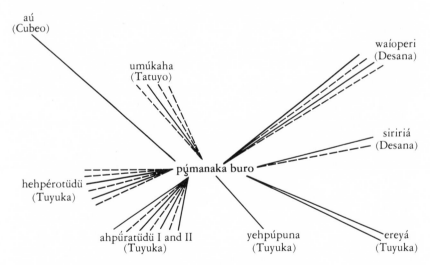

FIGURE 3. MARRIAGES DURING THREE GENERATIONS OF A BARÁ LOCAL LOCAL DESCENT GROUP.

Total marriages: 27 (13 women, 14 men). Total number of settlements participating in exchanges: 8. Solid lines represent men bringing women to *púmanaka buro;* dotted lines represent women marrying out.

TABLE 6. MARRIAGE BETWEEN SELECTED GROUPS IN THE VAUPÉS.

Husband's Language Group		Wife's Language Group								Row Total	Pct. Column
		Bará	Tuyuka	Tukano	Desana	Carapana	Tatuyo	Siriano	Yurutí		
Bará	N	0	55	0	7	2	12	1	0	77	
	%	0.0	71.4	0.0	9.1	2.6	15.6	1.3	0.0	100.0	(14.4)
Tuyuka	N	58	0	71	3	0	6	7	0	145	
	%	40.0	0.0	49.0	2.1	0.0	4.1	4.8	0.0	100.0	(27.2)
Tukano	N	0	47	1	45	4	5	20	5	127	
	%	0.0	37.0	0.8	35.4	3.1	3.9	15.7	3.9	100.0	(27.2)
Desana	N	5	2	36	0	2	0	10	0	55	
	%	9.1	3.6	65.5	0.0	3.6	0.0	18.2	0.0	100.0	(10.3)
Carapana	N	3	0	6	4	0	10	2	2	27	
	%	11.1	0.0	22.2	14.8	0.0	37.0	7.4	7.4	100.0	(5.1)
Tatuyo	N	10	0	5	1	2	0	0	2	20	
	%	50.0	0.0	25.0	5.0	10.0	0.0	0.0	10.0	100.0	(3.7)
Siriano	N	2	8	27	14	5	1	0	14	71	
	%	2.8	11.3	38.0	19.7	7.0	1.4	0.0	19.7	100.0	(13.3)
Yurutí	N	2	0	2	0	1	1	6	0	12	
	%	16.7	0.0	16.7	0.0	8.3	8.3	50.0	0.0	100.0	(2.2)
Column	N	80	112	148	74	16	35	46	23	534	
Column	%	15.0	21.0	27.7	13.9	3.0	6.6	8.6	4.3	100.0	(100.0)

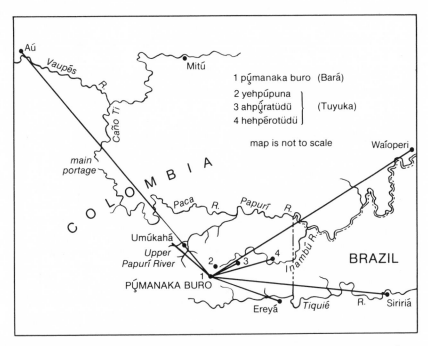

FIGURE 4. LOCATIONS OF SETTLEMENTS INTERMARRYING WITH *pǫ́manaka buro.*

riages do not generally occur between neighboring settlements. This is typical of the marriage patterns of the great majority of local descent groups. For the group residing at *pǫ́manaka buro,* some of the longhouse groups that exchanged women are quite far away. And it is interesting to note that many of the "potential affine" settlements that do not exchange women with *pǫ́manaka buro* are actually closer than some of those that do.

One type of measurement of geographical distance between marriage partners' settlements at the time of marriage gives a mean linear distance for a sample of 635 marriages of (very roughly) 22 linear miles, with a standard deviation of 19.8 miles. Some marriages occur between settlements as distant as 90 linear miles. This distance is actually much farther, taking into consideration the river and trail routes used by Tukanoans (see Jackson 1976 for a discussion of distance measures).

Thus the significance of distance between partners' settlements is not a question of a simple direct correlation between increasing distance and increasing undesirability of a prospective marriage alliance. For example, given that a specific settlement has married several of its women into one or two nearby settlements, it may be less "costly" from its point of view to make the next marriages with settlements relatively far away, even though this is less desirable from the point of view of the marrying individuals.

Lounsbury (1962:1307) discusses two general types of marital strategies. The first concerns the continuation and reaffirmation of an alliance already established, which continues to be seen as advantageous to both sides. Some of these advantages would be: geographical proximity, close kinship ties, facilitation of the ceremonial and economic exchanges generally characterizing neighboring longhouses that are on good terms, and maintenance of the welfare of the women already married into the respective affinal longhouses. The second type of marital strategy is that of establishing new alliances that might be economically, politically, militarily, or otherwise advantageous. In the Vaupés, alliance with more distant longhouses might be made for reasons such as: being assured of hospitality on various river routes or in certain mission towns, having one's close affines dispersed in order to have a wider range of individuals with whom they are linked in other affinal and neighboring relationships, and so forth. Furthermore, although raiding and feuding have ceased, in the recent past military considerations were very much an aspect of marital strategies. Distant marriages that are made today may be continuations of alliances formed originally for the purpose of having dispersed military allies. Given that open feuding did occur between affinal pairs of local descent groups, it was best not to have all of one's outmarried women and all of one's potential affinal allies located in a single settlement.

The influence of geographical distance is a crucial factor if one is to comprehend the way in which social structural principles actually influence decision making about marriage. For example, if a settlement considers itself owed a woman, its demands will not have much impact if it is located far away from the debtor settlement, and this distance is probably an important contributing factor in the debtor settlement's continued disregard of the claims of the other.

Conclusions

Many directions of further inquiry, both in the Vaupés during future fieldwork and with the data already gathered, are indicated in the preceding discussion of only four of the many characteristics of the marriage system. Numerous questions arise concerning previous marriage patterns in the region, and it is obvious that a greater time depth is needed for a comprehensive investigation into any area of Vaupés marriage. Other questions arise concerning the effects of the ecological setting of the Vaupés on its particular marriage system, such as (1) demography,

(2) subsistence patterns, and (3) social and spatial arrangements such as settlement pattern, multifamily longhouses, patrilineal sibs, etc.

Another question concerns the actual influence of so-called social structural principles as determinants of specific marriage behavior, rather than patterns resulting from the operation of other variables which are then reified by natives and anthropologists alike. For example, informants will discuss exogamy in terms of a phratric unit that is more inclusive than the language group level, containing as many as six specific language groups. A quick scanning of Table 6 also demonstrates that marriages are contracted between language groups in a regular pattern, for the sample of 534 marriages between members of eight language groups. Figure 5, using the data from Table 6, illustrates these patterns in terms of Euclidian space using three-dimensional scaling (Jackson and Romney 1973). To what degree do phratries exist in the Vaupés, in the sense that certain language groups do not intermarry in accordance with a phratric prohibition? It is certainly true that at present Tukanoans agree that Bará and Tukano do not and should not exchange women because they are "like brothers" to one another; this idea undoubtedly plays a role in making Bará-Tukano marriages highly unlikely. To what degree does this rule exist with respect to other pairs (such as Tuyaka-Desana)?

A final question has to do with whether certain sets of rules are so constructed that if one rule is followed, another is necessarily ignored, and the way in which such rules are ordered in terms of a given set of

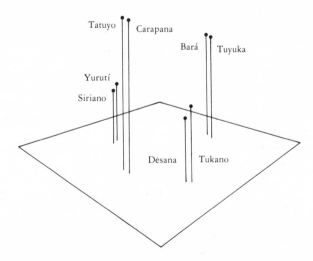

FIGURE 5. MARITAL DISTANCE BETWEEN LANGUAGE GROUPS. This figure is a three-dimensional spatial representation of marriage preferences among eight language groups (data from Table 6) (after Jackson and Romney 1973).

priorities. Evidence exists that such ordering produces what at first may appear to be rule-breaking behavior. An analogous situation is the fact that certain grammatical rules operate at a deeper level, taking precedence over more surface rules in speech. It is usually the latter, however, that native speakers are aware of as specifying what correct speech is. An example of this ordering of rules in the Vaupás is discussed by Silver-wood-Cope for the non-Tukanoan Makú. Although quite aware of Tukanoan rules, which they also use regarding the prescription to marry a person in the potential affine category, Makú have other rules relating to endogamous marriage within a bounded territory, and these take priority. Tukanoans do not have such rules and therefore see the higher frequency of improper Makú marriages with respect to kinship related-ness as far more serious than Makú themselves (1972:176). Like situa-tions undoubtedly also obtain for Tukanoans, who must similarly juggle the various principles and rules when deciding about a particular marriage.

One hopes that further research in the Vaupés and comparison of its marriage system with other tropical forest South American horticultural groups will result in answers to some of the many questions raised in this discussion.

NOTES

1. This paper is based on dissertation research in Colombia from Oct., 1968, to Nov., 1970, with support from the Danforth Foundation and the Stanford Committee for Research in International Studies. Eighteen months of this time were spent in the Vaupés territory with a longhouse group of Bará Indians living on the Inambú River. The term "Vaupés" is used rather than the more inclusive "central Northwest Amazon" because so little time was spent in the Brazilian sector. Conclusions are felt to apply to the larger region, but the degree to which this is so must await further research.

2. Excluded in this paper are (1) the nonriverine, non-Tukanoan Makú, (2) non-Indians, and (3) Cubeos. For further ethnographic information on the Vaupés, see Goldman (1963), Sorensen (1967), Reichel-Dolmatoff (1971), Silverwood-Cope (1972), S. Hugh-Jones (1979), C. Hugh-Jones (1979), and Arhem (1981).

3. The term "language group" is not an entirely satisfactory one, since it normally would refer to a linguistic rather than, as is the case here, a social unit. Use of terms specifically referring to marriage units has been avoided, however, since it has not been conclusively established that Vaupés language-affiliated social units are coterminous with the minimal exogamy-relating units in the same manner throughout the region.

4. "Kinsman" will henceforth be unmarked with reference to sex.

5. Of course, various stages exist which, if completed successfully, offer greater and greater assurance that a union is indeed evolving into a permanent marriage. Vaupés marriages, after a rather rocky preliminary period, are

highly stable and monogamous, characteristics not found for certain other South American horticulturalist groups, such as the Yanomamo (Chagnon 1968) or Sharanahua (Siskind 1973).

6. Classificatory siblings involved in marriage exchanges are almost always co-residents of the same local descent group; a man or a group of men have a minimal claim on a woman residing at another settlement compared to that of her co-residents.

7. Exchange marriages are spoken of as exchanges of women because this is the way Tukanoans talk about them and because it is the women who move at marriage. However, women are not to be thought of as pawns or "rubbish" as has been suggested for other strongly patrilineal systems (Fox 1967: 117). It is interesting to compare the position of Tukanoan women to that of such groups as the Yanomamo and attempt to discover the reasons for the relatively strong position of women in the Vaupés situation, with respect to marriage and other areas.

8. I did not collect systematic data on age at marriage, but most women are definitely not married at prepubescence or even at puberty. Some women do not marry until well into their twenties, but this is complicated by the fact that some will live with one or two men prior to settling down with their permanent mate, and this information tends not to be as easily remembered by informants when giving marriage histories.

9. For a discussion of Bará kinship terminology with respect to zero generation terms and marriage rules, see Jackson (1977).

10. The terms "MBD" and "FZD" are use in a classificatory sense unless otherwise specified.

11. Most of the literature following Homans and Schneider (1955), such as Needham (1962) and Schneider (1965b), has been concerned with refuting the point in Homans and Schneider which assumed that in prescriptive matrilateral marriage systems ego was most often marrying his real MBD. The point is well taken, but discussions concerned with whether or not people are responding to their own feelings of what is sentimentally appropriate when they marry a type of cross cousin are perhaps relevant to structural questions about the Vaupés, for, unlike unilateral systems, this one allows marriage with both types of cross cousins.

12. Meggitt, while attempting to demonstrate that subsection systems are not primarily concerned with the regulation of marriage, suggests that " . . . it may be that, in situations of European contact or declining population, the greater the failure of kinship-phrased marriage prescriptions to work, the more likely are the people to rely on the broadly based sections or subsections to define spouses" (1968:179). This may very well be applicable to the Vaupés situation.

8

Linguistic Exogamy and Personal Choice in the Northwest Amazon

ARTHUR P. SORENSEN, JR.

Introduction

The topic of this paper is what the prospect of marriage looks like to male ego in a society characterized first by prescribed exogamy among linguistic units, and then by preferential cross-cousin marriage, with sister exchange as a further preference.

The presentation of this topic will be descriptive rather than according to any specific social anthropological model. A pattern can be abstracted from the majority of case histories in terms of linguistic unit exogamy and of male ego's involvement in it as he proceeds toward marriage. It is this cultural pattern that will be presented in this paper, and as a generalization, with perhaps some idealization, not with specific case histories or exceptions to the rule.

To place the topic in its cultural context, a background will be sketched in first by some observations on male (versus female) roles and behavior, then by the sequence in male ego's life as he approaches marriage, and then by the actual process of selecting his bride.

The observations in this paper are based on visits going back more than twenty-three years, both among partially acculturated "mission Indians" and among unacculturated "backriver Indians" in both the Colombian Vaupés and the Brazilian Vaupés halves of the central Northwest Amazon. I came to enjoy a privileged, true participant-observer role such that I could check out impressions conversationally with informant-friends. In the course of these visits I was drawn into this society's nearest approximation of a "confidante" role with a number of individuals whose concerns, at times, were focused on one aspect or another of the topic of this paper. In addition, I have been able to keep track of a number of individuals over a period of time as they progressed into marriage. Because of the interactional mode of not crossing sex lines in their groupings, especially among individuals of the (nonformal) "age group" in which I fell until recently, I found the young male ego's viewpoint readily accessible, whereas I was more dependent on interviews for the young woman's viewpoint. The intention of this paper is to trace a gradually developing awareness of the prospect of marriage as it appears to male ego.

Statement of the Problem

In the culture of the riverine Indians of the Northwest Amazon, a marriage rule can be stated of prescribed linguistic group exogamy, with preferential cross-cousin marriage, desirably matrilateral for male ego, allowably patrilateral, and tempered with a desire for sister exchange. The preference is intensified if such cross cousins are also double cousins. This marriage rule is a social anthropological verity about their society. In fact, there are no unexplainable exceptions to the rule of linguistic exogamy, and many marriages are indeed cross-cousin ones, of which some also involve sister exchange; occasional sister-exchange marriages may occur without being cross-cousin ones.

But how does male ego perceive the prospect of fulfilling such an exogamous and hoped-for matrilateral cross-cousin marriage? How fully aware is he of the requirements of this marriage rule? Does he confront them all at once? Does he deliberately calculate marriage when he reaches marriageable age? Or does he go through stages of realizing more and more his growing readiness for marriage? After all, men marry rather late—often not until their mid-twenties or even into their thirties; some men never marry.

In the Northwest Amazon the question of marriage practices in a social environment of linguistic unit exogamy and preferential cross-cousin marriage is not verbalized per se as a social anthropologist's rule. Instead, its component aspects may crop up under variable conversational headings. Some aspects do not form verbalizable topics of conversation at all.

As suspected by now, a programmatic sequence of considerations to accommodate the marriage rule is not consciously conceived by male ego. Nor is the progress through a series of phases and conditioning factors consciously thought of as part of "marriage." The topic of this paper is delineated, then, in terms of an underlying curiosity about how consciously aware a young man may become of systematically following out these marriage rules.

Male versus Female Roles and Behavior

Some insight on the selection of a bride by male ego may be developed by viewing it in its context of male and female roles and behavior.

In the culture of the riverine Indians of the Northwest Amazon many activities and roles are clearly delimited within sex lines. Men hunt and fish (I have never seen a woman hunt or fish—despite Reichel-Dolmatoff's claim that fishing is "feminine" and hunting is "masculine"; see Reichel-Dolmatoff 1968[1]). Men weave fish traps and baskets; women make pottery. Men do foresting and make fields for manioc planting, which they then present to women. Women do horticulture, with occasional assists from men. Women prepare food; men smoke their own game and fish, but otherwise prepare food only in the absence of women. Certain ceremonial details are performed by men only, although women do have roles in other parts of ceremonies. In groupings larger than the nuclear family, men and big boys in a group are served food separately and first, with women serving themselves and their children in a group afterward. Men form the frequent evening discussion circle or council, sitting together in a semicircle, while women, who are free to participate in it once the men have begun, stay behind the men.

One of the characteristics of this society is that individuals strongly tend to group within sex lines. If there are several men and several women, they will most often be arranged in two groups, one all-male and one all-female. For many formal purposes men collect together and form a group vis-à-vis the women, or in the absence of women. This is even more marked for informal purposes—men bathe in groups together and almost disgustedly avoid groups of women bathers; men's bathing takes priority, and women wait and don't watch if they know men are bathing. Even in informal conversations that may include women, men sit together in a bunch or in bunches, in close physical contact, whether they are sitting side by side in rows, shoulder to shoulder and thigh to thigh; or hunkering in lines one behind the other, squeezed in by thighs and knees; or lolling two or three to a hammock. Any of this may be accompanied by some absent-minded pawing and even loose hugging—at least of the arms-around-shoulder variety. Especially of highly nubile youths, there is no public fondling across sex lines (though there is now male/female pair dancing in the Brazilian Vaupés, originally introduced and encouraged by missionaries; Indians of the Colombian Vaupés typically find this behavior uproarious[2]). Indeed, some young men initially may register squeamish shyness and embarrassment even to the point of blushing at having to be in close proximity to a young woman, as in entering a boat or in being served food. The public pairing off, cooing, and petting of young couples so common in North

American society and in some modernized, "liberated," levels of Latin American society is utterly absent.

Between males and females, there are a number of more subtly discernible differences in the area of personal traits. Men are more fastidious in their personal appearance; they dress up more, paint up more, primp more, and have more costumery and ceremonial effects. However, both men and women like nice clothes, and both are scrupulously clean and neat. In their physical activity—working, walking, paddling—men more often show up as almost self-consciously careful and graceful, in a musclebound sort of way perhaps, whereas women appear less studied about their movements and may at times be rough, gauche. A gourdful of beer proffered by a man to someone else is rarely sloshed, whereas a busy woman may thrust a gourdful or potful of liquid that splashes and runs from all around its perimeter. Men watch each other's physical movements and comment on them favorably. Some men may discredit women's physical movements, such as in paddling a boat, though most men receive women's help appreciatively. About the only feminine physical activity that really calls for favorable male attention is that of young women carrying pots of water on their heads up from a river—and, of course, young women are anxious to do this with very even and balanced motions, and to present especially erect posture.

Men are more formal, and formal more often, than women. This formality is a nonrigid preference to observe protocol. Men enjoy it, and some informal occasions may pleasantly be converted to formal ones as they proceed. Women are casual more often than men, and occasionally impromptu. Men, exhibiting more control in their movements as well as in their behavior, may be labeled "sedate." Women are more exaggerated in their movements and behavior. (Some of these traits provide for interesting three-way contrasts vis-à-vis North American behavior and Latin American behavior.) Men, as a group, exhibit and enjoy the more intense rapport. Perhaps the concept of "bonding" as suggested by Lionel Tiger (1969) may furnish an appropriate insight here.

Actually, a number of aspects of the culture of the riverine Indians of the Vaupés point to the potential importance of the concept of "bonding": presence of male's closest kinsmen in a patrilineal longhouse or other patrilineal community, with their spirit of cooperation and aid to each other; men's secret societies in those communities that have retained them; patterns of manning large, community fish traps and in hunting wild animals that herd; and patterns in the almost daily handling of boats, and especially in manning them when traveling.

Men in groups maintain very proximate, affectionate, even intimate behavior toward each other, inter- as well as intragenerationally. There is much companionableness—men almost always prefer to have companions

along, and the more the better. However, it should be pointed out, along
with this, there is no "star performer" role. Although superior skill is
acknowledged, individuals shy away from standing out; even the concept of leadership avoids self-assertive "outstandingness" but is imbued
with some sort of ethic of servility.[3] Males form groups in which they
are just individuals in a close, cooperative, interactional mode with
minimal competition. Women also regularly group, but appear to be
less intense in their interactional mode.

Some youths may develop a kind of "best friends" relationship for a
few months or even years; they may or may not go through a series of such
relationships. However, such a relationship lacks the exclusiveness, secretiveness, and jealousy that the North American (pre-hippie) version of
this can have. Two individuals in such a relationship are pleased to
"share" each other with still others, and invite them "in." A "best friends"
relationship does not happen for all individuals, nor is it actively sought.
Insofar as it may happen, it can take place within the home community
between classificatory brothers, or between individuals in traveling and
in the process of picking up new travel companions or meeting new individuals in new communities, or between individuals in work gangs away
from the home community. Most friends do become "close friends" but
not "best friends" ("close friends" here representing a stage or two closer
than "barracks buddies" or "team mates" in North America, or "com-
pañeros de la vida" among Latin Americans). In any case, the term for
someone in any of these relationships is an inalienable "my 'with-er'," or
"with-me-er," i.e. "my companion."

Such intimacy between friends and within groups at times leads to a
certain range of homosexual activity, normally limited to penis fondling
and masturbatory practices. Such occasional sex is regarded as expectable
behavior among friends; one is marked as nonfriendly—enemy—if he
does not join, especially in the youth "age group" (roughly 15-35). Males
at some time in their early youth are endowed with penis names by their
older peers, and these may be used in banter away from the presence of
women during group work or leisure time. Homosexual activity is limited
neither to within an "age group" nor to unmarried men. Actually, many
males contain their degree of participation in it by withdrawing to the
sidelines after receiving, and giving, an initial, single physical pass with
each who approaches them—the verbal substitute seems insufficient.
Otherwise they would remain outsiders. A good-natured willingness to
go at least part way in this can make all the difference between an arro-
gant, impatiently bossy Latin American or an icy, self-righteous North
American—both without penis names—and an open, empathetically
friendly almost-Indian, plus his penis name.

Homosexual activity represents a relatively uncharged item in the culture of the Northwest Amazon. It is not thought of as unusual or perverse. In fact, there is no direct name for it in the Indian languages of the area. If anything, it is regarded as normal, occasional behavior, though a nuisance value may also be acknowledged. This is despite the fact that while men's hugging and pawing are public, women are excluded from witnessing masculine homosexuality in its overtly sexual aspects. It is mentioned in this paper at all because it seems to function as a means of control of behavior to lessen tensions among males with respect to females, as will become more evident in the sections to follow. It remains an anxiety-free activity.

Resuming the contrast of male versus female traits, this time with even more implicitly two- and three-way comparisons and contrasts among them in Latin American and North American cultures, it is the women, who from the latter (Freudian?) point of view appear at first glance to sport the "more sexually aggressive" behavior, and it is the men who appear to be "sexually passive."

This may be restated (to assuage Freud?) as men being "aggressive" in making themselves available. Young men sit around enticingly sedate and formal in all their finery, or form troupes of panpipe-playing dancers. It is the young women who run around, trying to get the men to chase them to the nearest fields. Under other circumstances women may try to ambush men if they happen to see them going individually to bathe. Some older women may become quite ribald (also see Goldman 1963), doing such things as lifting their skirts over their heads in front of a shy young man in a public gathering.

Actually, quarrels seem more often to be based on women's "messing around" than on duplicity or original action by the male, and women are often more regarded as instigating such problems. Despite the "harmonious" tone being predicated in this paper, and the ideal generalizations being made, some of the worst fights, leading to killing, have been due to jealousies of married men over their wives' lovers or to wives' rages at their husbands' philandering. Regardless of who initiated it, for a man and a woman to indulge in an illicit affair can be quite threatening.

Huskiness, in both male and female, is found to be sexually attractive. The riverine Indians of the Northwest Amazon are a healthy, well-fed, and muscular people. Cleanliness and neatness enhance it for them. Young men's dancing in troupes while playing panpipes is regarded as an expression of sexual attractiveness. Young men as they return, glistening, from bathing are regarded as especially attractive by members of both sexes.[4] However, unlike in North American or Latin American culture, breasts on women are not found to be sexually stimulating by men, nor is a measure of hairiness on men found sexually stimulating by women; only their lack would call for comment.

The obvious "macho complex" of the Latins is viewed as impolite, unnecessary, and undesirable; the Indian youth who experimentally tries to adopt some of it is objected to and ridiculed—usually by being spoken to sharply. However, if asked verbally about masculine behavior, some mission Indians will repeat a number of imported Latin ideals as to how men should show off, even though in fact they themselves disparage doing it.

The consummation of sex is viewed as basically a daytime activity, and the preferred locality for it is in fields, especially in those made by a man for his wife. The longhouse is not the orgiastic sex playroom projected by missionaries. The rather rare, ritualistic, renewal-of-life "gang-rape" that Goldman (1963) and others report is highly circumscribed in its occurrence, and is ceremonially delimited. Sexual contact on the part of some in it may be more token than real, and selection of partners suspiciously seems to be prearranged.

Men, nevertheless, do not turn down the prospects of liaisons with women, by any means, and surreptitious relationships regularly occur. Premarital sex is expected and tolerated—even privately boasted—but not especially condoned. Extramarital sex is frowned upon but reluctantly accepted.[5]

Stages of Life up to Getting Married and Raising Family

Let me now place the prospect of his selecting a bride and getting married into the perspective of the young man's sequence of life.

In infancy he is closest to his mother and father—nuclear family—whether in longhouse or adobe hut village. If he has older sisters, they as well as his mother carry him around; older brothers and men in general may occasionally be seen carrying infants as well. Men as well as women are great babysitters. As the infant gets bigger, he comes to enjoy close, affectionate relationships with all individuals in his home community. The same is true of girl babies.

During childhood he alternates between accompanying his nuclear family in their activities and joining in with the other boys in his home community in their activities. Later childhood finds him helping his father more in his work, but he spends a proportionately larger amount of his remaining time with the other older boys of the community in packs that do not include girls. Girls, too, form packs, but spend more of their total time helping their mothers. The interactions that do occur between older boys and older girls are protective and cooperative, and can be playful.

In early adolescence the older boy may undergo initiation into the men's secret society or possibly some modified version of this. A few boys may undergo this in preadolescence; a few others, now men, may undergo it later in their youth. Initiation rites and other ceremonial activity have been under such repression from missionaries that there is now a whole generation of youth among mission Indians who have not undergone them.[6] Lack of undergoing such a *rite de passage* nevertheless does not seem to mitigate the aspect of bonding among such youth; in fact, if anything, its lack seems to beg it or something equivalent, such as participating in basketball and soccer teams, and perhaps carousing and fighting in Latin saloons when the youths can get in them in the two or three Latin towns on the fringe of the Indian area. In the case of initiation, the young man's father usually plays an important role.[7] Obviously the young man comes out of it with a further intensive link, intergenerationally within sex lines in general and with his age mates in particular.

He then enjoys a long, generally carefree period of youth—from about 15 or 16 to 35 or 40 (warrior age?)—and it is during this period that the in-group, male bonding shows up in its most intense form. (The inhibiting, minute age differences found between 15 and 35 in North American culture just do not exist.) During this period a youth explores, travels, and acquires goods, always counting on generous quantities of companionship. This period may be subdivided nonformally in a sequence going from exclusive male companionship, to "playing the field," leading to marriage, and then into early married life.

Youth, for the young man, whether a "mission Indian" or a "backriver Indian," seems to include a fairly well established period of working away from home on the fringes of Latin economy. Those who do not go away to this kind of work nevertheless do a great deal of traveling and visiting.

Such a stage, ranging in time from a several-month stint of rubber gathering or mission maintenance, to one of several years' duration of several such stints, importantly allows young men opportunities to acquire and accumulate some material goods, such as clothes, a few tools, phonographs, wrist watches, and—now—transistor radios. Some youths are able to acquire shotguns and—the chief prize at present—outboard motors.

During this stage of acquiring goods, another item or "good" that the youth will eventually want to have is his own manioc field. He does this by felling trees from a selected plot near his home community, with some help from friends and relatives. He will then turn over the planting of it to his mother or sisters. Manioc fields, though always made by men, are viewed as properly owned by women. However, this manioc field remains his in ownership; the same is true for older, unmarried men. His parents are very proud of him when they can count on this additional field. At the same time, making a manioc field marks him as a highly eligible bachelor.

Nor does he take it lightly. It represents a serious move calculated to letting up on his activities away from home, retrieving his accumulated goods entrusted to his close relatives, and settling down to some extent. He does not usually consciously have marriage in mind yet, and will laughingly retort that *he* is not going to get married! His resuming full-time residence in his father's house and his making a manioc field do not carry the overtones of emotional dependence upon his parents that would so often be implied in many North American contexts, especially in the nonrural ones.

During all this time he continues to have a great deal of companionable interaction with his friends. In those cases where there is a "best friends" relationship between two young men from different communities, there may be a lot of visiting in each other's communities and some semiserious joking about interest in each other's sisters. The traveling of young men now several years into their youth acquires an ulterior motive of seeing who the eligible, unmarried girls are. These young men continue to make themselves available for surreptitious liaisons with women while at the same time impressing their hosts with their easy-going formality, youthful charm, and graceful ability, whether initiated or not, to form troupes of dancers and to participate in at least the surviving, though still slightly "underground," ceremonies and social dances.

Observation has suggested that the older people of the host village appear relieved to the degree that the traveling youths fraternize with their own young men. Just as they do among the young unmarried men (classificatory and real brothers) of their own community, the young married men of the host community accompany the visiting youths when they go to bathe to try to induce them into homosexual activity. Whether either is consciously aware of it or not, this effectively lessens the chance that the visitors will be so vulnerable to the wiles of the hosts' young wives or sisters. Sometimes the younger, married hosts fall prey to their own machinations. In the course of all this, still newer friendships may be made, and some of the local young men may avail themselves of the opportunity of joining the traveling youths for their own urge to explore and travel. Surreptitious sexual liaisons with young women—and older women—may take place, but not so likely to such a disruptive degree.

Sometime during this leisurely period of his life a youth may become infatuated with a particular girl. If this infatuation endures, he finds himself really falling in love with her.

Actual Process of Choosing a Bride

The appropriate point has been reached now to pause and to review the questions being asked in this paper of how the prospect of marriage appears to male ego in terms of the marriage rule of linguistic exogamy, preferential cross-cousin marriage, with, if possible, sister exchange.

In childhood male ego identifies all girls of his generation at his home community as sisters. Classificatory sisters share the same kin terms ("elder sisters" and "younger sisters") as do the girls he knows to be his biological sisters. He also learns he has other sister-like relations—classificatory sisters—in other communities, and he ordinarily comes to meet many of them when his parents travel or when their families come to visit his community. He further comes to identify as sisters all those whose own patrilineal language is the same as his. (In the few exceptional cases where the families of such girls no longer speak their original language, the "tribal" identification remains, and the fact that they "should speak" the language identified with that tribe is highlighted.) In other words, early in his life male ego adopts a brotherly attitude and role toward girls of his own linguistically identifiable "tribe." Consequently, there will be no inclination on his part to look upon linguistic unit exogamy as a defiable rule—even though at times missionaries have tried to urge Indians to abandon it. A fact of social interaction in the Northwest Amazon is initial identification of unknown individuals according to language and tribe.

Male ego is also early aware that his mother is from another "tribe," one that is in turn identified by their speaking another language. Although his mother primarily uses his father's language with him, as it is his father-tongue, hence his own language, almost every boy comes to speak his mother's original language as well (his mother-tongue; see Sorensen 1967). It also becomes apparent to male ego, through attitudes and good-natured joking, that the girls of his generation in his mother's original home community, speaking his mother's language, are what (some rural) North Americans might call "kissing cousins"—though Vaupés Indians don't kiss—and potentially provide what could be a highly stable marriage with an individual of known and close relationship, if such were to occur. He also becomes aware that many marriages in his home community are of this sort, and he will know whether his parents are also cousins, or even double cousins because his grandparents were cousins; he further knows that double-cousin marriage is highly valued. The same is true, though less marked, in visits to his father's sisters' communities. Girls of most other tribes, then, will appear as nonsisters, and although they do not carry such a sanction of desirability as do his cross cousins, nevertheless they are regarded as potentially marriageable.

The young man bears all this in mind as he becomes more and more aware of his interest in girls, but not to such an extent that it becomes a screening device. He knows of the pleasant, jovial receptions at his cross cousins' places, and sometimes this induces him to stay with them for prolonged periods of time. He does not experience any undercover, obligating maneuvers here to put him and some girl into strategic and vulnerable positions for any parent-calculated marriage. True, certain cross cousins are suspected of high compatibility, and there may be some open suggestion that they should marry, but neither is pushed. Male ego is not discouraged from becoming interested in a girl of tribes other than those of his cross cousins. It is an independent decision that he makes in selecting his bride.

A youth, then, may find himself infatuated with some girl. The two may or may not have had sexual relations. If the infatuation becomes mutual, but, more important, if it is the kind of shared feeling that does not die away over a few months, then the young man and the young woman realize that they are in love. The Indians of the Northwest Amazon enjoy romantic love.

A new phase of activity on the young man's part comes into play now. He finds various reasons to visit the girl's community. He joins in more and more with the young men of her community, and he may especially cultivate friendships with her own (biological) brothers. If a "best friends" relationship develops, the young man may try urging the other young man to become more interested in his sister. From time to time the courting young man may provide the young woman's father with portions of fish and game, and he may even help her brothers and father fell trees for her mother's new manioc field.

By the time courtship has gone this far, it is quite evident that the young man and the young woman are thinking of marrying. The actual, formal request is initiated by the young man, first to the girl, then to her father and mother. A new series of actions then ensues.

In cases where the girl does not seriously reciprocate her suitor's ardor, she has first option to say "no," and the suit goes no further. The same is true for those few potential marriages that are straightforwardly set up, after all, by parents or elders of the individuals concerned. Otherwise, after the girl does indicate to her own family and lineage her desire to marry the young man, the latter in turn discuss the young man among themselves from a variety of angles: his personality, his evidence of being a good worker and provider, etc. If he does not stand in close kin relationship to them, they then try to reckon it, although in some cases no easily traceable relationship may be found.

The same goes on in the young man's family after he returns home to tell them of the seriousness of his desire, and of the mutuality of the girl's feelings. His family and his lineage discuss the case and try to find out more about the potential bride from others if they do not already know her. They, too, reckon or try to trace her relationship to themselves.

If for some reason the girl's family or lineage disapproves of the marriage, they discourage the young man, politely, and get him to leave. If his own family or lineage disapproves, they send him away, usually on an errand for his father of several months' duration to a place far away from the girl's place. Elopements are exceedingly rare. Older people comment that even in the case of bride capture, by a youth who had had his eyes on a particular girl for some time, if the ensuing marriage turned out to be incompatible, the bride was allowed to return to her original community. There seemed to have been some element of prearrangement even in bride capture.

If it is a cross-cousin marriage, then the brother, brother-in-law, sister, and sister-in-law bonds of the parents are further intensified and there is rejoicing. Youths comment on the favorability of this kind of marriage, but they do not feel personally obligated to fit into the mold.

Completion of Cycle of Raising Family

Let us resume tracing the stages of life for the young man. Marriage and bringing a bride home fit comfortably into the cycle. The young man usually already has prepared a manioc field, which he expands and turns over to his wife so she can start her own planting. If he lives in an adobe hut village, the young man, when he actually received approval for his marriage, most probably built his own adobe hut close to or adjoining his father's hut; if he lives in a longhouse, a section or a part of one is apportioned for him and his bride. His bringing a bride home, and its further implication of settling down, add to his parents' pride.

The marriage establishes itself gradually over a period of time. The newly married man does not keep himself at home all the time, and still may have occasional liaisons, especially when traveling with his companions. And no doubt the newly married woman may surreptitiously be able to consummate liaisons while he is away. He has various tricks to control his brothers' interest in her by deflecting their libidinous urges through the alternative of more easy-going homosexuality. But each spouse becomes reluctant to leave the other alone as they begin to accrue children. Now they try to arrange to travel together when the need arises. Otherwise, they spend most of their time together at home or in their fields. As their older children start growing up, their marriage becomes fully established. The father now can rely on his sons and daughters for real help at home and in the fields and, as his sons become young men, for their aid over several years in fishing and hunting. Taking pride in them, the generalized male ego of this paper has himself come full circle to the point where his own parents were when he was turning into a young man only distantly aware that some day he might get married. A cycle of raising a family is complete, in which context has lain the prospect of the young man choosing his bride. The man will go on to further stages of his larger life cycle—to becoming a grandfather, even great-grandfather, and a respected lineage elder, who then judges the prospective marriages of his descendants.

Summary

The main points being made in this paper are that male ego marries by choice a woman with whom he falls in love, and then, as if by default, he looks to see where the relationship between him and his bride falls. He is pleased if it turns out to be a "preferential matrilateral cross-cousin marriage," as often enough it does because of privileged visiting conditions in their communities, but he does not formulaically set this up in his thinking as he proceeds to select his bride. In fact, he has not consciously set himself up with the consideration of getting married at all; instead, he has approached the stage, phase by phase, where marriage occurs to him as a suitable vocation. Marriage has come to *him*. While there are crucial discussions of the suitability of the match at the family and lineage levels in both the young man's and the young woman's communities, these take place "after the fact" of the young man and the young woman falling in love with each other. If deemed suitable, and whether the groom and bride are cross cousins or not, their mutual choice is looked upon as a delightful surprise.

NOTES

1. Although he says that only men fish, Reichel-Dolmatoff claims that at another cosmological level, fish are female and going fishing is erotic. While this may be so among the Desana, it does not seem so among the Tukano, Pirá-Tapuyo, Tuyuka, etc.

2. Referred to here are the popular Latin dances. However, in the 1975 celebrations surrounding the *Día de la raza* (Columbus Day), the president of Colombia, Alfonso López, and much of the Congress made an unprecedented visit to Mitú, administrative capital of the Colombian Vaupés. In one sideline

presentation, Antonio Guzmán, Reichel-Dolmatoff's informant, who had recently arrived as a practical anthropologist, instructed high school–age Indian boys and girls to dance a traditional men's paired dance as male-female partners. I noted that the few Indian onlookers registered bewilderment and silent disapproval. Of interest is that in the eastern Tukanoan languages, men "dance" and women "follow." Although there is a suffixal derivation for "going first" or "preceding," it does not connote "leading" as in popular Western dances. This can be accomplished by adding an "order to" suffixal derivation, which would then impart a "Simon says" effect in this context.

3. A Big Man concept does not seem appropriate for the Vaupés, but *patrón*-like systems may sporadically be promoted by some local Colombians.

4. Skin which is naturally oily is highly rated by both sexes.

5. My impression through conversations with colleagues is that there is much less premarital or extramarital sex among the groups in the Vaupés region than among other lowland South American groups.

6. However, as of the late 1970s, more initiation and Yuruparí ceremonies were occurring, including in missionized communities. While there was little of the secretiveness that had characterized the height of the missionizing era, there was also less openness about allowing non-Indians to attend, much less expecting them to join the more secular dances.

7. He may be the one who puts whip stripes on the legs, torso, shoulders, and arms of the initiate. Fathers never strike their sons or daughters otherwise. Nor do mothers strike their children. In the Yuruparí ceremony best friends may give each other the heavy single whip stroke on the back which snaps around onto the abdomen causing a wound. Some missionaries also practiced whipping of adults as well as of their boarding-school children.

9

The Structure of Kinship and Marriage among the Canelos Quichua of East-Central Ecuador

NORMAN E. WHITTEN, JR., AND
DOROTHEA S. WHITTEN

The Canelos Quichua (also known as Canelo or Canelos—Karsten 1935, Oberem 1974, Harner 1972) number from 10,000 to 12,000 people who range through very rugged territory from the Andean foot-hills (3,000-foot elevation) near the town of Puyo eastward to the Peruvian border.[1] The contemporary culture area is bordered in the west by the Andean escarpment, in the north by the Villano and Curaray rivers, in the east more vaguely by the Peruvian border or the vicissitudes of contemporary movements of northeastern Peruvian peoples, and in the southeast by Achuar Jivaroans of the Copataza and Capahuari rivers and by the Shuar (Jívaro proper) (Harner 1972) on the right bank of the Pastaza River. They are distinguished from the Quijos Quichua (Quijo, Quijos—Oberem 1971, Porras 1974) and from other Quichua speakers of the lower Napo (see, e.g., Whitten 1976a, 1978, 1981, for more detail).

There is considerable diversity in biotope, degree of contact with national Ecuadorians and foreigners, level of population concentration, and specific interethnic marriage (Canelos Quichua–Zaparoan, Canelos Quichua–Shuar, Canelos Quichua–Achuar, Canelos Quichua–Quijos Qui-chua) among the Canelos Quichua. Indeed, each of the six major terri-torial divisions ("runa territories"), represented by the mission-adminis-trative sites of Puyo, Canelos, Paca Yacu, Sara Yacu, and Montalvo on the Bobonaza River, and Curaray on the Curaray River, has its own character, including specific mix of the above factors and an assertive ethos of dis-tinctive ethnicity.

The Canelos Quichua maintain a strong sense of ethnic identity based on concepts of descent from male and female ancestors who reputedly acquired souls from the Ancient Times People (*callari rucuguna runa*). A system of genealogical classification that derives from stipulated or demonstrated apical ancestors in the Times of the Grandparents (*apayaya rucuguna,* male ego; *apamama rucuguna,* female ego) links contemporary people directly descended from the Times of the Grandparents back to Ancient Times. Through the idioms of kinship reckoning and shamanic performance the Canelos Quichua maintain a clear sense of ethnic continuity through what they call Times of Destruction. Such continuity links families in their contemporary households (*huasi* refers to both nuclear family and household—Whitten 1976a:65-104) to ramifying kin ties of their current social networks. To understand Canelos Quichua marriage practices, it is necessary to sketch pivotal aspects of the repetitive patterning of consanguinity and affinity and their relationship to residence, territoriality, and cultural continuity.

Canelos Quichua referential kin classes (Whitten 1976a:106-24) provide them with a cognitive set of "relatives" that numbers 1,000 to 2,000 people for any ego. Out of such a lattice of living and dead people, which constitutes an inchoate cognitive set that no individual or group can manage as a totality, other structures are built. One of these is the maximal *ayllu,* a structure that links mythic (*unai,* "beyond time") dimensions, ancient time, and known and postulated history to the present and future. The reference points for this system are ultimately the stipulated souls (*aya*) of the known and stipulated ancestors who reputedly intermarried and acquired their substances from the Ancient Times People. The maximal *ayllu* is a relative constant, conceived of as an invariant structure by the Canelos Quichua. All of Canelos Quichua social organization, including relationships with other peoples, can be conceived of in terms of segments of maximal *ayllu*s linked by affinity.

Another system is an ego-centered network of ritual or mystical co-parents, called *gumba* (male) or *comari* (female, from the Spanish *compadre, comadre*). This connects a series of contemporary strategic partners for a given ego. The *gumba,* ego-centered system solidifies some relationships in the maximal *ayllu* but attenuates others. *Gumba* partners derive from affinal ramifications bound up with marriage procedures and from the ties that are built up among peers following the birth of children.

The two systems—*ayllu* and *gumba*—revolve around the processes of shamanic power and authority quests, in which successful acquisition of mystical skill and social support generates a localized stem kindred, also called *ayllu.* The shamanic processes involve both the metaphors inherent in the maximal *ayllu* (acquisition of souls, transformation into a jaguar—

see Whitten 1976a:141-63) and the strategies played out in expanding the *gumba* network. This dynamic, ego-centered system mediates the referential and address systems producing the polysemy and extension rules (Scheffler 1972, Scheffler and Lounsbury 1971) necessary to understand the fluctuations and shifts in kin class usage. Shaman alliances and duels affect the conceptualization, application, and transmission of both consanguinity and affinity.

Marriage itself must be understood as a process of spouse acquisition (for a man, *huarmiyuj,* "possession of a woman"; for a woman, *cariyuj,* "possession of a man"), which takes about three years to accomplish. During this period segments of maximal *ayllus* are linked, residence shifts, territoriality is somewhat redefined, *gumba* linkages are established, and a micro-universe *huasi* founded. All of these events take place within the constraints of the kin class system and the system of shamanism.

Kinship Idiom and Marriage Practices

Canelos Quichua affinal and consanguineal kin terms (Whitten 1976a: 106-24) quite clearly indicate an ideology of parental or grandparental cousin marriage, and a kin equation suggesting sibling exchange. Contemporary people practice sibling exchange under some circumstances. The concurrent rule, however, which prohibits marriage with double cross cousins—classificatory sisters with incest extensions—results in a complex structure that is often handled by cross-generational marriage.

Ego males and females often express marriage preferences in terms of related individual, household, and *ayllu* continuities of special attributes or substances. In such expression ego males try to marry so as to perpetuate their own male *and* female inherited and acquired soul and body substance, coming from *apayaya* (FF) through male transmission and *apamama* (FFW, FFWZ) through female transmission. A simple cognitive model that is often described to the field investigator is represented in Diagram 1, below:

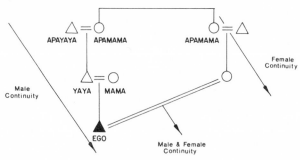

DIAGRAM 1

Women try to marry so as to perpetuate their own female *and* male inherited and acquired soul and body substances coming from *apamama* (MM) through female transmission and *apayaya* (MMH, MMHB) through male transmission. This model is portrayed in Diagram 2, below:

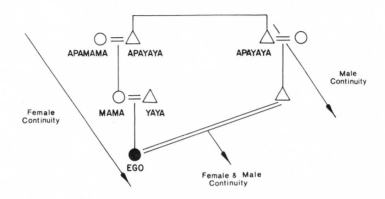

DIAGRAM 2

Apayaya, the father's father's soul or ancient male soul, is connected with an *ayllu* soul that exists in *unai,* beyond time. The first soul, *aya,* is simply inherited from the father, but the grandfather soul must be acquired. Such acquisition involves a process of status rise wherein the questing Runa moves upward in a hierarchy of shamans, embedded in competition with his brothers over the acquisition of ancient souls. As the quest for souls increases, so must knowledge (*yachana, ricsina*) of mythic structure increase, for it is within this structure that the metaphor necessary for the understanding of visionary experience (*muscuyu*) occurs (see Whitten 1976a, 1978).

Apamama, from the standpoint of any male Runa, refers specifically to the woman who gave birth to his inherited soul, his father's father's wife. And when he thinks of the future, he must think of transmission of *apamama* substance through his own wife. If he wants to transmit his inherited soul with the power and ancient life force that have come to him in the male line, then he can marry a woman from those descending from his father's father's wife's uterine relatives, all of whom he would class as *apamama* in the second ascending generation. Kinship statuses constitute an *idiom* of social transmission which, among other things, triggers metaphors that express a male-female parallelism *in* transmission, a mutual dependence *for* transmission, and a logic for cross-generational marriage.

Returning to the diagrams presented above, for a moment, if we take a brother-sister ego locus and combine these two models, we get the picture presented in Diagram 3:

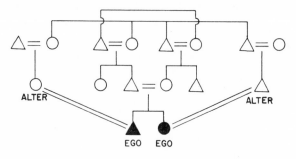

DIAGRAM 3

In this model ego male and ego female make a common marriage among the Canelos Quichua. For their partners, alter male and alter female, marriage is respectively male alter = FBDD (FZSD), female alter = MZSS (MBDS), which are also common marriages. Marriages such as the one indicated in Diagram 4, below, are also common:

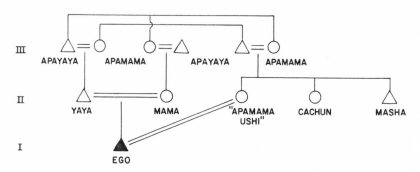

DIAGRAM 4

In generation III two men (ego's *apayaya*) exchanged sisters (ego's *apamama*). Another of ego's FFZ married another man, technically unrelated to the two men and two women from whom ego will inherit and acquire his soul substance. In generation II ego's father took a wife who is technically his FZD but was not so classed because FZH's parents lived in another runa territory and his father and mother had no kinship ties with his wife's immediate family. In ego's own generation ego also takes a wife who is technically both his FFZD and his FFWBD, a perfectly acceptable marriage class, although one that *could* be reckoned as an unacceptable double-cousin class. In Canelos Quichua kinship, extension of any consanguineal bond into the *apayaya-apamama* generation (by invoking a transmission rule) negates lingering taboos that can be applied by extending sibling bonds through filiation procedures. This is done by figuring each kin-type linkage. By invoking a matritransmission rule, ego simply uses an apical kin class designation *"apamama ushi"* (grandmother's daughter) and he has an acceptable and desirable wife class by which to reckon his chosen *huarmi*. He also maintains his male continuity from the father line, and marries into the *apamama* line of his mother. By making a common cross-generation marriage, he takes a spouse from a noncousin sector of genealogical space. Furthermore, by his marriage he creates a potential class of marriageable women, called *cachun,* and a potential class of marriageable men, called *masha,* for his classificatory siblings, should more marriages proceed into this group by ego's classificatory brothers or his father's or sons' classificatory brothers.[2] Finally, his new affinal *mama* (WM) is the sister of his father's affinal *mama* (FMW) and his new *yaya* (WF) is *masha* to his father's affinal *yaya* (FWF). By replicating some statuses in his father's *gumba-jauya* network (*jauya,* as "spouse negotiating category" centering on the parents of a marrying pair, is discussed below), his own segmental *ayllu* linkages become increasingly firm.

Linkage Classes

A fundamental principle of *ayllu* structure is the proposition that women in sister and wife kin classes, real and potential, link *ayllu* segments to one another. Sisters and wives invariably wind up in common kin classes. A woman is born into an *ayllu* reckoned from her mother to mother's mother and mother's mother's husband (MF). When she marries, she links ego to her father and mother, and brings into the *huasi* the MM *apamama* continuity. Ego is linked as a son to WF because of the female *huarmi* linkage, but because he is not *of* the wife's father's substance, transmitted through WM, this "father" uses the *masha* (affinal link) term for ego. The wife also links ego to her brothers and sisters in just the same way as ego's sisters link him to their spouses. All men so linked reciprocally share the kin term *masha.*

Ego is linked to his nonclassificatory (kin type) brothers and sisters through the common consanguinity created by the FF = FFW affinity, transmitted directly to ego. Brothers and sisters also share the special form of continuity brought to their common birth by M through her MM. Brothers transmit some of the same *yaya* substance to their children, but transmission of the *apayaya* substance depends on factors of shamanic acquisition discussed later. Sisters transmit their common *mama* substance to their children, but may differ on the *apamama* substance according to whether they took special pottery instruction from their own mother or from their husband's mother (see Whitten 1976a:82-95).

Within ego's generation the linkage classes through male and female transmission from common grandparents are potentially attenuated because of the *acquisition aspect* of soul substance possession from Times of the Grandfathers (male ego) and from the *choice involved* in women's learning of pottery traditions and associated continuity symbolism from Times of the Grandmothers (female ego).

Ayllu Structure

In his own generation ego male incorporates into his *ayllu* brothers, sisters, parents' siblings' children (classed as B, *huauqui,* and Z, *pani*), and female in-laws classed as *cachun.* Ego excludes the men whom he classes as *masha* from his maximal and segmental *ayllu,* for they belong to "another *ayllu.*" Women, then, span male *ayllu* divisions, for they are *pani* in one and *cachun* in others.

Ego male includes all people classed as *yaya, mama, jachi* (MB-FZH), and *miquia* (FZ) in his *ayllu,* as well as all classed as *apamama* and *apayaya.* Much merging takes place in such classification and the merging allows for choice in *ayllu* membership. For example, a man may reckon his descent from an *apayaya* who was, in effect, his WFF. Ego calls wife's father *yaya,* and even though the wife's father does not reciprocate with *churi,* son, in the living present, movement into the Times of the Grandparents introduces other factors. For example, if through dreams and soul acquisition Datura quests (Whitten 1976a:98-101; 1978) ego believes that he has acquired his WFF soul, then he begins to figure his position in maximal genealogical space in terms of other acknowledged descendants from this apical ancestor. Such a quest involves his wife as well, for she often refigures her *apamama* status.

Ego male readily classes his daughters, *ushi, ushushi,* as part of his *ayllu,* for they provide potential linkages to other *ayllu*s, as well as potential bonds to strengthen his *gumba* network. Ego's sons, *churi,* are part of his *ayllu.* His SS, SD, together with the children of his brothers and cousins, all *subriguna* (from the Spanish *sobrino,-a*), are all *potential ayllu* members, but ego male does *not abstractly* reckon *subriguna* as part of the *ayllu.*

Ego female includes her own children and those of her sisters and husband's sisters as *churi* and *ushi,* son and daughter. For a female ego the female *subriguna* are *very important ayllu members,* for they are the potential affines for future alliance and security.

Men divide *ayllu* structure along spatial lines as well as genealogical. *Ñuca ayllu,* "my *ayllu,*" refers to the set of people reckoned from the Times of the Grandparents residing in ego's "runa territory," one of the six territorial divisions of the culture area. This is the territorial clan. *Caru ayllu* refers to "distant *ayllu,*" meaning *ayllu* members residing in another runa territory or even a non-runa territory. Combination of territorial and panterritorial *ayllu* members constitutes the maximal clan, for male egos. Women reckon *ñuca ayllu* both in immediate and distant dimensions. They include their father's territorial and distant clan reckoning, together with the territorial and distant clan segments into which their sisters and mother's sisters have married.

Obviously, the *ayllu* is both ancestor- and ego-oriented. Convenient though it is to separate kin groups based on these contrastive orientations, the phenomenon of soul acquisition from Times of the Grandparents, which may merge affinal and consanguineal linkages for a given ego but not for others in his stipulated descent group, leads to a discussion of *ayllu* structure from both ancestor and ego perspectives.

Llacta Structure

Members who share *ayllu* bonds spread through a runa territory and subgroupings lay particular claims to named subdivisions, called *llacta,* which radiate out from the mission, trade, or administrative site of the territory to a distance of two to six hours' steady travel. Every territory contains from six to twelve generally acknowledged *llacta*s, and several more in the process of formation. *Llacta* formation coincides with *llacta* fission and realignment, the concept being a dynamic one that involves members in constant conflict and resolution. Each *llacta* has an original founder, a powerful shaman (*sinchi yachaj,* "strong one who knows") able to control generalized mystical power or danger and directed spirit attack (see Whitten 1976a:151-52).

*Llacta*s are consolidated around a nodal *ayllu* segment into which men and women representing one or more other *ayllu* segments are married. As the *ayllu* reaches a population of seven to ten male *huasi* founders, together with their wives and growing families, a currently maximal population of 70-100 people (including babes in arms) induces fission. Fission takes place through staggered *purina* (trek to a distant zone for swidden horticulture, turtle egg gathering, fishing, and hunting), by the out-movement of some members to another *llacta* or another territory, or even by out-movement to another culture such as Quijos Quichua or Achuar Jivaroan. By staggered *purina* we refer to a process by which a number of the families of a given *llacta* are on *purina* at one time, while other families are on *purina* at another time. Land scarcity, game scarcity, and shaman attack and defense are the voiced reasons leading to fission and dispersal of *llacta* members.

*Llacta*s are also depleted by diseases that sweep epidemically through runa territories, and probably by greatly increased parasite infections that accompany moderate crowding when contiguous *llacta*s near the administrative-trade site of the runa territory increase their populations. Epidemics lead to immediate dispersal to *purina chagra*s (cleared fields for swidden horticulture), and increased parasite infection leads to complaints of generalized mystical danger (contagion) and directed spirit attack. The latter is imputed to shamanic duels. Illness and ideas about spirit attack lead those who are ill to get out of the *llacta* territory for a time; *purina chagra*s and alternative opportunities for residence in another area provide refuge. Search for cures for illness and reconsideration of *ayllu* bonds necessitated by shaman duels (discussed briefly at the end of this paper; see also Whitten 1976a:141-63) also lead *llacta* members to move, realign, or elect a relatively isolated existence in a remote jungle area.

Ayllu members share their *llacta*s with members of other *ayllu*s. Ego male is linked to other men, with whom he cooperates in group hunting, group fishing, reciprocal labor exchange, trade expeditions, and territorial defense through affinal and consanguineal bonds. But equally important is ego male's linkage to potential competitors for *chagra,* forest, and river resources through affinal bonds as well as through consanguineal bonds. In two or three generations children and grandchildren of the original linked segments become a single residential segmental and extended *ayllu* descended from *apayaya-apamama* intermarried apical ancestors. These descendants continue to reckon other people, similarly descended from known and stipulated intermarrying ancestors in Times of the Grandparents, as part of their everlasting *ayllu* (maximal clan). Such *ayllu* consolidation (a stem kindred) is the core of a segment of an extended clan within a *llacta.* Constant recruitment of new members as children grow and marry gives to every *llacta* a symbolic duality of people "originally" of the *llacta* (those who reckon descent from founding apical ancestors) and those who have been recruited to the *llacta.* Even those who have been recruited to the *llacta,* however, often lay claim to membership on the basis of common *ayllu* bonds, reckoned through one or another linkage in the Times of the Grandparents.

People who are stipulated descendants from ancestors reckoned as crucial in *llacta* formation have claim to subdivided *chagra* land within the *llacta,* each claimant's land bordering another's. In order to recruit in-laws, a man offers a portion of the land that he claims to a son or son-in-law. By so doing the man loses part of his own *llacta* segment, but he gains a growing, strong ally. Furthermore, until such land has been subdivided two or three times, the man may not really be capable of exploiting or protecting it. He must recruit men who are in his debt and women who are in his wife's debt. If successful, he gains not only land-based allies to consolidate his intra-*llacta* zone against encroachment by *llacta* mates but also the woman- and manpower necessary to exploit his own established land claims.

Llacta structure also embodies two native concepts dealing with the politics of *llacta* maintenance vis-à-vis adjacent *llacta*s. These are the concepts that I translate and analyze as "embedding" and "outposting." Embedding refers to the placement of some *llacta* members near its named, symbolic focus, where they are socially circumscribed (Carneiro 1970:737-38) by the larger numbers of members. This involves the embedded *huasi* unit in more chicha giving, more intensive interaction and maintenance of good will, and greater jeopardy from directed spirit attack and shamanic duels. The Quichua concept of such embedding is simply *llactaimi causanchi*, "living there in the *llacta*."

Outposting refers to the placement of a *huasi* regarded by one *llacta* group as being *of* their *llacta* (*llactamanda*) adjacent to or even within the territory of another *llacta*. This is simply called *ñucanchi llactamanda* _____ *mayambi tian*, "one from our *llacta* is visiting (name of *llacta*)." Outposting removes the *huasi* members from intensive, frequent contact with their own other *llacta* members, and involves them more directly with alter *llacta* members. People who are outposted are capable of either going over to the adjacent *llacta* or forming their own *llacta*.

Through time *llacta* centers and boundaries shift and fluctuate as those outposted maneuver advantageously. Such maneuvering inevitably changes the nature of groupings in a runa territory. For example, let us consider the case of three brothers, sons of a shaman, who marry three women (often classificatory sisters) in three different, adjacent *llacta*s. Each of them has several residential alternatives within the *llacta* system. A man may live in his father's *llacta* near the *llacta* central locus, in which case he is clearly embedded and signals expansion of his father's *ayllu* in that *llacta*. Alternatively, he may live on the outer fringe of his own *llacta*, outposted to that of his father-in-law. He may live with his father-in-law near the central locus of this alter *llacta*, in which case he is regarded as outposted by his own *ayllu* segment and *llacta*, but embedded in his father-in-law's *llacta* by his father-in-law's *ayllu* segment and *llacta* mates. Or, a man and his father or father-in-law may be found near the fringe of one or the other *llactas*, both outposted, so to speak, but such a residential maneuver signals potentially new *llacta* formation.

If each of the three sons, mentioned above, arranges residence in such a way as to claim some outposted allegiance to different *llactas*, while at the same time locating his *actual residence* near the other sons, and if their father comes to live with them, then they become the central *ayllu* node of their own *llacta,* and anyone joining them from their previous *llactas* become "newcomers." Obviously, *llacta* dynamics necessitate further discussion of spouse acquisition, to which we now turn our attention.

Kindred and Marriage

Within *llactas,* shallow, three-generation stem kindreds represent the quasi-corporate segments of territorial clans as nodal, residential land-holding units. The stem kindred is ideologically predicated upon a shamanic node. Within each stem kindred adult male egos form their own personal kindreds. Both stem and personal kindred maintenance is dependent upon recruitment strategies and land allocation. Factors of *llacta* boundaries and membership, residence, and spouse selection vary, but certain structural aspects of the relationship between *ayllu* and *huasi* endure. Let us first turn to the common, repetitive variants and alternatives through which *ayllu* and *huasi* structures are maintained and adapted.

Residence

There are three residential alternatives practiced by a *huasi* unit among the Canelos Quichua at any given time. First, the man and his wife may go off to live on their own either in a remote jungle area or in another territory where *ayllu* members reside. This alternative is not common, but its possibility often keeps the couples' parents, *ayllu* or *llacta* mates, from becoming too "possessive," "bossy," or demanding.

The second alternative is to reside in the vicinity of one set of spouse's parents, leaving the other set with some sort of compensation. This is the most common option. Where two or more *llactas* border one another within a runa territory, interesting organization strategies are played out by a couple electing this option. If the boy comes from *llacta* A and the girl from *llacta* B and the couple elect to live in *llacta* A, then the girl's brothers (the boy's *mashas*) may well make special offers of land space, and allegiance, to the boy to see that he regards himself *of llacta* B (where his wife's parents reside), and potentially *outposted to llacta* A (where his own parents reside), even though he is regarded by his own *llacta* mates as *embedded* there (*llacta* A). Through time, residential changes of the couple may alternate between *llacta* A and *llacta* B, especially if they can establish a *chagra* within a couple of hours' walking distance from both *llactas*.

The third alternative occurs when two men who have married each other's sisters, or two (classificatory) brothers who have married two (classificatory) sisters, arrange some marriages of their children so as to fortify intra-*llacta*, inter-*ayllu* dominance. This normally occurs at the foundation of a *llacta*, and, after the second generation, powerful sanctions of incest accusation are applied if married double cousins attempt to re-enact this pattern by arranging intermarriages of their offspring. The pattern is most common when interethnic marriage takes place in the first generation. In fact, we know of no such arrangements between acknowledged Canelos Quichua intermarrying *ayllu* groupings. The ones we are familiar with involve Quijos Quichua marrying Canelos Quichua or bicultural Canelos Quichua–Achuar, in one generation, and perpetuating double-cousin marriage in the second.

Spouse Selection

Marriage choices and plans revolve around four alternatives. The first occurs when a man captures a baby boy from another people, out of Canelos Quichua territory, and rears him to marry one of his daughters. These arrangements are not common, but they have occurred in the past. Revenge stealing has also taken place, and the placation of aggrieved parties one or two generations later by gifts, or even by the sending of a marriageable spouse to a related member from the other culture, leads to some very strong alliances between some of the Canelos Quichua and members of other cultures (Achuar, Shuar, Zaparoan, and Cocama, that we know about).

The second alternative is either the outgrowth of the first or the result of diminution of hostilities resulting from a killing between members of different cultures. In this alternative a male child is sent to an aggrieved father who has lost a son or to a man who has lost a brother. The child is reared to marry the man's daughter, and further reciprocities again cement relationships between members of kindred segments of two different, normally antagonistic, cultures. A variant of this alternative occurs when a man with children escaping a killing in his cultural territory seeks asylum in the vicinity of a well-established Canelos Quichua man, or of a man endeavoring to consolidate his *llacta* territory. Such an escapee offers his young sons in marriage to the man's daughters, in return for asylum.

Children reared to marry under such circumstances are instructed in the origin of their *apamama* and *apayaya* substance, and encouraged to return to their natal territory to learn language and custom, taking their Canelos Quichua wife and a male and female unmarried youth or two from their wife's father's family with them.

The third alternative occurs where two sets of parents negotiate the marriage for a son and daughter, before the daughter reaches puberty. These marriages, in particular, cement relationships between strong men in different *ayllu*s and contribute to both *llacta* alliance (between members of often distant *llacta*s) and *ayllu* continuity when the affinal bond endures. But if the man abandons the woman, a life-long feud is initiated.

The fourth alternative involves the direct mutual choice of a young man and woman for one another as spouse. In this case, the most common one, the man asks his father to negotiate with his chosen mate's father for their marriage. Such negotiations can be interminable if not triggered by other factors, one of which is simply "capture" of the bride by the groom and flight to his father's household (and sometimes bride's father's brother's household in a different *llacta*), forcing negotiation to take place.

Canelos Quichua marriage stresses mutual, reciprocal possession of two individuals, *cari* and *huarmi*. The terms of affinity, or marriage, used by the *cari-huarmi* pair for each other, and applied to them by other *llacta* members, are *huarmiyuj*, possession of a woman, and *cariyuj*, possession of a man. The interactions of marriageable man and woman generate interdependent systems of obligation and responsibility, each of which is grounded in a primary dyadic relationship. For the man these are (1) the *cari-huarmi* relationship, which will become a *yaya-mama huasi* unit; (2) the *yaya-churi* relationship between ego's father and himself; and (3) the *yaya-masha* relationship between ego's wife's father and himself. For the woman there is (1) the same *huarmi-cari* dyad; (2) the *mama-ushi* relationship between ego's mother and herself; and (3) the *mama-cachun* relationship between husband's mother and herself.

Residential choice skews the relationship of one dyad or another. To satisfy the transactions involved in the maintenance of one dyadic system, *cari* or *huarmi* often create tension in another. Multiple, complex sets of transactions within each dyad cumulate and ramify, invariably modifying the quality of interactions in another. As the *cari-huarmi* union solidifies and maintains the impetus behind other dyadic and network transactions, the spouse-negotiating category *jauya* forms, its central focus being on the parents of the marrying pair.

A couple undertaking the task of reorganizing their lives and continuing to maintain their close ties with natal families, while developing the new ties with respective new families, face a set of social expectations that place severe strains on the affinal bond. Attenuated or weak affinal relationships simply do not stand up under such pressure. Affinity between man and woman signals a whole system of linkages, the ramifications of which are forcefully brought home to the young couple. The strains in their immediate kinship networks force the couple to symbolic activity attendant on creation of the *huasi* as a microcultural, microsocial universe embedded in Canelos Quichua symbolism and the maximal *ayllu*. Datura trials for man and woman, and subsequent instruction in spirit helpers and soul acquisition (man) and pottery tradition (woman), bring the couple into increased awareness of their role in cultural perpetuity as well as in socioeconomic affairs. A couple whose affinal bonds and *huasi* universe do not strengthen and persevere toward local *llacta* and inter-*llacta* interpersonal maintenance, or worse, a couple who find one another incompatible as a pair, simply break apart, each beginning anew the search for a viable partner.

A man is expected to take an active role in searching for a wife. All opportunities afforded by traveling are utilized to learn of spirit substances useful in attracting women, and in trying one's luck at attracting women as well. Ordinarily a man finds a compatible lover by the time he reaches 20 years of age. Sometimes, in his quest for knowledge, a man decides it is not so hard to love many different sorts of women, and makes his decision about a spouse on the basis of advantages offered by the girl's father. Women also actively seek a husband. They learn of secret magical substances to make themselves beautiful, perfect the female household tasks of chicha making and serving, and learn the bases of pottery manufacture. Many girls also travel with senior male relatives to distant territories or towns, and are not infrequently "stolen" by handsome beaus while there.

Regardless of how the selection is made—and the range is from thunderstruck "love at first sight" to courtship over a period of years—a man eventually tells his father that he intends to marry a particular girl. Whether he does this by simply bringing her home or by asking his father to negotiate their marriage, as any movement indicating pending affinity between a boy and a girl occurs, the respective *jauya* category between the couple's parents is signaled.

The *jauya* category starts to form on the boy's side, as his father begins the task of trying to structure the series of events making up the marriage episode, which take about three years to complete. At the same time, however, the girl's father and mother also begin to lay out strategies for the same episode series. In essence this is what occurs.

The boy's father arranges a visit to the girl's father. In such arrangements he asks one or two brothers or residential in-laws (ZH but never WB, as far as we know) to accompany him, and to share the burden of providing necessary gifts of food and drink. Today many gallons of raw cane alcohol are a crucial, indeed central, gift. Drinking goes on for a couple of days or more. Those accompanying the father of the groom are *jauya* vis-à-vis everyone who comes to drink in the girl's father's household, and (at least in Canelos and Puyo) they are *tentatively* or *potentially gumba* to the groom's father. Only later, when the bride's father has also selected one or two *gumbas* to continue to negotiate marriage arrangements, will the *jauya* term be reciprocally applied between individual members of the spouse-negotiating categories. When this occurs, ego's father strengthens his personal *gumba* network by close incorporation of some brothers and sister's husbands, differentiating this net from his WB *masha* statuses. Conversation about what a good hunter-provider the boy is, and what a good *chagra*-working chicha maker the girl is, goes on as people drink, eat, and dance; when the couple dance together, "marriage"—*cariyuj-huarmiyuj*—in its preliminary form is signaled. Thereafter, the couple begin to sleep together within the house of the bride's parents.

Most emphasis is in giving enough to the bride's father to compensate him for the loss of his daughter. At the end of a two- to three-day period (sometimes longer) the groom's negotiating set leaves. The married couple may stay on with the girl's father, in which case the groom is seen as paying off a debt of labor in compensation for his marriage to the girl. More often, the couple accompany the groom's parents, but it is understood that the groom still owes the girl's father his labor for from six months to a year. Two or three such visits by the groom's negotiating group may be necessary during the first year of marriage.

Many kin relationships are remembered during this period. Maximal *ayllu* members are recalled and discussed, and advice sought from knowledgable elders about grandparental origin nodes from which it is hoped that the man will acquire a soul and, on the female side, continuity will be transmitted through pottery tradition. Both spouses work for the parents in the house where they are residing. Although they would like to set up their own *chagra* and household, this is extremely difficult, for they are constantly involved in work within the *chagra* and residential unit of the parents.

Both sets of parents normally want their son or daughter to stay home, or at least to remain in the vicinity of the parental household. Each parental pair usually tries to make an attractive offer to the young couple to accept co-residence. Division of the man's or woman's father's *chagra* land is the basic offer made. But this in itself produces conflict among other *llacta* members, many of whom may object to a new youth holding land in their territory, when a father-in-law makes the offer. The youth may fare no better in his own father's territory, however, for those in his *yaya* and *jachi* categories may object to division of land of their brother (the youth's father).

Objections are usually based on the fact that there is, in practice, much overlapping in land claims. Given the system of swidden, slash-mulch

(and in some areas, slash-burn) agriculture, such overlapping is not
a critical point of contention until more and more of the land is worked.
When a father or father-in-law offers a son or son-in-law a segment of his
land, it is clear that more of the *chagra* territory will be worked, with
possible loss to holders of other *llacta chagra* territory.

Within the newly married man's father's *llacta* actual fights may break
out between him, or his brothers, and other residents. Although he is
important as a new adult to his father's expanding kindred, he also comes
to understand that he may not be able to live comfortably in an arena
of conflict. To remove himself from such conflict, and also to fulfill the
obligation to his father-in-law, he frequently goes to his wife's family's
huasi and begins a period of service to in-laws. Here he is obliged not
only to help clear land for his father-in-law's *chagra* but also to provide
firewood to his father-in-law's household, normally a woman's task.

A father-in-law often offers land to his new son-in-law as an inducement
for him to remain. Such an offer also produces conflict for those in the
youth's *masha* category, i.e. his wife's brothers, who see such land as
potentially theirs. Again, fights may break out, and accusations of sorcery
may also be reciprocally made between those in ego male's and ego female's *ayllu*s.

Instruction in pottery technique is a very important signal as to
where, and under what conditions, a girl will eventually reside. A mother
who took pains to train a girl in this difficult skill may insist that such
a continuity of *apamama* symbolism must remain in the vicinity of the
girl's natal *huasi,* convincingly maintaining that continuity of vision and
knowledge is tied to the girl's skill. The move of such a girl to the husband's parents' *huasi* is seen as a transposition of *ayllu* continuity to another territory. This is not necessarily negatively valued by the women
involved, but a relationship between the women in the *jauya* category
must be established where agreement as to the continuity of *apamama*
substance from Ancient Times to the present is reached. Should women
find conflict or discontinuity in their mythic structure, or histories, they
may object to the girl's movement and do everything possible to dissuade
her from joining her husband. Or, if they don't like the man's mother
or his family, they may invoke mythic or ancient discontinuity to instill
doubt in the girl's mind.

A woman who has not been so trained, however, may be taught techniques and symbolism by her husband's mother, learning to maintain
ayllu continuity from the *apamama* times through her affinal female
relatives. This, in turn, often involves her in other work and service to
her mother-in-law as she becomes more and more obligated to her and to
her husband's mother's sisters.

Sometime in the second year, occasionally earlier, the wife's family may visit the husband's family. If it is expected that the husband will reside with the wife's father for an indeterminate period, then the wife's spouse negotiators bring meat and alcohol. If not, then it is expected that the husband's spouse negotiators will provide chicha, food, and some cane alcohol. People party and recount *ayllu* history and legend, the hope being that accord in all aspects of spouse negotiating will occur.

If accord is reached, all well and good; but even fission may resolve some problems should the families not get along, for if one or the other spouse-negotiating group is displeased, it may leave, the couple then making a choice as to which side to take. Once again, a weak affinal bond simply cannot endure in such a conflict situation, and there is always the possibility of affinal fission within the second year.

By the end of three years more reciprocal visits, or even gifts sent by traveling Runas, cement whatever relationships have finally been somewhat tortuously worked out. By this time the husband has normally worked for his father-in-law for six months to a year, and he and his wife have established a *chagra* in some area. As soon as their *chagra* is planted, though, the couple is cut off from the parental food supply and forced to forage as best they can. Again, surviving this strain seems to strengthen the *huasi* unit. Furthermore, people who feel sorry for a struggling young couple may help them out, thereby cementing friendship bonds among a dispersed and localized network of people within consanguineal and affinal categories in a runa territory. Any time during this three-year period the couple may register their marriage with national officials, receive a church marriage at one of the *ayllu* ceremonies, or even be married in the Catholic church of Puyo or Canelos by special arrangement.

Occasionally, the Canelos Quichua perform some variant of the typical marriage dance of the Quijos Quichua (see Macdonald 1979). In such circumstances, as far as we can determine (since the practice is very uncommon), the couple signal the acquisition of high, personal prestige. Normally this ceremony is performed interstitially with the *ayllu* ceremony (Whitten 1976a:165-202), but sometimes it is performed in the absence of any other ceremony. Regardless of specific performance style, terrible fist fights often begin by late afternoon and sometimes continue for two or three days. Not infrequently, *llacta* fission, accusations of sorcery, realignment within a territory, and redistribution of *chagra* plots take place. Such ceremonies do, however, establish the couple as "equals" with their parents' siblings; the nature of the equality, though, must be determined or negotiated in each individual case.

The concept of one ceremony to cement the affinal bond, however, is not a Canelos Quichua one. The idea of at least three years of spouse negotiation and arrangement of the various peoples involved in a referential kin class system, constructed kinship network, and territorial-land claiming unit constitutes the reciprocal sense of *huarmi* and *cari* acquisition—*cariyuj, huarmiyuj*—which can be called "marriage." The end result is a structural unit—*huasi*—the nature of which is discussed elsewhere (Whitten 1976a:65-104; 1978).

The birth of the couple's first child, at least among the Puyo Runa and the Canelos Runa, is accompanied by the immediate establishment of a *gumba-comari* bond between the couple and another married pair. The man is usually F, B, ZH, or WZH to male ego, and the woman is HBW, HZ, or Z to his wife. We know of no cases of a WB serving as *gumba.* Of course, WB *becomes gumba to* ZH because the *gumba* co-parent class is reciprocally applied. But the bond is *formed* by ego asking ZH, not by a request to WB, as far as we know.

This *gumba* bond supersedes all other dyadic, classificatory, or categorical terminological designations, and is expected to establish a close, life-long, reciprocal, symmetrical relationship between the couples. The child becomes the *gumba*'s *llullucu marcashca,* "marked child," and the *gumba* is *marca yaya* (male) and *marca mama* (female). These bonds are also expected to endure throughout a lifetime. Ideally, the ritual co-parent chooses the child's first name, and the child's parent its second name. Men name boys, women name girls. Some of the secret spirit substance of the *gumba* is also conferred on the child, and if both father and co-father are shamans and there is reason to believe that the child has some special power, the child will be thought to have the potential for becoming *sinchi yachaj,* a powerful shaman. When such potential is thought to exist, the child's mother will softly address it as *sinchi yachaj runa* from time to time.

Extension of the *gumba* terminological designation is often made by co-parents' brothers, sisters, and children, though reciprocal maintenance of this term, and the implied symmetrical ties superseding kinship and affinity, is by mutual choice. Formation of such a *gumba* network within and beyond *llacta* boundaries signals the end, or nearly the end, of spouse negotiations. There is considerable variety, of course, much depending on when a woman has her first baby, where she has it, and whether or not it lives.

Canelos Quichua symbolize the enduring *ayllu* structure and its replication with each marriage by figuring ways in which a man can take a spouse from the same category from which his father took a spouse. Such acquisition assures the couple continuity of inherited soul substance and, equally important, a set of relatives who see themselves as replicating inter-*ayllu* exchange patterns taking place in Times of the Grandparents.

An ideology of structural replication seems to gloss over individual tendencies toward bellicosity during spouse negotiation, thereby reducing some potential strains on the *cari-huarmi* union.

There is also a tendency for distant *llacta* spouse acquisition, perhaps due to the difficulty of satisfying demands and expectations of both sets of parents.[3] The repetitive linking of *ayllu* segments in relatively distant *llacta*s, together with the consequent establishment of more *cachun* classes and an ideology of replication of structure from Times of the Grandparents, extends an awareness of *ayllu* and ethnic unity through *llacta* and territorial divisions. Furthermore, serial marriage and polygyny in the past, clearly evident in our genealogies, together with great fertility and fecundity of the acknowledged apical ancestors, create a large marriageable class for any ego. All such potential spouses *can* be reckoned as "cousins," and cousin marriage is ubiquitous. But individual choice of a desirable, compatible mate, as well as a need to bolster the affinal bond constantly in the face of strains produced by the spouse negotiators, leads to decisions far more complex than a cousin-marriage model can explain.

Kinship and Culture

The structure of *huasi* and the structure of *ayllu* are relative constants around which maneuvers involving *llacta, ayllu* segments, land, and social status revolve. Each *ayllu* segment maintains its special culture and special, sometimes secret, ethnic awareness. For example, every *ayllu* segment contains members who reckon descent from Jivaroan, Zaparoan, or Quijos origins and retain and perpetuate certain facets of these cultures through myth, design, medicinal secrets, or shamanic procedure. Such culture, including secrets, is transmitted to residential in-laws. In this transmission process, subterritorial, though inter-*llacta,* concentrations of knowledge exist. People in such intertwined *ayllu* segments trek together to the same general *purina* territory, and the male members trade with men of other cultures, particularly when they speak the requisite languages. Out-marriage from each intermarried center within a territory serves to concatenate knowledge within the maximal territory, producing the territorial runa. Further out-marriage, as well as movement of entire kindred groupings outward from one territory to another, disperses such knowledge among groupings in other territories who themselves transmit to one another.

The size of Canelos Quichua territory itself provides many large refuge zones for independent *huasi* units seeking to escape the pressures imposed by territorial clans. Moving into distant jungle territory and engaging in individual and household acquisition of soul power through Amasanga (male soul-master spirit) and Nunghuí (female undersoil spirit) is a viable alternative to either embedding or outposting within the *llacta* system. In time, the members of such a *sacha huasi* (jungle household) become particularly valuable to *llacta* members near an administrative center because of their greater knowledge of a jungle territory. Reincorporation of such Sacha Runa (jungle people) into certain *llacta*s ensures the territorial Runa of a diversity of knowledge that can be applied to *purina chagra*s, hunting territories, and the search for valued jungle products.

Death, Reorganization, and Shamanism

Death conjoins a world of souls of the dead, *huanushca aya,* with the living Runa. The living soul—that substance which maintained the life of the person—leaves the dying person through his mouth, and remains in the vicinity of the body. A corpse is brought to its own house and laid out in the center along a cardinal axis. Its soul then travels freely within the house. Both men and women resident in the house, and the brothers and sisters, begin immediately to chant a heart-rending wail. The women let their wail resound, and the men bottle theirs up in their throats, covering their mouths with their hands. The wail invokes memories of all the good things done by the deceased and also brings memories of the deaths of other loved ones. The grief that is projected and shared around the dead person is indescribably deep and moving.

Interspersed in such crying is a discussion of why the person died when he did. Illness, accident, or snakebite are usually dismissed as secondary causes, and the real reason for the death is explored as everyone tries to place blame. Frequently neglect or a mistake by people resident in the *huasi* is named, and quite violent arguments may result. These are usually resolved by projection outward, by an assumption of an evil "somewhere" that struck out at the beloved deceased. More and more people in the territory come bearing small gifts of tobacco, *copal* (for lighting), and chicha. Near the centers of trade they bring packs of cigarettes, candles, and cane alcohol. The general, terrible grief enactment goes on, interspersed with arguments over causality, until a couple of hours or so after dark.

By this time most sisters of the deceased, together with their close female relatives, move to the woman's section of the household where they continue to wail and visit with one another. Men, except for the actual brothers or sons of the deceased, begin to enact grief's opposition—uproarious humor. Such "play," *pugllana,* takes place near the corpse. Canelos Quichua exegesis of their play is that the soul of the deceased has become hungry and has sampled the chicha but cannot be satisfied. The games are played to entertain it, to allow it to flow in and out of the players, testing the relationship between the world of *huanushca* souls and living (*causan*) souls. Everyone must stay awake during the night of the wake, so that their souls do not travel as vision makers to conjoin directly with the fresh substance of the unsophisticated dead soul. Those who do try to sleep are rudely and loudly awakened. Throughout the night, and sometimes through a second and even third night, male *ayllu* members of the deceased, together with the in-married relatives, play within the contained universe of the *huasi* while women serve chicha, visit, and wail. Death conjoins the two invariant structures, *huasi* and *ayllu,* and touches each with the enduring soul substance of its own inevitability.

The appearance of the sun ends the intra-*huasi* ceremony and game playing, for the penetration of the yellow rays within the *huasi* destroys the closure of the household universe and opens the entire universe to the *huanushca aya.* Although the people may call the soul back for two or three nights, especially where people must travel for some distance to attend the wake, the coming of the sun itself signals time for burial. By the second or third signal—within two or three days—the corpse is interred.

The greatest reorganization occurring after the interment of a corpse takes place over the consolidated accusations of sorcery. People just do not normally believe that it is time for the deceased to go, and they search for, and reflect on, sources of killing power. To understand this process, and its relationship to kinship, it is necessary to understand the role of shamanism in family and kinship structure.

Let us turn, briefly, to Canelos Quichua concepts of time and linear history. *Ayllu* structure is conceived of by the Canelos Quichua as a postulated network of linked souls extending back before the Times of Destruction to the Ancient Times. Canelos Quichua oral history and cosmology impart demographic aspects to the different time periods and relate them to *ayllu* structure and to shamanism. In short, there were more ancient Runas than there are contemporary Runas and all of the Ancient People had some knowledge that was lost during the Times of Destruction. The totality of knowledge was considerable but is not completely irretrievable. Those *apayaya-apamama* ancestors emerging from the Times of Destruction were few in number. They intermarried among themselves to produce the living, and recently deceased, ancestors of the contemporary Runa who have once again begun to expand their population.

The contemporary Runa *ayllu*s (kindreds, segmental, territorial, and maximal clans) exist as expanding, outward-ramifying, consanguineal-affinal chains of linkage reckoned from contemporary shamans, and from the shaman-parents of the contemporary old people. The shamans, each of whom may muster the spirit power to kill, provide crucial linkages to the Ancient People—i.e. to the system of stipulated descent—through their acquisition of Ancient People's souls. To become a shaman (*yachaj*) involves a developmental sequence of soul acquisition that reunites *apa-yaya-apamama* substance with Ancient People substances and at least a partial regaining of knowledge lost in the Times of Destruction. The process of shamanic power quest also conjoins a Runa *ayllu* structure of partially controlled soul (*aya*) linkage with a world of spirits (*supai*). This process is partially described in Whitten (1976a:141-63; 1976c; 1978; 1981).

In Ancient Times, unlike the present, people knew how to direct the movement of the *huanushca aya* so that it could be reborn. When the Ancient People died, their souls entered rocks and enduring logs from which sources contemporary shamans acquire the living, encapsulated soul of the dead Runa ancestor in the form of a polished stone. Souls of the Ancient People are also captured by such spirit masters of forest and water domains, and powerful shamans acquire these ancient souls directly from these spirit masters. When a contemporary Runa considers his own soul substance, he must reflect on the ancient souls acquired by people in *yaya, jachi,* and *apayaya* kin classes, for souls of the same ancient substance form linkages to one another.

Many contemporary adult Canelos Quichua lack a *yaya* shaman, but none is without an *apayaya* shaman ancestor, and none is without one or more *jachi* soul possessors in the immediate ascending generation. In fact, recognition of shaman status for a man is signaled in the descending generation by an increasing number of men designating him by the term *jachi*. Even a man other than actual father (FB) previously classed as *yaya* by referential kin criteria becomes addressed as *jachi* when it is believed that his soul acquisition and mystical knowledge to cure and to kill are sufficient to regard him as a powerful shaman (*sinchi yachaj*). Because of postulated cousin marriage in the Times of the Grandparents, every ego knows that many *yachaj*s are related to him in the MB = FZH (*jachi*) kin class. Those whom ego calls *jachi* reciprocate the term *ala,* "mythic brother." An asymmetrical system is established wherein a powerful shaman is regarded in both a consanguineal and affinal kin class of the first ascending generation; he, in turn, lateralizes his terminology to that of the ethnic "mythic brother" for those who *call him jachi*. Use of the term *ala* by a shaman for younger, less powerful men symbolizes a present reawakening of lost souls in ego's generation; an expanding number of *jachi*s, for any ego, in the ascending generation symbolizes the acquisition of past power acquired for contemporary *ayllu* and ethnic continuity.

Powerful shamans are *llacta* founders, in which process they not only consolidate a stem kindred around themselves and firm up the extended clan segment throughout a territory but also establish sacred territorial markers throughout a runa territory, and beyond. For example, the stone or tree site where a powerful shaman reputedly made a depression by blowing a spirit dart (*supai biruti*), from which to drink Datura (*huanduj*) to gain more power from various spirits, is viewed as a permanent, sacred marker to a *llacta*. From the time of shamanic founding of such an area, *ayllu* members, reckoning from the shaman, defend their rights to the *llacta* against all adversaries, and come to stand in a position of higher rank (in their own eyes) than their in-married affines who are members of other *ayllu*s.

The relationship among shamanic power, death, *ayllu* structure, and territory is direct and clear. Shamans do harm by sending spirit darts toward an enemy. The enemy, if a shaman, also has spirit helpers who deflect the dart. When a dart cannot penetrate the enemy, it caroms off, follows *ayllu* lines in the immediate vicinity, and enters a more vulnerable person in the targeted person's *ayllu*. Such darts follow *ayllu* lines to the victim's *huasi*, and then on into the *huasi* to a vulnerable person. If they do not find a vulnerable person in that *huasi*, or if the resident spirits drive them out, then they move back into the *ayllu* structure and zoom toward another *huasi* until a vulnerable person is hit. Powerful shamans do not ordinarily send mere spirit darts at adversaries; they send spirits with living souls of dead humans winging at victims. Whenever a powerful shaman dies, it is due to the projection of such spirits by other powerful shamans collaborating in a kill.

Frequently, more than one powerful shaman lays claim to the same *llacta* near the trade locus of a runa territory. The children of such powerful shamans are often intermarried, and the shamans often cooperate. Sometimes, however, power acquisition results in enemy shamans occupying the same or adjacent territories, and the spirit darts and projectiles fly back and forth in shamanic death duels. No person can claim *ayllu* membership with both sides of a pair of warring shamans, or with their stipulated ancestors, for to do so would be to become vulnerable to the directed spirit attacks of both sides.

It is not possible in this paper to consider more than a few ramifications of the relationships among shamanism, kinship, and marriage systems. A few points, however, can be made briefly. First, powerful shamans acquire souls from grandparental shamans who themselves had acquired souls from the Ancient People. Only they know for sure what souls they acquire, and their outward flow of information to acknowledged *ayllu* and alter *ayllu* members varies, just as the interpretation of such information received by *huasi* members varies. Second, shamans directly acquire ancient shaman souls, and thereby provide symbolic continuity through the Times of Destruction—through stipulated descent and demonstrated filiation. Third, powerful shamans provide mechanisms for unifying and separating, expanding and contracting *ayllu* space according to criteria of soul power acquisition, defense from mystical danger and directed spirit attack, and the ability to counterattack.

Shamans also signal cooperation by transforming affinal to consanguineal status within a set of mystical cooperators. They commonly span ZH and WB statuses with the shaman kin class *huauqui* (brother), as shown in Diagram 5 below:

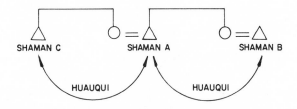

DIAGRAM 5

Shamans A, B, and C, each of whom is in the kin class *masha* with relation to one another, call each other *huauqui* to cement their mutual protection pact. Let us recall here another phenomenon introduced above, p. 215, illustrated in Diagram 6 below:

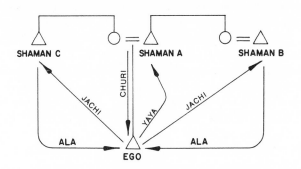

DIAGRAM 6

Ego places shamans B and C in kin class *jachi*, distinguishing the MB = FZH class as *ayllu* nodes distinct from *yaya*, his own *ayllu* node. Shamans B and C reciprocate *ala* to ego, classifying him as "mythic brother." In the next generation, as ego 1 transmits information on shaman nodes and *ayllu* structure to his offspring (ego 2), we find the situation occurring illustrated in Diagram 7 below:

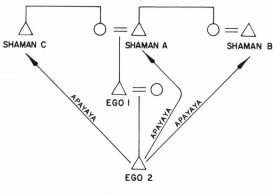

DIAGRAM 7

The shamans are all *apayaya* from the Times of the Grandparents, regarded as power extensions of primary (male ego FF) *apayaya* shaman power. From the shamans' perspective such male grandchildren are only *potential ayllu* members. Incorporation into shaman *ayllu*s will depend on factors of soul acquisition by the shamans' children and the children's children. By employing the MB = FZH kin class equation from the reference point of his own father (ego 1), ego 2 may combine grandparental nodes B and C as an *apayaya* node parallel to FF, necessitating a classificatory *apamama* affinal connection (FFWB or FFZH). The resulting structure can then be portrayed as in Diagram 8 below:

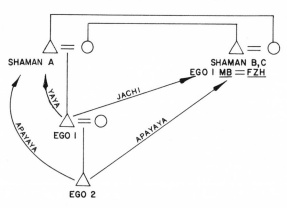

DIAGRAM 8

Shaman status B,C, now one referential position in *ayllu* space, becomes part of a dual apical structure from which ego 2 reckons descent. Recalling our earlier discussion illustrated by Diagram 1 on p. 196, we know that ego also seeks a wife classifiable as transmitting *apamama* substance from Times of the Grandparents. Considering shaman status in the domain of kinship offers multiple possibilities for the consideration of primary *apayaya* and *apamama* statuses. Let us again consider Diagram 1, but with shaman nodes added, as in Diagram 9 below:

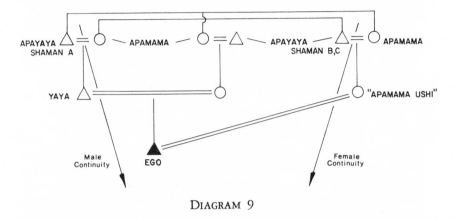

DIAGRAM 9

In this illustration ego figures a patritransmission node as shaman A and a matritransmission node as shaman B,C, an *apamama* affine. He marries so as to include in his own offspring the continuity of his own patri- and matri-inherited substances. What is crucial is the idiom of parallel transmission of shaman status and the role of marriage in uniting or recombining stipulated ancestral nodes of *ayllu* structure with imputed acquired power. When ego actually acquires power from the deceased shamans in the *apayaya-apamama* generations (if he moves into shaman status), he may change his name and further manipulate his *ayllu* membership so as to shift his descent position. This becomes necessary at times because of the inter-*ayllu* vendettas discussed above. For example, in Diagram 9, should stipulated powerful shaman descendants of shaman A's *ayllu* begin a killing feud with shaman B,C's *ayllu*, then fission of all people between A and B,C lines would take place, with people acknowledging membership to one or the other but not both. Or, should categorized B,C statuses come to be composed of actual shamans dueling with one another, either B or C would remain as *apayaya,* but the other would be denied such *apayaya* position. With some resolution of such a duel, however, merger may again take place. Resolution is particularly likely with the Canelos Quichua when the people as a whole, or a major segment of a runa territory, is faced with severe external pressures. These pressures currently exist (see Whitten 1976a, 1976b, 1978) but it is beyond the scope of this paper to discuss them, or the adaptive response of the Canelos Quichua to them.

NOTES

1. Fieldwork with the Canelos Quichua began in 1968 under the auspices of a Latin American Studies Committee grant, Washington University, St. Louis. Field research in 1970, 1971, 1972-73, 1974, and 1975 was supported by National Science Foundation grant no. GS-2999. Supplemental research stipends were also provided by the Research Board, the Center for International Comparative Studies, and the Center for Latin American and Caribbean Studies, University of Illinois, Urbana-Champaign, for fieldwork in 1974, 1975, and 1976. In Ecuador our research has been sponsored by the Instituto Nacional de Antropología e Historia (INAH) and the Museo del Banco Central, both under the direction of Hernán Crespo Toral. Sections of this paper are taken from *Sacha Runa: Ethnicity and Adaptation of Ecuadorian Jungle Quichua* (Urbana: University of Illinois Press, 1976) and are reprinted here by permission of the University of Illinois Press. The paper itself was prepared under the auspices of a John Simon Guggenheim Memorial Foundation fellowship. The basically Spanish orthography employed is that of Orr and Wrisley (1965). We wish to acknowledge here the editorial advice given by Kenneth M. Kensinger and F. K. Lehman in the preparation of the paper for publication, while reserving all responsibility for lack of clarity, or other faults, for ourselves.

2. The categories *masha* (male) and *cachun* (female) are affinal terms that are asymmetrical between parents and children-in-law and relatively symmetrical between brothers- and sisters-in-law. In the former ego calls S *churi*, DH *masha*, D *ushi*, and SW *cachun;* both *churi* and *masha*, and *ushi* and *cachun*, reciprocate *yaya* (to a male) and *mama* (to a female). See Whitten (1976a:106-18) for analysis of the kin class terminology.

3. Bicultural, bilingual Achuar Jivaroans intermarry with the Canelos Quichua and maintain a clearly articulated proposition, or rule, that affects marriage choice and the tendency to take spouses from distant *llactas*. When a father succeeds in arranging a marriage between his daughter and a man from his own natal territory (such arrangement includes movement of the man to the father-in-law's residential *llacta*), he is obliged eventually to send one of his sons to marry a sister of the daughter's husband. This "exchange of brothers," as it is commonly called, will be discussed in a future publication. Suffice it to say here that the "brother" and "sister" terms are classificatory and extendable, and the concept of natal terriory is somewhat fluid. As a result, there is considerable concern given to pending marriages by the Achuar–Canelos Quichua, whether arranged or not, to see whether they may satisfy this reciprocity principle.

10

An Emic Model
of Cashinahua Marriage

KENNETH M. KENSINGER

In this paper I present an emic model of Cashinahua marriage, i.e., a model that takes into account what informants said about marriage in casual conversations among themselves, in the more formal discussions that took place when disputes arose about particular marriages, and in the more structured discussions with the ethnographer, and the facts of their marriage practices as gleaned from genealogies, gossip, and personal observations.[1] The model is an attempt to account for (1) the ways in which the Cashinahua classify any particular marriage as "real" or "unreal" and as "good" or "bad," and the criteria they seem to have in mind when they classify marriages; (2) the rules implicit in their behavior and the explicit statements made about choosing a spouse; and (3) the variability within the systems of classification, within the behavior they call "marriage," and between the stated norms and ideals and their actual behavior. Since the analysis focuses on the social phenomena the Cashinahua label *ainwan*, to marry (male speaker), literally "wife-do/make," and *ainyan*, to be married (m.s.), literally "wife-have," *benewa*, to marry (f.s.), literally "husband-do/make," and *beneya*, to be married (f.s.), literally "husband-have,"[2] the resulting definition applies to the Cashinahua only and is not presented as having any universal cross-cultural applicability. However, it is hoped that this analysis will contribute to the refinement of "our etic concepts" and increase "our potential for systematic comparison" (Goodenough 1970:113).

The meaning of the terms "etic" and "emic" follows in the tradition of the linguist Pike (1954), who coined the terms, and Goodenough, who further refined the definitions as they specifically applied to ethnographic analysis, rather than in the tradition of Harris (1964, 1968, 1971, 1979). Wallace (1980:423-24), in his recent review of Harris's *Cultural Mate-*

rialism: The Struggle for a Science of Culture, has succinctly summarized the differences between the two traditions:[3]

> The emic/etic distinction was originally invented and has been generally used by linguists and cultural anthropologists to distinguish between two kinds of models of discriminant behavior that the *observer* may construct for his own use in understanding what he observes. The etic model describes the behavior in categories already familiar and convenient to the observer (and ideally such categories have a "universal" scientific currency, like metric units of measurement or Murdock's "kin-types"). The subject may or may not be using the observer's etic categories but the etic observer is not concerned with whether or not that is so. The emic model, however, sets out deliberately to describe the same discriminant behavior in the categories actually being employed, consciously or unconsciously, by the subject (which again may be the same as the observer's but usually are not).

Cashinahua Marriage as Process

The four linguistic terms—*ainwan* and *benewa, ainyan* and *beneya*—focus on the process of establishing and maintaining a marriage, not on the act of marrying or the state of being married.[4]

Ainwan and *benewa* refer to the totality of a series of activities that occur over a period of months and even years, and that vary depending on the sex of ego, on whether or not it is a first monogamous marriage or a subsequent one, and on whether or not it is the first or succeeding marriage in a polygamous union.[5]

Ainwan

Males generally marry for the first time between the ages of 14 and 17 years, although some have first married at 10 or 11. This marriage is arranged by his father or his father's brother. In the absence of these, a mother's brother speaks with the girl's father and obtains his approval. Once permission has been granted by the girl's father, the prospective husband begins to visit her in her hammock after the rest of her family has gone to sleep or at least are all settled in their hammocks for the night. These visits may last all night, but he must not be with her when the family wakens in the morning. He may also meet with her surreptitiously in the forest during the day. During these visits the couple engage in fondling, tickling, pinching, sexual intercourse, or simply sleeping in one another's arms.

About the time the boy's visits begin, he asks his father's sister to weave a new cotton hammock for him, which when completed he leaves under her hammock when he departs before daybreak. The same day he moves his possessions to where his wife hangs her hammock. This move places him under the authority of his father-in-law rather than that of his father. For the first month he daily leaves the village at daybreak either to hunt or to work in his or his father-in-law's garden, returning after 4 P.M. During this period he is supposed to be embarrassed when his peers tease him, making bawdy comments about his sexual activity. Most informants say that this is the point at which the process of *ainwan* ends. Others argue that it continues for a year, until the onset of his wife's first pregnancy, or until the birth of their first child.

If death or divorce terminates his first marriage, which is highly likely, the process leading to any subsequent marriages is less standardized unless it is the first marriage for a man's new wife. A kinsman of the groom seeks the wife's father's permission only for a man's first marriage; the groom must get the agreement of the woman's father himself if it is her first marriage but not his. If both have been married before, *ainwan* refers to the period during which he is trying to convince his lover to marry him, ending when they take up residence together.[6] In cases of polygyny *ainwan* refers to the period of courtship and the initial weeks and months of co-residence, differing from primary marriages in that there is no residential shift for the male; the wives who are added to an already established monogamous union usually join their husbands at his place of residence.

Benewa

Women generally marry for the first time between the ages of 9 and 14. During the period of amatory nocturnal visits from the prospective spouse, a woman may be reluctant or even hostile and may reject a man's advances, refusing him admittance to her hammock.[7] Whether or not the process runs full cycle depends on her satisfaction with the male; she is free to give or withhold sexual favors and all favors granted must be rewarded by gifts, which usually consist of meat sent to her through an intermediary—a younger sibling or parallel cousin of her lover. Gifts of trade goods such as beads, cotton cloth, scented soap, and perfume are signs that the romance is progressing well.

For the first month after her husband takes up residence with her, a woman is expected to stay in her house near her hearth being shy and embarrassed. When not engaged in household chores, she sits in the new hammock given to her by her new husband. She may establish a new cooking hearth near that of her mother or continue to use her mother's hearth. During the next several months she makes her own set of cooking pots, bowls, corn and peanut toaster, and water jars. If her husband has already made a garden, she becomes its owner and harvests the crops when ripe or as needed. In general, marriage brings little change to her daily routine unless there is a change in her place of residence. For example, if she becomes the new wife added to an already existing monogamous or polygamous union, she would normally be expected to move to her husband's household. Such a residential shift requires her to establish a new network of working cohorts but does not significantly change the nature of her working day. (For a fuller discussion of residence rules, see pp. 233-35.)

Ainyan and *Beneya*

Ainyan and *beneya* refer to the ongoing processes of maintaining a relationship between a pair of co-residential spouses. These include economic cooperation based on a series of reciprocal exchanges of services and goods, shared responsibilities for child rearing, and a continuing, but not exclusive, sexual relationship. Males are responsible for making two gardens per wife annually (see Kensinger 1975a for discussion of gardening); women harvest the gardens and cook food. Men hunt and provide meat for their wives; women cook the meat. These reciprocal exchanges of goods and services are closely related to and support the ongoing sexual relationship between the spouses. Cashinahua spouses do not gain exclusive access to their partner's sexual services. Both may engage in extra-marital affairs as long as they are discreet and do not create a public scandal that would embarrass their spouse. Neither may repeatedly and over prolonged periods deny their partner's conjugal rights, except during periods of ritually prescribed sexual abstinence, without risking the withdrawal of economic supports and possible divorce. This does not mean that couples never limit their sexual activities to their spouses—many do, but they can neither demand nor expect exclusive sexual services in return.

There is no single unambiguous point at which spouses refer to their relationship as *ainyan/beneya* rather than *ainwan/benewa,* but there are points before and after which it is deemed inappropriate to use the terms *ainyan/beneya* and *ainwan/benewa,* respectively. The former may not be used prior to establishing co-residence and the latter may not be used after the termination of the first pregnancy, either through the birth of a child or through a spontaneous or induced abortion.

Four Taxonomic Devices

The Cashinahua use four binary contrasts or polarities for classifying actual or potential marriage and most but not all other aspects of their life[8]: Polarity 1, $kuin_1$ versus $kuinman_1$; Polarity 2, $kuin_2$ versus $bemakia_2$; Polarity 3, $kayabi_3$ versus $bemakia_3$; and Polarity 4, pe_4 versus $chaka_4$.[9] $Kuin_1$, $kuin_2$, and $kayabi_3$ can all be glossed real, true, known, familiar, actual, primary, proper, etc.; $kuinman_1$, $bemakia_2$, and $bemakia_3$ can be translated unreal, false, unknown, unfamiliar, hypothetical, secondary, improper, etc. Pe_4 and $chaka_4$ can be glossed good and bad, respectively. Because of the significance of these taxonomic devices for understanding not only Cashinahua marriage but the meaning of kin terms as they relate to marriage rules, I discuss them here in abstract terms before discussing their specific application to the classification of marriages.

Polarity 1, $kuin_1$ versus $kuinman_1$, divides a semantic domain into two categories, those things that are "real" and those that are "unreal." The categories are strictly and rigidly defined and form a diametric opposition. Membership in them is closed, fixed, unchangeable. The criteria for deciding if objects, behavior, relationships, etc. are $kuin_1$ or $kuinman_1$ are highly idealistic cultural norms and values. Informants rarely disagree on the classification of items within a domain. Even informants who publicly disagreed, because they were at the time attempting for personal reasons to maneuver public opinion using Polarity 2 (see below), either to justify their errant behavior or to establish their lack of culpability for an infraction of a norm, often indicated in private discussions with me that the classification of a domain as the others had stated it was correct.

Polarity 2, $kuin_2$ versus $bemakia_2$, also divides a semantic domain into two categories, real and unreal. Except for a small residual core of items that must always be $kuin_2$ or $bemakia_2$, things are classified as either $kuin_2$ or $bemakia_2$ by individuals; things are what an individual calls them because that is what the individual says they are. Others may agree, disagree, or be neutral depending on their own motives and goals or simply out of indifference or disinterest. Thus classifications based on the use of Polarity 2 are highly individualistic, idiosyncratic, and existential. They serve as the basis for reality bargaining between individuals.

Polarity 3, $kayabi_3$ versus $bemakia_3$, also divides a semantic domain into two categories, real and unreal.[10] The categories are diametrically opposed and membership is mutually exclusive; they are relatively closed, fixed, and unchangeable. Rather than being idealistic, they are pragmatic, based on the knowledge that the vicissitudes of life often require accepting the less-than-perfect as inevitable without abandoning the ideal represented by Polarity 1. There is a high degree of agreement between informants on what is $kayabi_3$ and what is $bemakia_3$.

Polarity 3 does not resolve the dialectical opposition between the rigid idealistic sociocentric classification produced by Polarity 1 and the existential, almost anarchistic egocentric classification produced by Polarity 2. Polarity 3 serves as a kind of mediating synthesis that makes social action possible.

Polarity 4, pe_4 versus $chaka_4$, divides a domain into two categories or subdomains, those things that are good and those that are bad, each of which may be further subdivided. This creates a continuum from very

TABLE 1a. RELATIONSHIP BETWEEN POLARITY 4 AND POLARITIES 1, 2, and 3.

		Polarity 1		Polarity 2		Polarity 3	
		$kuin_1$	$kuinmam_1$	$kuin_2$	$bemakia_2$	$kayabi_3$	$bemakia_3$
pe_4	pebaida	+	−	+	−	+	−
	pe	+	−	±	±	+	−
	pepishta	−	+	±	±	+	−
$chaka_4$	chakapishta	−	+	±	±	−	+
	chaka	−	+	±	±	−	+
	chakabaida	−	+	−	+	−	+

Polarity 4

Read as follows: If an item is classified as pe_4 and pe, it is obligatorily classified as $kuin_1$, obligatorily not classified as $kuinmam_1$, optionally classified as $kuin_2$ and $bemakia_2$, etc.

good, *pehaida,* to good, *pe,* to a little good, *pepishta,* to a little bad, *chaka-pishta,* to bad, *chaka,* to very bad, *chakahaida.* Polarity 4 establishes the relative moral value within a behavioral domain; in contrast, Polarities 1, 2, and 3 establish the structural order. Table 1a shows the relationship between the categories produced by using Polarity 4 and the categories resulting from Polarities 1, 2, and 3. Table 1b shows the same relationship with the columns rearranged as a Gutman scale.

The four polarities are merely linguistic devices for labeling categories within semantic domains. The criteria by which these discriminations are made have their roots in the implicit and explicit rules that underlie Cashinahua thought and behavior. We turn now to an examination of the rules and their social contexts.

Cashinahua Marriage Rules and Social Organization

Cashinahua informants often classified and evaluated specific marriages, both actual or potential. They also made statements about what they customarily do or generally expect. However, they did not explicitly formulate a set of rules regulating the choice of a spouse, list the criteria by which they evaluate a marriage, or indicate any particular order in which the rules are applied or considered. Therefore, the rules, as presented below, are a distillation of many hours of discussions with a multiplicity of informants. The order of presentation was heavily influenced by a conversation I had with one of my best informants about the selection of a wife for his orphaned sister's son, who several years later married that informant's daughter—a marriage that all informants agreed was $kuin_1$, $kuin_2$, $kayabi_3$, pe_4, and *pehaida.* Quotation marks set off my translations of the informants' statements from my restatement of them in anthropological terms.

Rule 1: Cross-cousin marriage

Rule 1a: *Preferential actual first cross-cousin marriage.* "He will marry his *ainkuin.*"[11] Marriage is preferred with an actual double first cross cousin (FZD *and* MBD) or an actual first cross cousin (FZD or MBD).[12]

This rule reflects the Cashinahua ideal model of the society, where each local group is based on sister exchange between two focal males, replicated by their sons, their son's sons, etc. Each of these males must be a member of the opposite moiety and the appropriate linked marriage section. Actual genealogical connections are a prime consideration. (See Figure 1 and Kensinger 1977).

Rule 1b: *Prescriptive "cross-cousin" marriage.* "He must marry one of his *ainbuaibu.*" Marriage is prescribed with a member of the kin class

TABLE 1b. RELATIONSHIP BETWEEN POLARITY 4 AND POLARITIES 1, 2, and 3 ARRANGED AS A GUTTMAN SCALE.

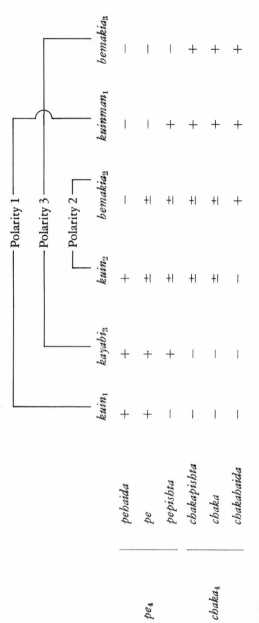

Polarity 4		$kuin_1$	$kayabi_3$	$kuin_2$	$bemakia_2$	$kuinman_1$	$bemakia_3$
pe_4	pehaida	+	+	+	−	−	−
	pe	+	+	±	±	−	−
	pepishta	−	+	±	±	+	−
$chaka_4$	chakapishta	−	−	±	±	+	+
	chaka	−	−	±	±	+	+
	chakabaida	−	−	−	+	+	+

Polarity 1
Polarity 3
Polarity 2

Read as in Table 1a.

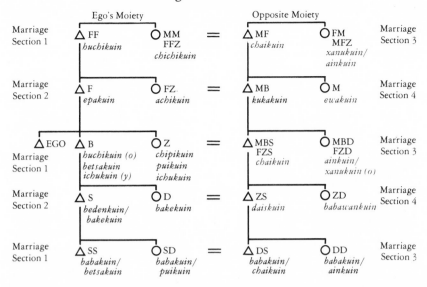

FIGURE 1. DISTRIBUTION OF FOCAL KIN TYPES AND *kuin*₁ KINSMEN FOR MALE EGO—an idealized model of Cashinahua society.

"female cross cousin," i.e. with a person of the opposite sex in the opposite moiety and linked marriage section.[13]

This rule reflects a pragmatic version of the Cashinahua ideal model of the society, with groups of male moiety and section mates exchanging "sisters" with the males of the opposite moiety and linked marriage section; actual genealogical connections are not significant. (See Chart 1 and Rules 2 and 3 below.)

Marriage and/or sexual intercourse with women who are not members of the social category *ainbuaibu* constitutes incest. However, sanctions against incest vary depending on the degree of genealogical closeness. Incestuous relations with a *kuin*₁ kinswoman[14] are strongly prohibited and generally are prevented or terminated by beating and death; they are strongly disapproved and discouraged with *kayabi*₃ kinswomen who are not also *kuin*₁ kinswomen.[15] With all other kinswomen, i.e. any other Cashinahua women not included in the *kuin*₁ or *kayabi*₁ categories, they are neither disapproved nor strongly discouraged—they are the topic of gossip, as are any illicit affairs—but are subject to negative sanctions by spirit beings only.

Rule 2: Moiety exogamy

"He (a *duabake*) will marry an *inanibake*." Marriage must be exogamous with reference to the moieties.

Moiety 1

	Male	Female
O1	*epabu*	*achibu,*m
		*yayabu,*f
Yr	*bedenbu,*m	*babawanbu,*f
	*daisbu,*f	
	*bakebu,*m	
O1	*huchibu*	*chichibu/*
		chipibu
NA	----- *betsabu* (same sex) -----	
	puibu (opposite sex)	
Yr	*ichubu/* ·	
	bababu	

Moiety 2

	Male	Female
	kukabu	*ewabu*
	*daisbu,*m	*babawanbu,*m
	*bakebu,*f	
	*chaiiabu,*f	*xanubu,*m
	----- *chaibu,*m	*aimbuaibu,*m
	*benebu,*f	*tsabebu,*f
	bababu	

Marriage Section 1   Marriage Section 2   Marriage Section 3   Marriage Section 4

CHART 1. Referential Kinship Terms Distributed by Moiety and Marriage Sections. Ego is a member of moiety 1, marriage section 2.

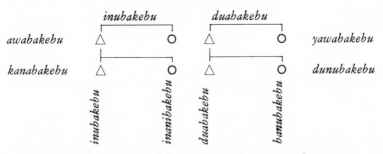

FIGURE 2. CASHINAHUA MOIETIES AND MARRIAGE SECTIONS.

All Cashinahua are members of one of two moieties, *inubakebu* and *duabakebu,* each of which is subdivided by sex. The female counterparts are *inanibakebu* and *banubakebu* respectively (see Figure 2). A male is a member of his father's moiety; a female is a member of her mother's mother's/father's father's sister's moiety. The male term is used to designate the male and female members of a moiety as a group.

The moieties are the social structural entities that unite all the autonomous local villages into a single society. Along with the marriage sections (see Rule 3 below), the moieties provide each Cashinahua with an immediate social identity in every other community, they limit marriage choices, and they operate as social groups for ritual and ceremonial occasions. The members of the moiety within each village are the local representatives of the entire moiety; they do not constitute subgroups such as localized clans, lineages, etc. (cf. Mundurucú phratries, clans, and lineages in Murphy 1960).

Rule 3: Marriage section prescription

"He (a *yawabake*) will marry an *awabake.*" Marriage is prescribed with reference to a specific marriage section.

All Cashinahua are members of one of four marriage sections or alternating generation-namesake groups, *xutabuaibu;* they are all either *awabakebu, kanabakebu, yawabakebu,* or *dunubakebu* (see Figure 2). A male is a member of the marriage section of his FF or FFB from whom he receives his names; a woman is a member of the marriage section of her MM, who ideally is also her FFZ, from whom she receives her names. Each marriage section consists of all the members both male and female of a person's moiety and generation and of those moiety mates two generations senior and junior. This group is further subdivided into two subgroups, those who are older than ego (i.e. those from whom he receives his names) and those younger than ego (i.e. those to whom he gives his names). The other members of ego's moiety are members of another marriage section consisting of persons one generation senior and junior to ego (i.e. those who sired ego and those whom ego sires respectively). Persons who are *awabakebu* and *kanabakebu* are members of the *inubakebu* moiety, and persons who are *yawabakebu* and *dunubakebu* are members of the *duabakebu* moiety (see Figure 2). Furthermore, *yawabakebu* should only marry *awabakebu* and vice versa; *dunubakebu* should only marry *kanabekebu* and vice versa.

Under normal circumstances the rule of section prescription coincides with that of Rule 1, which prescribes marriage with a real or classificatory cross cousin. However, in cases where there have been violations of Rules 2 and 3, adjustments must be made in the marriage section and/or moiety membership of all female offspring; male offspring are not affected. A woman may not be a member of her father's marriage section as she would be if her father's marriage violated Rule 3. Nor may she be a member of the marriage section from which her father should have selected a spouse or of her mother's moiety, which would be the case if her father had violated both Rules 2 and 3. And finally she may not be a member of the same moiety as her mother, as would be the case if her father violated Rule 2. The adjustments in group membership of a female required by the violations of these two rules are shown in Table 2. Therefore, her social identity based on her moiety and/or marriage section membership places her in kinship categories that do not coincide with her placement through genealogical reckoning, a discrepancy that can be actively manipulated by all but her *kuin₁* kinsmen.

Rule 4: Village endogamy

"He will marry a woman from his own village." Marriage should be endogamous with reference to the village.

Rule 4 states a clear preference; it reflects the Cashinahua view of what constitutes a well-ordered society. The ideal Cashinahua village, *maekuin₁*, consists of a *social core* composed of two *focal males* who are members of the opposite moieties and of marriage sections of the same generational levels who have exchanged sisters in marriage—an exchange that is replicated by their sons and son's sons in perpetuity, plus the primary cognates of the focal males, i.e. their *nabukuin₁*.[16] This arrangement would coincide, of course, with the ideal of marriage with a double first cross cousin.

No Cashinahua village meets the requirements for being classified *maekuin₁*. However, a village may be classified as proper *maekayabi₃* if the two males, either actual or classificatory cross cousins, have exchanged sisters or classificatory sisters in marriage, and have established themselves as the political leaders of their village.[17]

Only when no spouses are available in his village does a man consider going to another village in search of a wife. In such cases there is fre-

TABLE 2. ADJUSTMENT IN MOIETY AND MARRIAGE SECTION MEMBERSHIP
OF DAUGHTER WHOSE PARENTS' MARRIAGE VIOLATES RULES 2 AND/OR 3.

Moiety-Section Male		=	Moiety-Section Female		Moiety-Section Daughter		Condition
inu	awa		banu	yawa	inani	kana	Normal
inu	awa		banu	dunu	inani	*kana*	SV
inu	awa		inani	awa	*banu*	*dunu*	MV
inu	awa		inani	kana	*banu*	*dunu*	MV&SV
inu	kana		banu	dunu	inu	awa	Normal
inu	kana		banu	yawa	inu	*awa*	SV
inu	kana		inani	kana	*banu*	*yawa*	MV
inu	kana		inani	awa	*banu*	*yawa*	MV&SV
dua	yawa		inani	awa	banu	dunu	Normal
dua	yawa		inani	kana	banu	*dunu*	SV
dua	yawa		banu	yawa	*inani*	*kana*	MV
dua	yawa		banu	dunu	*inani*	*kana*	MV&SV
dua	dunu		inani	kana	banu	yawa	Normal
dua	dunu		inani	awa	banu	*yawa*	SV
dua	dunu		banu	dunu	*inani*	*awa*	MV
dua	dunu		banu	yawa	*inani*	*awa*	MV&SV

Read: if a male who is a member of *inubakebu* moiety and *awabakebu* marriage section
marries a female who is a member of *banubakebu* moiety and *yawabakebu* marriage
section, their daughter is a member of *inanibakebu* moiety and *kanabakebu* marriage
section; the marriage is normal.
SV   Violates marriage section rule
MV   Violates moiety exogamy rule
Italics indicate the changes required.

quently heavy pressure on him to marry a local woman even if the marriage requires violation of either Rule 3 or Rule 2, or both, in that
order of preference, so long as he does not marry a *kuin₁* kinswoman.
Such marriages would be *kuin₂*, *kuinman₁*, and *bemakia₃* but not *kuin₁*
or *kayabi₃*.

Rule 5: Residence rules

"He will live with his *achi*." Postmarital residence is matrilocal or
uxorilocal.

Under normal circumstances a man takes up residence at marriage with
his wife in the household of her parents, his *achi* and *kuka,* i.e. with his
actual or classificatory father's sister and/or his actual or classificatory
mother's brother. However, if the wife's actual father[18] is deceased, other
residential options are open to the couple, depending on their individual

circumstances: (1) they may reside with his parents, especially if the wife was residing there at the time of her marriage; (2) they may reside with the husband's older sister and her family, especially if his father is deceased, or with a brother if he has no actual sisters; or (3) they may establish an independent household near any close kinsman of either spouse.[19] The decision almost always results in their living with or near a cross-sex sibling of one of the spouses.[20]

Postmarital residence practices also vary if either spouse has been married before or if the wife is becoming a secondary wife in a polygynous union. In polygynous unions secondary wives generally become part of the households of their husbands unless they are the last surviving daughters of their fathers, in which case the father may demand that her husband and his other wife or wives join his household. If either spouse has been married before, economic factors involving gardens and hunting territories generally influence the decision. Although marriage is entered into with the assumption of permanence, it is very fragile during the early months, so much so that the Cashinahua speak of the dissolution of a marriage as divorce (*ain puta,* "wife-throw away," or *bene puta,* "husband-throw away") only if the marriage has lasted more than a year.[21] Because of this, my data on divorce (only 10 of 93 marriages ended in divorce) give poor indication of the residential mobility of some males and females. But such affairs, whether or not the Cashinahua call them marriages terminated by divorce, do influence residential decisions.

Although Rule 5 is not a criterion in the classification of marriages, informants always discussed residential arrangements when we talked about marriage rules and classification. The reasons why residence rules play such a prominent part in these discussions of marriage are clear. First, marriage includes an actual or a potential change of locus of authority. Prior to marriage a male lives with and is subject to the authority of his father. By authority here I mean that he has obligations of respect, loyalty, economic and political support, but not necessarily obedience (Kensinger 1974b). When a man marries, he comes under the authority of his wife's father,[22] and change of residence is symbolic of this change in locus of authority. Even if a man does not change his place of residence, he still has obligations to cooperate with and economically support his father-in-law, to show him deference and respect, to support him politically except in disputes involving his primary agnatic kinsmen. Only with the death of father-in-law, or if a man becomes a focal male, is he free from the authority of his wife's father.

Second, there may be a change in his factional alignment. Until he becomes a focal male, each male is normally part of the political faction of his father and father-in-law or that of his brother and/or brother-in-law (cross cousin). Unless he marries a woman who is part of his faction, he must align himself with the political faction of his father-in-law or brother-in-law, especially if either of them is politically ambitious and active, or he risks putting his marriage in jeopardy. (See Kensinger 1974b for a discussion of the political manipulation of marriages.)

These are the principal rules of the Cashinahua marriage system. However, other considerations bear on the selection of a spouse, including physical attractiveness, industriousness, sexual and personal compatibility, political realities, economic advantage, etc. Although these factors play a not insignificant part in a man's decision to marry a particular woman, they are not factors in the classification of his marriage.

Taxonomies, Rules, and Practice

We turn now to an examination of the marriage taxonomies and rules as they relate to each other and to Cashinahua behavior. Table 3 shows the relationship between the classification of marriages using Polarities 1, 2, and 3 and adherence to the marriage rules; Table 4 shows the relationship between the classification of marriages using Polarity 4 and adherence to the marriage rules.[23] Table 5 shows the frequencies of marriage by classification.

Polarity 1: $kuin_1$ versus $kuinman_1$

$Kuin_1$ marriages are those with an actual double first cross cousin (simultaneously FZD and MBD) or an actual first cross cousin (FZD or MBD),[24] who is a member of the opposite moiety, the appropriate marriage section, and ego's village. All other marriages are classified as

TABLE 3. RELATIONSHIP BETWEEN CLASSIFICATIONS OF MARRIAGE USING POLARITIES 1, 2, AND 3 AND ADHERENCE TO MARRIAGE RULES.

		Rule 1a	Rule 1b	Rule 2	Rule 3	Rule 4
Polarity 1	kuin	+	+	+	+	+
	kuinman	−	±	±	±	±
Polarity 2	kuin	+	±	±	±	±
	bemakia	−	±	±	±	±
Polarity 3	kayabi	+	+	+	+	±
	bemakia	−	−	−	−	±

+ Obligatory adherence
− Violation
± Optional adherence

TABLE 4. RELATIONSHIP BETWEEN CLASSIFICATIONS OF MARRIAGE USING POLARITY 4 AND ADHERENCE TO MARRIAGE RULES.

		Rule 1a	Rule 1b	Rule 2	Rule 3	Rule 4
pe_4	*pehaida*	+	+	+	+	+
	pe	+	+	+	+	+
	pepishta	−	+	+	+	±
$chaka_4$	*chakapishta*	−	±	+	−	±
	chaka	−	±	−	−	±
	chakahaida	−	−	−	−	±

+ Obligatory adherence
− Violation
± Optional adherence

*kuinman*₁. Five of 77 marriages are classified as *kuin*₁, 72 are *kuinman*₁. Data are not available on adherence to Rule 4 for 16 of 93 marriages.

Polarity 2: *kuin*₂ versus *bemakia*₂

Only marriages that adhere to Rule 1a are obligatorily *kuin*₂ and only marriages with an actual M, MM, FFZ (if his MM), FM, Z, D, ZD, SD, and DD are obligatorily *bemakia*₂. Apart from these restrictions, ego is free to manipulate his classification of particular marriages and attempt to manipulate others' classifications in order to justify his violation of social

TABLE 5. FREQUENCIES OF MARRIAGES BY CLASSIFICATION.

Polarity 1		*kuin*₁	5/77[a]		
		*kuinman*₁	72/77[a]		
Polarity 2	Obligatorily	*kuin*₂	5/93		
	Obligatorily	*bemakia*₂	0/93		
	Optionally	*kuin*₂	88/93		
	Optionally	*bemakia*₂	88/93		
Polarity 3		*kayabi*₃	76/93[b]		
		*bemakia*₃	15/93[b]		
Polarity 4	*pehaida*	2/93			
	pe	3/93	pe_4	76/93	
	pepishta	71/91[b]			
	chakapishta	4/93			
	chaka	11/93	$chaka_4$	15/93	
	chakahaida	0/93			

[a]No data on adherence to Rule 4 for 16 of 93 marriages.
[b]Insufficient data on two marriages.

norms and/or his failure to carry out his social obligations. Because of the highly manipulable and idiosyncratic character of Polarity 2, only five of 93 marriages (two with actual double first cross cousins, two with actual FZDs, and one with an actual MBD) are indubitably $kuin_2$. None of the 93 marriages is obligatorily $bemakia_2$; such unions would be forcibly terminated by a severe beating, resulting in death, for either of the guilty parties, or excommunication of the couple from the society.

Polarity 3: $kayabi_3$ versus $bemakia_3$

$Kayabi_3$ marriages adhere to Rules 1, 2, and 3, and optionally adhere to Rule 4. Marriages that violate Rules 1a and 1b, 2, and 3 are always $bemakia_3$. Some informants argued that marriages which violate Rules 2 and 3, but not 1a and 1b, could also be classified as $kayabi_3$. Most insisted that since violations of Rule 3 results in confusion vis-à-vis the social status of the offspring of such a marriage, they were *chakapishta* and therefore could not be $kayabi_3$. Seventy-six of 93 marriages are classified as $kayabi_3$; 15 are $bemakia_3$ (I do not have sufficient data on two). The marriages classified as $bemakia_3$ include 12 that violated both Rules 2 and 3 (six males married women from their own moiety and section, six married women from their father's section of their own moiety) and three in violation of only Rule 3.

Polarity 4: pe_4 versus $chaka_4$

Use of Polarity 4 results in marriages that are classified as pe_4 or $chaka_4$, that is, good or bad. These two categories are each further sub-divided into three subcategories so that marriages are *pehaida, pe, pepishta, chakapishta, chaka,* or *chakahaida,* i.e. they are very good, good, a little good, a little bad, bad, or very bad.

Marriages classified as *pehaida* are between actual double first cross cousins who are members of opposite moieties, linked marriage sections, and the same village; that is, they abide by the ideal rules. Only two of 93 marriages are classified as *pehaida.* The key to understanding the low frequency of such marriage lies in the strict, narrow requirement that actual double first cross cousins marry. Few persons have potential spouses who meet these qualifications, since it requires a prior *pehaida* marriage, so that FZ = MBW *and* MB = FZH. An examination of my genealogical data leads me to conclude that few *pehaida* marriages have existed in the recent past, if ever.

Pe marriages are those between spouses who are actual first cross cousins but not double first cross cousins, who are members of opposite moieties, linked marriage sections, and the same village. Three of 93 marriages are *pe.* Even with this relaxation of the strict ideal, most persons reaching marriageable age find no actual first cross cousins available.

One informant told me that he had very much wanted to marry well or very well, *ainwan pehaida* or *ainwan pe,* but all of his first cross cousins, his *ainkuin*$_1$, were either infants or already married.

Marriages classified as *pepishta* are between classificatory cross cousins who are members of opposite moieties and of the appropriate marriage sections but who reside before marriage in the same village *or* in different villages.[25] The overwhelming majority of Cashinahua marriages, 71 of 91 (I do not have sufficient data on two marriages), fit the category *pepishta.* Although such a marriage falls short of the ideal, it is an acceptable compromise because it often is required by demographic realities. Informants insist that although such marriages are not *pehaida* or *pe,* they are *pe*$_4$ as opposed to *chaka*$_4$.[26]

Marriages classified *chakapishta* are those between persons who are not members of linked marriage sections, who are members of opposite moieties, who may or may not be cross cousins, and who may or may not be village co-residents. Four marriages of 93 were classified as *chakapishta.* Of these marriages, one was between cross cousins who were co-residents, but whose marriage violated the marriage section rule because the wife's father had married badly; two were between persons who were neither cross cousins nor village co-residents; I have insufficient data on the fourth case.

Marriages classified as *chaka* are those between persons who may or may not be cross cousins,[27] who are members of the same moiety and therefore are members of inappropriate marriage sections, and who may or may not be village co-residents. Eleven of 93 marriages are classified as *chaka;* none of them was between actual cross cousins, six of them were with members of the same marriage section, five were with persons belonging to father's marriage section, and all of them involved village co-residents. One informant told me "They say I married badly (*ainwan chaka*), but I have a good marriage (*ainyan pe*)." He agreed, however, that the classification *ainwan chaka/ainyan chaka* was appropriate from a moral perspective and speculated that his failure to realize his political ambitions was a result of his bad marriages.

Marriages classified as *chakahaida* violate all four marriage rules with the possible exception of village endogamy and are further characterized by being with prohibited *kuin*$_1$ kinsmen, namely with an actual M, FZ, MM, FFZ (if also MM), FM, Z, D, ZD, SD, or DD.[28] Strong sanctions including physical violence are used to terminate such marriages; none of the 93 marriages is classified as *chakahaida.*

Taxonomies, Rules, and Cashinahua behavior

The marriage rules and elaborate taxonomies seem to have little direct impact on daily behavior. Except for those marriages classified as *chaka-*

haida, the Cashinahua do not shun individuals or couples whose marriages are improper, nor do they subject them to negative sanctions. Furthermore, the rules do not seem to be a serious consideration in a couple's decision to marry or not; other than arranged first marriages, most marriages are but formalizations of ongoing sexual liaisons entered into without consideration of any rules and taxonomies, except possibly those against sexual activity with prohibited *kuin₁* kinsmen. However, a young man contemplating marriage does take the marriage rules into consideration while surveying his prospects; he chooses to marry an *ainbuaibu* if one is available. He does so because of the supernatural sanctions he risks if he marries improperly.

The spirit world of the Cashinahua is concerned with maintaining harmony and balance in the universe including within and between society, nature, and spirits. Bad marriages, by causing social confusion, are disruptive, resulting in suspicions and claims of supernatural intervention such as unexplained illness and accidents to the members of one's close circle of kin, bad luck at hunting, the cracking of one's kinswomen's pottery during firing, strange nighttime noises, apparitions of deceased kinsmen, etc.[29] I observed and my informants reported no cases where bad marriages were dissolved to placate the spirits; medicine is used (Kensinger 1974a). Thus bad marriages, except those classified as *chakahaida,* are tolerated and preferred to no marriage at all. Most females are married for the first time by the age of 13, males by 16. Widows and divorcées, even elderly ones, rarely remain unmarried for more than a few days; widowers and divorcés remarry as soon as a spouse is available and rarely have difficulty getting a new wife if they have a reputation as a good hunter, worker, and provider. Unmarried adults, whatever the reasons for their being unmarried, are viewed as potentially more disruptive to the society than is a bad marriage.

An Emic Model of Cashinahua Marriage

An emic model of Cashinahua marriage must account for all of the data presented above. It cannot be merely a translation or restatement of informants' statements nor can it be restricted to such statements. It must be based both on what they say *and* on what they do; it must define marriage as opposed to nonmarriage within Cashinahua society and as compared to marriage in American, Nuer, Trobriand, or Japanese society. These criteria exist not as isolated, discrete traits but as constellations or bundles of traits that define the discrete class or classes of social behavior called marriage. In addition, an emic definition of Cashinahua marriage must indicate the range of acceptable variation, both free or conditioned, present both in actual behavior of the members of Cashinahua society and in their statements of acceptability. Furthermore, it must also include a statement of the distribution of the emic class or classes in larger structures or groups of which they form a part. Thus, for example, in Cashinahua society the married pair, husband and wife, is a basic structural unit that forms the nucleus of a nuclear family or constitutes part of the nucleus of a polygynous and/or an extended family. They may also be part of an atom of social organization, the social core, or the social periphery of a village.

The taxonomies resulting from the use of Polarities 1, 2, 3, and 4 are not emic. Although I was prepared at first to argue that Polarity 3, $kayabi_3$ versus $bemakia_3$, and/or Polarity 4, pe_4 versus $chaka_4$, are isomorphic with an emic model, closer examination showed that they are not and cannot be so. They fail to make explicit certain factors that are crucial to an emic model of Cashinahua marriage and that all informants implicitly assume to be true but never state. It was equally clear that Polarity 1, $kuin_1$ versus $kuinman_1$, cannot be emic because it is too idealistic, restrictive, and inflexible to account adequately for much of Cashinahua behavior; only about 5 percent of the marriages are classified as proper, $kuin_1$. Nor can Polarity 2, $kuin_2$ versus $bemakia_2$, be emic. It is too idiosyncratic, unrestrictive, and flexible to account for most of the constraints on Cashinahua marriage behavior. However, it does reveal both the range of variability possible within the system and the manner in which individuals are able to manipulate the system to their own advantage. Thus, although the four Cashinahua polarities provide us with taxonomic data essential for an emic analysis, individually and collectively they do not constitute an emic model.

My emic model of the Cashinahua marriage system consists of three emic classes—Legitimate-proper, Legitimate-improper, and Illegitimate-improper, hereafter L-p, L-i, and I-i respectively—and a two-phase emic process.

Table 6 summarizes the defining characteristics of each emic class. Table 7 summarizes the essential elements of the emic process; it indicates the obligatory and optional sequence of events that together define the process of Cashinahua marriage.[30] Table 6 includes three elements, which were not discussed in connection with the informants' taxonomies and rules because they are not criteria relevant to the Cashinahua classifications, namely cohabitation, a sexual relationship, and economic cooperation. However, they must be made explicit in an emic analysis because they are part of the behavior that defines marriage as opposed to other nonmarriage relationships.

An L-p marriage is defined as the process of establishing and maintaining a socially recognized and approved relationship characterized by

TABLE 6. MATRIX SHOWING DISTINCTIVE FEATURES OF EMIC CLASSES OF CASHINAHUA MARRIAGE.

Emic Class	Cohabitation	Sexual Relationship	Economic Cooperation	Cross-Cousin Class Prescription	Moiety Exogamy	Marriage Section Prescription	Village Endogamy
L-p	+	+	+	+	+	+	±
L-i	+	+	+	±	±	−	±
I-i	+	+	+	−	−	−	±

+ Obligatory presence of feature
− Obligatory absence of feature
± Optional presence or absence of feature

cohabitation, a sexual relationship, and economic cooperation between a male and female who are actual or classificatory cross cousins and members of opposite moieties and appropriate, linked marriage sections. The parties to the relationship may or may not be co-residents of the same village prior to their marriage. An L-p marriage may form the nucleus of a nuclear family, and/or be part of the nucleus of a polygynous

TABLE 7. THE PROCESS OF MARRYING AMONG THE CASHINAHUA.

	First Marriage	Subsequent Marriages
Establishment Phase *aimvan*	± Arrangement by proxy + Nocturnal visits/daytime trysts ± Requesting hammock ± Giving hammock to bride + Husband changes residence + Period of being ashamed + Regular hunting—catch to wife/wife's mother + Making garden ± First pregnancy and birth	+ Sexual liaison with giving of gifts to woman + Change of residence by one spouse
Maintenance Phase *ainyan*	+ Annual garden making + Regular hunting—catch to wife + Marriage of first daughter and shift from being son-in-law to father-in-law	+ Annual garden making + Regular hunting—catch to wife

and/or extended family, and/or be part of the social core or periphery of a village. Only L-p marriages, however, may form the nucleus of an atom of social organization.[31] All those marriages the Cashinahua classify as *pe₄*, *kuin₁*, and *kayabi₃*, and some they classify as *kuinman₁* or *kuin₂* (namely, those included in *pe₄* and *kayabi₃*), are L-p marriages.

An L-i marriage is defined as the process of establishing and maintaining a socially recognized and accepted but not approved relationship between a male and female, characterized by cohabitation, a sexual relationship, and economic cooperation, by violation of the rule of marriage section prescription, and by optional adherence to the rules of village endogamy, moiety exogamy, and/or cross-cousin class prescription.[32] The variant forms of L-i marriages are products of the particular options followed. An L-i marriage may form the nucleus of a nuclear family, and/or be part of the nucleus of a polygynous and/or extended family, and/or be part of the social core or periphery of a village. An L-i marriage *may not* form the nucleus of an atom of social organization. L-i marriages include all the marriages the Cashinahua classify as *chaka* and *chaka-pishta* and some they classify as *kuinman₁*, *bemakia₂*, and *bemakia₃*, namely, those included in *chaka* and *chakapishta* but not *chakahaida*.

An I-i marriage is defined as the process of establishing and maintaining an acknowledged but socially unrecognized and unapproved relationship between a male and a female who are *kuin₁* kin to each other but not cross cousins (and who thus violate all the marriage rules with the possible exception of the rule of village endogamy), characterized by cohabitation, a sexual relationship, and economic cooperation. I-i marriages include all those unions classified *chakahaida*, those obligatorily classified *bemakia₂*, and some of those classified *bemakia₃* and *kuinman₁*. Although such unions are forcibly terminated or couples are forced to leave both their village and Cashinahua society to live with outsiders, they are defined as marriage rather than nonmarriage. And although I-i marriage can form the nucleus of a nuclear family, it cannot be part of a Cashinahua village.

Thus the Cashinahua marriage system consists of a two-phase process— taking a spouse, *ainwan/benewa*, and having a spouse, *ainyan, beneya*— that is, the process of establishing and continuing a marital relationship, which is the primary relationship in the formation of a family unit, which in turn serves as an integral part of larger social units. The process is loosely regulated by a series of rules or understandings, and the relationships resulting from them are evaluated in terms of their adherence to and/or violation of these rules. An examination of both the taxonomies and Cashinahua behavior reveals an underlying tripartite model that reflects and can be used to generate the system but does not coincide with any Cashinahua taxonomies.

Discussion and Conclusions

The foregoing description has focused on the Cashinahua system of marriage. It is based on, but not limited to, what the Cashinahua said and what they did. These observations were informed and illuminated by concepts that are part and parcel of my anthropological training. Thus, when I write about moiety exogamy, village endogamy, marriage section prescription, etc., I am translating informants' statements and behavior into words and concepts that are part of the ethnographer's etic tool kit. Goodenough (1970:112) has argued that "emic description requires etics, and by trying to do emic descriptions we add to our etic concepts for subsequent descriptions. It is through etic concepts that we do comparison. And by supplementing our etic concepts we contribute to the development of a general science of culture." What, then, are the implications of an emic analysis of the Cashinahua data for the development or refinement of our etic concepts and an etic definition of marriage?[33]

(1) An etic definition of marriage must distinguish between marriage and sex. Anthropologists, like the Cashinahua, have assumed that although sex and marriage are not synonymous, a sexual relationship is an integral part of marriage. However, we need to examine how a marriage relationship differs from sexual relationships both within marriage and outside of marriage.

The Cashinahua word for sexual intercourse, whether inside or outside of marriage, is *chuta;* the term refers both to the act of intercourse and/ or all the attendant activities. *Beyus* (play) is frequently used—perhaps euphemistically—in place of *chuta* in the sense of sexual play but never refers to the sexual act alone. A sexual relationship outside of marriage, *atiwa/atiya* (to make or have a lover), does not involve co-residence as does marriage, nor does it create the social bond that is integral to the establishment of a social unit, although it may be the prelude to marriage. Furthermore, the meat, trinkets, trade goods, etc. given by the male to his partner in an *atiwa/atiya* relationship in exchange for sex do not constitute the economic cooperation that characterizes the marriage relationship. The reciprocal exchange of goods and services that is one of the defining features of Cashinahua marriage is expected to endure whether or not there is an active, ongoing sexual relationship between the spouses. The termination of sexual relations does not spell the end of a marriage; the termination of economic cooperation does. In contrast, the cessation of sexual activity marks the end of an *atiwa/atiya* relationship. Furthermore, some informants classify *atiwa/atiya* relationships using the same polarities and the same criteria they use to classify marriage, indicating the structural and moral appropriateness of the lover relationships. On the other hand, they only use Polarity 4 to classify *chuta,* a classification filled with semantic ambiguity. For example, *chuta chakahaida* can mean either that the sexual activity was highly incestuous or that it was very unpleasant or unsatisfactory. Thus sex as an act is differentiated from sex as part of marriage or lover relationships.

(2) An etic definition of marriage must deal with the question of the extent to which marriage limits sexual access to and/or establishes control over the sexual activities of one or both spouses.

Although the Cashinahua expect a sexual relationship within marriage, they do not expect that it will be an exclusive relationship. The husband and the wife have neither an exclusive right of sexual access nor control over the partner's sexual activities. The expectation holds both that affairs will be carried on with discretion so as not to embarrass their spouses and that the adulterous individual will not withhold sexual services from the spouse in favor of the lover. In theory, every Cashinahua has rights of sexual access to all those persons who are members of the kin class "opposite-sex cross cousins," and every female has the right to accept or reject the sexual advances of any or all males, including her husband. However, the Cashinahua acknowledge that the economic relationship established by marriage places limits on this freedom, giving spouses prior claim but not exclusive control over or sexual access to each other's sexuality.

(3) An etic definition of marriage must reflect the fact that in all marriage systems some elements or features are obligatory and essential while some are optional, thus creating variability within the system. The obligatory features frequently will not be mentioned overtly by informants, who simply assume their listener knows what these elements are and therefore take them for granted, just as my informants assumed that I knew that marriage included a sexual relationship, co-residence, and economic cooperation and so never mentioned them during our discussions.

(4) An etic definition of marriage must distinguish marriage from nonmarriage.[34] In most societies the expectation exists that most, if not all, individuals will marry and be married most or all of their adult lives. Unmarried individuals often are considered aberrant and potentially dangerous. The Cashinahua prefer that a person marry in violation of highly valued norms rather than remain single, since they view unmarried individuals, especially males, as potentially disruptive. Understanding why this is so often the case should contribute to a more precise etic definition.

(5) An etic definition of marriage must not imply that marriage is only an act, an institution, a state of being, or a social process; it may be one or more of these. Unfortunately, the vocabulary we use for discussing marriage reflects our society's views. Thus my use of the noun "marriage" when talking about Cashinahua marriage does violence to the Cashinahua conception of marriage as process, expressed with verbs rather than nouns.

Given the nature of natural language, I do not know how to resolve this problem. We clearly need to develop an etic meta-language that will allow us to discuss marriage in any society with as little ambiguity as possible, while conveying whatever ambiguity exists in the system itself.

(6) Although an etic definition of marriage cannot be a legal or moral definition—law and morals are culture-specific and thus must be dealt with in emic terms—it must include provisions for dealing with the legal and moral dimensions of marriage. Like other and perhaps all societies, the Cashinahua distinguish between those marriages that are legitimate/legal and those that are illegitimate, and between proper and improper. However, if the relationship is characterized by cohabitation, a sexual relationship, and economic cooperation, for the Cashinahua it is marriage. This is not the case in American society, where a social relationship characterized by cohabitation, a sexual relationship, and economic cooperation without the appropriate religious and/or legal rituals may or may not be defined as marriage,[35] and is frequently considered amoral if not immoral.

(7) Given the complexity of all marriage systems, a valid etic definition must reflect this complexity and therefore cannot focus on one factor to the exclusion of all others even if that factor can be shown to be common to all marriage systems. Thus I suspect that an etics of marriage may in the end look something like the International Phonetic Alphabet; that is, it will be not a unitary definition but a matrix chart wherein various constellations of features can be identified as particular kinds of marriage, just as each symbol in the IPA represents a constellation of phonological features.

If we are to develop a more adequate definition of marriage, we must realize that:

> . . . we have been the victims of our ethnocentrism, taking a functionally significant unit of our society—one that we regard as basic to our society —and treating the nearest functional equivalent elsewhere as if it were, in some fundamental way, the same thing.
> . . . if our purpose is to develop a set of concepts to describe and compare *all* human societies—*all* distinct cultural communities then the traditional concepts of marriage and family are unsatisfactory, serving only as a negative standard of comparison, one that emphasizes degrees of difference from our own institutions and obscures what is common and basic to human societies generally. (Goodenough 1970:5)

NOTES

1. The Cashinahua are a Panoan-speaking tribe living along the Curanja and Upper Purus rivers of southeastern Peru. In 1968 they numbered about 400 people, distributed among seven villages ranging in size from 22 to 98

persons. Although villages are politically, socially, and economically autonomous, the Cashinahua consider themselves to be one people, *huni kuin* ("real men"). (This unity is somewhat ephemeral; the cordiality and generosity characteristic of intervillage contacts is but a thin veneer over the suspicion, distrust, and dislike felt toward all outsiders.) Being *huni kuin* sets the outer limits of membership in kinship categories, the patrimoieties and the marriage sections. For an introduction to the Cashinahua, see Kensinger (1975a).

This paper is a heavily revised version of the one originally presented in New Orleans under the title "Fact and Fiction in Cashinahua Marriage." I have benefited from comments and suggestions from many of the participants in the symposium, especially Gertrude Dode, Jean Jackson, Patricia Lyon, and Judith Shapiro. Michael Brown, Gillian Feeley-Harnik, Rhoda Halperin, Martha Hardman de Bautista, Harriet Klein, Waud Kracke, Hal Oringer, David Price, the members of the South American Indian Caucus of Columbia University, Charles Wagley's South American Seminar at the University of Florida, and two of my classes at Bennington College also made helpful suggestions. What flaws remain are a result of my failure to follow their advice.

2. The suffixes *-wan* and *-yan* are the phonologically conditioned forms of the morphemes *-wa* and *-ya,* which occur following a nasalized final syllable. The Cashinahua orthography used throughout this paper is a practical modification of the phonemic orthography. Consonants *p, t,* and *k* are pronounced like their counterparts in the English words *spy, sty,* and *sky; b, s,* and *sh* as in *buy, sigh,* and *shy; ch* and *ts* as in in*ch* and ca*ts; m, n, w,* and *y* as in *met, net, wet,* and *yet; d* in word initial position is pronounced as in English, between vowels it is pronounced like the Spanish *r; x* is pronounced like the English *sh* with the tip of the tongue turned back. Vowels *i, a,* and *u* are pronounced like the vowels in b*eet,* f*ather,* and b*oot; e* is pronounced like the English *oo* in b*oot* but with the lips flat as when one smiles. Nasalization of vowels is indicated by writing *n* after the vowel or sequence of vowels; e.g. *kain* is /kai̧/ and *kanka* is /ka̧ka/. Phonemic pitch is not written. Words have a primary stress on the first syllable; words with more than two syllables receive secondary stress on odd-numbered syllables, counting from the beginning of the word.

3. For additional discussions of the difference between Pike's and Harris's definitions of etic and emic, see Burling (1969), Fisher and Werner (1978), Goodenough (1970:esp. 113-14, n. 15), Kay (1970), Kensinger (1975b), and Merrifield (1968).

4. These terms only roughly correspond to the English glosses "marriage," "to marry," and "to be married," used throughout the paper. The slippage in translation is further compounded by the polysemy of the English terms. For example, "marriage" can refer to the ceremonial act of marrying, as in "their marriage took place at the Church of the Immaculate Conception last Saturday," or to the relationship between the couple, as in "I have had a good marriage for thirty years." The verb forms "to marry" and "to be married," which seem to be less ambiguous referents to the act of marrying and the state of being married respectively, become ambiguous in the statement "He was mar-

ried four times." I discuss the significance of this problem further in the conclusions.

5. Although polygyny is considered desirable by most Cashinahua, both male and female, only 17 of 64 married males are polygynous; one man has four wives, one has three wives, and 15 have two wives. The ideal polygynous marriage consists of a man's marrying two or more women who are actual sisters; nine of the polygynous males married in this way. Availability of wives is the primary limiting factor on polygyny. Almost as significant, however, is the attitude of a man's wife. Many wives object to the addition of a co-wife unless she is a full or half sister. However, I know of two instances where women exerted considerable pressure on their husbands, including refusal of sexual relations, until a new co-wife, not a sister, was brought into the household.

Male informants frequently said that they do not have or want more than one wife because of the added economic responsibilities and the greatly increased workload polygyny entails; they preferred to have extramarital affairs, which are easily arranged and carry with them no long-term responsibilities. Beside, his wife's approval of extramarital partners is not needed, as in the case with co-wives.

6. The Cashinahua draw a clear distinction between *ainwan/benewa* and *atiwa*, that is, between marriage and mere sexual liaisons, either fornication or adultery; the point at which an *atiwa* relationship becomes *ainwan/benewa* is not sharply defined. Although both relationships involve sexual intercourse, *chuta,* only in *ainwan/benewa* is this activity ever referred to as *bakewa* ("baby-make/do"), a period of intensive sexual activity aimed at producing pregnancy. Although both *atiwa* and *ainwan/benewa* (at least in its early stages) are characterized by secrecy, privacy, and discretion, there is the general expectation that the latter will gain public recognition and approval when the couple establish co-residence. *Atiwa* relationships are often public knowledge and the topic of gossip; however, they are not publicly acknowledged, the couple never appear together in public, and the relationship is not discussed in a public forum unless their behavior becomes so scandalous as to result in public dispute and recriminations.

7. All informants, both male and female, told me that women never reject their suitors because of fear of the sexual act, about which even young girls are well aware. From an early age they have accompanied older sisters or parallel cousins to the forest for amorous liaisons. Women may reject suitors for failing to be sufficiently tender and loving or for being too rough or impatient. Women expect their lovers to be aggressive but no more so than they themselves are. Cashinahua men like their women to be sexually aggressive and proudly wear scratches and bite marks as badges of honor.

8. See Kensinger (1975a) for a general discussion of these polarities, Kensinger (1977) as they apply to the classification of local groups (villages), and Kensinger (1981) as they apply to the classification of foods and food taboos.

9. The subscripts indicate the polarities to which the terms belong. They are used throughout this paper to reduce for the reader the ambiguity inherent in the polysemic character of *kuin, bemakia, pe,* and *chaka.* In natural discourse, of course, the ambiguity may or may not be resolved by the linguisic and/or nonlinguistic context, depending on the speaker's intention; a speaker frequently wants to maintain the ambiguity of statements in order to leave room for manipulation of and/or maneuvering within the social situation.

10. With the added meaning of central versus peripheral, Polarity 3 may also be used to subdivide the categories created by Polarities 1 and 2. However, only the more analytical of my informants use Polarity 3 in this way. They argued that when applied to the categories *kuin* and *kuinman,* Polarity 3 highlights those items that are quintessential and therefore indubitably and always *kuin$_2$* or *bemakia$_2$.* These also correspond to those items that are always *pehaida* and *chakahaida* respectively (see discussion of Polarity 4 below).

11. The term *ainkuin* differs from *ainwankuin* in that it involves the application of Polarity 1 to the kin term *ain* rather than to the marriage term *ainwan.* It designates a class of women who are actual first cross cousins as opposed to women who are merely members of the kin class female cross cousin, *ainbuaibu* (see Rule 1b). (Some informants were reluctant to classify first cross cousins who are MBD but not simultaneously FZD as *ainkuin$_1$* but were even more reluctant to classify them as *ainkuinman$_1$.*)

A note about the nature of Cashinahua kinship terminology seems relevant at this point. All kinship terms are morphologically bound forms; they must bear either a possessive pronominal prefix, the vocative morpheme {Y̧}, or the generic suffix *-bu.* For example, the kin term *epa,* which can be glossed "father or fathers" (Cashinahua nouns are not marked for the singular-plural distinction; this information is carried by the context or is left ambiguous), can occur in the following forms with different implications: *en epa* means my father, or my kinsmen whom I call father, i.e. FB, FFS, and any of the other males my father calls brother; *en epakuin$_1$* means my actual father—no distinction is made between pater and genitor unless it is general public knowledge that pater and genitor are not the same, in which case pater may be called *en epakayabi$_3$* or *en epakuin$_2$; epabu* means all the males who are members of my father's marriage section and moiety, i.e. my fathers, etc.

Thus the kin term *epa* is the label for a class of kinsmen—a social category defined by membership in the major social groups that define the individual's social persona, the moiety and marriage section. Ego has rights and duties with all members of the category. However, *epa* is not an undifferentiated category, nor are ego's rights and duties the same with regard to all. Polarities 1, 2, and 3 may be used to discriminate between the various members of the category; the criterion used to sort out the differences is for the most part the degree of genealogical closeness or distance. *En epa kuin$_1$* can only refer to the actual pater-genitor; *en epa kuin$_2$* always includes pater-genitor but may include a step-father toward whom ego has strong affective ties; *en epa kayabi$_3$* always includes ego's pater and/or genitor. *Epa kuin$_1$* is clearly the focal kin type within the social category *epabu.*

12. For a female ego, read: "She will marry her *benekuin*$_1$," i.e. her FZS *and* MBS, FZS *or* MBS.

13. For a female ego, read: "She must marry one of her *benebu*," i.e. any male of the opposite moiety and linked marriage section.

14. These include his actual M, MM, FZ, FFZ (if also MM), FM, Z, D, ZD, SD, DD. For female ego: her actual F, FB, FF, MMB (if also FF), MF, B, S, BS, SS, DS.

15. These include the *kuin*$_1$ kinsmen of one's *kuin*$_1$ kinsmen. For example, father's brother is ego's *kayabi*$_3$ kinsman because he is a *kuin*$_1$ kinsman to ego's father. All of ego's *kayabi*$_3$ kinsmen are part of ego's *nabukuin*$_1$, which consists of the members of ego's families of orientation and procreation, i.e. his *kuin*$_1$ kinsmen, and the members of the families of procreation and orientation of ego's lineal kinsmen, i.e., the *kuin*$_1$ kinsmen of ego's M, F, S, D, FF, FM, MM, MF, SS, SD, DS, DD, etc.

16. Two focal males, their wives, and their offspring constitute the basic structural unit of Cashinahua society, what I have called (Kensinger 1977) an *atom of social organization.* Thus the social core of an ideal village consists of an atom of social organization plus their primary cognates. Persons who are residents in a village but are not part of the social core are part of the social periphery; they generally have actual direct genealogical and/or affinal ties to members of the social core. Persons with only putative ties are defined as visitors until actual ties have been established by means of marriage.

17. Under these circumstances, there is a good likelihood that one or more other pairs of competing focal males might emerge, leading to the development of political factions. Therefore, although the Cashinahua speak simply of village endogamy, I suspect that the more accurate phrasing of the rule should be that one should marry within one's own political faction as well as within one's village (Kensinger 1974b). My data are inconclusive on this point; I did not realize while in the field the potential significance of this distinction and so failed to follow up the clues contained in my notes (see note 25).

18. I.e. either her actual father or a step-father who has raised her. It should be noted that although the wife's father is the pivotal figure in determining residence, Cashinahua males always speak of matrilocal residence as being with *achi,* FZ, a moiety mate, rather than with *kuka,* MB, a member of the opposite moiety.

19. This ordering represents the sequence in which the options are considered.

20. The brother-sister bond is the strongest dyadic relationship in Cashinahua society, especially the bond between an older sister and the male siblings she cared for as a young girl.

21. One young male was "married" to seven different women during a 16-month period. None of these is counted as marriage or divorce in my data.

22. Although a man is under the authority of his father-in-law, his wife's mother, his *achi,* plays a significant role in the success of his marriage in the early years. If she is not satisfied with him as a worker, provider, and member of the household, she will agitate for termination of the marriage. She may

either order him out of the house or make life so miserable for him that he will leave.

23. Since Rule 5 is not used as a criterion in the classification of marriages, it is not included in Tables 3 and 4.

24. I suspect that the addition of actual first cross cousin as opposed to double first cross cousin is a compromise necessitated by demographic realities because all informants agreed that a woman who was a FZD or MBD, but not both, was *ainkayabi$_3$* but not *ainkuin$_1$*; in practice, many of them classified a FZD who was not also MBD, and vice versa, as their *ainkuin$_1$*.

25. Two informants occasionally classified one of the *pe* marriages as *pe-pishta* because, although the spouses were village co-residents, they were members of different and antagonistic political factions. They argued that marrying a person from another political faction at odds with one's own faction is tantamount to violating the rule of village endogamy (see note 17).

26. Many informants also used *pe* and *chaka* to refer to the quality of the relationship between a couple. Therefore, statements about marriages being *pehaida, pe,* etc. are ambiguous, and intentionally so, since it allows the speaker to judge the response of the hearer before indicating whether one is making an impartial moral judgment or merely gossiping.

27. If they are cross cousins, the marriage of the wife's father and mother violated the moiety exogamy rule and/or the rule of marriage section prescription.

28. Many informants argued that marriage with an actual MM, FM, SD, or DD would be *chaka* but not *chakahaida,* since sexual activity with these persons is tolerated. For the perspective of the female ego, read: F, MB, FF, MMB (if also FF), MF, B, S, BS, SS, or DS respectively.

29. Birth defects are not included in this list; the Cashinahua believe that birth defects and multiple births are caused by incubi.

30. In an earlier formulation based on linguistic distinctions made by the Cashinahua, I viewed this process in terms of a 2×2 matrix that differentiated between establishment and maintenance and between first and subsequent marriages. Closer examination forced me to abandon that analysis for several reasons. (1) Although first and subsequent marriages may differ in terms of the inventory of events that occur during the establishment phase, the essential features are identical, namely the establishment of a sexual relationship and the residential shift of one partner, and the establishment of economic cooperation. The differences are a result either of conditioned variation based on the age of the partners, their marital histories, the presence or absence of significant kinsmen such as the spouses' parents, parents' marital histories, etc., or of free variation, depending on which sequence of optional activities is selected. (2) Although the Cashinahua distinguish between the phases of establishing a marriage (*ainwan* and *benewa*) and maintaining a marriage (*ainyan* and *beneya*), they do not sharply define when these phases begin or end. For example, a male may use the term *ainwan* at the onset of marriage negotiations, with the inception of sexual activities, or later in the process. Or he may deny that he is even married, asserting that he is merely having an affair,

atiwa. He may continue to use the term *ainwan* to describe his relationship until the birth of his first child, indicating a certain tentativeness about the relationship. On the other hand, he may begin to use the term *ainyan* as soon as co-residence and economic cooperation have been established. Others, including his parents, spouse, and siblings, tend to use *ainwan* after co-residence has been established and *ainyan* after economic cooperation has been clearly established, indicated by the husband's planting a garden and his wife's caring for and harvesting the crops. His parents-in-law tend to use *ainwan* with the initiation of sexual activity, especially if it is their daughter's first marriage, and *ainyan* only after the birth of the couple's first child.

31. In my original analysis I divided L-p marriages into two emic classes, legitimate-ideal and legitimate-proper. The significant contrasting criteria were actual versus classificatory cross cousin and obligatory versus optional village endogamy. The analysis, however, broke down when I considered distributional criteria—their distributions were identical.

32. L-i marriage between actual cross cousins is the result of improper marriages by their parents; it results in the social identity of one or both parties, based on moiety and marriage section affiliation, being at variance with their personal identity, based on actual genealogical ties. In the classification of marriages, social identity takes precedence over personal identity.

33. Like Goodenough, I am assuming that it is possible and desirable to attempt to develop a cross-culturally applicable definition of marriage; c.f. Leach (1961), Needham (1971a, 1971b), and Rivière (1971).

34. I was reminded of this point by Robert F. Murphy, whose sage advice has been stimulating and helpful on other points in this paper as well.

35. Marriage in the United States is defined by legal statute; all states require a license before marriage, and some require a religious ceremony. In addition, 14 states (Alabama, Colorado, Florida, Georgia, Idaho, Iowa, Kansas, Montana, Ohio, Oklahoma, Pennsylvania, Rhode Island, South Carolina, and Texas) and the District of Columbia recognize common-law marriages, either by statute or on the basis of judicial decision (case law); the remainder do not, although Delaware, Indiana, New Hampshire, and Wisconsin will grant exceptions under certain circumstances. (For legal sources see Clark 1968: 45-46, especially nn. 9 and 11.) Thus in at least 15 jurisdictions there are two kinds of marriage—Legal-proper (regular) and Legal-improper (irregular).

I gratefully acknowledge the legal research done by my former student, Sharon Jacobs, of the Miami law firm Chaykin, Karlan, and Jacobs, which made this note possible.

11

Change in Wachipaeri
Marriage Patterns

PATRICIA J. LYON

Introduction

Studies of the formal aspects of marriage sometimes overlook the fact that this institution is basic to the continuation of any culture. Marriage legitimates, and often requires, childbearing, thus providing the individuals who will bear the culture; it further provides protection and sustenance for these children until they can sustain and protect themselves. In many cases the parents of the child, or the mother(s) and her husband(s), are largely responsible for inculcating much of the knowledge of both nature and culture that a child receives in its early years. Thus any drastic change in marriage practices within a given culture should have drastic repercussions on that culture and might even endanger its continued existence. In this study I shall examine the effects of a devastating epidemic, compounded by growing pressure from European culture, on Wachipaeri marriage patterns. I shall indicate how these changes, especially as they affect the role of women, place Wachipaeri culture in severe danger of extinction.[1]

General Background

The group now called Wachipaeri is the remnant of a number of closely related bands who formerly occupied most of the valleys of Q'osñipata in the Department of Cuzco, Province of Paucartambo, District of Cosñipata, in eastern Peru. The area comprises five major river valleys, the lower reaches of which are separated only by low hills. These rivers (Q'eros, Cosñipata, Pilcopata, Tono, and Piñi-piñi) join just above the Pongo de Coñec, which is the head of navigation of the Alto Madre de

252

Dios River. The Wachipaeri belong to an isolated linguistic family that I have called Háte, which contains several mutually intelligible dialects (Lyon 1975). The groups belonging to this family once occupied much of the Alto Madre de Dios drainage, but many no longer exist (Lyon 1975, in press). To the west of the Wachipaeri are the Machiguenga, an Arawak-speaking people who differ in both culture and language from the Wachipaeri. Although the Machiguenga once occupied the northwestern portion of the valleys, they, like the Wachipaeri, have now been forced back to the margins of the region.

The Wachipaeri are also in contact with the Quechua-speaking highland Indians, and have oral traditions of such contact prior to the European conquest. The Spanish appropriated Inca coca plantations in the valleys shortly after their invasion, and since that time the Wachipaeri have been in more or less continuous contact with the land owners and laborers in the region, who are generally Spanish-speaking or bilingual in Spanish and Quechua (Lyon in press). In spite of the long contact, the Wachipaeri have been highly resistant to outside influence, clinging stubbornly to their culture in the face of various attempts either to wipe them out or convert them. Since 1948, however, they have had to face great pressure with very few people to carry on the culture; at that time the group was reduced from about 200 to about 70 individuals by a smallpox epidemic.[2]

Traditional Patterns

Prior to this disaster, the choice of a marriage partner was largely in the hands of the man, and he had a wide selection of prospective mates. Marriage was permissible between Wachipaeri "not of the same family," and with non-Wachipaeri of groups who were not classified as "enemy." Although cross-cousin marriage was said to be preferred, I found no cases of such matches (see, however, Appendix I).[3] Opportunities to meet prospective spouses were provided by extensive visiting throughout the valleys and by drinking parties. Drinking parties were held for various reasons by one or another house in the valleys about once a month, and all Wachipaeri in the valleys were invited (Lyon 1967: 38-41).

A number of Machiguenga women were incorporated into the Wachipaeri groups as wives. Some had been captured in raids and others seem to have been acquired by more pacific means. I heard of no case of a Machiguenga man marrying a Wachipaeri woman and living with the Wachipaeri. There were, however, two groups of Háte speakers, the Toyeri and the Sirineri, some of whose men married Wachipaeri women and settled among the Wachipaeri. I have no evidence that this arrangement was reciprocal. Both of these groups were located downriver from the Wachipaeri, but it is unclear exactly how many specific culturally defined groups were involved.

Once a man decided which woman he wanted to marry, he approached her parents for permission. If they consented, the pair was married, even over the woman's objections. Both parents were involved in the decision, and they apparently seldom consented to a marriage if their daughter was vehemently opposed, or if they thought she would be unhappy. If an unmarried man and woman were found to be having a sexual affair, however, they were forced to marry each other.

There is no indication that any Wachipaeri woman remained single throughout her lifetime. Some men did, however, and I knew one bachelor about 70 years old. I was told that a man might meet an animal spirit in the forest who would appear to him in the form of a woman. If the man established a sexual relationship with such a spirit woman, he would never marry. I do not know if this was the only reason given for men remaining single, nor if all single men were believed to have established such a relationship.

Although the Wachipaeri are officially monogamous today, they have practiced polygyny within the last two generations. The extent of the polygyny is not clear, nor is the reason for its abandonment, although a shortage of women may have been a major factor.[4]

The Wachipaeri lived in large communal houses separated from one another by a walk of one-half to two hours, and occupied by a numerous extended family plus occasional unrelated hangers-on. Residence after marriage depended on various factors. In the case of cross-cousin marriage, since both parties would originally be living in the same house, there was no change of residence. In the case of marriage between houses patrilocality was preferred unless the husband came from far away, for example, from another group such as the Toyeri or Sirineri, in which case he would move into his wife's house. The critical distance may have been that distance beyond which regular contact could no longer be maintained. Wherever residence was established, the newly married couple became part of a large interacting household that could exert a certain amount of influence in the case of difficulties arising between man and wife. They were in a position to both observe and be helped by older, established married people who served as examples and could be approached for advice on how to avoid the many pitfalls present in a new marriage.

If a woman found her married life unhappy, she might run away. In such a case her father was expected to help apprehend her and return her to her husband. On the other hand, her husband was expected to keep her happy so that she would not run away. Women frequently appealed to their brothers for help, and might even visit them for extended periods in case of trouble.

Among the songs sung at drinking parties are a number sung by women complaining about marital problems. Since such songs were sung before the assembled company, the listeners were in a position to help resolve such problems once they were out in the open. Help might take the form of advice to the complainant and/or the object of her complaint. This advice was frequently couched in song, since direct criticism in any other form was not permitted (Lyon 1967).

If all efforts to make a marriage function failed, divorce was possible. Indeed, it appears that Wachipaeri marriages were quite brittle, and many individuals passed through several before settling down for life. On the other hand, I found most older Wachipaeri couples to be affectionate toward each other and to maintain a happy and egalitarian relationship. There appears to have been little bad feeling between divorced spouses, and the decision regarding disposition of children was made by mutual consent. When one marriage partner died, the survivor was not required to remarry, but remarriage with a sibling of the deceased spouse was common. If the survivor remained single, he or she would be aided when necessary by grown children and/or other close relatives.

Causes of Change

Virtually all the practices outlined above have changed, most of them quite recently. Probably the single most important factor in the changes was the sudden sharp drop in population as a result of the 1948 smallpox epidemic. At about the same time there was an increase in the presence of outsiders in the valleys attracted by the road that was being constructed into the region.[5]

In about 1946 a North American Baptist mission was established on Wachipaeri territory. In 1955 a Dominican mission was established on the Alto Madre de Dios below the head of navigation, and in 1958 was moved to its present location at Shintuya (Secretariado de Misiones Dominicanas n.d.:74). Each of these factors has influenced Wachipaeri marriage practices.

Present Situation

The Wachipaeri have traditionally been divided into two major groupings, one in the southeast part of the valleys and one farther north. During my studies the southeastern group (25 people in 1965) was gathered on the Baptist mission lands, which occupied the territory of three Wachipaeri houses. The northern group was scattered in from three to five small clusters. Although I visited one of the northern settlements briefly, my data were obtained almost entirely from the southeastern group.

In 1955 I gathered, from informants, a count of all known living Wachipaeri. The total was 71, 60 of whom were living in the valleys of Q'osñipata.[6] I do not have exact ages for these individuals, but they can be divided roughly in two groups, those below the age of about 10 years and those above.[7] The breakdown by sex is as follows:

	Over 10 years old		*Under 10 years old*	
women	21	girls	4
men	27	boys	8
Totals	48		12

At that time there were three Wachipaeri men and one woman living at the Catholic mission.

The population drop alone was sufficient to cause a number of problems in maintaining Wachipaeri culture, but to complicate matters further, there was a definite shortage of women. The figures presented do not tell the entire tale. Of the 21 women in the valleys, 4 were living with non-Wachipaeri. Thus, of a total of 48 individuals over 10 years old, there were 10 males with no immediate possibility of marriage, or a ratio of approximately 1.5 men for each woman. The sex ratio of 2 to 1 among children under 10 did not bode well for the future. I know of no reason why the epidemic should have affected women more than men, and there is no way to determine the population structure prior to the epidemic. I have, however, no data indicating a shortage of women prior to that time.

Besides the reduced number of women, chances to meet them were also reduced. Since the last drinking party to encompass the whole region was held in 1955, there no longer were opportunities for all Wachipaeri to gather. The discontinuance of the all-inclusive drinking parties seems to have resulted from the effect of the Baptist missionaries on the southeastern group; their culture was greatly affected by the missionaries following the epidemic. Although the missionized Wachipaeri could, and did, attend parties given on the other side of the valleys, they could not reciprocate. I was told that the northern groups continued to have occasional drinking parties but no longer invited the Wachipaeri living on the mission. Although the Baptist missionaries had little effect prior to the epidemic, their later efforts were particularly noticeable among the many children who were orphaned, some of whom had no surviving close relatives (see Appendix II). By 1964 all Wachipaeri living on mission land appeared to be converted, and one result was that the converts no longer established contact with animal spirits. None of the young unmarried men had ever had such contact, thus removing at least one culturally approved reason for remaining unmarried.

Informal visiting among the various Wachipaeri groups has gradually declined; I noted a great difference between 1954 and 1960. While the reasons for this decline are not obvious, one important factor is probably the increased number of outsiders in the region. At the same time that the two divisions of the Wachipaeri have been gradually pushed out to the margins of the habitable region, the intervening region has been occupied by outsiders; thus any Wachipaeri wishing to visit another group would have to pass through a number of properties owned by outsiders. Such passage may be not only distasteful but actually dangerous, since many land owners assume the right to order any Wachipaeri to work for them, running errands or performing other tasks, generally without pay. Failure to accede to such "requests" might result in very unpleasant consequences. The role of the missionaries in the decline in visiting is not entirely clear. The personnel of the Baptist mission changed from time to time with concomitant differences in attitude. Sometimes visiting between the converted and "heathen" Wachipaeri was discouraged, while at others there was no objection. Some contact was maintained between the Wachipaeri of the valleys and those of the Catholic mission; however, the distance is sufficient that such visits have never been frequent and the Catholic missionaries have never encouraged them.

If a young Wachipaeri man had problems finding a Wachipaeri wife, the situation was no better outside his group. The number of Machiguenga in the valleys had also declined, and the Háte-speaking groups who had previously intermarried with the Wachipaeri were, as noted, virtually extinct. One young Wachipaeri from the southeastern group secured a young Amarakaeri wife from the Catholic mission at Shintuya and returned with her to the valleys. The Amarakaeri are one of several Háte-speaking groups represented at the Shintuya mission who were previously either enemies of the Wachipaeri or unknown to them. This particular marriage caused the missionaries to institute very careful watch over the remaining young women, not permitting them to marry off the mission. Thus, to get a wife from this source, a Wachipaeri man would have to settle there, and many feel the cost too high.

What, then, are the possible solutions available to the unmarried Wachipaeri man? In the face of similar sex imbalance, other groups have resorted to some sort of polyandrous arrangement (e.g. Laraia 1963, Clastres 1970:19-25). I observed one Wachipaeri household composed of two men and one woman in 1955, and another such flourished at least from 1965 to 1968. The proximity of the missions, as well as many Christian settlers, tends to militate against such arrangements as a general solution. Were polyandrous households to become common, outsiders would surely learn of them and could exert strong social and economic pressures against persons involved in such un-Christian groupings. I knew of a single case of two young men who seemed to have established a homosexual relationship. While this solution might relieve the sexual tensions of the pair involved, it would not contribute to the Wachipaeri birthrate. Another young man tried to steal his uncle's wife. Not only was this move unsuccessful, but it almost led to the dissolution of the entire community through the tensions aroused.

There was some talk of trying to get together with some of the smaller independent remnants of downriver groups, but nothing positive was done. There is also no assurance that such groups would either have surplus women or welcome the idea of such a coalition. The other possible source of women is among the Quechua-speaking highland Indians, especially those now living in the valleys. One young Wachipaeri whom I asked about the possibility of marrying a highland woman replied that it would not work. He noted that highland women do not know how to cultivate lowland crops, how to prepare the food, or how to do all the other things that a Wachipaeri woman must do to keep the family economy going, entirely aside from the language difficulty.[8] There is also the question of how willing such a woman would be to marry a Wachipaeri. On the Peruvian social scale the highland Indian is generally considered at the bottom, but the tropical forest Indian is even lower.

The problems raised by the young man were real ones. The man who had tried to steal his uncle's wife left the valleys and lived in Cuzco for a couple of years. During that time he married a highland woman and returned with her to live with the Wachipaeri. The arrangement did not last, however, and no offspring resulted.

If a young man succeeds in finding a Wachipaeri wife, further problems may arise. If she runs away, who will bring her back? Her father probably died in the epidemic. Furthermore, she may take shelter with the outsiders. An attractive young woman seldom has trouble in finding someone to take her in, especially in a frontier situation with a shortage of women in the general population. As a direct result of the woman shortage, there is an increasing likelihood that a man may try to steal another man's wife, and such actions are very disruptive of the social fabric. The probability that a new wife will run away may be greater now that there are fewer opportunities for problem resolution open to women. Without drinking parties, a woman has no acceptable forum for expressing her problems and seeking advice. Since the epidemic few have brothers to visit until problems can be resolved. The few communal-type houses that still exist often contain no more than a nuclear family and one or two additional people, so that the large supporting group that used to help newly married couples with their problems is no longer available. In fact, in about 1961 the southeastern group abandoned their communal houses and joined together in a settlement of nuclear family dwellings around a central plaza in imitation of the white pattern.[9]

Although widowed women have no problem finding a spouse today, a man who is widowed or abandoned by his wife is unlikely to be able to remarry. Such a man will not starve; even if he does not cultivate his own fields, his fellow Wachipaeri will feed him. If, however, his wife has either died or gone to live with the outsiders, he will probably be left to care for his children. Although other members of the community will aid in taking care of such children, they will not constitute the close family group that would have been present in pre-epidemic days (see Appendix II).

Conclusions and Some Questions

The basic problem is the continuing survival of Wachipaeri culture. The survival of the culture demands both the continuance of those cultural practices that mark the Wachipaeri off as a unit from the outsiders who surround them, and a population to carry on these cultural practices. The Wachipaeri have a long history of resistance to outside influence. Such resistance is obvious in the minimal amount of either indigenous highland Peruvian or European cultural influence observable in their culture in 1954, and the fact that most such influences were material objects (steel tools, chickens, the use of Western clothing in the presence of outsiders) and some use of Spanish by young men. Now, however, the Wachipaeri are under growing pressure to change, and there are ever fewer of them to resist such pressure. In view of the foregoing account of recent changes, one might ask what remains of the culture. And does anyone care whether it survives or not? The question of what will persist is one that will require time to answer, since at the moment the entire culture is in a state of flux. It is clear that what will emerge will be different from what has gone before, but the exact form it will take remains to be seen. The question of whether anyone cares can be answered with a resounding Yes. The Wachipaeri care. They feel themselves to be a distinctive people, standing in sharp contrast to outsiders. They are aware, and their awareness is expressed especially in their songs, that their way of life and their uniqueness are in danger. This awareness is more obvious among the older people, but the younger ones also feel the pressure to change from the outside; although they are willing to change in some respects, they do not feel themselves at one with those to whom they always refer as "the people from outside."

Although I have no quantitative data, my impression is that the Wachipaeri population has grown somewhat since 1955. There is no apparent drop in birthrate, and more children are surviving owing to the recent availability of medical care, especially through the missions. Thus the population can probably survive as a biological unit. The main question, then, is whether the culture can hold together long enough for the children being born today to grow up as Wachipaeri rather than as cholofied Peruvians. Obviously Wachipaeri culture must change, and it is changing, but the problem of maintaining *a* Wachipaeri culture will be more severe if Wachipaeri men must seek wives from outside the group. Women are important in the transmission of Wachipaeri culture. They are responsible for most plant lore and much in the way of oral tradition, among other things. The influence of the many Machiguenga women who married into the group may be seen in the considerable number of people bilingual in Wachipaeri and Machiguenga as well as in the many Machiguenga loan words in the language. The introduction of highland women, probably bilingual in Quechua and Spanish, combined with the fact that most men who would marry such women would be bilingual in Spanish and Wachipaeri, could lead to the abandonment of Wachipaeri as a language in favor of Spanish, a tendency that would be reinforced by the presence of the ever-encroaching settlers.

At the moment the breakdown of a series of traditional institutions tends toward the removal of Wachipaeri women from the marriage pool. The lack of surviving parents, combined with the shortage of women, has shifted the decision on a marriage partner from the men to the women. Women may now choose freely among the various suitors available to them, and may even prefer to marry out of the group. Superficially, life among the outsiders may seem very appealing to a young Wachipaeri woman, surrounded as it is by the glamor of the unknown. Not until she is involved in such an arrangement does she realize that she does not have the freedom to leave if she is unhappy that she would have had among her own people, nor does modern Peruvian culture include any expectation that a man should do his best to keep his wife happy so she will not want to run away (see Appendix I). Even those women who initially choose to marry within their own culture may end outside of it. Since running away from an unhappy marital situation has always been culturally acceptable for women, it will probably continue. Now, however, the options have changed. A woman may have no brothers or parents to run to, but she may seek refuge with either a settler or the Catholic mission (see, for example, Appendix II).

Some of the problems I have discussed will presumably be resolved in time. It is only the generation immediately following the epidemic that suffers so from the lack of family, and all the problems relating to that particular factor may be resolved in a maximum of two generations. On the other hand, will the families that are formed now function in the same way families have functioned in the past, especially in the solution of marital problems? At the moment the question of the survival of Wachipaeri culture hinges on the decisions made by Wachipaeri women. And the decisions reached by these women will not simply provide a change in formal aspects of social organization but, rather, will be the key to the continuation or extinction of an entire culture.[10]

NOTES

1. The fieldwork upon which this study is based encompassed some 20 months in 1954-55, 1960, 1962, 1964, 1965, and 1968. Support for this work was provided variously by the American Museum of Natural History; the Graduate Division of the University of California, Berkeley; the National Institutes of Health (National Institute of General Medical Sciences), training Grant no. GM-1224; and the Johnson Fund of the American Philosophical Society. Unless otherwise noted all statements are based on field data.

2. Population data for the period prior to the epidemic are based on informant statements, specifically on the number of houses with a modest estimate of 25-30 people per house. This latter figure is based on counts of the number of people recorded as living in the houses of informants. The population was probably considerably larger around the turn of the century when my oldest informant was a boy. A conservative estimate for that time would be 500-700 people.

3. The Wachipaeri are uncomfortable discussing close kin who are dead and have stringent prohibitions against mentioning the names of the dead. Since, at the time I gathered these data, virtually no one had a complete family, and many had only a single living relative, it was impossible to collect genealogies. The same prohibitions prevented close inquiry into the traditional social organization, which had broken down almost entirely by that time.

4. Johnston et al. (1969) note a similar shortage of women among the younger Peruvian Cashinahua. It will be interesting to see if this sexual imbalance affects their practice of polygyny.

5. The influx of settlers and exploiters preceded the completion of the road, which was finally opened as far as the head of navigation only in 1960. The source of the epidemic was not the settlers themselves but the young daughter of a mule driver who trafficked with the inhabitants of the valley, exchanging provisions for cane alcohol.

6. Aside from four individuals at the Catholic mission, the other Wachipaeri outside the valleys were too far away to maintain any contact (e.g. Lima and Puerto Maldonado) and are therefore irrelevant to the present discussion.

7. The breakoff point of 10 years is insignificant culturally, since Wachipaeri marry relatively late, between 18 and 25 for both men and women.

8. Most highland Indians in the valleys are somewhat bilingual in Spanish and Quechua, but the women know less Spanish than do the men. Few Wachipaeri speak more than a few words of Quechua, although most of the young men are relatively fluent in Spanish and frequently Machiguenga.

9. The reasons for this change in settlement pattern are complex and not directly germane to this paper.

10. I am indebted to Alex Georgiadis and John H. Rowe, both of whom read the original version of this work and offered many valuable suggestions. They are not, however, responsible for any of its shortcomings, which are mine.

Appendix I: Pilar

When I met Pilar in 1955, she was about 45 years old. Although Wachipaeri, she was living with a Greek hacienda administrator and had been doing so for some 20 years. They had four living children, three girls and a boy. She told me the following story of how she came to settle down with this man.

As a girl she had lived in a communal house among her people. Living in the same house was her mother's brother's son, Salomón, whom she was expected to wed. When she was about 19, the families began to exert some pressure for the marriage to take place. Salomón, however, was in love with a tall, handsome Machiguenga girl, Irma, and did not want to marry Pilar. Since Pilar and Salomón were good friends, they discussed this problem and devised a solution. One night they met Irma and her brother, Carlos, and all four fled downriver, out of the territory of their family groups.

For a couple of years the four lived happily together, and then Carlos died. Pilar finally took refuge on the hacienda of the Greek, who was living nearby. Later Salomón and Irma returned to the Q'osñipata valleys, where they still dwelt in 1954. In time Pilar and the Greek also moved to the valleys.

In 1960 Pilar's children were exerting pressure on their parents to get married so that the children could be legitimized, and they requested that I try to convince their mother. I had assumed that their father opposed the marriage but found I was wrong. Pilar told me that she would have left the Greek any number of times to return to her people, but stayed because of the children. She had, in fact, run away from him twice, but he had pursued her and brought her back. Now she was waiting for the children to become independent in order to leave him for good. Under no circumstances would she be legally tied to this man with whom she had lived for 25 years but who was still an outsider to her.

Appendix II: Manuel

I first knew Manuel in 1954 when he was about 18 years old. He was one of the many young Wachipaeri orphaned by the epidemic. His only surviving kin were a half-brother and an aunt who was raising them. A number of such children were then living on the Baptist mission, more influenced by the missionaries than by any other factor in their surroundings. Manuel, in particular, had been acting as linguistic informant for the missionary, since he spoke a little Spanish. Through his close association with the mission, Manuel developed not only a taste for trade goods but also the idea that cash money was easily obtained. For example, the missionaries paid ten centavos per bug to the children for catching cockroaches. Although Manuel was considered to be rather lazy, he was paid ten *soles* a day to work as an informant at a time when the average daily wage for agricultural labor was two and a half *soles*. The missionaries also allowed the Wachipaeri under their tutelage to buy trade goods and canned food on credit, using the same debt bondage system that was current among the local haciendas. At one time Manuel was said to owe the mission several hundred *soles* (with an exchange of about 19 to the dollar).

I again encountered Manuel in 1960. By then his aunt had died and he had married and had two sons, but I never met his wife.

In 1964 Manuel was still living on the Baptist mission lands, but his wife had left him and he had taken his older son, Jorge, to the Catholic mission for schooling. He lived with his younger son, Juan, in a house he had never quite finished building (it had only two and a half walls). He had planted some coffee that he neglected, with a resultant poor yield. He had not planted a subsistence plot, although the other single men in the community had done so. He occasionally went hunting but seldom with any success, since he usually did not get up early enough to take advantage of the early morning hours when hunting was best. Manuel and Juan ate with the other families in the settlement in a sort of rotation. They would eat with one family until they got tired of the fare, or until the family had no meat for several days, and then move on to eat with another family. So they survived. No one complained of this freeloading, but the group often joked that Manuel was the laziest man alive. Juan wandered around with his father and was occasionally left in the care of his maternal aunt, who also lived in the settlement. I inquired about what had happened to Manuel's wife and was told that she had left him and gone to live with one of the outsiders. She had been, I was told, a fine, hard-working, pleasant woman. He, however, had beaten her so often and so severely that she finally could not stand it and had left him.

Manuel could not understand that one did not receive something for nothing. When he visited Jorge at the Catholic mission, he complained that the padres wanted him to work for them while he was there. He could see no reason why he should pay either for his son's schooling or for the food he himself ate during his visits. Although Jorge was a fine lad, Juan, who was living with Manuel, showed every sign of following in his father's footsteps, which had been directed so much earlier by the benevolent Baptist missionaries.

Bibliography

ACKERMAN, CHARLES
    1964   Structure and statistics: The Purum case. *American Anthropologist* 66:53-65. (GD)

ÅRHEM, KAJ
    1981   *Makuna social organization: A study in descent, alliance and the formation of corporate groups in the North-Western Amazon.* Uppsala Studies in Cultural Anthropology, no. 4. Uppsala. (JJ)

ARNAUD, EXPEDITO
    1975   *Os índios Gaviões de Oeste: Pacificação e integração.* Museu Paraense Emílio Goeldi, Publ. Avulsa 28. Belém. (WC)

ARNAUD, EXPEDITO, AND ANA RITA ALVES
    1975   A terminologia de parentesco entre os índios Galibí e outros groupes Karib. *Boletím do Museu Paraense Emílio Goeldi,* N.S., Antropologia no. 60. Belém. (GD)

ARNAUD, EXPEDITO, ROBERTO CORTEZ, AND ANA RITA ALVES
    1977   A terminologia de parentesco dos índios Gaviões de Oeste (Parkateyê)—Tocantins, Pará. *Boletím do Museu Paraense Emílio Goeldi,* N.S., Antropologia no. 63. Belém. (WC)

ARVELO-JIMENEZ, NELLY
    1971   Political relations in a tribal society: A study of the Ye'cuana Indians of Venezuela. Latin American Studies Program Dissertation Series. Ithaca, N.Y.: Cornell University. (JK)

Atlas de Colombia
    1969   Instituto geográfico "Agustín Codazzi." Bogotá: Litografía Arco. (JJ)

BALDUS, HERBERT
    1970   *Tapirapé: Tribu Tupi no Brasil central.* São Paulo: Companhia Editôra Nacional. (WK)

BAMBERGER, JOAN
    1979   Exit and voice in central Brazil: The politics of flight in Kayapó Society. In *Dialectical societies: The Gê and Bororo of central*

265

Brazil, ed. David Maybury-Lewis. Cambridge, Mass.: Harvard University Press. Pp. 130-46. (WC)

BARNES, J. A.
1960   Marriage and residential continuity. *American Anthropologist* 62:850-66. (GD)

BASSO, ELLEN B.
1970   Xingu Carib kinship terminology and marriage: Another view. *Southwestern Journal of Anthropology* 26:402-16. (JS, GD)
1973   *The Kalapalo Indians of central Brazil.* New York: Holt, Rinehart and Winston. (GD, JS)
1975   Kalapalo affinity: Its cultural and social contexts. *American Ethnologist* 2:207-28. (JS, GD)

BECK, BRENDA E. F.
1972   *Peasant Society in Konku.* Vancouver: University of British Columbia Press. (JK)

BECKER, ELLEN R.
1969   Xingu society. Ph.D. dissertation, University of Chicago. (GD, JS)

BETTS, LAVERA, AND HELEN PEASE
1966   *Morongita.* Rio de Janeiro: Summer Institute of Linguistics. (WK)

BLOCH, MAURICE
1973   The long term and the short term: The economic and political significance of the morality of kinship. In *The character of kinship,* ed. Jack Goody. Cambridge: Cambridge University Press. (JS)

BOHANNAN, PAUL
1957   An alternate residence classification. *American Anthropologist* 59:126-31. (GD)

BUCHLER, IRA R., AND HENRY A. SELBY
1968   *Kinship and social organization: An introduction to theory and method.* New York: Macmillan. (JJ, JS)

BURLING, ROBBINS
1969   Linguistics and ethnographic description. *American Anthropologist* 71:817-27. (KK)

CARDOSO DE OLIVEIRA, ROBERTO
1959   Matrimônio e solidariedade tribal Terêna. *Revista de Antropologia* 7 (1 and 2). São Paulo. (WK)
1961   Aliança interclânica na sociedade Tukuna. *Revista de Antropologia* 9 (1 and 2):15-32. São Paulo. (WK)

CARNEIRO, ROBERT L.
1970   A theory of the origin of the state. *Science* 169:733-38. (NW)

CARNEIRO DA CUNHA, MANUELA
1978   *Os mortos e os outros: Uma análise do sistema funerário e da*

noção de pessoa entre os índios Krahó. São Paulo: Editora Hucitec. (WC)

CARRASCO, PEDRO
1963   The locality of referent in residence terms. *American Anthropologist* 65:133-34. (GD)

CARTER, WILLIAM E.
1977   Trial marriage in the Andes? In *Andean kinship and marriage,* ed. Ralph Bolton and Enrique Mayer. Special publication of the American Anthropological Association, no. 7. (JS)

CHAGNON, NAPOLEON A.
1968   *Yanomamö: The fierce people.* New York: Holt, Rinehart, and Winston. (JJ, JS)

CLARK, HOMER H., JR.
1968   *The law of domestic relations in the United States.* Minneapolis–St. Paul: West Publishing Co. (KK)

CLASTRES, PIERRE
1970   Ethnographie des indiens Guayaki (Paraguay-Brésil). *Journal de la Société des Américanistes* (Paris) 57:8-61. (PL)

COMAROFF, J. L.
1980   Bridewealth and the control of ambiguity in a Tswana chiefdom. In *The meaning of marriage payments,* ed. J. L. Comaroff. New York: Academic Press. (JS)

COMAROFF, J. L., AND SIMON ROBERTS
1977   Dialectics of legal change among the Kgatha. *Journal of African Law* 21:97-123. (JS)

CROCKER, J. CHRISTOPHER
1977   Why are the Bororo matrilineal? In *Actes* 2:245-58, XLII Congrès International des Américanistes, Paris (1976). (JK)
1979   Selves and alters among the Eastern Bororo. In *Dialectical Societies: The Gê and Bororo of central Brazil,* ed. David Maybury-Lewis. Cambridge, Mass.: Harvard University Press. (JK)

CROCKER, WILLIAM H.
1961   The Canela since Nimuendaju: A preliminary report on cultural change. *Anthropological Quarterly* 34:69-84. (WC)
1962   A method for deriving themes as applied to Canela Indian festival materials. Ph.D dissertation, University of Wisconsin. Ann Arbor: University Microfilms. (WC)
1964a   Extramarital sexual practices of the Ramkokamekra-Canela Indians: An analysis of socio-cultural factors. In *Beiträge zur Völkerkunde Südamerikas: Festgabe für Herbert Baldus zum 65. Geburtstag,* ed. Hans Becher. Völkerkundliche Abhandlungen des Niedersächsischen Landesmuseums Abteilung für Völkerkune, vol. 1. Hannover: Münstermann-Druck GMBH. Pp. 25-35. (Also in Lyon 1974:184-94.) (WC)

1964b   Conservatism among the Canela: An analysis of contributing factors. In *Actas y Memorias,* vol. 35, Congreso Internacional de Americanistas. México, D. F.: Editorial Libros de México. (WC)

1971   The Canela (Brazil) taboo system: A preliminary exploration of an anxiety-reducing device. In *Verhandlungen* 3:323-31, XXXVIII Internationalen Amerikansterkongresses, Stüttgart-München (1968). Munich: Klaus Renner. (WC)

1972   The non-adaptation of a savanna Indian tribe (Canela, Brazil) to forced, forest relocation: An analysis of factors. In *Anais,* vol. 1, Encontro Internacional de Estudos Brasileiros, I Seminário de Estudos Brasileiros (1971). São Paulo. (WC)

1974   Extramarital sexual practices of the Ramkókamekra-Canela Indians: An analysis of socio-cultural factors. In *Native South Americans: Ethnology of the least known continent,* ed. Patricia J. Lyon. Boston: Little, Brown. Pp. 184-94. (WC)

1977   Canela "group" recruitment and perpetuity: Incipient "unilineality"? In *Actes* 2:259-75, XLII Congrès International des Américanistes, Paris (1976). (WC, JK)

1978   Estórias das épocas de pré e pós-pacificação dos Ramkókamekra e Apãniekra-Canelas. *Boletím do Museu Paraense Emílio Goeldi,* n.s., Antropologia no. 68. Belém. (WC)

1979   Canela kinship and the question of matrilineality. In *Brazil: Anthropological perspectives* (*essays in honor of Charles Wagley*), ed. Maxine L. Margolis and William E. Carter. New York: Columbia University Press. Pp. 225-49. (WC)

DA MATTA, ROBERTO

1971   Uma breve reconsideração da morfologia social Apinayé. In *Verhandlungen* 3:355-64, XXXVIII Internationalen Amerikanistenkongresses, Stüttgart-München (1968). Munich: Klaus Renner. (WC)

1973   A reconsideration of Apinayé social morphology. In *Peoples and cultures of native South America,* ed. Daniel R. Gross. New York: Doubleday. (WC)

1976   *Um mundo dividido: A estrutura social do índios Apinayé.* Petropolis: Voces. (WC)

1979   The Apinayé relationship system: Terminology and ideology. The Gê and Bororo of central Brazil. In *Dialectical societies,* ed. David Maybury-Lewis. Cambridge, Mass.: Harvard University Press. (JK, WC)

DESCENT IN LOWLAND SOUTH AMERICA

1975   Symposium held at the annual meetings of the American Anthropological Association, San Francisco (Judith Shapiro, organizer). (JS)

DILLINGHAM, BETH W., AND BARRY L. ISAAC

1975   Defining marriage cross-culturally. In *Being female: Reproduc-*

tion, power and change, ed. Dana Raphael. The Hague: Mouton. Pp. 55-63. (GD)

DOLE, GERTRUDE E.
1957   The development of patterns of kinship nomenclature. Ph.D. dissertation, University of Michigan. Ann Arbor, Mich.: University Microfilms. (GD)
1966   Anarchy without chaos: Alternatives to political authority among the Kuikuru. In *Political anthropology,* ed. Marc J. Swartz, Victor W. Turner, and Arthur Tuden. Chicago: Aldine. Pp. 73-87. (GD)
1969   Generation kinship nomenclature as an adaptation to endogamy. *Southwestern Journal of Anthropology* 25:105-23. (GD, JS)

DREYFUS, SIMONE
1977   Propositions pour un modèle sud-américain de l'alliance symétrique. In *Actes,* XLII Congrès International des Américanistes, Paris (1976). (JS)

DUMONT, LOUIS
1953a   The Dravidian kinship terminology as an expression of marriage. *Man* 53:34-39. (JS, JK)
1953b   Dravidian kinship terminology. *Man* 53:143. (JK)
1957   *Hierarchy and marriage alliance in South Indian kinship.* Occasional Papers of the Royal Anthropological Institute, no. 12. London. (JJ, JS, JK)
1961   Marriage in India, the present state of the question. *Contributions to Indian Sociology* 5:75-95. (JK)
1975   *Dravidian et Kariera: L'alliance de mariage dans l'Inde du Sud, et en Australie.* Paris: Mouton. (JK)

ELKIN, A. P.
1953   Murngin kinship re-examined and remarks on some generalizations. *American Anthropologist* 55:412-19. (JJ)

FISHER, LAWRENCE E., AND OSWALD WERNER
1978   Explaining explanation: Tension in American anthropology. *Journal of Anthropological Research* 34:194-218. (KK)

FORTES, MEYER
1953   The structure of unilineal descent groups. *American Anthropologist* 55:17-41. (GD)

FOX, ROBIN
1967   *Kinship and marriage.* Middlesex: Penguin. (JJ)

GARCIA DE FREITAS, JOSÉ
1926   Os indios Parintintin. *Journal de la Société des Américanistes* (Paris) 18:67-73. (WK)

GOLDMAN, IRVING
1948   Tribes of the Uaupés-Caquetá region. *Bureau of American Ethnology Bulletin* 143:763-98. (JJ)

1963   *The Cubeo: Indians of the Northwest Amazon.* Illinois Studies in Anthropology, no. 2. Urbana: University of Illinois Press. (JJ, AS)

GONDIM, JOAQUIM
1938   *Etnografia indígena: Estudos realizados em várias regiões do amazonas, no período de 1921 a 1926,* vol. 1. Fortaleza, Ceara: Editôra Fortaleza. (WK)

GOOD, ANTHONY
1980   Elder sister's daughter marriage in South Asia. *Journal of Anthropological Research* 36:474-500. (JK)

GOODENOUGH, WARD H.
1956   Residence Rules. *Southwestern Journal of Anthropology* 12:22-37. (GD)
1970   *Description and comparison in cultural anthropology.* Chicago: Aldine. (KK, JS)

GOUGH, KATHLEEN
1959   The Nayars and the definition of marriage. *Man* 89:23-34. (JS)
1971   Nuer kinship: A reexamination. In *The translation of culture,* ed. T. O. Beidelman. London: Tavistock. (JS)

GREENBERG, JOSEPH
1966   (ed.) *Universals of language.* 2nd edition. Cambridge, Mass.: M.I.T. Press. (JS)

HARNER, MICHAEL J.
1972   *The Jívaro: People of the sacred waterfalls.* Garden City, N.Y.: Natural History Press/Doubleday. (NW)

HARRIS, MARVIN
1964   *The nature of cultural things.* New York: Random House. (KK)
1968   *The rise of anthropological theory.* New York: Thomas Y. Crowell. (KK)
1971   *Culture, man and nature: An introduction to general anthropology.* New York: Thomas Y. Crowell. (2nd ed., 1975.) (KK)
1979   *Cultural Materialism.* New York: Random House. (KK)

HEINEN, H. D.
1972   Residence rules and household cycles in a Warao subtribe: The case of Winikina. *Antropologica* 31:21-86. (GD)

HENLEY, PAUL
1979   The internal social organization of the Panare of Venezuelan Guiana and their relations with the national society. Ph.D dissertation, Cambridge University. (JK)

HOMANS, GEORGE C., AND DAVID SCHNEIDER
1955   *Marriage, authority, and final causes: A study of unilateral cross-cousin marriage.* Glencoe, Ill.: Free Press. (JJ)

HUGH-JONES, CHRISTINE
  1979   *From the Milk River: Spatial and temporal processes in North-west Amazonia.* Cambridge: Cambridge University Press. (JJ, JK, JS)

HUGH-JONES, STEPHEN
  1979   *The palm and the Pleiades: Initiation and cosmology in North-west Amazonia.* Cambridge: Cambridge University Press. (JJ, JK)

JACKSON, JEAN E.
  1972   Marriage and linguistic identity among the Bará Indians of the Vaupés, Colombia. Ph.D dissertation, Stanford University. (JJ)
  1974   Language identity of the Colombian Vaupés Indians. In *Explorations in the ethnography of speaking,* ed. R. Bauman and J. Sherzer, Cambridge: Cambridge University Press. Pp. 50-64. (JJ)
  1976   Vaupés marriage: A network system in the Northwest Amazon. In *Regional analysis,* vol. 2, *Social systems,* ed. Carol A. Smith. New York: Academic Press. Pp. 65-73. (JJ)
  1977   Bará zero-generation terminology and marriage. *Ethnology* 16:83-104. (JJ, JS)
  1983   *The fish-people: Linguistic exogamy and Tukanoan identity in the Northwest Amazon.* Cambridge: Cambridge University Press. (JJ)

JACKSON, JEAN E., AND A. KIMBALL ROMNEY
  1973   A note on Bará exogamy. Unpublished paper. (JJ)

JAKOBSON, ROMAN
  1941   *Kindersprache, Aphasie und Allgemeine Lautgesetze.* Uppsala: Mouton. (JS)

JAKOBSON, ROMAN, AND MORRIS HALLE
  1956   *Fundamentals of language.* Janua Lingarum, series minor, no. 1. The Hague: Mouton. (JS)

JOHNSTON, FRANCIS E., ET AL.
  1969   The population structure of the Peruvian Cashinahua: Demographic, genetic, and cultural interrelationships. *Human Biology* 41:29-41. (PL)

KAPLAN, JOANNA OVERING
  1972   Cognation, endogamy, and teknonymy: The Piaroa example. *Southwestern Journal of Anthropology* 28:282-97. (JK, JS)
  1973   Endogamy and the marriage alliance: A note on continuity in kindred-based groups. *Man* 8:555-70. (JK, JS)
  1975   *The Piaroa, a people of the Orinoco basin: A study in kinship and marriage.* Oxford: Clarendon Press. (JK)
  1977a   Orientation for paper topics. In *Actes* 2:9-10, XLII Congrès International des Américanistes, Paris (1976). (JK)

1977b   Comments. In *Actes* 1:387-94, XLII Congrès International des Américanistes, Paris (1976). (JK)
1981   Review article: Amazonian anthropology. *Journal of Latin American Studies* 13:151-65. (JK)
n.d.   I saw the sound of the waterfall: Gods, shamans and leadership in Piaroa society. (JK)

KAPLAN, J. O., AND M. R. KAPLAN
In press Los dea Ruwa. In *Encyclopedia des los Indígenes Venezuelanos.* Caracas: Fundación la Salle. (JK)

KAPLAN, M. R.
1970   Death and sex in the Piaroa world ordering. Paper presented at the annual meetings of the American Anthropological Association, San Diego. (JK)

KARSTEN, RAFAEL
1935   *The head-hunters of western Amazonas: The life and culture of the Jíbaro Indians of eastern Ecuador and Peru.* Helsinki: Societas Scientiarum Fennica, Commentationes Humanarum Litterarum, II, I. (NW)

KAY, PAUL
1970   Some theoretical implications of ethnographic semantics. *Bulletin of the American Anthropological Association* (special issue) 3:19-31. (KK)

KEESING, ROGER M.
1972   Simple models of complexity: The lure of kinship. In *Kinship studies in the Morgan centennial year,* ed. Priscilla Reining. Washington, D.C.: Anthropological Society of Washington. (JK)

KENSINGER, KENNETH M.
1974a   Cashinahua medicine and medicine men. In *Native South Americans: Ethnology of the least known continent,* ed. Patricia J. Lyon. Boston: Little, Brown. (KK)
1974b   Leadership and factionalism in Cashinahua society. Paper presented at the annual meetings of the American Anthropological Association, Mexico City. (KK)
1975a   Studying the Cashinahua. In *The Cashinahua of Eastern Peru.* Haffenreffer Museum of Anthropology, Brown University, Studies in Anthropology and Material Culture, vol. 1. Providence, R.I. (KK)
1975b   Data, data and more Yanomamö data. *Reviews in Anthropology* 2:69-74. (KK)
1977   Cashinahua notions of social time and social space. In *Actes* 2:223-44, XLII Congrès International des Américanistes, Paris (1976). (JK, KK)
1981   Food taboos as markers of age categories in Cashinahua. In *Food taboos in lowland South America,* ed. Kenneth M. Kensinger

and Waud H. Kracke. Working Papers on South American Indians, vol. 3. Bennington, Vt.: Bennington College. (KK)

n.d.   Dual organization reconsidered. Paper presented at the Conference on Anthropological Research in Amazonia, Queens College, CUNY. (1975). (WK)

KIRCHHOFF, PAUL

1931   Die Verwandtschaftsorganisation der Urwaldstämme Südamerickas. *Zeitschrift für Ethnologie* 64:47-71. (JJ)

KOCH-GRUNBERG, THEODORE

1909-10   *Zwei Jahre unter den Idianern Reisen in Nordwest Brasilien.* Berlin: Otto Zerries. (Reprinted, Graz, Austria: Akademische Druck–U. Verlagsanstalt, 1967.) (JJ)

KOPYTOFF, IGOR

1977   Matrilineality, residence and residential zones. *American Ethnologist* 4:539-58. (GD)

KRACKE, WAUD H.

1978   *Force and persuasion: Leadership in an Amazonian society.* Chicago: University of Chicago Press. (WK)

KRIGE, EILEEN

1974   Woman-marriage, with special reference to the Lovedu: Its significance for the definition of marriage. *Africa* 44:11-37. (JS)

KROEBER, ALFRED L.

1938   Basic and secondary patterns of social structure. *Man* 68:299-309. (GD)

LARAIA, ROQUE

1963   Arranjos poliândricos na sociedade Surui. *Revista do Museu Paulista* 14:71-75. (Also in Lyon 1974:370-72.) (WK, PL)

LARAIA, ROQUE, AND ROBERTO DA MATTA

1967   *Indios e Castanheiros: A empresa extrative e os indios no medio Tocantins.* Corpo e Alma do Brasil, no. 21. São Paulo: Difusão Européia do Livro. (WC, WK)

LAVE, JEAN

1967   Social taxonomy among the Krikatí (Gê) of central Brazil. Ph.D. dissertation, Harvard University. (WC)

1971   Some suggestions for the interpretation of residence, descent and exogamy among the Eastern Timbira. In *Verhandlungen* 3:341-45, XXXVIII Internationalen Amerikansterkongresses, Stüttgart-München (1968). Munich: Klaus Renner. (WC)

1977   Eastern Timbira moiety systems in time and space: A complex structure. In *Actes,* vol. 2, XLII Congrès International des Américanistes, Paris (1976). (WC, JK)

1979   Cycles and trends in Krikatí naming practices. In *Dialectical Societies: The Gê and Bororo of central Brazil,* ed. David Maybury-Lewis. Cambridge, Mass.: Harvard University Press. (JK)

LEACH, EDMUND RONALD
1951   The structural implications of matrilateral cross-cousin marriage. *Man* 81:23-55. (JS)
1955   Polyandry, inheritance and the definition of marriage, with particular reference to Sinhalese customary law. *Man* 54:182-86. (JS)
1961   Rethinking anthropology. In *Rethinking anthropology*. London School of Economics Monographs on Social Anthropology, no. 22. London: Athlone Press. (JS, GD, KK)
1970   *Lévi-Strauss*. London: Fontana. (JS)

LÉVI-STRAUSS, CLAUDE
1943   The social use of kinship terms among the Brazilian Indians. *American Anthropologist* 45:398-409. (JS)
1948   The Tupi Cawahib. In *Handbook of South American Indians, III: The Tropical Forest Tribes*, ed. Julian Steward. Smithsonian Institution, Bureau of American Ethnology Bulletin no. 143. Pp. 299-306. (WK)
1949   *Les structures elementaires de la parente*. Paris: Presses Universitaires de France (2nd ed., Paris: Mouton, 1967). (JS)
1953   Social structure. In *Anthropology today*, ed. Alfred L. Kroeber. Chicago: University of Chicago Press. (JS)
1956   Les organisations dualistes existent-elles? *Bijdragen tot de Taal-, Land- en Volkenkunde* 112:99-128. (Published in English as Lévi-Strauss 1963a.) (WK)
1958   Documents Tupi-Kawahib. In *Miscellanea Paul Rivet Octogenaria Dicata*, vol. 2. Mexico City: Universidad Autorómina Nacional. Pp. 323-38. (WK)
1960   On manipulated sociological models. *Bijdragen tot de Taal-, Land- en Volkenkunde* 116:17-44. (Reprinted as: The meaning and use of the notion of model, in Lévi-Strauss 1976:71-82.) (WK)
1961   *Tristes tropiques*. Trans. John Russell. New York: Atheneum. (WK)
1963a   Do dual organizations exist? In *Structural anthropology*. New York: Basic Books. (KK, WK)
1963b   *Structural anthropology*. New York: Basic Books. (WK, JS)
1967   Preface to *Les structures elementaires de la parente*. 2nd edition. Paris and La Hague: Mouton. (JS)
1969   *Elementary structures of kinship*. Trans. James Bell and John von Sturmer. Boston: Beacon Press. (JK, WK)
1976   *Structural anthropology*, vol. 2. New York: Basic Books. (WK)

LIZOT, JACQUES
1971   Remarques sur le vocabulaire de parenté yanomami. *L'Homme* 11:25-83. (JK)
1977   Descendance et affinité chez les Yanomami: Antinomie et com-

plémentarité. In *Actes,* XLII Congrès International des Américanistes, Paris (1976). (JS)

LÖFFLER, LORENZ, AND GERHARD BAER
1974   The kinship terminology of the Piro, eastern Peru. *Ethno-
logische Zietschrift* (Zürich) 1:257-82. (GD)

LOUNSBURY, FLOYD G.
1962   Review of *Structure and sentiment,* by Rodney Needham.
American Anthropologist 64:1302-10. (JJ)
1964   The formal analysis of Crow- and Omaha-type kinship terminologies. In *Explorations in cultural anthropology,* ed. Ward H.
Goodenough. New York: McGraw-Hill. Pp. 351-93. (WC)
1968   The structural analysis of kinship semantics. In *Kinship and
social organization,* ed. Paul Bohannan and John Middleton.
Cambridge, Mass.: Harvard University Press. Pp. 125-48. (JK)

LOWIE, ROBERT H.
1927   *The origin of the state.* New York: Harcourt, Brace. (GD)

LYON, PATRICIA J.
1967   Singing as a social interaction among the Wachipaeri of eastern
Peru. Ph.D. dissertation, University of California, Berkeley.
(PL)
1974   (ed.) *Native South Americans: Ethnology of the least known
continent.* Boston: Little, Brown. (WC)
1975   Dislocación tribal y clasificaciones lingüísticas en la zona del
Río Madre de Dios. In *Actas y Memorias* 5:185-207, XXXIX
Congreso Internacional de Americanistas, Lima (1970). Lima:
Instituto de Estudios Peruanos. (PL)
In press   The attackers or the attacked? The invention of "hostile" sav-
ages in the valleys of Paucartambo, Cuzco, Peru. In *Proceedings*
of the colloquium "The Defense of the Latin American Indian
Cultures and Its Present Projections." Terre Haute, Ind.: Uni-
versity of Notre Dame Press. (PL)

MACDONALD, THEODORE
1979   Processes of change in Amazonian Ecuador: Quijos Quichua
Indians become cattlemen. Ph.D dissertation, University of Illinois, Urbana. (NW)

MACDONALD, J. FREDERICK
1965   Some considerations about Tupi-Guarani kinship structures.
Boletím do Museu Paraense Emílio Goeldi, Antropologia no.
26. Belém. (JS)

MAYBURY-LEWIS, DAVID
1960   The analysis of dual organisations: A methodological critique
Bijdragen tot de Taal-, Land- en Volkenkunde 116:17-44.
(WK)
1965   Prescriptive marriage systems. *Southwestern Journal of Anthropology* 21:207-30. (JJ, JS)

1967   *Akwĕ-Shavante society*. Oxford: Clarendon Press. (Reprinted in paperback, New York: Oxford University Press, 1974.) (JS, WK, WC)

1979   *Dialectical societies: The Gê and Bororo of central Brazil*, ed. David Maybury-Lewis. Cambridge, Mass.: Harvard University Press. (WC, JK)

MEGGITT, M. J.
1968   Marriage classes and demography in central Australia. In *Man the Hunter*, ed. Richard Lee and Irven DeVore. Chicago: Aldine. Pp. 176-84. (JJ)

MELATTI, JULIO CEZAR
1970   O sistema social Krahó. Tese de Doutoramento na Anthropologia da Universidade de São Paulo. (WC)

1972   *O messianismo Krahó*. São Paulo: Editora Herder. (WC)

1977   Estrutura social Marubo: Un sistema Australiano na Amazônia. In *Anuario Antropologico/76*. Rio de Janeiro: Tempo Brasilerio. Pp. 83-120. (JS)

1979   The relationship system of the Krahó. In *Dialectical societies: The Gê and Bororo of central Brazil*, ed. David Maybury-Lewis. Cambridge, Mass.: Harvard University Press. (JK, WC)

MERRIFIELD, WILLIAM R.
1968   Review of *The rise of anthropological theory*, by Marvin Harris. *Current Anthropology* 9:526-27. (KK)

MILES, DOUGLAS
1970   The Ngadju Dayaks of central Kalimantan, with special reference to the upper Mentoya. *Behavior Science Notes* 5:291-319. (GD)

MOERMAN, MICHAEL
1971   A little knowledge. In *Contributions of Ethnomethodology*, ed. Harold Garfinkel and Harvey Sacks. Bloomington: Indiana University Press. (First published in Tyler 1969.) (JS)

MURDOCK, GEORGE PETER
1949   *Social structure*. New York: Macmillan. (JS, GD)

MURPHY, ROBERT F.
1959   Social structure and sex antagonism. *Southwestern Journal of Anthropology* 15:89-98. (JS)

1960   *Headhunter's heritage. Social and economic change among the Mundurucu Indians*. Berkeley: University of California Press. (KK, WK)

1972   *The dialectics of social life*. New York: Basic Books. (WK)

1979   *An overture to social anthropology*. Englewood Cliffs, N.J.: Prentice-Hall. (KK)

MURPHY, YOLANDA, AND ROBERT F. MURPHY
1974   *Women of the forest*. New York: Columbia University Press. (JS)

MURRAY, COLIN
1976   Marital strategy in Lesotho: The redistribution of migrant earnings. *African Studies* 35:99-121. (JS)

NEEDHAM, RODNEY
1958   The formal analysis of prescriptive patrilateral cross-cousin marriage. *Southwestern Journal of Anthropology* 14:199-219. (JS)
1962   *Structure and sentiment: A test case in social anthropology.* Chicago: University of Chicago Press. (JJ)
1971a   Introduction. In *Rethinking kinship and marriage,* ed. Rodney Needham. A.S.A. Monographs, no. 11. London and New York: Tavistock and Barnes & Noble. (KK, JS)
1971b   Remarks on the analysis of kinship and marriage. In *Rethinking kinship and marriage,* ed. Rodney Needham. A.S.A. Monographs, no. 11. London and New York: Tavistock and Barnes & Noble. (KK, JS)
1973   Prescription. *Oceania* 43:166-81. (JK, JS)
1974   The evolution of social classification: A commentary on the Warao case. *Bijdragen tot de Taal-, Land- en Volkenkunde* 130:16-43. (JS)
1975   Polythetic classification: Convergence and consequences. *Man* n.s. 10:349-69. (JS)

NEWTON, DOLORES
1971   Social and historical dimensions of Timbira material culture. Ph.D dissertation, Harvard University. (WC)

NILES, BLAIR
1931   Introduction. In *Djuka, the Bush Negroes of Dutch Guiana.* by Morton C. Kahn. New York: Viking Press. (GD)

NIMUENDAJU, CURT
1924   Os indios Parintintin do Rio Madeira. *Journal de la Société des Américanistes* (Paris) 16:201-78. (WK)
1942   *The Sherente.* Publications of the Frederick Webb Hodge Anniversary Publication Fund, vol. 4. Los Angeles: Southwest Museum. (WK)
1946   *The Eastern Timbira.* Trans. and ed. Robert H. Lowie. University of California Publications in American Archaeology and Ethnology, no. 41. Berkeley: University of California Press. (WC)
1952   *The Tukuna.* Trans. William D. Hohenthal, ed. Robert H. Lowie. University of California Publications in American Archaeology and Ethnology, no. 45. Berkeley: University of California Press. (WK)

NOGLE, LAWRENCE ELWAYNE
1974   *Method and theory in the semantics and cognition of kinship.* The Hague/Paris: Mouton. (WC)

Notes and queries in anthropology
1951   6th ed. London: Routledge and Kegan Paul. (JS)

OBEREM, UDO
1971   *Los Quijos: Historia de la transculturación de un grupo indí-
          gena en el oriente Ecuatoriano (1538-1956)*. 2 vols. Madrid:
          Memórias del Departamento de Antropología y Etnología de
          América, Facultad de Filosofia y Letras de la Universidad de
          Madrid. (NW)
1974   Trade and trade goods in the Ecuadorian montana. In *Native
          South Americans: Ethnology of the least known continent,* ed.
          Patricia J. Lyon. Boston: Little, Brown. Pp. 346-57. (First pub-
          lished in 1967.) (NW)

OBOLER, REGINA
1980   Is the female husband a man? Woman-woman marriage among
          the Nandi of Kenya. *Ethnology* 19:69-88. (JS)

O'BRIEN, DENISE
1977   Female husbands in southern Banta societies. In *Sexual stratifi-
          cation: A cross-cultural view,* ed. Alice Schlegal. New York:
          Columbia University Press. (JS)

ORR, CAROLYN, AND BETSY WRISLEY
1965   *Vocabulario Quichua del oriente del Ecuador.* Serie de Vocabu-
          larios Indígenos, no. 1. Quito: Instituto Lingüístico de Verano.
          (NW)

ORTIZ, ALFONSO
1969   *The Tewa world.* Chicago: University of Chicago Press. (WK)

PEREIRA, NUNES
1967   *Moronguêtá: Um decameron indígena.* Rio de Janeiro: Editôra
          Civilização Brasileira. (WK)

PIKE, KENNETH L.
1947   *Phonemics: A technique for reducing language to writing.* Ann
          Arbor: University of Michigan Press. (WC)
1954   *Language in relation to a unified theory of the structure of
          human behavior.* Preliminary ed., vol. 1. Glendale, Calif.: Sum-
          mer Institute of Linguistics. (2nd ed., The Hague: Mouton,
          1967.) (KK)

POPJES, JACK, AND JO POPJES
1982   *Ortografia Canela-Krahô.* Edição experimental. Brasília, D. F.:
          Summer Institute of Linguistics.

PORRAS GARCES, P. PEDRO I.
1974   *Historia y arqueología de ciudad España Baeza de los Quijos,
          siglo XVI.* Estudios Científicos sobre el Oriente Ecuatoriano,
          vol. I. Quito: Centro de Publicaciones de la Pontificia Universi-
          dad Católica. (NW)

PRICE, DAVID
 1977   Comercio y aculturación entre los nambicuara. *America Indígena* 37:123-35. (JS)

RADCLIFFE-BROWN, A. R.
 1952   On social structure. In *Structure and function in primitive society*. New York: Free Press. (JS)
 1953   Dravidian kinship terminology. *Man* 53:112. (JJ)

RAMOS, ALCIDA
 1972   The social system of the Sanuma of northern Brazil. Ph.D. dissertation, University of Wisconsin, Madison. (JS)

RAMOS, ALCIDA, AND BRUCE ALBERT
 1977   Yanomama descent and affinity: The Sanuma/Yanomam contrast. In *Actes,* XLII Congrès International des Américanistes, Paris (1976). (JK, JS)

RAO, M. K.
 1973   Rank difference and marriage reciprocity in South India: An aspect of the implications of elder sister's daughter marriage in a fishing village in Andhra. *Contributions to Indian Sociology* n.s. 7:16-35. (JK)

REICHEL-DOLMATOFF, GERARDO
 1968   *Desana, simbolismo de los Indios Tukanos del Vaupés.* Bogotá: Ediciones Universidad de los Andes. (AS)
 1971   *Amazonian cosmos: The sexual and religious symbolism of the Tukano Indians.* Chicago: University of Chicago Press. (JJ)

RIVIERE, PETER G.
 1966a   Oblique discontinuous exchange: A new formal type of prescriptive alliance. *American Anthropologist* 68:738-40. (JK)
 1966b   A note on marriage with the sister's daughter. *Man* 1:550-56. (JK)
 1969   *Marriage among the Trio.* Oxford: Clarendon Press. (JK, JS)
 1971   Marriage: A reassessment. In *Rethinking kinship and marriage,* ed. Rodney Needham. A.S.A. Monographs, no. 11. London and New York: Tavistock and Barnes & Noble. (KK, JS)
 1973   Lowland South American culture area: A structural definition. Paper presented at the 72nd annual meetings of the American Anthropological Association, New Orleans. (JS)
 1974   Some problems in the comparative study of Carib societies. In *Proceedings* 2:639-43, XL International Congress of Americanists, Rome (1972). (JK)
 1977   Some problems in the comparative study of Carib societies. In *Carib-speaking Indians: Culture, language, and society,* ed. Ellen B. Basso. Anthropological Papers of the University of Arizona, no. 28. Tucson. (JS)

ROBERTS, SIMON A.
 1977   (ed.) *Law and the family in Africa.* The Hague: Mouton. (JS)

RODRIGUES, ARYON
1965   A classificação do troncolinguistico Tupi. *Revista de Antropologia* 12 (1 and 2):99-104. São Paulo. (WK)

ROSENTHAL, ROBERTA L.
1979   Homosexuals' right to marry: A constitutional test and a legislative solution. In *University of Pennsylvania Law Review* 128: 193-216. (JS)

SANTOS, EURICO
1952   *Da eme ao beija-flor.* Zoölogia Brasileira, vol. 4. Rio de Janeiro: F. Briguiet et Cie. (WK)
1960   *Passaros do Brasil.* Zoölogia Brasileira, vol. 5. Rio de Janeiro: F. Briguiet et Cie. (WK)

SCHEFFLER, HAROLD W.
1971   Dravidian-Iroquois: The Melanesian evidence. In *Anthropology in Oceania,* ed. L. R. Hiatt and C. Jayawardena. Sydney: Angus and Robertson. (JK, JS)
1972   Kinship Semantics. In *Annual Review of Anthropology* 1:309-28. Palo Alto, Calif.: Annual Reviews. (JK, NW)
1977   Kinship and alliance in South India and Australia. *American Anthropologist* 79:869-82. (JK, JS)
1978   *Australian kin classification.* Cambridge: Cambridge University Press. (JK)

SCHEFFLER, HAROLD W., AND FLOYD G. LOUNSBURY
1971   *A study in structural semantics: The Siriono kinship system.* Englewood Cliffs, N.J.: Prentice-Hall. (WC, JK, NW)

SCHNEIDER, DAVID M.
1965a   American kin terms and terms for kinsmen: A critique of Goodenough's componential analysis of Yankee kinship terminology. *American Anthropologist* 67:288-308. (Reprinted in Tyler 1969.) (JS)
1965b   Some muddles in the models: Or, how the system really works. In *The relevance of models for social anthropology,* ed. Michael Banton. London: Tavistock. Pp. 25-86. (JJ, GD, JS)
1968   *American kinship. A cultural account.* Englewood Cliffs, N.J.: Prentice-Hall. (JS)

SCHNEIDER, DAVID M., AND JAMES BOON
1974   Kinship vis-à-vis myth: Contrasts in Lévi Strauss' approaches to cross cultural comparison. *American Anthropologist* 76:799-817. (JS)

SECRETARIADO DE MISIONES DOMINICANAS
n.d.   *Alma de la selva.* Lima. (Probable date of publication 1971.) (PL)

SEEGER, ANTHONY
1974   Nature and culture in the cosmology and social organization of

the Suya, a Gê-speaking tribe of central Brazil. Ph.D. dissertation, University of Chicago. (WC)

1981   *Nature and society in central Brazil: The Suyá indians of Mato Grosso.* Cambridge, Mass.: Harvard University Press. (WC)

SHAPIRO, JUDITH
1968   Tapirapé kinship. *Boletím do Museu a Paraense Emílio Goeldi,* Antropologia no. 37. *Belém.* (JS)

1972   Sex roles and social structure among the Yanomama of northern Brazil. Ph.D. dissertation, Columbia University. (JS)

1974   Alliance or descent: Some Amazonian contrasts. *Man* 9:305-6. (JS)

1979   Cross cultural perspectives on sexual differentiation. In *Human sexuality: A comparative and developmental perspective,* ed. Herant Katchadourian. Berkeley: University of California Press. (JS)

1981   Anthropology and the study of gender. *Soundings* (Vanderbilt University). (JS)

in press Kinship in the Great Basin. In *Handbook of North American Indians,* vol. 11. Washington, D.C.: Smithsonian Institution. (JS)

SHAPIRO, JUDITH, AND DONALD HUNDERFUND
n.d.   Descent constructs in lowland South American societies. In preparation. (JS)

SILVERSTEIN, MICHAEL
1976   Shifters, linguistic categories, and cultural description. In *Meaning in Anthropology,* ed. K. Basso and H. Selby. Albuquerque: University of New Mexico Press. Pp. 11-55. (JS)

SILVERWOOD-COPE, PETER
1972   A contribution to the ethnography of the Colombian Makú. Ph.D. dissertation, University of Cambridge. (JJ)

SISKIND, JANET
1973   Tropical forest hunters and the economy of sex. In *Peoples and cultures of native South America,* ed. Daniel R. Gross. New York: Doubleday. Pp. 226-41. (JJ)

SORENSON, ARTHUR P., JR.
1967   Multilingualism in the Northwest Amazon. *American Anthropologist* 69:670-84. (WK, JJ, AS)

SOUTHALL, AIDAN
1971   Ideology and group composition in Madagascar. *American Anthropologist* 73:144-64. (GD)

SPENCER, BALDWIN, AND F. J. GILLEN
1927   *The Arunta.* London: Macmillan. (JJ)

SUÁREZ, MARÍA MATILDE
1971   Terminology, alliance, and change in Warao society. *Nieuwe West-Indische Gids* 48:56-122. (JS)

1972   *Terminología, alianza matrimonial y cambio en la sociedad Warao.* Caracas: Universidád Católica Andrés Bello. (JS)

TAYLOR, KENNETH, AND ALCIDA RAMOS
1975   Alliance or descent: Some Amazonian contrasts. *Man* 10:28-30. (JS)

THOMAS, DAVID JOHN
1979   Sister's daughter marriage among the Pemon. *Ethnology* 18: 61-70. (JK)

TIGER, LIONEL
1969   *Men in groups.* New York: Random House. (AS)

TOWNSEND, PATRICIA K., AND PATSY JEAN ADAMS
1973   From wives to peccaries: Marriage conflict among the Culina. Paper presented at the 72nd annual meetings of the American Anthropological Association, New Orleans. (Published in Spanish in 1975 as: Estructura y conflicto en el matrimonio de los índios Culina de la Amazonia Peruana, *Folklore Americano* 20:139-60.) (JS)

TURNER, TERENCE S.
1966   Social structure and political organization among the northern Cayapó. Ph.D dissertation, Harvard University. (WC)
1979   The Gê and Bororo societies as dialectical systems: A general model; Kinship, household, and community structure among the Kayapó. In *Dialectical societies,* ed. David Maybury-Lewis. Cambridge, Mass.: Harvard University Press. (WC)

TYLER, STEPHEN A., ed.
1969   *Cognitive anthropology.* New York: Holt, Rinehart and Winston. (JS)

VIDAL, LUX
1977   *Morte e vida de uma sociedade indígena brasileira.* São Paulo: Editora Hucitec. (WC)

WALLACE, ALFRED RUSSEL
1889   *Travels on the Amazon and Rio Negro.* London: Ward, Lock & Co. (JJ)

WALLACE, ANTHONY F. C.
1980   Review of *Cultural materialism,* by Marvin Harris. *American Anthropologist* 82:423-26. (KK)

WEDGWOOD, C. H.
1952   An annotated glossary of technical terms used in the study of kinship and marriage. *South Pacific* 6:450-58. (GD)

WHITTEN, NORMAN E., JR.
1976a   (with the assistance of Marcelo F. Naranjo, Marcelo Santi Simbana, and Dorothea S. Whitten) *Sacha Runa: Ethnicity and adaptation of Ecuadorian jungle Quichua.* Urbana: University of Illinois Press. (NW, JS)

1976b   *Ecuadorian ethnocide and indigenous ethnogenesis: Amazonian resurgence amidst Andean colonialism.* IWGIA Document 23. Copenhagen. (NW)

1976c   Structure and transformations of contemporary Canelos Quichua spirit relationships. In *Festschrift for Dr. H. C. Hermann Trimborn,* ed. Udo Oberem. *Antropos* (special ed.) (Bönn). (NW)

1978   *Amazonian Ecuador: An ethnic interface in ecological, social, and ideological perspective.* IWGIA Document 34. Copenhagen. (NW)

1981   (ed.) *Cultural transformations and ethnicity in modern Ecuador.* Urbana: University of Illinois Press. (NW)

WITHERSPOON, GARY J.

1977   *Language and art in the Navaho Universe.* Ann Arbor: University of Michigan Press. (JK)

WORDICK, F. J. F.

1975   Review article: Siriono kinship terminology. *International Journal of American Linguistics* 41:242-85. (JK)

YALMAN, NUR

1962   The structure of Sinhalese kindred: A re-examination of the Dravidian terminology. *American Anthropologist* 64:548-75. (GD)

1967   *Under the bo tree.* Berkeley and Los Angeles: University of California Press. (JK)

YENGOYAN, ARAM A.

1968   Demographic and ecological influences on aboriginal Australian marriage sections. In *Man the hunter,* ed. Richard Lee and Irven DeVore. Chicago: Aldine. Pp. 185-99. (JJ)

Contributors

ELLEN B. BASSO is associate professor of anthropology at the University of Arizona. She has been engaged in research among the Kalapalo since 1966. She is the author of *The Kalapalo Indians of Central Brazil.*

WILLIAM H. CROCKER has been the curator of South American ethnology at the Smithsonian Institution since 1962. He began his studies of the Ramkókamekra-Canela and the Apanyekra-Canela in 1957 and has returned frequently since then, most recently in 1979. He is the author of numerous articles on the Canela.

GERTRUDE E. DOLE is a research associate at the American Museum of Natural History. She did fieldwork among the Brazilian Kuikuru in 1953-54 and among the Peruvian Amahuaca in 1960-61. She has published a number of articles based on her fieldwork.

JEAN JACKSON is associate professor of anthropology at the Massachusetts Institute of Technology. She has carried out fieldwork in Mexico and highland Guatemala in addition to her research with the Bara between October 1968 and November 1970. In addition to several articles, she has written *The Fish People: Linguistic Exogamy and Tukanoan Identity in the Northwest Amazonia* (1983).

JOANNA OVERING KAPLAN is lecturer in the social anthropology of Latin America with a joint appointment at the London School of Economics and the Institute of Latin American Studies, University of London. She began her Piaroa fieldwork in 1968 and has returned to the field for two additional periods of work, most recently in 1981. She is the author of *The Piaroa: A People of the Orinoco Basin, a Study in Kinship and Marriage,* and editor of the symposium *Social Time and Social Space in Lowland South American Societies.*

KENNETH M. KENSINGER is a member of the anthropology faculty at Bennington College. He is editor of *Working Papers on South American*

285

Indians and author of *The Cashinahua of Eastern Peru.* He began his fieldwork with the Cashinahua in 1955.

WAUD H. KRACKE is associate professor of anthropology at the University of Illinois, Chicago. He began his research with the Kagwahiv in 1967, returning in 1973. He is the author of *Force and Persuasion: Leadership in an Amazonian Society.*

PATRICIA J. LYON has done extensive archaeological, ethnohistorical, and ethnographic research in Peru beginning in 1954; her paper is based on fieldwork between 1954 and 1965. She is a research associate at the Institute of Andean Studies and the University of California, Berkeley, and the co-editor of *Ñawpa Pacha.* Her list of publications includes *Native South Americans: Ethnology of the Least Known Continent.*

JUDITH R. SHAPIRO is chairman of the anthropology department at Bryn Mawr College. She has done fieldwork with the Northern Paiute, Walker River Reservation, Nevada, with the Yanomama of the Rio Catrimani and Serra dos Surucucus, Roraima, with the Tapirape in Mato Grosso, and is currently completing studies of the Little Sisters of Jesus in Brazil, Italy, France, and the United States.

ARTHUR P. SORENSEN, JR., began his studies on the languages of the Vaupés in 1959, returning most recently in 1975. He is the author of "Multilingualism in the Northwest Amazon" and other articles.

NORMAN E. WHITTEN, JR., is editor of *American Ethnologist,* head of the anthropology department at the University of Illinois, Urbana-Champaign, and co-founder of the Sacha Runa Research Foundation. Together with his wife he has been working with the Canelos Quichua since 1970. He is the author of *Sacha Runa* and the editor of *Cultural Transformations and Ethnicity in Modern Ecuador,* both published by the University of Illinois Press.

DOROTHEA S. WHITTEN is research associate in the Center for Latin American and Caribbean Studies at the University of Illinois, Urbana-Champaign, and co-founder of the Sacha Runa Research Foundation, Urbana. She is the author or co-author of several articles on Canelos Quichua lifeways, including "Ceramics of the Canelos Quichua" published by *Natural History.* She has been working with these native Upper Amazonian peoples since 1968.

Index